CENTER FOR JEWISH STUDIES

HARVARD JUDAIC TEXTS AND STUDIES

III

HARVARD UNIVERSITY
CENTER FOR JEWISH STUDIES

Christian Hebraists and Dutch Rabbis

Seventeenth Century Apologetics and the Study of Maimonides' *Mishneh Torah*

AARON L. KATCHEN

Distributed by
HARVARD UNIVERSITY PRESS
Cambridge, Massachusetts and London, England
1984

Library of Congress Cataloging in Publication Data

Katchen, Aaron L., 1942-
Christian Hebraists and Dutch Rabbis.

(Harvard Judaic texts and studies; 3)
Bibliography: pp. 338-367
Includes index.
1. Hebrew language—Study and teaching—Netherlands—History—17th century. 2. Netherlands—Intellectual life. 3. Humanism. 4. Jews—Netherlands—Intellectual life. 5. Maimonides, Moses, 1135-1204. Mishneh Torah. 6. Netherlands—Ethnic relations. I. Title. II. Series: Texts and studies ; 3.
PJ4538.N4K3 1983 296.3'872'09492 83-22736
ISBN 0-674-12865-6

Publication of this book is made possible by funds from the
Alan M. Stroock Fund for Advanced Research in Judaica
Harvard University Center for Jewish Studies

Printed by
Harvard University
Office of the University Publisher

To

my mother
and
the memory of my father, z"l

Preface

"Rabbi Moyses Aegyptius," or Rabbi Moses ben Maimon (1135–1204), called Rambam by Jews and Maimonides by the world of scholarship, first owed his fame and stature in the West to his *Guide of the Perplexed,* or *Dux neutrorum,* as it was entitled. This work, a complex exposition of Jewish philosophical methodology and doctrine completed in 1190 and translated from Arabic into Latin within three decades of the author's lifetime, made him a widely celebrated figure in the scholastic capitals of Europe. By contrast, his other masterpiece, the *Mishneh Torah,* a Hebrew codification of Jewish law and tradition composed during the 1170s, waited more than four and a half centuries before any substantial portion of it was Latinized. Though its existence became known to Christians just as rapidly as that of the *Guide,* its use and study was long confined essentially to anti–Jewish controversialists, many of whom were converted Jews and may therefore have had both a facility with Hebrew and a prior knowledge of the work. Until the seventeenth century and, indeed, until the 1630s, when the first translations of complete sections of the *Mishneh Torah* began to appear in Amsterdam, the code was available to a wider Latin audience only through brief and disconnected citations. By that point already, the balance between the two works had begun to be rectified, and the *Mishneh Torah,* the codification of law, was on its way to becoming the sourcebook par excellence for an intense and still growing Christian interest in "normative" Judaism.

The respective stages in the history of the two works as representatives of Judaism abroad reflect, in some ways, the basic distinction between them in their original setting. To be sure, both the philosophical treatise and the halakhic *summa* or compendium comprised and constituted authentic, even magisterial statements on the nature of Judaism. Both were, moreover, innovative and intellectualistic in conception, formulation and content. Despite their correspondence in doctrine and goal, however, each had proceeded from an ostensibly different vantage point and each had been addressed to a different audience; each, for reasons independent of the other in some respects, would meet with strictures in certain Jewish quarters. In the end, though, the *Guide of the Perplexed,* the more esoteric of the two, while translated from the original Arabic into Hebrew even before Maimonides' death, would remain the work restricted in readership and acceptability among Jews. The *Mishneh Torah,* on the other hand, which had compassed and charted the whole of Jewish life and thought and had been written for a broader public, had both an immediate and an enduring impact on Jewish life overall. It proceeded, almost within Maimonides' lifetime, to become totally identified with the very mainstream of Jewish tradition.[1]

Some recognition of their contrasting function and status at home would seem to be implied in the contrasting ways in which the two works were taken up and treated in Christian Europe. For Christians of the High Middle Ages and later, cognizant though they were of the predominance of the halakhah in Jewish life, were probably more often preoccupied themselves with details of belief and doctrine. For that reason they tended to focus more on ideological parallels or differences when they stopped to consider the nature of Judaism. They thus turned more readily to the work that, on the surface at least, was more devoted to such issues. Neither were converts from Judaism responsible for this emphasis, nor were Jewish teachers whom Christians engaged able to or even interested in changing it. Initially, then, when they had recourse to Maimonides' works, it was to the *Guide* as an example of philosophical methodology and theological investigation that Christians turned first. When they did turn to the *Mishneh Torah,* though, it was, at this early stage, first and foremost for the purpose of examining what might be called its doctrinal aspects. It is easy to understand, then, why there was, at the outset, greater demand for a complete translation of the *Guide* than for any extended one of the *Mishneh Torah.*

Eventually, as we have said, the balance would be redressed. Indeed, it may fairly be said that the ultimate impact of the *Mishneh Torah* on Christian scholars was far greater than that of the *Guide.* It is with that impact, that is to say, with the understanding of the work by its Christian students, and also with the repercussions of their study of it on the history of the Jewish community, in sum, with the impact of its study on Jewish–Christian relations, that the present work deals. Our focus is largely on the place and period where the *Mishneh Torah* began to be translated widely, seventeenth–century Holland, and especially on Leiden and Amsterdam during the first half of that century. Not only was this setting uniquely conducive to such an enterprise, it was also a place of rather free exchange between Christian and Jew. Despite the anti–Jewish animus that persisted in many quarters, Holland provided, *de facto,* one of the freest such environments in early modern times. In general, then, Maimonides' code rapidly became the prism through which Judaism was most often perceived and the life of the Jewish community analyzed. Moreover, given the *Mishneh Torah*'s longstanding importance in both dialogue and disputation, it was natural that it should assume a significant role in Jewish–Christian interchanges at this period. The Amsterdam Jewish community was well aware of the uses to which the code could be put, and it attempted to exercise whatever influence it could on Christian perceptions of the work. The best known among those who courted Christian students was, of course, Menasseh ben Israel, the rabbi who saw himself as his people's advocate before the gentile world. His efforts and those of other Amsterdam rabbis to influence the attitudes and productions of the Dutch Christian Hebraist students of the *Mishneh Torah* are not merely of fundamental importance for any study of the Hebraists, but also of major import for Jewish history.

It is probably fair to say, in fact, that Christian Hebraism rarely, if ever, existed in a scholarly, religious, or political void. Sometimes Hebraists became directly involved with a Jewish community, as in the famous Reuchlin–Pfefferkorn affair; sometimes, they had little to do with Jews, but were, nonetheless, important figures in their own society; John Selden, the English jurist, is a good example. 'Hebraist' can refer variously to one concerned with the "Hebraica veritas" of Scripture, to a student of the Hebrew language, whatever his or her intellectual interests, or even to a student of rabbinic literature with only minimal language skills. The designation does not, to be sure, carry any connotation of or imply any allegiance to any specific or more general *Weltanschauung*. Nor does it attribute to its practitioners any specific attitude to Judaism or relationship to the Jewish community, although certain attitudes were endemic, and the use of Jewish teachers frequent. More than anything else, Hebraism was a tradition of study and learning, one that maintained itself among scholars and even laymen from the time of Jerome to the nineteenth century. This tradition ultimately came to have a threefold character. As summarized most succinctly by Altmann, it would eventually denote: rabbinic learning, a veneration for Maimonides, and an allegiance to "the Renaissance concept of the essential unity underlying all human thought," a unity that allowed classical pagan sources to appear as testimony side by side with Christian and Jewish ones.[2]

To be sure, specific collaboration between Christians and Jews was not an infrequent phenomenon. Grabois remarked on its character in the High Middle Ages, showing how some Christian scholars, primarily concerned with philological and historical explanations of Scripture through reliance on the "Hebraica veritas," were, in effect, collaborating both intellectually and in person with their Jewish "masters."[3]

In fact, the significance of Hebraism in the Western intellectual tradition is far richer and with far greater range and depth than we can possibly suggest here. Not merely were prominent individuals Hebraists of one degree or another, but their learning and the learning of lesser known scholars became widely disseminated among the general literary public. Down through the period of the Enlightenment the influence of rabbinic literature persisted, largely through the productions of some of the Christian Hebraists with whom this study deals. If any changes in attitude toward the Jews resulted from the study of Jewish literature—and attitudes toward the Jews certainly had their vicissitudes even in the eighteenth century—it was this literature, the literature translated and commented upon by the greatest seventeenth–century Hebraists, that is to say, it was, first and foremost, the *Mishneh Torah* that brought about these changes.

ACKNOWLEDGEMENTS

I have been the beneficiary of much learning, expertise, and generosity from teachers, colleagues, and friends. Although no one, as the rabbinic dictum says, ever learns except out of the musings of his own heart and mind, the wisdom, counsel, and firm friendship proffered by my teachers Isadore Twersky and Yosef Yerushalmi have sustained and supported me throughout. Moreover, in his capacity as editor of this series, Professor Twersky has manifested an exemplary measure of patience with a most recalcitrant author. His persistent, yet gentle encouragement has given me the courage to submit to the printer and the light of day a work that must surely still stand in great need of emendation.

There are many others to whom I am also indebted. Frank Talmage read through the entire piece with great care. I have learned much from his animadversions on matters both technical and substantive and I hold his friendship very dear. James Kugel read through with a keen eye and made many a valuable suggestion. Frank Manuel made himself available on short notice and helped me greatly with his comments and judgments. I can only hope that the result is worthy of the efforts of all of the above.

I have had much satisfaction in the warm friendship of colleagues at the University of Toronto, Indiana University and Brandeis University. I am particularly grateful to Marvin Fox, the director of the Philip W. Lown School of Near Eastern and Judaic Studies and to Leon Jick, the chairman of the Department of Near Eastern and Judaic Studies at Brandeis for their many kindnesses and, especially, for a confidence in me that I hope they have not misplaced.

I should also like to thank the National Foundation for Jewish Culture, the Memorial Foundation for Jewish Culture, and the Canadian Foundation for Jewish Culture for their assistance at an earlier stage of research. The staffs of the Harvard University Libraries and the Brandeis University Libraries and of other institutions have been unfailingly courteous. Cynthia Schweppe and her staff in the Feldberg Computer Center at Brandeis have always been "up"; in answering queries and solving problems, they have guided me toward computer literacy, and I cannot thank them enough. Miriam Palmerola, and now Hagop Sarkissian, and the staff of the Office of the University Publisher at Harvard have been painstaking in their efforts; Shirley Siroka of the Center for Jewish Studies and Carolyn Cross of the Department of Near Eastern Languages and Civilizations have helped me in ways both large and small. To them and to and all the many others too numerous to mention who have read, commented and otherwise been of assistance—I hope to have slighted no one—my warmest thanks.

My children Yonatan, Medinah, and Hillel have had to yield me repeatedly to my "ivory tower." As their understanding has been without measure, so is my love and gratitude. Beyond my power of expression is the debt I owe to my wife Rosalie. She has often perforce singlehandedly kept our household going and has done so with a grace beyond compare. This book is a tribute to her, even if it is but a small token of my love and devotion. Without her faith in me, it would never have been brought to completion. And, without the love and example given by our parents, it would never have been possible in the first place. My indebtedness to them is unending.

Contents

CHRISTIAN HEBRAISTS AND DUTCH RABBIS

INTRODUCTION:

The Vicissitudes of "Rabbi Moyses Aegyptius" the Jurist: The Christian Study of *Mishneh Torah* Down to the Seventeenth Century

Such concern with law as was shown by Christians of the early thirteenth century was most often with the spiritual or symbolic sense of biblical law, or with the rational basis for a given commandment. And so, when they had recourse to Maimonides' works, it was to the *Guide* as an example of philosophical and theological methodology and doctrine rather than to the *Mishneh Torah* that Christians turned. A distinction in Book III of the *Guide* between judicial and ceremonial law was adopted, for example, by the philosopher Alexander of Hales (d. 1245), the founder of the Franciscan School in Paris about 1231. He deemed the judicial laws still useful for Christians. His remark, though deriving ultimately from a Jewish source, constituted, strikingly enough, a veiled attack on Christian heretics who negated the continuing value of any kind of biblical law for contemporary morality. Another student of the *Guide*, William of Auvergne (d. 1249), who became Bishop of Paris in 1228, also acceded to some Maimonidean interpretations. Yet he took issue with a view he attributed to Maimonides, according to which the whole sacrificial cult was a concession, "because of [the people's] being accustomed to idolatry."[1]

Despite this interest in certain aspects of law, there is no indication that such writers pursued their study even of the so-called "judicial" laws from the *Guide* into the *Mishneh Torah*. To be sure, neither were Christians so inept in legal matters nor was their own canon law so divergent methodologically from the halakhah that they were unable to handle a halakhic compendium. Still, though they sometimes gleaned of the fruit of rabbinic thought from its philosophical branches, and even more often imbibed from the well of Jewish biblical exegesis, their recourse specifically to halakhic literature was far less frequent. In this period prior to the mid–thirteenth century, when men such as the aforementioned scholastics did inspect the Talmud, the source book of rabbinic Judaism, they did so most often in order to condemn it for its "blasphemies" and for many of its aggadic or ideological aspects.[2] Their actions were hardly unconventional, and William of Auvergne even oversaw the burning of the Talmud. Such condemnation often came to be extended as well to rabbinic literature at large and militated against its study, except by those who wished to attack it further. And, indeed, the thirteenth century saw attacks on Judaism stepped up specifically with reference to the contents of rabbinic literature, turning from outright criticism to the argument that Christian interpretations, though denied by Jews of the century, "had the support of ancient tradition—Targum, Talmud, Midrash—whose authority the Jews could not dispute."[3]

This is not to say that Christians were unfamiliar with the halakhah. Some of their interest centered on specific ordinances or on rulings that they deemed directed against Christians, or that were so in fact. The various libels against the Jews are not our concern here, but rather, the kinds of accusations Rabbi Yeḥiel of Paris (fl. 1224– ante 1267) attempted to refute in his disputation there in 1240; specifically included were restrictions on business dealings with Christians, supposedly unequal compensation by Jews for loss or damage to the property of Christians, and the alleged refusal of Jews to teach Torah to Christians. It is not clear, though, that any of their information had been derived from a direct study of the *Mishneh Torah.*[4]

Nonetheless, after study of the code began, it quickly began to manifest the whole variety of approaches shown by Christians toward Jewish literature and Judaism in general. They focused first on Maimonides' statements about doctrine and heresy, as well as on his supposed blasphemies and abusive remarks about Christians and Christianity. Their earliest forums for such inquiries were, again, the public Jewish–Christian disputations. At Barcelona in 1263, the convert Paulus Christiani (d. 1274) attempted to cite a passage from the work, but failed to find one corresponding to the one he was looking for, which was actually to be found in another work of Maimonides', his *Commentary on the Mishnah.* Paulus's Jewish interlocutor, the exegete and mystic Rabbi Moses ben Naḥman (1194–c. 1270), then made his own citation from the *Mishneh Torah,* intending, of course, to embarrass his opponent.[5]

The code would also be cited at the disputation of Tortosa in 1413–14, but, by that point, reliance could be had on quotations from it in anti-Jewish literary polemics. The classic *Pugio Fidei* [*Dagger of the Faith*] (1278) by Paulus's pupil Raymund Martin (1220–85), probably of Jewish ancestry himself, was the earliest and most significant of these. The *Pugio*'s few references to the *Mishneh Torah,* as, indeed, the *Pugio* as a whole, became a major source for other Christian polemics, the character of which is of enough interest to be dealt with further below. Half a century after Martin, though, the contents of the code were criticized in great detail by the notorious apostate Alfonso of Valladolid, formerly Abner of Burgos (1270–1346), who was instrumental in the then impending ruin of Spanish Jewry. According to Baer, Abner, toward the end of his *Moreh Tsedek* (*Mostrador de Justicia* in its Spanish version) [*Teacher of Righteousness*], which seems to have appeared in the 1320s, "reviews all the books of Maimonides' code . . . in an attempt to prove that Christian morality and custom are superior to Jewish law and ethics."[6] Though the scope of this "review" is not clear, it would appear that apostates from Judaism like Abner generally had a far greater interest in Jewish legal materials than did other Christians, and understandably so. Still, there were others with a curiosity about Jewish law; the brief enumeration of the traditional 613 Commandments of the Torah that Maimonides had made and prefixed to his code was, very early on, translated into Latin as an independent piece, with additional versions appearing several times before 1600.

Noteworthy from a different standpoint is the 1383 order by King Pedro IV of Aragon that the Jews of Barcelona, Gerona, and Perpignan produce a Catalan version, of the entire code presumably, "with the greatest diligence." Though the decree had been promulgated under penalty of loss of royal favor, no explanation had accompanied it. Yet the Jews did contest the demand, undoubtedly as one detrimental to their interests, and the translation seems never to have been made.[7] Indeed, strictures against the work in Jewish quarters had aroused the suspicions of the non–Jewish authorities and had led to the general scrutiny of Jewish books by the Dominicans and others as early as the 1230s. (It must be said, though, that there is no specific reference to the *Mishneh Torah* in this context of scrutinization.) Aside from the active encouragement of Pope Gregory IX and William of Auvergne as well, the moving force was probably Raymund of Pennaforte (1176–1275), who was among the first to advocate the study of Hebrew for the purpose of converting the Jews and who counted both Paulus Christiani and Raymund Martin among his pupils. By the fourteenth century, we find inquisitors like Bernard Gui of Provence condemning the *Mishneh Torah* in 1321 for its "blasphemies" and its references to Christians as "heretics." Such judgments again led to censorship and to the burning of at least one book of the work, this time *Sefer ham–Madda‘*, the first book of the code and the one most concerned with doctrinal matters. To be sure, much of this activity was due to allegations of Jewish influence on certain Christian heresies, with the suppression of which the Church was more concerned than it was with Judaism per se.

On the basis of the foregoing, it can hardly be said that the *Mishneh Torah* was unknown, even if its readership was still limited to Hebraists. Also, from the rather sporadic intervals at which it was quoted and the brief and unconnected nature of the passages cited, there is little to suggest any sustained or systematic study of the compendium as an integral piece. The portion most frequently drawn upon was Maimonides' treatment of the Messiah and the messianic age, which constitutes chapters 11 and 12 of *Hilkhot Melakhim,* itself the last of the eighty–three individual sections of the fourteen books. Raymund Martin had recourse only to these chapters, and the one reference by Bernard Gui, who must at least have been familiar with *Madda‘* also, was, similarly, a paragraph from *Melakhim* 11. This paragraph, later censored, had first been cited by Martin. It speaks of Jesus' having failed and led people astray; the citation is worth quoting since its context is Gui's overall opinion on the *Mishneh Torah* in his *Manual for Inquisitors:*

> In a certain book that the Jews call the *Glosses of Moses of Egypt* and the author of that book entitled *The Exposition and Restoration of the Law* are contained the abuses and falsifications of the Talmud and also many errors and blasphemies against the Christian faith, especially, that all

those who follow the way and the faith of Christ are called and said to be heretics [or], as it is said in Hebrew, "minim." Moreover, [in] that book it is said that Jesus Christ erred and acted against God and against the Law and that Jesus erred more than Mohammed and that it was Jesus who brought the rest of the world into error, both that of worshipping another God, who is not the one God, and that of undoing the law that God gave; and it contains many other blasphemies against Christ.[8]

It is also of interest that Martin, who actually both quotes the Hebrew original of the passage and makes his own Latin translation, had varied Maimonides' text, so that the words that we may translate as "Jesus, who imagined that he would be the Messiah," [she–dimmah she–yihyeh] read in the *Pugio:* "who was," "she–hayah."

Still, no translation even of chapters 11 and 12 of *Melakhim* in their entirety was made public, to say the least, until 1572, when Gilbert Génébrard (1537–97), originally a friar of Cluny, who was professor of Hebrew at Paris and himself a controversialist, included them in an anthology of other works. All in all, of the extracts or citations of the code prior to the late sixteenth century, it is probably fair to say that most of them owed a great deal to renegade Jews, if they were not actually citations by apostates who had studied the *Mishneh Torah* in Hebrew prior to their conversion. Only at the end of the sixteenth century did such a Hebraist as Hugh Broughton (1549–1612), the English divine who debated with Jews at Frankfurt and Amsterdam, show much greater familiarity with the work, using it as an ancilla in his Latin treatise *Seder Olam* (1594), a work in which he attempted to show that biblical chronology is compatible with Jesus' having been the Messiah. Prior to Broughton, then, and aside from a few odd citations that may have been reproduced or followed through from Maimonides' own citation or reference to them in the *Guide of the Perplexed,* that was it. In sum, Christians already had such access to the *Mishneh Torah* as they deemed necessary for their polemical and conversionist purposes. With regard to any broad knowledge of or interest in the work as a comprehensive unit, this still remained completely lacking.

Nonetheless, even prior to the Renaissance that began in the fifteenth century and brought in its wake changing religious and humanistic currents, there had begun to appear a certain shift in the Christian stance toward rabbinic literature. By no means did attempts to disprove Jewish tenets and confute and convert the Jews diminish, to be sure; indeed, the scope of anti–Jewish polemic became even broader. The twofold approach to Jewish texts alluded to above now became paradigmatic for Christians. It had been articulated best by Martin in his *Pugio* and is worth describing in detail here. Martin's position is the following: The Jews believe that the traditions they call Oral Torah, that is, "legem ore tenus," the law by [word of] mouth, were handed down by God to Moses "simul cum lege," i.e., right along with the written Torah, and passed on down by his successors until they were committed to writing by the ancient rabbis. To believe, however, that everything in the Talmud was handed down to Moses at Sinai must be considered madness, in view of the innumerable absurdities it contains. (Others, like Gui, had more simply referred to its contents as "lies and falsifications.") And yet, continued Martin, it cannot be disputed that those things that smack of truth, breathe of the teachings of the prophets and patriarchs and "in an exceedingly wonderful and incredible way" give expression to the Christian faith, but, in truth, demolish and confound the perfidy of present–day Jews,[9] those things were able to come down successively from Moses and the prophets and patriarchs to those who wrote them down; indeed, such traditions are wholly contradictory with those that the Jews, from the time of Jesus until "now" [Martin's day], hold about the Messiah and many other things, and in no way can we believe that they come from anywhere else than the prophets and patriarchs. In short, "truth is not to be rejected wherever it may be found; nor from wherever [it may come]; but one must look to what is said." As Baron summarized it, Martin was arguing that some Hebrew books "contained genuine rabbinic traditions going back to Moses and that they could actually serve to reinforce the truth of Christianity."[10]

The Christian kabbalism of the Renaissance was a further manifestation of this attitude. It grew in part out of a renewed emphasis on spirituality in certain Christian quarters, new ways having been sought through which Christianity might be validated or affirmed.[11] Christian kabbalism was thus the successor in some respects to the scholastics' recourse to Jewish philosophy. If there were Christian kabbalists in Martin's time, many of them were converted Jews who had rebelled against philosophy and also followed their own antinomian tendencies through Jewish mysticism and on out of Judaism. By the mid– to late fifteenth century, even native Christians began to consider the kabbalistic teachings more than just proofs of Christianity: they saw them as guides to magic, the occult and even the future, in line with newly revived Pythagorean and neo–Platonist modes of thought. In this way, the kabbalah became more specifically part of the reaction to scholasticism and the revolt against it.

Recourse to and reliance on Jewish teachers became even more frequent than heretofore, though these teachers still saw their own teachings turned against them almost constantly. The teachers were further unsuccessful in a simpler sense: their pupils regularly confused the two senses of the term 'kabbalah', the one referring to an authoritative oral tradition about a specific practice and the manner of its observance, the other meaning an esoteric doctrine revealed only to the initiated. Among the foremost Christian kabbalists was the well–known Pico della Mirandola (1463–94), who has been described as more of a religious thinker than a humanist of the new breed. Like many of his counterparts, he too saw all the great Christian doctrines revealed in the books of the kabbalah. And he too wrote that "there is absolutely no controversy between ourselves and the Hebrews on any matter, with regard to which they cannot be refuted and gainsaid out of the cabalistic books, so that there will not be even a corner left in which they may hide themselves."[12]

Nevertheless, such reinforcement of Christianity was no longer directed only at Jews or wavering Christians. Moreover, an understanding or knowledge of rabbinic law, that is, of the halakhah, was now seen to promote an increased comprehension of biblical and Christian antiquity and even of Christianity itself, however defined. For, with the coming of the Protestant Reformation, many of the new denominations and even many of those individuals who remained faithful to the Roman church came to view an understanding of Jewish law and practice as basic to inter– and even intraconfessional debate or defense.

None of these developments, however, and especially not the growth in the study of the *Mishneh Torah* that was about to begin, can be understood fully apart from the larger context of Hebraism in general.[13] Hebraism had already had a long and colorful history before the Renaissance. It need not always necessarily have implied a knowledge of Hebrew; it was, in the long run, most closely tied to the study of Scripture and to a certain Biblicism that intensified toward the end of the sixteenth century. Initially, it had meant an interest in the *Hebraica veritas,* i.e., Jerome's Latin version of Scripture, which was presumed to be so closely tied to the original Hebrew that it had an authority of its own. This approach did not necessarily presuppose or invite a knowledge of the language. Moreover, Christian exegetes, even those who did not learn Hebrew, often managed to learn something of Jewish exegesis. They were especially interested in the *peshat,* that is, the simple sense of the biblical text, and they frequently had this communicated to them by Jews. The apologetic dimension of these often informal contacts must not be underestimated for either side. Indeed, Christians were quite likely offered a good measure of homiletics along with more literal interpretations. At any rate, they soon became familiar with many of the great Spanish and Franco–German Jewish exegetes of the High Middle Ages: Rashi (1038–1105), Abraham Ibn Ezra (1089–1164) and David Kimḥi (c. 1160–1235), to name but a few. There were of course those who did take up the study of the language; Roger Bacon (1213–94), the English monk, was among the most famous of these. He studied Hebrew (and Greek too, which was unusual for his day) in order to come closer to the original revelation, which he identified with philosophical truth, and to revelation in general. His views were hardly unique and he too had conversionist aims with regard to the Jews, though he also sought their help as teachers. The impact of Jewish biblical exegesis on Christian exegetes from the Victorines of the twelfth century through Nicholas of Lyre (c. 1270–1349) to Martin Luther and even John Calvin in the sixteenth century and on down to their successors in the seventeenth was substantial. Though it is impossible to dwell on this phenomenon and its changing character in any detail, it may be pointed out that the study of the Hebrew language, even for the purpose of studying Scripture in the original, did not always lead to a more direct study of Jewish exegesis. Nor did it always lead to polemics. Yet this progression necessarily played a role in the growing interest in rabbinic literature at large, and its place in these developments must be noted.

Aside from the study of Scripture, Hebrew language study itself was an important factor; this hardly needs be said. Yet the study of the language often tried to remain self–contained and free of its Jewish connections. It was unable to so for a number of reasons, the first being the somewhat revolutionary associations such studies held in the minds of many. Its advocacy by both humanists and even nonhumanists after 1450 shows many of the same strains and tensions to which the study of the classical languages, Greek and Ciceronian Latin, were subject. Yet, if there was widespread hostility to the renewed emphasis on classical antiquity and scorn for the paganism of the Greeks and Romans, there was much fiercer opposition to Hebrew and Jewish literature. Contrary to the position of Raymund Martin and his successors, many not only condemned the study of Jewish literature, specifically for its *lack* of Christian truth, they even extended their opposition to the study of Hebrew. They felt that, even for biblical studies, Hebrew had no real value over the existing Latin.[14] As a way out, many tried to represent Hebrew language studies as an independent enterprise; but most of the opposition finally died down when the forensic necessities of Reformation biblical scholarship diverted men's minds.[15]

Many of those who did take up the study of Hebrew continued to do so out of a missionary goal, promoted originally by Raymund of Pennaforte, advanced by Martin and, finally, encouraged and even established in several colleges at Oxford, Paris, and Salamanca by the decrees of the ecclesiastical council of Vienne in 1311. Many of these students wished, like Martin, to argue against the Jews on the basis of Jewish literature and its evidence, such as they would interpret it. They and most Christian Hebraists of the fifteenth and sixteenth centuries remained firmly on guard against any sort of "judaizing," meaning against Jewish "glosses" and "corruptions" of Scripture, as Jewish interpretation was often called.[16] The epithet "judaizer" was one of general reproach, both Catholics and Protestants hurling it at their opponents. A most notable instance of its use was by and against John Calvin (1509–64) and not merely with reference to his legalism. As Protestants in general looked for a new, biblical basis for their respective teachings, rejecting the Roman teachings on the one hand and leaning toward a new fundamentalism and sometimes even a legalism on the other, as they sought to counter confessions opposed to theirs, they were especially wary of the charge of "judaizing," which might discredit them completely. Hardly to be overlooked is the frequent use of the charge by the Spanish Inquisitors, who began to operate in the late fifteenth century. They invoked it against both *conversos,* or New Christians of Jewish ancestry who had allegedly "relapsed," and others whom they wished to prosecute on suspicion of heresy in general, though there was often, of course, a similarity between the two uses.[17]

The most important way polemicists and just plain philologists from about 1500 on hoped to forestall "judaizing" in Christian writings was to free Christians from the need for Jewish teachers of Hebrew. Implied in this aim is a certain hostility to converted Jews as well, but there was certainly a greater willingness, if not an absolute one, to make use of converts. At any rate, many Christians continued to believe that Jews were both reluctant and prohibited from teaching Torah to non–Jews, the opinion long since discounted by R. Yeḥiel of Paris. Yet, in his Hebrew primer, the *Rudimenta hebraica* of 1506, even Johannes Reuchlin (1455–1522), the noted humanist and kabbalist, and, later, the defender of the Talmud against its being burned, complained of this Jewish attitude. He himself, of course, had studied with Jews, yet he, too, extended this Jewish refusal and "inexperience" in teaching Torah to Christians to the very teaching of Hebrew as a language.[18] Reuchlin argued on the basis of the use of "verba" in his reading of the standard talmudic proof–text:

> Our Jews, whether out of hatred or out of inexperience in teaching, are unwilling to instruct any Christian in their language, on the authority of a certain Rabbi Ammi, who says in the Talmud as follows: the words of the law may not be expounded to any gentile, as it is written: he makes his words known to Jacob, his regulations and his judgments to Israel; he has not done likewise to any other nation.[19]

Reuchlin and others felt that Hebrew lexicons and grammars by and for Christians would enable them both to surmount these difficulties and to study both the Bible and even postbiblical Jewish literature for its Christian truths as well as for its Jewish errors without being beset or overcome by Jewish interpretations. Among grammarians, the names of Sebastian Münster (1489–1552), Santes Pagnini (c. 1470–1536), and, later, the great rabbinic scholar Johannes Buxtorf the Elder (1564–1629) of Basel are most familiar. It is hardly even ironical, though, that the first Latin manuals of Hebrew grammar were generally based on the work of Jews, particularly David Kimḥi, mentioned above as a biblical exegete, and Elias Levita (c. 1468–1549), who gained his fame from his proofs for the posttalmudic origin of the vowel points as well as from his several grammatical texts. He was also the teacher of several prominent Christian scholars. Though the usefulness of the Latin primers and more advanced grammatical and lexical works continued to grow, recourse to Jewish teachers remained a fact of life for Christians who really wished to progress. And so, too, did disagreement among Christians continue about the appropriateness of such instruction, quarrels that were tied to larger issues of change that many were reluctant to see coming about.

Still, some of the emphasis of earlier centuries did begin to be displaced. Older attitudes to Jewish ideology and custom gave way before newer cultural emphases. The overall widening in the cultural horizons of the age, as overseas exploration and expansion gave rise to the study of non–European societies and their mores, contributed in some measure to a revised picture of the culture of the Jews. Yet more important, perhaps, was the growing search by humanists, with their mass of rhetorical, philological, historical and moral concerns, for new texts, new models and new ways to "illustrate" both Scripture and the Greco–Roman classics, which had already given a major impetus to the study of Hebrew, both biblical and rabbinic. The majority of humanists,[20] though not all of them, saw Hebrew as one of the three pivots of civilization, right alongside Latin and Greek. "Trilingual erudition" had become the mark of the educated person. Trilingual colleges were established throughout Europe, the first at Louvain in 1516. In sum, this growth in the knowledge of Hebrew and, in general, the cultural and religious shifts of the Renaissance that were followed by a new biblicism and fundamentalism in the Reformation were all necessary prerequisites for the new way in which the *Mishneh Torah* began to be regarded and treated at the end of the sixteenth century.

Hebraists of this time specifically commended the code on several grounds, most often its own 'auctoritas' as well as that of its author, its omission of the dialectic and fable of the Talmud, and its clarity of language. It was also said that the *Mishneh Torah* contained many things of value for the explication of Scripture. In other words, Maimonides' halakhic compendium came to be viewed as a most accessible and appropriate source of primary information on the religious and civil traditions and institutions of the Jews. For the scope of Christian attention to Judaism was becoming increasingly comprehensive, with interest growing rapidly in the ancient and the more recent also: temple and synagogue; priesthood and rabbinate; sacrifice and worship; government and jurisprudence; education, marriage; indeed, all the halakhic aspects of Jewish life, in addition to the ideological ones. These subjects constituted the expanding field of "biblical antiquities." Also, biblical exegetes as well as others who wished to see the institutions of their own society structured in accordance with the practice of the Jewish state of old now had recourse to the *Mishneh Torah.* The continuity that was sensed between the biblical period and postbiblical Jewish life was extended more frequently now to Jewish institutions in general. No longer was the emphasis primarily on Christian truths that might be discovered in Jewish texts. Issues of continuity and discontinuity between the ancient world and that of the Renaissance and of early modern times in general had been fundamental to the humanists' revision in attitude and approach toward the past as a whole, that is to say, toward ancient Judaism as well as Greco–Roman antiquity and ancient Christianity. Despite the discontinuity sensed by humanists with respect to the other two, however, the chain of authority and tradition in rabbinic Judaism was understood to include the *Mishneh Torah,* perceived as an abridgment and synthesis of the most authoritative Jewish works, the Mishnah and Talmud. And so, from this point on, the format and methodology of scholarship and commentary on or using the *Mishneh Torah* was usually of a piece with the modes of scholarship on the other classics. This refers, to be even more explicit, to the Jewish classics and to editions of Mishnaic and talmudic tractates; to commentaries on the Greco–Roman writers and on the Oriental, i.e., Arabic and Persian classics; to a new type of scholarship on the Greek Testament, which came to rely with increasing frequency on rabbinic parallels; and, of course, even if the Latin versions often served as the foundation, to the study of the Hebrew Bible. In this, Christians continued to make use of Jewish exegesis both early and late, and to this the *Mishneh Torah* began to make its contribution. The new methodological approaches with which the polemical and dogmatic ones were often supplanted were also both the result of a new "love of learning for its own sake," as George Foot Moore put it, and the manifestation of a growing antiquarianism, to the general outlines of which Momigliano has frequently called attention.[21]

Moreover, as the general purview of Christians continued to change and as their scholarship began to move beyond the disciplines of language, literature, law, or philosophy to new social sciences such as anthropology, the mores of the Jews and the evidence of rabbinic literature, and particularly of the *Mishneh Torah*, began to be viewed more and more dispassionately as merely pieces of evidence in the study of culture. This was not universally the case, to be sure, and Frank Manuel provides cogent illustration both of the initially favorable reception of rabbinic learning in the halls of the Enlightenment and of the subsequent perverse aversion. He does note, however, that it was through the Christian Hebraists that the *philosophes* derived their initial, largely sympathetic view of Judaism.[22] Moreover, while the religious views of Isaac Newton did not, according to Manuel, exert any major influence, Newton provides an excellent example of the extended influence that Hebraism enjoyed, even in apparently remote quarters of men's minds and of scientifically oriented ones at that. Newton's "belief in the sacral nature of science" ultimately led him to the biblical books for his investigations of the early history of man and the history of science, and to Maimonides for a definition of the true prophet. For his studies in this area, Newton had recourse to many of the leading Christian Hebraists of the seventeenth century, among whom Manuel mentions Dionysius Vossius and John Spencer, two of the most prominent Hebraist students of the *Mishneh Torah*.[23] In sum, there was hardly any lessening among believing Christians in the value of rabbinic learning, at the same time as there was hardly any lessening of their longstanding hopes or efforts toward the conversion of the Jews. In other words, neither the supposedly more dispassionate method nor the widespread dissemination of rabbinic literature had effected any changes on Christian goals. In point of fact, hopes for Jewish conversion became linked even more strongly at this period with a growing millennialism, one that saw the conversion of the Jews as an indispensable preliminary. The twofold Christian posture toward the Jews and their religion and culture remained essentially unchanged, even as it grew in sophistication.

I

Hebraism and the Dutch Republic

The dual approach that seventeenth–century Christian readers still manifested toward Jewish literature was a pan–European phenomenon. So too was the broader philological, cultural and historical interest in rabbinic learning that had begun to flower by the turn of the seventeenth century. Nowhere in Europe, however, were these phenomena more apparent than in the Netherlands. More particularly, nowhere was the study of Maimonides' *Mishneh Torah* more cultivated than there. Now the historical features of the life and society of the Dutch Republic, that is, of the United Provinces of the Netherlands, were such as to produce an environment far more receptive to the open practice of Judaism than that found almost anywhere else at this time. To be sure, the intertwining of theology, culture, and politics that shaped seventeenth–century Dutch life was by no means unique in its day. Yet the specific mix that characterized the Dutch setting was rather remarkable, allowing as it did such extensive interchange between Christian and Jew while, at the same time, often prompting rather defensive postures from the two vis–à–vis each other. The extent to which this mix was determinative for and determined by the phenomenon of Hebraism is our subject at present and, ultimately, at large in this work.

The Culture and Politics of the Dutch Republic

Before considering the character of the Christian Hebraist study of Maimonides and its impact on the Jewish community of Amsterdam, it would be well to consider the tenor of Dutch society and culture more generally, and to examine the ways in which the attitude or approach of representative students and scholars to Hebrew and rabbinic literature emerges from and is characteristic of the tendencies of that society.

Dutch Humanism and the Politics of Theology

We must turn first to Leiden University, the oldest institution of higher learning in the United Provinces, for, even though the premier Latin editions of the *Mishneh Torah* would appear in Amsterdam, they were a direct product of the training and traditions of Leiden.

Leiden had been founded in 1575, in the flush of enthusiasm at the early victories by Dutchmen over their Spanish overlords, "as a protestant university, . . . to fill the need for an intellectual and spiritual centre on which the budding [Dutch] nation could draw for its political leadership and religious autonomy."[1] There was a practical as well as a spiritual purpose implicit in this founding, one that soon allowed Leiden to develop the strong tradition of humanistic scholarship that made it a center of learning second to none in its day. It attracted some of the greatest scholars of the day in both the arts and the sciences. Justus Lipsius (1547–1606), a product of the Collegium Trilingue of Louvain, whose neo–Stoicism, political theories, and rhetorical ideals set the tone for much early–seventeenth–century thinking in all disciplines, taught there from 1579 to 1591, when he returned to Louvain. Joseph Justus Scaliger (1540–1609), Lipsius's successor, arrived from Avignon in 1593 with a great reputation. Not only was he known as the son of Julius Caesar Scaliger (1484–1558), who, from Italian beginnings, had come to rule French humanism, ordering it away from the Hellenism of Guillaume Budé (1467–1540) and making it Latinate, the younger Scaliger was already famous in his own right as well. The author of the 1583 *De emendatione temporum,* it was he who had singlehandedly begun to revolutionize the study of chronology. Though he never lectured, Scaliger became the true luminary of Leiden, known as a historian and a jurist, and, ultimately, as the founder of modern classical philology.

Now Scaliger did not think highly of Franciscus Junius (1545–1602), but almost everyone else did. Junius held a chair in theology from 1592 to his death and was known for his peace–loving and tolerant qualities, despite his overall orthodoxy. It was probably due to Junius that Leiden achieved its reputation in "theology," which implied both the training of young men for the ministry and the academic investigation of the sources of religious knowledge. To be sure, there was at Leiden, as elsewhere at this time, a subjective purpose to the latter of these two enterprises; at Leiden, there were also, from the very outset, numerous controversies on the nature of Protestantism, i.e., Calvinism, between the stricter Calvinists and their more moderate opponents. Junius did not become particularly embroiled himself, but the mildly heterodox views of his successor Jacob Arminius (1560–1609) aroused the wrath of one who had been Junius's rather silent colleague from 1595, Franciscus Gomarus (1561–1641). The conflicts between Arminius and Gomarus over such matters as the origin of sin and the irresistibility of grace would become even more heated after Arminius's death. Though Gomarus himself would leave Leiden in 1611, the debates would come to a head with the victory of the Gomarist faction at the national Synod of Dort in 1618 and the condemnation and orders of restraint and restriction placed on their opponents. Yet Arminianism managed to retain its influence and its adherents. The major issues of Arminianism have recently been put as follows: "freedom of conscience; the responsibility of man before God; and the universality of grace."[2] These and the questions that grow out of them, such as the rights (or power) of temporal government in (or over) Church affairs and the general issue of toleration, go to the very roots of both humanism and Protestantism.

Yet, both prior to and in the long aftermath of the Synod of Dort, there were ongoing attempts by the Gomarists (or, to identify them by church affiliation, the Counter–Remonstrants) to exclude their more liberal Calvinist counterparts, that is, the Remonstrants, as the Arminians were more frequently referred to—not to mention the other dissenting non–Calvinist Christian groups to which the orthodox group was opposed—from Dutch society. Their goal, never realized, was to make their own Dutch Reformed Church the sole legitimate religious body in the Netherlands and to have that church established as a full–fledged partner in the affairs of state.

Dutch Christian Hebraism drew some of its forcefulness from this strife. The foremost propagandists on either side were often Hebraists whose interest in and use of rabbinic literature stemmed as much from their internal squabbles as it did from any of the other purposes cf Christian humanist scholarship. It also stemmed in part from the growing Jewish presence in the Netherlands, to which settlement Calvinists in general, and not merely the Hebraists, paid particular attention. The Jews, in return, paid particular attention as a community to the various nuances in the Christian approaches.[3] Moreover, if members of the Jewish community became especially close to leading members of the Arminian wing and Remonstrant Church, it was perhaps because Jewish interests were, in some respects, more closely identified with those of the more liberal group.

For the rising bourgeoisie that dominated the Sephardic Jewish community of Amsterdam bore somewhat the same character as the membership of the Remonstrant Church. The mostly middle–class origins of the latter, the sympathy accorded them by the regent class, with its broad economic interests, and even the extensive social links between Remonstrant and Regent, not to mention the basically middle–class Remonstrant values, all gave the Remonstrants an affinity of sorts with the Jewish community. Contact between intellectuals in the two groups was only a natural concomitant, even though absolute religious toleration of either side by the other was generally out of the question. It should be noted here that the Jews did not limit their contacts to the Remonstrants. Nor did the Remonstrants show any greater leniency toward the Jews based on their own having been and continuing to be an oppressed minority.

The life of the Dutch Republic, in which Hebraism played an integral role, was not merely at the background, but was itself the very theater in which all of this took place. Let us examine its character in somewhat closer detail. There were three major forces or power blocs in the society: the Regent class, the House of Orange, and the Reformed Church. Before the mid–seventeenth century, no one of these groups gained total supremacy, due to a strong, constantly shifting balance of power between the three of them. Strong traditions of local autonomy continued to ward off the establishment of a strong central power such as the House of Orange. The firm opposition of the Church prevented the Regents from really gaining the upper hand.[4] It was the Church that usually held the balance of power, though; responsiveness to its dictates demanded, even from the Regent class, a certain degree of external orthodoxy,[5] particularly in view of the firm support from the Church among the lower classes. Even the more liberal opponents of the Church were inclined to stress their own adherence to the principles of Calvinism,[6] although they differed, sometimes rather strongly, over what those principles should be. They were, after all, still Calvinists. In the end, to be sure, the Church remained, technically and de facto, with power only over its own affairs;[7] although there was intense pressure on liberal Calvinists to display external fidelity to the demands of the Church, the liberals were still able to defend their own, inward liberalization and their personal freedom from coercion on points of dogma. The Church was not at all satisfied with this imperfect state of affairs. They tried to harass their opponents and to have them banished, and in this they sometimes succeeded. There was little, however, that they could do to enforce complete control. While the cloak of Calvinism covered Dutch culture more and more as the century progressed, it also became less and less effective in stemming freedom of expression.

In fact, the extent of Calvinist influence in Dutch culture is very much a matter of dispute.[8] There is no question, though, that the actual disputes within Calvinism played a central role in Dutch life. Politics often became tied up with obscure points of religious doctrine, debated heatedly. Though the issues, mentioned earlier, were complex, contemporaries were certain that they understood them and their significance clearly, and there is no reason to assume that this "race of amateur theologians"[9] did not have a clear grasp of the interpretation or point of view they were defending.

There were, to be even more explicit, only a few major issues, even if the detailed form of expression was far more complicated. The points mentioned above can, in effect, be reduced to two: man's role in his own salvation and the role of the church in a society composed of both the saved and the fallen.[10] The corollaries, again, included the issues of: the respective functions of Church and state, the possibility of freedom of the will, or of freedom of conscience with regard to certain propositions. The Remonstrant article on the irresistibility of grace is a good touchstone for the whole controversy.[11] It states that the grace of God is indispensable in the life of the spirit, but that it is not irresistible. This means that, in order for the grace of God to insure salvation, man has to be an active partner in accepting that grace. An opening is left for human initiative. By contrast, the strict Calvinist interpretation offers no option. Grace, if it is predestined by God—and the Remonstrants, too, generally accepted the idea of predestination—is granted, and the individual is saved, categorically. There is no flexibility on the question, no latitude for the possibility of falling from grace. In short, there are two positions with far wider implications than the propositions themselves articulate. The one position, particularist or "precieze," argues very carefully, scholastically as it were, for a stringent application of the principle of God's supremacy, indeed, His absolute supremacy. The other view, that of the "rekkelijken," the more flexible or tensile of the groups, also pays homage to the idea of the sovereignty of God. It insists, however, on a place for man in the working out of his own salvation. The pattern of expression is strongly humanistic in both method and implications, and, also, in the materials with which it articulates and defends its position.

With respect to the relationship between Church and state,[12] the Remonstrants generally supported the "Erastian" doctrine of the supremacy of the needs of the state over those of any clerical body or power (one might say of civil power over ecclesiastical power). While the Calvinists of the more stringent position gave the state complete control over affairs of state, they expected the magistrates to be responsive to the needs of the clergy, and they tried increasingly to identify their own affairs with those of the state.

The Remonstrants had closer links to the Regent class than to the House of Orange. The House of Orange, which was generally without religious opinions—Maurice is often quoted as having said that he did not know whether predestination was blue or green—and which stood in theory to benefit more from the Arminian position, tended to favor the orthodox Calvinists, because they usually lent the stadholder greater support in his wars with Spain and in his attempts to centralize power in his own hands. Ultimately, the Calvinists proved to be monarchist in their views, provided the ruler would defend their religious interests; this the stadholders were often prepared to trade off, as their own designs became progressively more monarchist. Many orthodox Calvinists desperately wished to see a "theocracy" established where people would have to attest to their beliefs.[13] The Church hoped to have the stadholder as the arm of enforcement in a truly Christian state. Yet, while Maurice was more yielding in this regard, Frederick Henry, the period of whose tenure, from 1625 to 1647, has often been termed the Dutch Golden Age,[14] was himself of an outlook more sympathetic to the Remonstrants. In fact, the cultural and intellectual character of the Golden Age, not to mention its lasting achievements, were shaped, in many instances, by men and ideas that were at variance with the reserved, moralizing piety which orthodox Calvinism stood for.[15]

Hugo Grotius (1583–1645) embodied the essence of that age. Though he spent the last twenty–four years of his life in exile, he was still the outstanding Dutch man of letters in the seventeenth century and had a major influence at home. Johann Huizinga, the cultural historian, once capsulized him as follows: "the simple–hearted teacher, the gentle optimist, the universal peace–bringer, one who put his trust in the strength of honest argument, in the spirit of harmony and religious tolerance, the opponent of unyielding orthodoxy—in short, the Remonstrant."[16] Remonstrant is too restrictive a term, perhaps; the general flowering of culture and learning during this period has more often, and rather loosely, been called Arminian instead. Arminianism claimed adherents far and wide, not merely within the Remonstrant brotherhood itself.[17] Its "humanistic" emphasis on the value of individual initiative and on practical ethics was probably subscribed to openly or implicitly by the majority of Dutchmen.[18] The burgers, especially, acted as if their own efforts could affect their material as well as their spiritual well–being, and not merely as if their personal success was a demonstration of their salvation.[19] Increased prosperity rendered these members of the bourgeoisie increasingly at odds with the tenets of strict Calvinism[20] and its emphasis, for example, on frugality. It was often the case that, as bourgeois merchants became members of a more cultured élite,[21] they adopted a culture that was far from denominational or strict. The arts and secular culture were, indeed, looked upon askance and their pursuit frowned upon by the puritanical Calvinist *predikanten.* The worldly character to which the visual arts, for example, sometimes gave expression and that material prosperity itself tended to promote was disparaged by the spokesmen for orthodoxy, with their emphasis on piety and their horror of "idolatry."

As a result, there was a growing gulf between the two expressions of Calvinism, both of which insisted on predestination, yet each of which viewed it in a different light. For the "preciezen," salvation or damnation had been completely predetermined; no real achievement was possible in this life except, ironically, in view of thc foregoing, a chance demonstration, in the form of material success, that one was among the saved. Such a doctrine seems to have appealed greatly to the lower classes, themselves lacking any sense of the potential for achievement, looking instead to the ruler for a vicarious embodiment of their success or salvation.[22] The "rekkelijken," the latitudinarians, on the other hand, had a far more middle–class perspective: although material success may have been a demonstration of spiritual salvation, the danger of losing one's grasp on this success was ever present; the human factor was an essential component, in tandem, to be sure, with the workings of the Holy Spirit, in insuring final victory over sin: one could fall from grace. The potential for achievement was easily enough transferred from the spiritual plane to the human one and back again; it was, in all respects, an article of faith.

The doctrine of a potential for achievement, which favored and was in harmony with the dynamic conception of a growing mercantile society, was at odds, therefore, with the older traditions of a stable society that orthodox Calvinism sought to defend.[23] Even though the Calvinists became identified at a very early stage with the party that sought independence from Spain, they also represented traditions of local autonomy (which worked, in some respects, to their own disadvantage); they stood, in other words, for the preservation of privilege. Calvinism had supplanted Roman Catholicism as the defender of tradition in the Netherlands, using the call to liberty and independence as a prelude to its later invocation of the name "true Israel" for the United Provinces of the Netherlands. All Calvinists, the liberals included, espoused this idealized conception that the Church was probably responsible for originally.[24] None bandied the idea about so vehemently as the orthodox Calvinists, however. They wielded it as a weapon and, with the appellation, claimed the prerogatives of the *ecclesia* in a theocracy, seeking to suppress any dissent from their dogmatic and ethical ideals. They sought, in other words, to convert the nation to their faith and their way of thinking; in the process, they sought to become transformed from a sect into the national church of a united state. Although, as noted above, sovereign authority would remain vested in the civil government in political matters and even in ecclesiastical ones, sovereignty, as the *predikanten* and even some of their academic defenders had hoped to have it, was to be defined by God's word as interpreted by the Church. "The ruler was to do the will of God in the same way as the kings of [the united] Israel had served the Lord; by preventing heresy and punishing idolatry."[25] "The orthodox ministers," wrote Pieter Geyl, "regarded themselves as the watchmen on the turrets of Zion,"[26] but neither the Regents nor certain other influential groups in society necessarily acceded to that view. Some groups tended to prefer the image of Batavia, in fact, as the Netherlands had been known in ancient Roman times, which usage harked back to a different set of ideals. Moreover, though the image of "Israel" was used,[27] for example, by Arminius himself,[28] by the great playwright Joost van den Vondel (1587–1679),[29] and even by "the oracle of Delft,"[30] Hugo Grotius, none of these men associated the idea of ecclesiastical power with it. They held patriotic sentiments in favor of the emerging republic, to be sure, and they expressed them in religious guise. Even the poet Jacob Cats (1577–1660), the arbiter of Dutch taste, if not also its bellwether, and Constantijn Huygens (1596–1687), the cosmopolitan but definitely Protestant *littérateur,* invoked the *typus* or *figura* of Israel.[31] Their works generally reflect and defend Calvinist ideals. Yet, while they themselves defended the Church, they were still far from shackled to its rigid preachings. Cats invoked the parallel of the Hebrew republic during the Grand Assembly of 1651, in an address on behalf of republicanism and a stadholderless regime; his view went counter to the position of the Church.[32] All this fabrication and use of the myth of Israel, then, reflects the famous "biblical tint," in Busken Huet's phrase, that overlay the totality of Dutch life throughout the seventeenth century.[33]

The vehemence with which the Reformed Church took up the idea can be seen particularly well in a broadside dating from 1631. Its anonymous author drew a "Comparison, both in Government and Church, of the blessed and rebellious State of these United

Netherlands with the State of the Israelites, when God bestowed the promised Canaan upon them, and they lost the same through disobedience."[34] Not unexpected is the pamphleteer's argument that the chosenness of Israel applies to the people of the Netherlands, and that the state should be run according to God's word. Abraham the patriarch, he says, was the first to reject and destroy idolatry; Abraham is set up as the *exemplum.* The Republic of the United Netherlands is obligated to follow in his footsteps and in those of his descendants: to destroy idolatry lest the state itself be destroyed. Among the groups to be banished, therefore, as enemies: "Arians, Socinians, Papists, Mennonites, Martinists, and, most of all, the Arminians, who are apostates and traitors, who live without religion, and who are not to be tolerated."[35] They are to be equated with the heathen whom Abraham and the Israelites were commanded to destroy; the Israelite failure to root out the heathen completely resulted in their own disobedience and in their banishment from the promised land. As for the Jews, there is no question that they are excluded from the state. Having rejected Christ, they do not share in salvation.[36] Yet the focus in this pamphlet, as in all the many such arguments at this period, is really on the Arminians.

The slogan 'idolatry' was also, however, a rallying cry for the Reformed Calvinists in their war against Spain and the Catholics.[37] 'Idolatry' was well–nigh the standard term for Catholicism in Calvinist writings, even if it was also applied to the Remonstrants both frequently and stridently. As a result, its expropriation called forth a strenuous response from the liberal camp. They were, they insisted, neither idolators nor Catholics. They might have dissented from the views of the "preciezen," but they had by no means made their peace with Catholicism, and they resented the label. They continually stressed that they had no allegiance to the Pope or the Spanish king and had not been influenced by Catholic or, especially, Jesuit ideology and doctrine.

Scholarship would have to come to their defense. A treatise setting forth the nature of idolatry was clearly a great desideratum. In 1641, having drawn upon the resources of his phenomenal erudition, Gerardus Johannes Vossius, the great Remonstrant polyhistor and Grotius's closest friend, produced an immense work and his true magnum opus, *De Theologia Gentili et Physiologia*

Christiana, sive De Origine ac Progressu Idololatria. It was, in effect, though not expressly, a vindication of the Arminians from the accusation of idolatry. By specific intent, it was a monument to his son Dionysius, who had died of smallpox in 1633 at the age of 21 and who had stimulated his father's interest in the subject even further with his own edition of Maimonides' *Hilkhot 'Avodah Zarah.* This appeared bound together with his father's work and was entitled *De Idololatria.*[38] It was, in other words, an added *testimonium.* Nowhere is it mentioned, but it is not impossible that this Maimonidean treatise, which begins with the history of Abraham's opposition to idolatry and his discovery of true religion, was, in some ways, a response to the anonymous pamphlet just discussed. It was certainly, however, a major contribution to the displays of source material that were a great Arminian weapon in the war of propaganda with the Reformed Church.[39]

Vossius the Elder and his fellow scholars, no matter how antiquarian their métier, were more than mere practitioners of *Altertumswissenschaft.*[40] As adherents of a tradition that has been characterized as "the bastard child of faith and free inquiry,"[41] they too took biblical and even classical models as examples for the present. They did not necessarily become shackled by them, though.[42] The Arminians were broad in their interests and unfettered in studying other cultures. They looked to the broader past for models or examples for the Dutch burger to emulate as he tried not merely to achieve or excel, to be himself at his best, but even to transcend his own limitations. The portraiture of the period, which, as indicated above, was often condemned by the *predikanten* for its too worldly character, even though its representations did not always necessarily clash with their ideals, shows some of the influence of this thinking especially well, in attempting to capture the subject's aspirations, rather than his previous achievements alone.[43] This portraiture, also, looks outside the biblical world to the Greco–Roman classical tradition for models. If the Arminians were moralists, however, as they almost invariably were, they were empiricists by methodology. They were willing to lay out evidence without always necessarily passing judgment on it, without always feeling compelled to reconcile all discrepancies. The Arminian mind, like Amsterdam itself, was an entrepôt of diverse ideas.[44] The Arminian faith was one of "intellectual assent";[45] it was possessed of an "antipathy to Calvinist theology" and to the scholastic dogmatics that the precisians lived by.[46] Arminianism was in the direct line of the return "to the sources." It looked back beyond Calvin, beyond Augustine even, to the early church fathers, to Greek and Roman literature, and, also, to Jewish tradition. It was not anti–Calvin; it was, though, if anything, Erasmian.[47] Trevor–Roper considers Arminianism a forerunner of the Enlightenment.[48] Yet Arminianism was part of the whole cultural movement that had begun with Renaissance humanism and that was not limited to Arminianism, to Protestants, or to theology at all. It may even be pointed out that many an otherwise "orthodox" Calvinist was often an unconfessed or latent Arminian in scholarly method. And almost all Calvinists were beneficiaries of scholarship by Arminians.

One of the major tools of cultural self–discovery and expansion for both the classically oriented Arminians and the more fundamentalist Calvinists was the study of rabbinic literature. When either group wished to explicate the Hebrew or the Greek Testaments, they frequently looked to rabbinic literature for help in understanding the source materials, and for traditions and a knowledge that they did not themselves possess. They also looked to rabbinica to learn about the Judaism of more recent times, for both polemical purposes and sheer curiosity. If, for the Calvinists, rabbinic literature was a help in the exposition of their own tradition, for the Arminians it was also a valuable source of more general cultural information.[49] Yet, even for those who might otherwise be classified as humanists, there would be clear disagreement on certain points, especially the theological ones, and even they did not always eliminate polemics from their scholarly treatises. It must be stressed again that, even among Arminians there was little momentum toward an absolute tolerance of their Jewish contemporaries as Jews.

In short, rabbinic literature was excluded less and less often as a subject of study, even by more conservative scholars. It became accepted as part of the training, or 'requirements for membership' in the 'Christian Republic of Letters', the formula by which this period designated the international body of learned individuals.[50] Leiden was but one home of the group; indeed, education and culture were not necessarily associated with the academy at this point in time.[51] Moreover, the famous struggle of the "ancients" and the "moderns" was only in its incipient stages, and the loss of faith in the classics had not yet set in. Soon reverence for the past would be undermined by a general shift to the various vernaculars and by the scientific revolution.[52] Until mid–century at least, though, biblical and classical wisdom and values held sway; even afterwards, scholars would select materials from the stores of antiquity and from ancient wisdom as proof either for or against the new truths, and also as source materials for vernacular creations.

Latin was still the international language, and this facilitated communication. Also, rhetorical traditions stretching back to Renaissance times were still firmly entrenched, perpetuating the methods of study.[53] There were, as has already been made clear, three mainstreams of thought, with these methods applied equally to all three. We may again emphasize here for a moment the special importance of the biblical tradition. It has been said, though not with reference to the Netherlands, that "much Hebraic thought, [that is,] thought of which the original expression was in Hebrew, was, in translation, behind the characteristic movement of the seventeenth century."[54] In the Netherlands, as elsewhere, though, the translations were usually still into Latin, and the translations and scholarly studies of rabbinic literature, and their diffusion, helped further the overall biblicism of the century. Though there is a distinction to be made between biblicism and Hebraist scholarship, there were certainly links between them, and the readership of the works that the Hebraists produced was very broadly based.[55] And not all the Hebraists were professionals either; many of them were nonspecialists. A distinction we may draw, however, even if it does not always hold, is one between the types of works composed. The editions and commentaries on rabbinic literature were, more often than not, the work of scholars; the original compositions, that is, treatises on more general themes or issues, dependent on the former in many instances, were the work of interested amateurs.

What linked the two groups even more closely in the Netherlands was their Calvinism, of course. Calvinism has been called a "life–system,"[56] and Judaism can be seen to be very much the same. In fact, from no religion did Calvinism borrow as many symbols as it did from Judaism. Calvinists, therefore, both "craved" and felt an antipathy toward the Jewish sources.[57] It may be that the Arminian approach to rabbinics was probably less doctrinaire in the long run. Yet even the Arminian humanist, while seeking to expand his understanding and application of his own life–system and to compare, contrast, and learn from rabbinic Judaism, also sought to confront it. The leading Arminians, such as Vossius the Elder and Grotius, eagerly looked forward to the Jews' conversion.[58] The difference, though, must be stressed. The prime context of their learning and of their literary productions, and, consequently, those of their disciples who did the more scholarly work on rabbinic literature, was cultural, philological, and historical. One might call it humanistically religious, rather than doctrinal, ecclesiastical, or missionary, regardless of the original inspiration. The contrary, of course, was more often true of the stricter Calvinists. But the boundaries here are obviously imprecise, and in either camp there were those whose methodological views cut across party lines. The Vossius family's own self–perception on this question shows the inherent complexities.[59] Their motivation toward rabbinic studies was as much missionary as utilitarian or, generally, religious. Missionary and conversionist aims were attributed to Dionysius specifically. Yet he himself argued vocally at one point the usefulness of Jewish sources for scholarship and theology.

Nor were the defenders of orthodoxy necessarily unscholarly or crudely propagandist. As a matter of fact, the theological faculty at Leiden, that bastion of orthodoxy after Dort, prided itself on its ability to carry on its controversies with the Remonstrants and Catholics "acute, subtiliter ac perspicue," i.e., with sharpness, precision, and clarity, and, at the same time, to set forth its arguments "sine ira et studio."[60] Still, despite their erudition, most of these precisians had been and remained theologians and theologians alone, not humanists. More important, they were scholastics and defenders of an idealized *status quo ante* that had probably never existed; they were men hardly receptive to the broader currents of humanistic education. Their interest in Jewish materials was more often directly controversialist or narrowly exegetical. The latter of these was, to be sure, a respectable humanistic enterprise, yet, as carried out in precisian hands, tended to reflect a doctrinaire point of view. And the *Statenbijbel,* the 1637 'Authorized Version' of the Dutch Reformed Church that was the work of numerous Hebraists, was a particularly reactionary rather than progressive book, having excluded certain scholars from participating in its creation and, it has been argued, closing off a system rather than inspiring a new series of creative developments.[61]

Still, as indicated, it was not uncommon for Remonstrant and Counter–Remonstrant to exchange works of scholarship. Constantijn l'Empereur, for example, whose "extraordinary" appointment as professor of Jewish controversies at Leiden is an important part of the story of Dutch Hebraism and will be treated at some length below, was a careful scholar, highly respected in all circles. He remained a friend and correspondent,[62] and was even a visitor of the Vossii after they had transferred from Leiden to Amsterdam in 1631. He was also a correspondent of Grotius's, and his editions and commentaries were a major source for the great jurist and biblical commentator.[63] Just as the Dutch and Spanish continued to trade throughout the Eighty Years War, with only rare interruptions, despite severe embargoes on such activity, and surely against the will of the Reformed clergy, who railed quite frequently against any truce,[64] so Remonstrant, Counter–Remonstrant, and even non–Calvinist all took advantage of each other's scholarship. The Christian Republic of Letters incorporated diverse factions, and the political and religious differences of individual Dutchmen did not destroy it. It may even be that the divisiveness that existed was a major factor in creating the kind of environment in which the libertarian faith and freedom of inquiry that were ultimately the essence of Arminianism were able to flourish at all.

It cannot be denied, though, that such controversies also transformed and even helped diminish the status of Hebrew. At Leiden, as elsewhere at this time, the study of Hebrew was reduced from its initial position as a component of *eruditio trilingualis* into an essentially ancillary one as a subdivision of theology; it was hardly any longer a discipline independently pursued unto itself.[65] That most of the individuals who have been mentioned to this point were Hebraists (of greater or lesser ability, which does not matter) is beside the point, even though not all Hebraists were theologians and not all theologians Hebraists. While the quality of Hebrew instruction and learning at Leiden was among the best of its day, the language soon came to be studied almost exclusively for its application to learned theology or to 'historical' investigations that might defend one or another set of ideals. If the apologetic and even polemical background and impetus did not necessarily preclude dispassion or precision in the actual pursuit of these investigations, it did mean that the humanists' ideal of *bene loquendi,* with all that implied, as well as the grammatical or more purely literary productions that might have resulted more routinely from a detached set of ideals were brought to fruition with comparative infrequency. So the traditions developed with an emphasis on the *utilitas* of Hebrew study. Though the later Christian humanists were obviously following the thinking of their predecessors, the earlier stress on the usefulness of language and literature as tools for history and politics, and the formerly more detached function of history and historical investigation themselves, had given way to a more conscious application of theological dogmatics. To be sure, the actual skills of the Hebraists were not necessarily diminished and may even have shown an advance on those of their predecessors. Yet, as the dogmatic approach masked the others with increasing frequency, the discontent of scholars in the Remonstrant and even in the Counter–Remonstrant camps grew apace. Christian Hebraism came to be regarded by many as a theological enterprise only, although in some quarters it remained almost strictly a philological pursuit. The gamut of approaches is reflected well in the study of the *Mishneh Torah,* and it is to that study that our inquiry now turns.

Rabbinic Studies Out of Leiden and Franeker: The Early Study of *Mishneh Torah* in the Netherlands

While the study of Hebrew by Dutchmen waxed and waned as the century went on, and even as the several modes of Hebraist scholarship alternated among themselves, the frequency of *Mishneh Torah* study, once it had been entered upon in earnest, grew fairly consistently throughout the century. The extent to which it was translated and commented upon and, indeed, the very nature of the translations and commentaries flowed directly from an intricate interdependence among these Hebraist scholars that was one of the predominant characteristics of this period. Aside from the usual and natural affinity of teacher and pupil, there was, during the seventeenth and eighteenth centuries, both in the Netherlands and abroad, a large body of students of the *Mishneh Torah;* moreover, the very connectedness of the Republic of Letters helped stimulate and give form to the translations. This is not to say that only one point of view or dogmatic tendency was to be found. Rather, the views were as multifarious as the practitioners. It was, perhaps, more than anything else the richness of Maimonides' code that afforded commentators the possibility of treating it in so many different ways and of deriving or seeming to derive material consistent with their individual needs and goals.

Among the predecessors and contemporaries of the earliest translators, Scaliger's name comes immediately to mind as the one whose Hebraic accomplishments deserve first mention. As the colossus of learning associated with the early years of Leiden, Scaliger exercised a role, to be sure, but the real impetus to the study of Hebrew and rabbinics there was provided by Johannes Drusius (1550–1616), though he would move from Leiden to Franeker in 1584–85. Moreover, Drusius and Scaliger only laid the foundations. On their work other scholars would build, from such generalists as Hugo Grotius and Petrus Cunaeus (1586–1638) to such specialists as Johannes Coccejus (1603–69) and Constantijn l'Empereur, right down to the very first translators and commentators on the *Mishneh Torah.* It is these translators, the aforementioned Dionysius Vossius (1612–1633), Guglielmus Vorstius (c. 1610–1652), and Georgius Gentius (1618–87), on whom the present study ultimately comes to focus and turn, particularly with respect to their attitudes and opinions on Judaism and, especially, their relations with members of the Jewish community. But the scholarly milieu from which they took their start and in which they grew and developed as individuals was the academy at Leiden, and it is there that we too shall begin.

Drusius, Scaliger and Other Forerunners

Johannes Drusius the Elder, the leading Hebraist of the early days of Leiden, found it difficult to tolerate the conditions that promoted dogmatics there.[66] After seven years at the new university, he found that his resolutely antitheological view of *eruditio*

Hebraica had made his position virtually untenable. Indeed, Leiden had had and always would have difficulty establishing a Hebrew chair, even within the faculty of theology, as a separate position; usually the teaching of Hebrew was held as an added responsibility by someone whose primary duties lay elsewhere, in mathematics, for instance. In 1584, Drusius left Leiden and, with the opening of the new university in Franeker the following year, took up residence there, quickly making his new home the foremost center of its time for the philological study of the Hebrew Bible. Even if, for most students, the goal was still theology, for Drusius the prerequisite of theology always remained philology. He himself specifically rejected the designation "theologus," aspiring instead to the appellation "grammaticus," implying with this that different methods and even different spheres of activity belonged to each area.

Drusius was also an avid student of rabbinic literature, acquiring the Talmud and other Jewish books from a Jewish bookseller of Emden. Letters from that bookseller to Drusius dating from the 1590s have been preserved.[67]

Drusius read the books he received and did so with care: his *Annotationes in totum Jesu Christi Testamentum . . . [quô] consensus ostenditur synagogae Israelitae cum ecclesia Christiana* (Franeker, 1612) refers to a wide range of talmudic tractates, midrashim, and Jewish biblical exegetes. Further, Drusius cites: the *Turim,* the halakhic code of Jacob ben Asher (1290–c. 1343); Abraham ibn Daud's (c. 1110–c. 1181) historical overview of the chain of rabbinic tradition, *Sefer hak–Kabbalah* (1161), perhaps in one or another sixteenth century Latin abridgment, though the Latin title Drusius uses for the work does not correspond to either Münster's or Génébrard's; *Sefer Yuḥasin* (c. 1510) of Abraham Zacuto (1450–1515), also a historical work on the rabbinic tradition; and, repeatedly, the kabbalistic and ethical treatise *Sefer ham–Musar* by the Spanish exile Judah Kalats (16th Century) of Tlemçen [?], Algeria. For this last–named work, Drusius probably used the Cracow edition of 1598, though the work had appeared first in Constantinople in 1536–37.

Though I have spotted no reference to Maimonides in Drusius's commentary, it is clear that he was quite conversant with a broad spectrum of rabbinic literature. Nonetheless, he still had recourse to the works of such of his predecessors as Pietro Galatini (1460–1540), whose aims in the famous *De Arcanis religionis Christianae* (Ortona, 1518 and frequently reprinted), an important treatise in the history of Christian kabbalism, were more strictly polemical than Drusius's ever were. (Galatini, incidentally, as Drusius's friend Scaliger discovered, had plagiarized heavily from the *Pugio Fidei* of Martin.) And yet, if it was in any way Drusius's intention here, as it had been in his commentaries on the Old Testament, to keep himself "as independent as possible from Jew[ish interpretations]," he certainly wished in most cases to be independent of the opinions of his Christian predecessors as well. His use of Jewish sources was, moreover, for illustrative, rather than controversial purposes.

A recent study has called Drusius's attitude to Hebrew and Hebrew literature objective. This is fairly accurate. For, while not blind to the *utilitas* of Hebrew for theological studies, he was quite disinclined to spend his time pointing out the errors of the rabbis or engaging in Christian apologetics. This attitude, we may add, caused him a great deal of grief, even at Franeker. His posthumously published *Commentarium ad loca difficiliora Pentateuchi* (1617) is resolutely opposed to anything but the grammatical or lexical type of explanation, or, sometimes, "illustrations" of *realia* or of a basic concept. Drusius disavows any attempt to look for the spiritual sense, which so many others were preoccupied with. "What I deal with," he wrote, "pertains mostly to grammar. I do not claim for myself any deeper knowledge. I do know this: 'I am neither a prophet nor the son of a prophet'."[68]

Drusius has been viewed as an original scholar in advance of his time. Perhaps he was merely a holdover from the humanism of the Renaissance, a person trying to advance on humanistic scholarship in an age when theology had become paramount; perhaps he was a forerunner, laying the groundwork for the new biblical criticism that would appear at the end of the seventeenth century. Whatever the case, Drusius's hand–picked assistant and successor Sixtinus Amama (1593–1629) attempted to carry on his master's traditions. He, too, became a noted philologist and a defender of the study of Hebrew as the proper foundation for theology. He often railed against the widespread ignorance of Hebrew, calling such a state "barbarism." A knowledge of the language was to him "humanitas," and he spent a good deal of his efforts trying to ensure that future theologians and others would study it. Yet, despite Amama's philological orientation, he looked upon progress in the study of rabbinic literature by Christians as an indication of the imminence of the conversion of the Jews. So he said of his student Coccejus's edition of Mishnah *Sanhedrin,* for which he himself appears to have been directly responsible. There is no reason to doubt that Amama had a good measure of rabbinic learning. Moreover, like Drusius, and whatever his own goals, he too refused to let these ultimate goals compromise the necessary stress on correct philological method.[69]

Neither did Scaliger, whose positions are almost too well known to require much discussion here. His own study of Hebrew; his view of Hebraism as a part of general erudition and his criticism of its being pursued only superficially in his day; not to mention his attaching great importance to having Jews as teachers and his welcoming the possibility of their settlement, precisely because he was hoping to engage one of them for his own instruction; his own brief reliance on the converted Polish Jew, Phillipus Ferdinandus (c. 1555–1599),[70] who had come to teach Arabic at Leiden and died quite suddenly shortly after his arrival, to Scaliger's great bereavement; and, lastly, both his friendship and his disputations at Rome and Avignon with living Jews and even with one Jewish woman; all these were cited and discussed a century ago by his biographer, Bernays.[71] They have even been reviewed again recently in detail, though probably in too positive a light in at least one case.[72] We may still draw attention, however, to the following comment from the *Secunda Scaligerana,* which date from 1603–6:

> One who wishes to refute and confute a Jew must be very expert in Judaism. . . . The Jews are learned and subtle; they must have demonstrations made out of the Talmud, not out of the New Testament, [which they will] ridicule; it is astonishing that no one treats this subject in earnest; what a pity how we Christians write against other [Christians] and not one [of us] against the Jews. The Jews are very subtle in their exposition of Scripture; it is stimulating to read their books, which contain much wit . . .[73]

His twofold attitude to Jewish literature shows through clearly here, especially his emphasis on the need for anti–Jewish argumentation out of the appropriate sources. And yet, at the same time, there is his characteristic and corresponding stress on the usefulness of the Talmud, which he had studied with Phillipus Ferdinandus. Scaliger had "refused to elucidate the New Testament without having the Talmud at hand," alongside the pagan authors: "read good authors, the *Metamorphoses* of Ovid, the Talmud; they are necessary for [the study of] the Bible."[74]

Scaliger's equally well known comments on Maimonides' *Guide* also merit quotation:

> The *Moreh Nevukhim* can not be commended enough. I rate not only that book but also all the works of that master so highly that I would say that he alone among the Jews has given up talking nonsense.[75]

Here, too, is the twofold attitude: general disdain and selected praise. Now, while it is not impossible that the mention of "all" Maimonides' works includes admiration for the *Mishneh Torah,* I am inclined to doubt it, for Scaliger fails to mention the work by name anywhere else and, more important, because it appears that those of Scaliger's students who would subsequently use the work seem to have come upon it some other way than through Scaliger. He may have owned a set of *Mishneh Torah*—he did donate a large number of books to the Leiden University library—but if he ever became a serious user of the code, it is not apparent from his writings or from any specific encouragement to its study that he may have provided his students.

Before considering the use of the *Mishneh Torah* by Scaliger's students, we must recognize the first Christian Hebraists not of Jewish origin with an extensive knowledge of the work. Hugh Broughton's familiarity with it has been mentioned, yet his *Seder Olam* of 1594 is quite short and its subsequent impact hard to judge. The one who truly deserves the laurel is Henry Ainsworth (1571–1622). This English-born Bible commentator was one of the leading spokesmen of the Separatist community of Amsterdam and, after 1609, of Leiden, that is, of the future Pilgrim fathers of Plimoth Plantation; his *Annotations on the Pentateuch,* which began to appear in Amsterdam in 1616, would exercise specific influence on the form of religion and society in the new colony. Ainsworth is said to have been in contact with the rabbis of the young Jewish community of Amsterdam, but I have found no evidence to either prove or disprove this contention. Ainsworth's annotations are filled with longish citations, in English translation, from the "Maimony," as the *Mishneh Torah* was often popularly referred to by Jews, and other rabbinic works, most frequently Menaḥem Recanati's mystical commentary on the Torah; for this latter work, he may have availed himself of Pico della Mirandola's Latin translation. Concerning his recourse to "the Rabbines," Ainsworth wrote at length:

> . . . I allege their expositions for two causes: the one, to give light to the ordinances of Moses touching the external practice of them in the commonwealth of Israel, which the Rabbines did record, and without whose help, many of those legal rites (especially in Exodus and Leviticus) wil not wel be understood. By their records also, many particulars about the *Passover* which Christ kept, . . . the *Phylacteries* which the Pharisees wore, . . . and other things mentioned in the Evangelists, wil much be cleared; . . . As for the theological exposition, therein the later Rabbines are for the most part blinde; but we are inlightned by the Apostles of Christ, whose writings (especially Pauls) doe unfold the mysteries of the law. An other reason why I cite the Rabbines, is to shew how in many words, phrases, and points of doctrine, they approve of the new Testament; though somtime to the condemning of themselves: and so the testimony of the adversary against himself, helpeth our faith. . . . [Here follows a series of examples of various types.] . . . wherefore the evidence brought frô the learned Iewes, wil help both to understand some scriptures, and to end some controversies. But *Jewish* forbidden *fables,* of which there are too many, them I pass over as unprofitable: some things also I note from them, not as approving them my self absolutely, but leaving them to further consideration of the prudent.[76]

His reasoning is not novel, even if his use of Maimonides is. The interest in ordinances is part of the history of Calvinism, the distinction between the observances and the doctrine not without precedent. The usefulness of rabbinic literature for the explication of the life of the early Christians is an increasingly popular idea at this period, of course. Two other points deserve mention: the way in which "the Rabbines . . . approve of the new Testament" and in which Ainsworth is willing to cite or "note" from rabbinic "fables." As to the former, the mention of the Jew as adversary seems tangential, as does their "condemning of themselves." Their "approval" appears to lie more in the illumination of the Christian Scriptures by rabbinic examples and parallels. As for his intention of citing the "fables" without rendering judgment, this probably applies most to Recanati and his mystical interpretations. In any case, such an explicit suspension of judgment is a fresh voice of moderation. Ainsworth also mentions, by the way, his plans for citing "the Christian Fathers & Doctors," but only briefly, since so many others cite them, and "the testimonie of hethen writers," but also "more sparingly, as of whom we have least need." They were, he admits, useful for some things, "ancient histories, and religious exercises, and for the witness which they bear unto the trueth of God."

Ainsworth, for all the inspirational hopes of his commentary, tends to adopt a nonpolemical approach, though. When he cites Maimonides, he rarely editorializes, taking even points of doctrine from *Sefer ham–Madda'* (and from *Hilkhot Yesode hat–Torah* in particular) to illuminate points of creed common to both Judaism and Christianity and then quoting them without comment. Also, with respect to the Pentateuchal narrative and its significance, he says that "in [its] propounding, Moses hath a veil drawen over his bright and glorious face: for in the histories are implied Allegories, & in the lawes are types and shadowes of good things that were to come . . ." Ainsworth does go for the deeper sense and uses the rabbis to help him get there; yet he also believes that "by a true and sound literal explication, the spiritual meaning may the better be discerned." The understanding of "types and shadowes" here is of a different variety from that seen elsewhere, but it is part of the same tradition as the one that wishes to have the law concretized anew in Calvinist society according to the ancient example and practice.[77] For an understanding of those "types," Maimonides would likewise be invoked by Ainsworth's more literal–minded contemporaries and successors. However, Ainsworth's impact on the Leiden university community is not certain, despite the fact that both addressed themselves to similar issues. There is no explicit reference to him in subsequent studies of biblical antiquities, and he himself takes no account of the university milieu.

Petrus Cunaeus: *On the Commonwealth of the Hebrews*

The true Leiden pioneer in the study of *Mishneh Torah* was Cunaeus, and his introduction to the work was from another source entirely. A scholar of jurisprudence by profession, he had as his avocation a strong interest in and devotion to theology.

Cunaeus had quite a reputation in the seventeenth and eighteenth centuries for his *De Republica Hebraeorum,* first published in Leiden in 1617 and often reprinted. This study of Jewish antiquities was the first by a non–Jew to make extensive use of the *Mishneh Torah.*[78]

Cunaeus's background and training are of some interest. Enrolled at Leiden in May 1601, when not yet fifteen years of age, he began his studies of Hebrew and Greek with a cousin, Ambrosius Regemorterus, himself a young man, and traveled with him to England in 1603. Regemorterus stayed in England to become the emissary of the Flemish Church, but Cunaeus returned to Leiden to take up his studies again, under the tutelage of Scaliger, Daniel Heinsius (1580–1655), the classical and New Testament scholar who was also the librarian of Leiden, and others. He also made the friendship of Grotius at this time. At the urging of his teachers, probably Scaliger first and foremost, he went off to Franeker in 1605 to study Hebrew with Drusius, staying there until about 1608. Drusius's philological approach to Hebrew and rabbinics was a major influence on the young scholar. It was probably of this period in his life that Cunaeus wrote in the Prolegomena to Book III of the *De Republica Hebraeorum:*

> We had extremely great delight from the writing of this book. For we were taking up again those studies to which we were so exceedingly given over at one time during our adolescence. We had repeated pleasure in thinking how much enjoyment our heart derived from Hebraism, when we would study the volumes of the Bible [with] the rabbinic commentaries and many other erudite works written by the Jews. We have, indeed, never regretted this effort.[79]

Having enrolled again at Leiden, he became professor of Latin in 1611; subsequently, he was appointed to the chair of politics, later adding the teaching of jurisprudence to his duties.

Sometime shortly before 1615, he happened to acquire a set of the 1574 Venice edition of the *Mishneh Torah.* It was given him by his friend Johannes Boreel (Borelius) (1577–1629), a Leiden graduate and himself a Hebraist and a man of many capacities. He served as a member of the Middelburg clergy and translated a work of Broughton's from English into Latin. Also a good friend of Grotius's, he became well known in his own right, as a diplomat and a statesman, and as the holder of a series of public offices in Zeeland from 1613 until his death. He was also a world traveler.

On one of his tours to Italy and the Near East, he had acquired "a large store of those Oriental books that our region has never or rarely seen," according to Cunaeus. Some of this treasure went to Thomas Erpenius (1584–1624), the famous Leiden Arabist. The *Mishneh Torah* edition, as we have said, went to Cunaeus.

In 1615–16, Cunaeus went on leave from Leiden to study law. During that year, he devoted some of his time to reading the *Mishneh Torah,* a reading that proved little short of revolutionary for him:

> . . . at the Hague during that time . . . I ran through the splendid treatises of Rabbi Maimonides with great enthusiasm in the most pleasant and leisurely fashion . . . I was so affected that I nearly turned my pen around and erased all my previous animadversions on things Jewish. [1:9]

Cunaeus thus appears to have revised his previous knowledge of rabbinics almost completely. "Most learned Maimonides" (2:23) became for him "the most distinguished of the rabbis" (2:20). Nevertheless, said he, when Maimonides yielded, as it were, to the doctrines of his fellow Jews, "I never hesitated to censure his errors" (1:8). In fact, the passage most often cited as an indication of Cunaeus's positive attitude toward Maimonides is really rather restrained and more representative of the standard dual approach:

> Admired among men is a great writer, Rabbi Moses ben Maimon, who has put aside the nonsense and successfully grasped hold of the teaching of the Talmud in that divine work that he himself calls *Mishneh Torah.* We can never speak so highly about that author that his own excellence will not surpass it. By a certain fate and accident of birth he first and he alone among that people rightly perceived what it is not to talk nonsense. We shall often cite him in these [three] books as a most distinguished witness. . . . His authority will be most useful for us. [1:2]

Though Cunaeus was suspected of Remonstrant sympathies on account of the work, *De Republica Hebraeorum* is an essentially conventional presentation of the traditional Calvinist views on biblical antiquity and on Judaism and the Jews. There are, to be sure, several exceptions to this rule, such as his understanding for the causes of Jewish sufferings at the hands of the nations.[80] The true novelty of his work, however, consists in its quarrying of the *Mishneh Torah* for the study the ancient Jewish commonwealth. Cunaeus himself was aware of this difference between himself and his predecessors. The two he mentions are Sigonius and Bertram.

Carlo Sigonio (1524–84) had published his *De Republica Hebraeorum* in 1565 and it had been frequently reprinted. Cornelius Bertram (1531–94) had come out with his *De Politia Judaica* (which would later reappear under the title used by Sigonio and Cunaeus) in 1574. These were largely compilations by topic of biblical passages; they covered various aspects of religion and politics in the Jewish state of old, in fairly straightforward fashion, with only an odd mention of one or another Jewish source.

Cunaeus, of course, had come to his work almost by accident, apparently never having had a Jewish teacher, but still managing to sense the importance of the *Mishneh Torah.* It seems, moreover, to have been the very reading of the *Mishneh Torah* that was the major stimulus for his own work. He had already read Sigonius and Bertram and did not wish to repeat what they had said.

> We wished to touch on other things pertaining to the constitution of this republic. Indeed, we have omitted those things that Sigonio and Bertram made widely known, and, in a totally independent [*liberrimâ*] composition, have gathered herein things that we had at hand from elsewhere. These were really rather numerous and appeared altogether worthy of attention. A good part of them, moreover, were suggested by Rabbi Moses ben Maimon the Egyptian, whose diligence and sagacity is beyond praise.
> [From the Preface to the Reader]

In another sense of the word "liberrima," it might also be noted that Cunaeus "freely" heaped ("congessimus") source upon source in composing his work.

The *De Republica Hebraeorum* was to be a guide for the magistrates of Holland and West Frisia to whom it was dedicated. It was based on the thoroughgoing Hebraism advocated by Scaliger. Cunaeus takes up his teacher's position: The Dutch, he says, do not always understand the need for the study of Hebrew:

> We have learned the words and the sayings of the Spaniards, the French, and the Italians: and, since our fleets went out to discover another world, we even speak in the barbarian language with the Indians. As talented as we are, the one language we do not understand is the one that it would truly have been worth while learning. For, if there are any who turn their intellects to this most noble pursuit, it is for the most part in an entirely perfunctory fashion. In fact, the majority approach the gates of Hebraism, which is the easiest thing, but do not wish in the least to enter into the interior of the sanctuary, the study of Syriac and Rabbinic. Certainly it is not for them to judge how many and how great the treasures are in

Hebraism, not for those who, content to know only the words of the biblical text, consider themselves sufficiently learned that they even wish to teach others. They are mistaken, to my mind at least. One must proceed further, one must investigate and see what the Jews, the vernacular interpreters of the Bible, already said long ago, either rightly or wrongly.

[Prolegomena to Book III]

Cunaeus recognized both the importance of rabbinic Hebrew and the Jews' abilities as native students of that language. A thorough knowledge of their biblical criticism was therefore essential.

If he himself pursued "sacra sapientia," i.e., theology, with a zest, it was with the humanistic approach to which he had been educated. His defense of his right to use this humanistic approach against those professionals who claimed theology as their private domain and spent their time lashing out at each other's positions is a strong one:

. . . amid the business of public instruction and of jurisprudence, and even at leisure from time to time, we deal with a certain theology, not the kind [that is] subject to some party or master, but the kind that is independent and temperate and moderate, one which, supported by our knowledge of Greek, Hebrew, and Latin letters, contemns the excessive passion and disputatiousness of the other kind. [Ibid.]

He would rely on the solid knowledge he had gained of the three languages and on his not being beholden to any particular school of thought, his aim being a dispassionate, yet useful description of the Hebrew "theocracy," a state rich in "bona exempla." As such, he argues at the beginning of his treatise, the Hebrew commonwealth was much more worthy of imitation than either the Greek state or the Roman republic. For the magistrates could learn from the Hebrew state the true meaning of the maxim (taken, in fact, from a Roman historian, Sallust,[81] but not identified as such): "in concord small states become great, in discord the greatest ones tumble." Cunaeus saw the foundations of the Dutch Republic being rocked:

Very many of your citizens have already become schismatized and divided into petty factions contending among themselves over contrary propositions. This has all taken place since there arose among them a useless disagreement on religious mysteries that most of them do not understand.

[From the Dedication]

The majority of disputants, in his view, do not have a clear understanding of the obscure points of doctrine that are constantly being raised. But he himself is certainly not interested in honing his skills for either duelling with them or supporting one side against the other.

At this point, however, the Synod of Dort was only a year away. Cunaeus anticipates it in some ways by advocating a uniformity in religious doctrine as the best guarantee of the unity of the state. He urges the magistrates, accordingly, as the official guardians of the pure worship of God, to take strong and timely action against the schisms and superstitions that could destroy the state entirely. He thus lines himself up on the side of the more stringent Calvinists, even though methodologically he seems to have had less in common with them. As he was suspected of liberal leanings, perhaps this is an attempt to ward off further criticism. At any rate, he betrays here the characteristic mixture of retiring academician and public functionary that Leiden regularly produced. Finally, his presentation of the practices and mores of the Hebrew commonwealth of old was, he writes, meant to be allusive enough for those magistrates whose "learning is such that, if anything at all is said that sheds light on antiquity or on the written works of its celebrated authors, they are eminently capable of drawing conclusions" (ibid.).

According to Cunaeus, the Israelite commonwealth was the most perfect, because of the harmony and, especially, the indivisible bond between Church and state that existed in it. Inasmuch as the two were separate entities, however, he devotes separate discussions and sections of the work to the nature of each. He adopts the traditional division of the biblical laws into the political, moral, ceremonial, and spiritual ones, devoting the first two books of his treatise to the institutions of the people and the last book to the "Ecclesia." Nowhere does he stop to define "ecclesia" precisely, but it obviously refers to the community of faith, shared belief, and piety. Cunaeus's commentator Nicolai, probably with a good measure of justification, called it the "genus hominum electum," 'the class of men [that is] chosen'.

An important source of information throughout the work was Josephus.[82] But in the first two books, which are concerned with law, the *Mishneh Torah* is ever present also, though it is nowhere to be found in the last one. Cunaeus was not out to refute Maimonides; he wanted the illumination that the *Mishneh Torah* could provide. If, on specific points, Cunaeus expended a great deal of energy advancing a view to the contrary of Maimonides', it was often because he sensed disagreement with Maimonides in Jewish quarters as well. In discussing the institution of the sabbatical and jubilee years, for example, as a demonstration of the greatness of the ancient theocracy, Cunaeus quoted various passages from *Hilkhot Shemittah ve–Yovel* on the methods of their enumeration and calendration. He appears to have engaged in extensive discussions with colleagues, themselves experts in rabbinic literature, about the several methods.[83] As Cunaeus tells it in *De Republica Hebraeorum,* though, it was after comparing other Jewish interpretations and considering the possibility that—as the rabbis knew and Maimonides himself says in *Hilkhot Shemittah ve–Yovel*—there were discrepancies between the first and second Jewish commonwealths as to procedure, and after examining the logic and reasonableness of the several views, not to mention comparative evidence from the Greco–Roman world, that he finally concluded that Maimonides was slightly in error on a few points (1:6 and 7). Ziskind cites a letter in which Cunaeus says that he had been inclined initially to follow Maimonides, but yielded after reading Scaliger's observations on the several rabbinic opinions. In the *De Republica,* however, Cunaeus felt compelled to reassert how much respect he had for Maimonides as the greatest of the rabbis:

> To our mind, the latter opinion [i.e., the minority view of Rabbi Judah] has greater merit. We are unable to approve of Maimonides' [position] here, though elsewhere we esteem and are in exact agreement with his rulings. For he is the kind of man who compensates for a few small, trifling mistakes of this kind with considerable and admirable accomplishments everywhere [else], and with a legacy of the choicest teachings. [1:6]

That is what he had to say in this instance. Cunaeus did like to quibble, however. On one occasion, he chided Maimonides for offering a biblical proof–text ("testimonium") to legitimate what Cunaeus himself recognized as a postbiblical innovation. Nonetheless, he relied on Maimonides' description of the subject, which was the Levites and their duties. After detailing the various watches as listed in *Hilkhot Bet hab–Beḥirah,* Cunaeus went on to praise the "majestas" of the temple service and the scrupulousness with which the Levites carried out their "sacred obligations" ("religio"). The passages from *Bet hab–Beḥirah* are found in chapters 4 and 8; the biblical text is Num. 3:38. Though the issue might appear to be one with great ramifications, it is not. Cunaeus's criticism was neither a general condemnation of the Jewish use of proof–texts nor a specific rejection of Maimonides' conclusions. It is, rather, a scholarly quibble:

> We consider the procedures we spoke about with respect to the watches to have been instituted rather late and during the decline of the [Second] Commonwealth. At that time, there were put into effect many different things of which there had existed neither trace nor sign beforehand. So it is by all means a mistake for the great Egyptian rabbi to invoke certain testimonies out of the Pentateuch. It is certainly very unwise to transfer things that were ordained in the second and third chapters of Numbers about the measurements that were appropriate in the desert for the area around the tabernacle to the city of Jerusalem, where there was a secure spot for the divine services and sacred rites. [Ibid.]

It is interesting to compare another approach. Though writing a century or so after Cunaeus, but certainly without a knowledge of his work, Judah Rosanes (d. 1727), of Constantinople, in his *Mishneh lam–Melekh,* his posthumously published commentary on the *Mishneh Torah* (Constantinople, 1731), also saw problems in Maimonides' use of the biblical text. His problem was not a historical one, but rather one with Maimonides' use of the rabbinic sources. The difference reflects the completely different orientations of the two critics.

Generally, though, as we have already indicated, Cunaeus uses the *Mishneh Torah* without criticizing it, in order to explain or illuminate the subject at hand. He finds the ancient rabbis to have been rather disinterested in the military prowess of the Israelites (2:18), though he judges that prowess to have been considerable. Nonetheless, he recognizes that the rabbis did discuss the subject of war and did distinguish between two different types, the optional war and the obligatory one (*milḥemet reshut* and *milḥemet mitsvah*). For his definition of these, Cunaeus turns to *Hilkhot Melakhim.* The obligatory war, for example, was to be waged

against the Canaanite nations. The various commands to annihilate these peoples might be modified, according to Cunaeus, on the basis of Maimonides' explication of several verses in Deuteronomy 20. The decision to make peace rather than destroy a city depended on that city's willingness to adopt the "seven commandments [given to] the children of Noah." Such an agreement was viewed by some Jews, including Maimonides, as the necessary basis for any civilized society.

Cunaeus's explanation of these laws is also drawn from *Melakhim* 2:18. Writes Cunaeus: one of the seven things proscribed by the "Talmudici" was idolatry. "And, as Maimonides shows quite clearly in *Hilkhot 'Avodat Kokhavim u–Mazzalot,* corruption in religion implanted [itself] at the very beginning [period] of the world." Since, in Cunaeus's own view of the origins and growth of idolatry, mortals erred in honoring a variety of things besides God ("numen" is the term used by Cunaeus), he gives a condensed paraphrase of the first chapter of *'Avodah Zarah.* Following Maimonides faithfully, he tells how Abraham finally "recognized his maker . . . and . . . fostered the knowledge of [the God] of heaven so successfully among his followers, that Maimonides rightfully calls him *'ammudo shel 'olam,* the pillar and support of the world."[84] The summation with which Cunaeus concludes this chapter helps demonstrate his overall method:

> These are most discerning observations by the very sagacious author. We were not reluctant to record them, because they could shed light on the talmudic [rabbis'] ruling that we referred to concerning those seven precepts that were obligatory for the descendants of Noah. The liability was such that, if by chance any nations were to refuse to accept their observance among the terms of a peace [treaty], the Jews are bidden to extirpate them entirely, on the ground of their being uncivilized and monstrous savages. [2:19]

Maimonides makes the opinion of the Talmud clearer and sheds light on the halakhah; on account of these benefits, Cunaeus has a strong predilection for his code as the source of his own explanations.

Yet this "summus Rabbinus," this "greatest of the rabbis," (1:17 and 2:14) is only one among many authorities quoted, especially in the first part of the treatise. Cunaeus is not concerned so much with a "correct presupposition about God," he says, since "we tend toward ("spectamus") those [views] that [have an] affinity to history" (2:24). Nonetheless, in these para–historical investigations, other writers, both Jewish and non–Jewish, do not fare nearly so well at the author's hands—for a variety of reasons, philological and doctrinal both. Cunaeus is firm in his criticism, but certainly respectful toward Scaliger. After reproducing Maimonides' version of a formula used in rabbinic ordination, Cunaeus mentions that

> . . . the talmudists devised another formula also, the words to which that celebrated personage Joseph Scaliger brought down in his *Refutation of Trihaeresius,* but did not take correctly. Wherefore we shall transcribe that passage hither and interpret it as it ought to be understood. [1:12]

Similarly of a disagreement with his teacher Drusius:

> I know, of course, that even that most illustrious individual Johannes Drusius, whom we once had as a teacher, agreed [on a certain point] with the author of the *Arukh.*[85] But he, in his equanimity, showed indulgence toward my frank sincerity. And, indeed, professing genuine freedom of speech, without love, without hate, we try to find out the most correct [meaning of] what is said. [3:5]

Like Drusius, Cunaeus was beholden to no one, refusing to show partisanship for or against any view. He took exception to the church father Eusebius of Caesaria's interpretation of the Shiloh passage in Genesis 49 and to Isaac Casaubon's (1559–1614) defense of Eusebius. Casaubon was a classical scholar for whom Scaliger had great admiration, and Cunaeus himself had developed cordial relations with Casaubon on a visit to England, so Cunaeus was reluctant to criticize:

> Now we do not take pleasure in disagreeing with Eusebius, whom we have always reckoned among the greatest writers, or with the man we have mentioned, a leading figure of our century, who followed Eusebius. We venerate him so thoroughly that, in our eyes, no one is great compared with him. He is truly the person under whose guidance admirable progress has been made in this generation toward the perfection of knowledge in every [field]. But simple honesty bids us dispassionately find out the plain truth. [1:9]

Such is Cunaeus's attitude to his fellow Hebraists.

As for the rabbinic writers cited on questions of dogma and biblical exegesis, in Book III primarily, the occasional use of "hallucinatio," "vanitas," "insania," and other such classic descriptions of rabbinic views[86] is of less interest than the ways in which Cunaeus asserts Christian views in response to Jewish interpretations. His method shows up particularly well in an account he offers of a personal attempt at using rabbinic interpretation in the explication of Hebrews 7.

> I will not employ circumlocution. At first, when I was endeavouring to resolve difficulties of such a kind with as little effort as possible, I did not doubt at all that this epistle at least had been deservedly rejected in times past by the Roman churches; moreover, I construed David's words about Melchisedek not as referring to the Messiah, but in a different sense. Indeed, I followed the Jewish teachers, whose diligence in interpreting the biblical text is very frequently to be admired. [3:3]

The verse in question is Ps. 110:4, and Cunaeus cites the interpretations of Ibn Ezra, Naḥmanides, and Kimḥi at length; they all apply the reference to King David.

> While I was using this approach to the subject at hand, a splendid passage in divine Matthew, 22:44, opportunely came to our notice. There Christ himself ensnares the Pharisees through questioning . . . [the Greek and a Latin version of the verse follow]: "How is it that David, directed by the divine spirit, calls Christ Lord, saying sit at my right hand, until, etc." We require no other proof to refute the mad falsehood that the rabbis thrust upon us unawares. Through that whole psalm, it is not the singer [referring to] David, as they hold, but David speaking of the Messiah. [Ibid.]

The rabbinic view is thus summarily cast out in favor of the Christian one in which he has faith:

> This is what our supreme master, with whom faith shall be, teaches the Pharisees in this book of the Gospel. Ibn Ezra was mistaken, [as were] Rabbi Moses and Kimchi, and the Chaldean Targum, and all words anywhere. There remains and there will remain the truth of the mystery uttered about Melchisedek by David, followed by the apostle [Paul], whose Epistle to the Hebrews is most sacred and breathes of nothing but God. [Ibid.]

Here ends Cunaeus's willingness to be convinced by others. He had said:

> . . . we are ready, as soon as someone shows us something better, to change our mind. Not for us the attire of obstinacy as a reputation.
> [Prolegomena to Book III]

This apparently did not apply in cases where Christian truth was at stake.

The approach is hardly new, to be sure. Its persistence in Cunaeus is hardly surprising either. Yet there is another remarkable passage where Cunaeus criticizes both the Jewish expositors and his fellow Christian Hebraists:

> A great and memorable crime is committed by one who has set his mind to searching out and airing publicly all the mistakes in the rabbinic writings. For when the Hebrew [authors] gave us their thoughts on the sacred book, in their native language, and, with extraordinary erudition and keen ingenuity, they discovered many fruitful things that had always escaped the comprehension and diligence of others. But, on the other hand, from time to time either their arrogance or their selfish ambitiousness led them to put forth certain explanations close to the true ones, but with a falsity not at all easy for the heedless to detect. I am not speaking now about allegorical, mystical, or narrative [i.e., aggadic] interpretations. . . . [Here follows a brief tirade against these supposed defamations of Scripture.] Rather, I am speaking about those interpretations in which *hap–pashut* [Cunaeus uses Hebrew letters here], as they call it, that is the *simple sense of the words,* is explained. For in this area the Jews alone, against the will of all the nations, hold, as it were, first place. [3:5]

The Jews may be the masters of *peshat,* but their interpretations should be considered with caution; Drusius himself, Cunaeus claims, was not critical enough of the errors of the Jews in *peshat.* Like other Hebraists, Cunaeus respects the Jews' devotion to the simple sense and admires their findings, but refuses to accept unquestioningly every interpretation of theirs in this mode. The difficulty, he argues, is the apparent verisimilitude of many of the explanations.

The subject in this chapter of the *De Republica Hebraeorum* is circumcision; along with the Sabbath, which Cunaeus deals with elsewhere (2:24), it is one of two fundamental problems in biblical law that Calvinism addressed. Cunaeus treats the issue in Book III, the section on "Ecclesia," since, in biblical times, circumcision determined membership in the community of the faithful. His explication of the institution revolves around a semihistorical investigation of the evidence in Jer. 9:25–26. In Cunaeus's partial translation, this reads: "Ecce, prope adsunt dies, cum animadvertam in omnes, qui circumcisi sunt cum praeputio, In Ægyptios, & in Judaeos, in Edomitas, & in Ammonitas, Moabitasque."[87] His understanding and his view run counter to an interpretation advanced by the "most learned rabbi, whose book, called *Arukh,* is well known to all men." The *Arukh,* dating from 1101, is a lexicon of the Talmud and midrashim by Nathan ben Yeḥiel of Rome (c. 1035–1106). The details of Cunaeus's criticism need not concern us. Of interest, though, is Cunaeus's citing the testimony of Herodotus and Strabo as to the elimination or continued presence of this rite among the Egyptians and others. He does this in order to assert the Calvinist view that the elimination of circumcision as a sacrament was intimately bound up with the crucifixion: "Among those things that prefigured the sacrifice of the Messiah was even that blood that was shed in the circumcision of the foreskins." In the process, Cunaeus notes, almost in passing, how the Jews, "although the people repeatedly fell into impiety, slighted God, and learned to defile all things sacred and profane, nevertheless kept the rite of circumcision most steadfastly . . ." (Are there foreshadowings here of some more recent views on the continued cohesion of the Jewish people?)

The tone adopted here by Cunaeus and the type of investigation he conducts is quite representative of Book III, which tries in essence to deal with the major issues in Calvinism by showing how faith grows out of and is ultimately freed from the law. In truth, this is probably the aim of his treatise as a whole, and elements of criticism of the law are scattered throughout. Not at issue here are such remarks as the following, a disparagement of the Jewish Sabbath that merely rehearses the traditional postures:

> But the Jews, whose wont it is to undo all the most sacred undertakings, added to the biblical ordinance many restrictions that Moses had not established. And thus the festival of the most sacred day was transformed into a troublesome superstition, sometimes to the hurt of [the Jews themselves]. [2:24]

The issue is really one of a different order. Cunaeus is arguing that, while the institution was at one time necessary and good and commanded by God himself, the spiritual meaning that grows out of it has always been paramount. This, in his view, was true for the days when the law was first given and is still true for his own. Under the guise of biblical antiquities, then, Cunaeus offers a traditional Christian view. Yet the question of the observance of the Sabbath and of the ceremonial law in general was still at the forefront of Calvinist consciousness. So it is hardly a passing comment when Cunaeus remarks:

> . . . the celebration of the Sabbath, which was ordained at the very beginning of the world and has always been observed by pious people, has at last most recently, when a law was proposed, been confirmed anew. [Ibid.]

There are two aspects to the Sabbath question. One is its significance as part of the ongoing discussion in Calvin and his followers on the role of the Ten Commandments in the life of the present-day church, a question made more acute by the presence of a ceremonial commandment among the "hominum munia & officia," the "duties and obligations of men," that is, the latter half of the Decalogue. The debate over the meaning and manner of observance of the Sabbath would continue—this is the other ramification of Cunaeus's remark—down through the second half of the seventeenth century as a major source of Dutch religious strife, with the Coccejans, who wished to spiritualize its meaning, under attack by the Voetians, who tried to take the biblical prescriptions literally.

Though the rabbis were hardly invoked either pro or con in the chapter on the Sabbath, they were made to contribute to the spiritual interpretation in other instances. The extent of this was determined, of course, by the degree to which their elucidations were at specific variance with Christian doctrine.

One such instance is the following. After discussing Ezekiel's prophecies on the future Temple, Cunaeus puts forth the standard Calvinist view of the day: that, contrary to what the Jews say, the rebuilt Temple is not a material one, as the explicit formulas in Ezekiel might seem to imply. Cunaeus turns to and quotes *Hilkhot Ma'ase hak-Korbanot* 2:14 for a summary of the talmudic discussion at *Menaḥot* 45, in order to show that the specifications Ezekiel gave for the sacrifices applied to a future, i.e., Messianic Third Temple. It is certain, Cunaeus argues, that Ezekiel's descriptions refer to the Temple that would exist "during the reign of the Messiah." Wherefore the Jews say that its form is not clearly understood and that Ezra, when he built the Second Temple, for the most part executed Solomon's plan, but also included as much of Ezekiel's as he could comprehend, "in a matter that is obscure and perplexing." This, says Cunaeus, is the meaning of the statement by the "summus rabbinus" in *Hilkhot Bet hab-Beḥirah* 1:4, which he quotes in Hebrew only. He then continues:

No small delusion is the Jewish hope that the Messiah will build a temple of the kind that can be looked upon, approached, and trodden under foot. That it is otherwise we, who have been born under the reign of the Messiah, surely perceive. All the things that were said there on the measurements of the building and its offices have a rather hidden sense: what the individual components signify or how they are to be interpreted is difficult to say. [1:17]

The evangelical sense is the one to be followed, he claims, but it is better not to inquire into such matters in the first place:

For, although in this elucidation of the Gospel enormous progress has been made toward recognition and knowledge, something is still left, however, to wonder at. Wherefore, in these things hidden from the eyes, it is the part of obtuseness and audacity to reach beyond that which the Holy Spirit has placed at hand. [Ibid.]

Maimonides' statements are introduced to explain the position to which Cunaeus is opposed, not specifically to be refuted. The view of his own contemporaries to which he is opposed has it that Ezekiel's prescriptions can be understood with precision at present. And so, if he introduces criticism of the Jewish view of a future physical reconstruction, it is in some ways tangential to his main thrust, which is directed against his fellow Christians.

In some ways, however, such criticism of the Jewish point of view is central. In the penultimate chapter of the work, Cunaeus identifies the "mystical sense of those things that are concealed in the sacred books" (1:12), the "true Cabala," with the truth of the Holy Spirit as exposited in the New Testament. He claims his is a novel view, though it hardly appears to differ from the views of Christian kabbalists in general. Cunaeus expresses it with exceptional force, though. A tight bond is forged between tradition as law and tradition as spirit (i.e., secret tradition as contained in the law). Except for the Gospel–as–fulfillment aspect, this view is hardly different from that of Jewish kabbalists who see the halakhah and the mystical interpretations thereof interpenetrating one another.[88] The meanings of "kabbalah," as a [legal] tradition transmitted orally—Cunaeus takes it as equivalent to oral law as a total entity—and as a secret mystical tradition were perhaps confused by him. As he takes it, for example, the Sanhedrin was empowered by "Cabbala" to do their work:

The senators of the Sanhedrin had the job of going through all of Judaea, observing the courts of the people, and establishing magistracies in the towns. And although a certain *kabbalah* and knowledge of things mystical had already been transmitted from hand to hand since the very beginning of the state, they had the power and authority over [the *kabbalah*] in their possession. [1:12]

The two meanings are also fused conceptually as part of an overall schema, the standard Calvinist view of law as a "preparation for the gospel," containing the spiritual sense to which the Gospels give full play. The view was not new with the Calvinists, to be sure; we have seen elements of it in William of Auvergne and others. Now, though, its support comes from the complete portrayal of Jewish institutions out of rabbinic literature.

Cunaeus also draws an implicit parallel (at 1:18) between the preservation of the law and the preservation of the biblical text by the Jews.[89] Here too his views differ little from those of pre–Reformation Christianity. The Jews, he says, were blind to the "sacred and true meanings," but they did preserve the text and not corrupt it, which would indeed have been in their power, since no one else had a knowledge of Hebrew like theirs. For that, the Christian world owes them a debt. The veil will be lifted and they will regain their former glory: "The light of day will shine again for them too." On that account, writes Cunaeus, "we cannot in the future justly turn away from the Jews as victims of public hatred, since such great hopes still remain for them." This is party–line Calvinism, based, of course, on Romans 9–11, from which Cunaeus quotes. He even sees the possibility that "some favor of God will restore them to Canaan," though they will have to pay the penalty for their obstinacy. If their status is reduced and their spirit demeaned now by their long suffering, says Cunaeus, this is part of the cycle of history: "quemadmodum temporum vices, ita & morum vertantur," that is to say, their customs and character will change with time. This approach is somewhat rationalistic and is a bit unusual as well. Cunaeus considers the oppression that the Jews have suffered to be responsible:

Surely, the day that removed the bright light of freedom from them and shook power from their hands, that same day thoroughly subdued their noble spirits so that they now have nothing left of their vital energy.

His view is indebted to his reading of the *Sefer hay–Yuḥasin* of Abraham Zacuto, a favorite of Drusius's also. Cunaeus cites the list of persecutions and asks:

> How can they breathe, they who have been vexed with such great abuse for so many years throughout the whole world, whom children already long ago dragged by the corner of their garment and adults by their beard? At long last the rage of all the kings against them has finally subsided.

Christians, he says, should act differently from the pagans:

> Let us, who are joined to them with a rather short chain, love them in our midst and hold this in common, that we obey the dictates ("jussa") of the same God.

Most of this echoes Romans 11:16, which he cites, but his mix is novel. It is hard not to wonder whether he has any particular circumstance or group in mind, but he gives no indication of any such. Also, to his somewhat offhand observation that both Christians and Jews obey the "jussa" of God, the commandments or ordinances, no specific legal sense can be imputed, even if the choice of language is not inappropriate to Dutch Calvinism. Despite this glimmer of understanding and even sympathy for the situation of his Jewish contemporaries, then, Cunaeus's vision throughout this excursus is the standard one: the Jews will see the light so that their light will shine again, though not, to be sure, as Jews in the flesh.

In any case, these concerns are submerged in others. Jews were not the focus of Cunaeus's remarks, even if rabbinic literature was his main vehicle. The final chapter of the work again points up the Calvinist goals that were its real object and concern. It was the more or less conventional demonstration that the gospel was there in the law and that the law was superseded with the advent of the Messiah; it is based on a more or less traditional reading of Galatians 3 and 4 and Hebrews 8. The covenant, writes Cunaeus, has not been abrogated. Formerly, there were two covenants, one containing the promises to the patriarchs about the Messiah, the second, promises in the form of legal obligations upon the people as a whole to maintain them in the faith. The New Testament came to deal only with the latter one: " . . . the covenant of the New Testament is not in contrast with the promise that was given to the patriarchs, but with the one that was long afterwards confirmed by the law." The apostle Paul viewed the promises in the laws as the inferior ones, says Cunaeus, because the people were insufficient to the task: "the legislator added a stipulation to [the laws] that no one was able to abide by. 'He who performs them will live in them.'" But Paul knew that the people had faith, Cunaeus goes on, and he came to free this faith from its tie to the law. The promises, which the gospels record, were fulfilled. The Jews of the period preceding the advent of the Messiah did have some knowledge of Him—this is one major question Cunaeus comes to answer—but their "incredulitas" proved to be an insurmountable obstacle, both to the fulfillment of the law and to faith and the recognition of the Messiah. "The end of the law is Christ," quotes Cunaeus from Romans 10:4. The Jews, in his reading of the several Pauline Epistles, did not know what God intended for them in giving them the law:

> In fact, the law and all the religious ceremonies had Christ in view; that was a wonderful mystery and one that the Jewish populace of old did not at all comprehend. And yet all learned, from the prophets especially, not from the law, that the Messiah would come and restore things fallen away and worn out.

In some ways, Cunaeus undercuts his whole argument by saying that the people learned the promises of the messianic future from the prophets and not from the law. He had, after all, been claiming all along that there was an indissoluble link between institutions and faith. On the other hand, he had just disparaged the law for its inability to convey the promises to people, with their "weakness of nature." Like most Calvinists, though, he believed that, because of the spiritual sense contained in the law, a description of the institutions such as his was of absolute value. Where he went beyond his fellow scholars was in his extensive use of rabbinic *legal* materials as "testimonia," that is, as a major vessel out of which the spiritual truth, the truth of Christianity, could be shown to emanate. It can even be argued that this approach parallels and supplements the earlier Christian use of Maimonides' *Guide*. The *Guide*, having been used from the first as a source of spiritual truth, was still widely known, though Cunaeus makes no mention of it. Now the *Mishneh Torah* was perceived by Cunaeus as a new source of higher spiritual truth, in a manner more characteristic of the seventeenth century. We refer here, of course, to the fact that Calvinism and its institutions were understood primarily as a source of spiritual meaning, though that, to be sure, was true of Judaism as well in many respects. There is no indication of Cunaeus's having had any contact with Jews, though; his importance for Jewish history, therefore, consists in his having been read by those who had such contact.

Hugo Grotius as Hebraist

With Hugo Grotius, we encounter one such person. Though he probably never achieved Cunaeus's proficiency in either Hebrew or rabbinics, his was certainly the more original mind, and he was the greater overall scholar. We may conjecture, though, that his interest in Maimonides developed out of his friendship with Cunaeus or out of his reading of *De Republica Hebraeorum,* a copy of which he had in his library. Grotius's importance for the Jews of the Netherlands lies in his *Remonstrantie* of 1616. In this "judicial opinion," he offers a justification for the admission and toleration of Jews in Holland and West Frisia and he proposes certain conditions for their residence there. As such, certain attitudes toward the Jews must have developed in his mind before the appearance of Cunaeus's book in 1617. Yet his fluency, such as it was, in Hebrew and his eventual passing familiarity with Maimonides' code appear to have come later. It is possible, therefore, that certain attitudes of his toward rabbinic literature may have been at least reinforced by his reading of Cunaeus. There is no necessary connection, however, between Grotius's rabbinic studies and his attitudes toward the Jews.[90]

As was the case with Cunaeus, there were two spheres of interest that dominated his life: jurisprudence and theology. Sometimes the two overlapped; in this, he, too, was very much Scaliger's disciple. The *Remonstrantie* shows his training and the thinking of his mentor. As he proceeded to consider both legal precedent and prospective status, i.e., the rights and privileges the Jews might be permitted or granted, he relied, for some points, on the charters that had already been granted the Jews in Haarlem and Rotterdam. But he also relied on several of the classic arguments for a Jewish presence, most notably the value and benefit Jews might confer on the Hebrew studies of Christians. The *Remonstrantie* is Grotius's most extensive statement on the Jews, but, from its style, tone, and general lack of reference to Jewish sources,[91] it appears to have predated his rabbinic studies. It is impossible to be certain, of course. Any recourse to such works in such a context might have compromised the value of his arguments. Moreover, only those who generally advocated some form of toleration of Jews to begin with would have argued on the basis of the need for Jewish teachers, "which," as Baron says, "by stressing the self–interest of the Christian peoples, reduced the risk that its authors would be considered promoters of the Jewish interest."[92] It is difficult to determine whether Grotius had had any experience prior to this date with a Jewish teacher or whether he had even tried to secure one. It seems unlikely. From the *Remonstrantie,* then, it is impossible to judge the state of Grotius's Hebraic learning at that time.

Nonetheless, Grotius did attain some measure of competence in the field. At the same time, throughout his life, he continued to maintain roughly the same mixture of openness and restriction vis–à–vis the Jews as he had first shown in the *Remonstrantie.* He was never rabidly anti–Jewish nor was he ever completely free from some negative bias. His personal maturity did grow with time, though, his response to an inquiry from Lublin about the charge of ritual murder being indicative of this. In the *Remonstrantie* he had given credence to that familiar libel, but he dismissed it in his 1636 letter as an accusation inspired by hatred.[93] In the letter, he also made a few incidental remarks about the Jews themselves, noting sympathetically: "The Jews are undoubtedly exposed to false accusations because they are exiled from their homeland and subject to hostile rulers."[94] This comes from the pen of a banished patriot, one who referred to himself as "Batavum Captivus et Exul,"[95] and it has both the matter–of–factness and the poignant ring that come from personal experience. Yet it is hardly different in voice from the observation in the *Remonstrantie* that the Jews are regularly mistreated because, in part, learned opinion considers the Jews to be slaves of the princes and exposes them to ill treatment.[96] Even if it seems appropriate to balance Grotius's credence, when writing the *Remonstrantie,* in the charge that the Jews are permitted to break a Christian woman's head just like that of a serpent[97] with his judgment on ritual murder charges that "not a single one of them is to be believed,"[98] he is, we find, still capable in the same 1636 letter of using the canard that, according to the Talmud, the Jews consider it just and right to hate Christians. Scandalous, moreover, is his judgment in this letter as to the reasons for an absence in his day of the blood libel: "No Jews are suspected there of the charge, whether because, treated gently, they are becoming tame, or whether, as recent arrivals, they are rather circumspect."

On the other hand, there are statements of an anti-inflammatory nature even in the *Remonstrantie.* Though Grotius wrote in 1615 that the specific maltreatment of the Jews—and he loses little affection on them as a group—was not due to the offenses of any one individual, but "only to their race ut dentes filiorum obstupescant quia patres emphacen comederunt," (" . . . the fathers have eaten sour grapes, and the children's teeth are set on edge,")[99] this classic line appears in the context of a larger appeal for better controls on others to prevent further maltreatment. And the famous line with which he renders his overall judgment: "It is clear that God wishes that they live somewhere. Why not, then, here?"[100] is a measure of the fact that he had never been truly harsh to them in legal terms.

Still, Grotius's often reproduced 1640 remark about the Amsterdam Parnassim shows a certain prejudice. Grotius was responding to a letter in which Vossius had announced the imminent departure for Brazil of Menasseh ben Israel (1604–57), the Amsterdam rabbi with many Christian friends, who would also become famous for his advocacy of the readmission of the Jews to England. Menasseh had become anguished over the *Mahamad*'s refusal to grant him the munificent salary he had requested. Grotius wrote Vossius: "I had thought that the men of the Amsterdam synagogue were both rich and generous. As for the latter, I now see I was wrong. With regard to the former, I'm not at all sure whether they're telling the truth or whether they want to be thought poorer than they are in order to avoid taxes."[101] This response discountenances Vossius's suggestion that the Jews were, in fact, telling the truth, but more on Vossius below in another context.[102] In short, Grotius's attitudes toward the Jews seem to have borne little correlation one way or another with his growing rabbinic knowledge. He is still quoting the Talmud adversely toward the end of his life, and there are no grounds for arguing that, whereas his earlier mere "toleration" had only had recourse to Roman law and Christian lore, a certain later sympathy is of a piece with his growing rabbinic knowledge. Grotius's growing interest in Jewish traditions, even as transmitted through Menasseh ben Israel, toward whom he always bore a friendly countenance, did not in any way mask his enduring hope that the Jews would all soon be converted.

This was one of his goals in print as well. His apologetic treatise *De veritate religionis Christianae,* published in Dutch in 1622 and in Latin in 1627, was composed as a missionary handbook for Dutch traders overseas (Cunaeus had also mentioned them) and was used as a manual of inspiration by generations of Dutchmen at home. It is suffused with his own Arminian spirit, even though he was not necessarily the most liberal of his group of friends. Book 5 of the work is the section where "Judaism is confuted." Though obviously a defender of Christianity, Grotius does not appear truly intolerant here either.[103] He was able to evince respect for the Jewish people: as the bearers of revelation, "the preservers of the oracles of God" (5:1); for their endurance in the face of adversity (1:14); for the ancient Jewish religion, which "afforded *testimonia* for Christianity" (3:16); and for the Jews' faithful preservation of the Hebrew Scriptures (ibid.). In all these areas, his arguments are reminiscent of Cunaeus's, though probably because of their similar Calvinist views and their common reliance on certain passages in the New Testament. Grotius's overall attitude toward the Jews appears hardly more open than Cunaeus's, though; he, too, speaks of the day when the blindness of the Jews will fall away and they will see the truth of Christianity. Grotius himself cites Romans 9–11 as the source of his views, just as Cunaeus had. If the Jews, he argues, having remained all this time in such an abject state, have not turned to idolatry and, against all reasonableness, have continued to observe, e.g., the law of circumcision (1:14) and (5:16) to pray to God in order to placate Him, they are not heard,[104] due to their sin, "that sin of despising the Messiah."[105] These views remained characteristic of Grotius; they were even fleshed out with footnotes for the 1640 edition. (They can also be compared to views expressed elsewhere in Grotius's writings, e.g., in *De Iure Belli ac Pacis* [1625, etc.], 1.2.8.)

In the *De veritate,* Grotius, like Cunaeus, found the writings of the Jews about ancient Judaism as valuable and as authoritative as those of Christians about the Christian religion. But he, too, was concerned with the standard issues of Christianity as it applied to ancient Judaism: the law and its fulfillment in the spiritual sense; the obsolescence of the sacrifices and other ceremonial laws—he discusses those related to diet, the Sabbath, and the holy days in detail; the abolition of circumcision; and the form of the covenant. All these were fairly standard in their treatment. By the time of the 1640 edition with its annotations,[106] he was able to adduce the support of the "Talmudistae" and to make vague references to various tractates of the Talmud.

He has been criticized for the apparently derivative nature of most of these references.[107] It is clear, though, that he was able, by this point, to find his way around in the talmudic literature, even if his major sources of help were the works of his fellow Hebraists and even if he himself probably read the original with great difficulty. As for the presence of Maimonides in this group of citations, incidentally, the only certain reference in the first edition had been to the *Guide* (*De ver.* 1:15), but it was not by title. The 1640 notes have one or two more odd references to the *Guide* and only one certain one to the *Mishneh Torah:* "in Maimonides' works, in the book *On Idolatry*" (ad 5:9);[108] Dionysius Vossius's translation had not yet appeared, of course, at this time, but Grotius was well aware of the imminence of its publication. There is, it may be added, a group of references to Menasseh ben Israel's *Conciliator,* which had also been translated by Dionysius Vossius and which was published in Amsterdam in 1633. One of these references (ad 5:5) contains a mention of Menasseh's citation of Maimonides; the reference proves to be *Yesode hat–Torah,* though it is not listed by Grotius. The general impression one derives is that of a multiplication of source references that are in no way related organically to the main text of the *De veritate.* And they tend to support the view that much of Grotius's knowledge of the literature was derivative.

There are, however, other important works by Grotius, after an examination of which we may be less certain that his learning was derivative. Recently, there has been a great deal of discussion about the use of rabbinic materials in his most enduring book, the *De*

Jure Belli ac Pacis.[109] Though this too is clearly the work of a religious thinker, it is based on principles of law and is itself, of course, the foundation of modern international law. Grotius rests his case not only on natural law, but also on the mutual respect of nations: despite his strongly held views, he hardly presents himself as a dogmatist. Rather, what he demonstrates is his trilingual erudition; consequently, Hebraic and rabbinic sources are by no means excluded. Already in the first edition of 1625, there are several references to the *Guide of the Perplexed* (as *Dux dubitantium*) and at least one, though not by title, to the *Mishneh Torah.*[110] It is found in the discussion of sovereignty in 1.3.20 and comes from *Hilkhot Melakhim* 3:7. It is completely without context, however, and reflects no particularly extensive study or understanding of the code as a whole or even of Maimonides' discussion in that particular section. Yet it is integrated, in the style of Grotius's times, as one of a series of authorities or *exempla* drawn from various sources, classical, Christian, or Jewish, to substantiate entirely secular considerations. We are no longer in the arena of sacred history alone: Grotius's is the wisdom of his day relying on ancient truths, through such intermediaries as rabbinic literature, to buttress his own views. He devoted more than a few paragraphs of his "Prolegomena" to the question of sources. Some of what he says shows how rabbinic literature has its place:

> 46. History in relation to our subject is useful in two ways: it supplies both illustrations and judgements. The illustrations have greater weight in proportion as they are taken from better times and better peoples; thus we have preferred ancient examples, Greek and Roman, to the rest. And [the] judgements are not to be slighted, especially when they are in agreement with one another; for by such statements the existence of the law of nature, as we have said, is in a measure proved, and by no other means, in fact, is it possible to establish the law of nations.
> 48. I frequently appeal to the authority of the books which men inspired by God have either written or approved, nevertheless with a distinction between the Old Testament and the New. There are some who urge that the Old Testament sets forth the law of nature. Without doubt they are in error, for many of its rules come from the free will of God. And yet this is never in conflict with the true law of nature; and up to this point the Old Testament can be used as a source of the law of nature, provided we carefully distinguish between the law of God, which God sometimes executes through men, and the law of men in their relations with one

another. . . . the early Christian writers used the witnesses of the Old Testament.

49. The Hebrew writers, moreover, most of all those who have thoroughly understood the speech and customs of their people, are able to contribute not a little to our understanding of the thought of the books which belong to the Old Testament.[111]

The primary role of the rabbinic sources is still to help elucidate the Hebrew Bible. However, Grotius's statements to the contrary notwithstanding, the authority of the Bible has hardly become subsidiary to that of the other ancient *testimonia.* But the theological mode of thought has become intermingled with the antiquarian and has been freed up from the view that all aspects of the human condition are part of sacred history. Thus, in some respects, the rabbinic sources might seem to be freed from the odium that formerly attached to them. But there had not been any real diminution of faith in Scripture, and many of the biases still remained.

Incidentally, these characteristics and these attitudes were not restricted to Grotius, but were even characteristic of John Selden (1584–1654), who would later become Grotius's arch–rival in the area of the international law of the seas. Selden was also a rabbinic scholar of some accomplishment himself. His studies of biblical institutions were antiquarian rather than doctrinal, but were also utilitarian in purpose.[112]

Grotius's interest in rabbinics expanded between 1625 and 1642, when the fourth edition of *De jure,* the first annotated one, appeared. The text had, during prior revisions, been slightly expanded by additional rabbinic and, specifically, Maimonidean references, particularly in the 1631–32 editions. The notes contained several more citations, not all of them necessarily derivative; a series of translations of rabbinic and talmudic literature during the 1630s probably helped increase the jurist's ability in handling these sources. We may suggest that the notes of the 1640s to both the *De veritate* and the *De jure* were ways of adding new *exempla* for a new edition without having to alter the body of the text. They are thus a measure of Grotius's reading over the period since the previous edition had been prepared.

One such reference has recently been called into question. It is a reference to Maimonides' *'Akkum* under the name *De Idololatria.* Grotius could not have seen Dionysius Vossius's edition, however, because he had already sent his own manuscript off to the printer before receiving his copy of Vossius's translation.[113] Yet he may well have been stimulated to examine the original Hebrew himself by Vossius *père*'s constant stream of references to his late son's work over the eight–year period between the time of its completion (and the younger Vossius's death) and its publication.

Grotius did have other sources for translations of portions of the *Mishneh Torah,* however, even if they did not include the *De Idololatria.* Joseph de Voisin (c. 1610–85), a theologian and controversialist who would be the editor of Martin's *Pugio Fidei* for its first appearance in print in 1651, had, in 1635, translated several sections of the *Mishneh Torah:* Maimonides' introduction to the code as a whole; chapters one and two of *Yesode hat–Torah;* and chapter one of *Tefillah.* Along with the copies of his work that he sent along in manuscript to Grotius for his approval, Voisin explained his intention. He expected that, by comparing the Jewish and Christian regulations and points of view in these areas, he would be able to discredit and invalidate the Jewish ones.[114] Several months after his first letter, he announced to Grotius that he had abandoned this project and was proceeding instead to the "ordinances of the synagogues and the academies," ("institutos synagogarum academiarumque,") that is, several sections of Book Two, *Ahavah.* Grotius replied at last in April 1636: "The versions of Maimonides that you prepared deserve very much to be read, and rouse in me a desire to see many such [translations]." He had, he wrote, found the part "on synagogues and their government" most useful, but he did not mention the first letter or its contents at all. Later that year, Grotius would write of Maimonides that, "of the Jews," he was "almost the sole one of sound judgment."[115]

Grotius mentioned and used Maimonides most frequently in his other major works, the *Annotata ad Vetus Testamentum* of 1644, the *Annotata ad Evangelia* of 1641, and the complete *Annotationes ad Novum Testamentum* of 1644. These works were also composed, that is, written and revised, over a long period of time. It is sometimes difficult to evaluate the character or intent of these citations of Maimonides, since they frequently consist of just one word: "Maimonides." No reference or quotation is given, no indication that the interpretation is really Maimonides' own. Often, Grotius merely seems to be saying: "Maimonides supports my view." The overall pattern of these three sets of annotations makes them direct descendants of Scaliger's and, especially, Drusius's. Neither inclined to dogmatics nor directly concerned with the mystical or spiritual sense, they focus on and are mostly interested in the technical aspects of the original, that is, generally, the simple sense, based on language, contextual background, and history. They are, in short, philological. In the commentary on the Old Testament, Grotius has freed himself and, implicitly, posterity from always looking for the fulfillment of the Old in the New. If Grotius adds a reference from time to time to the "sensus sublimior," "the deeper meaning," of a *locus,* it is, in Diestel's view, a concession to popular tastes or tendencies; and Grotius himself does not delve deeper.[116]

In these *Annotations,* he often uses Maimonides and other rabbinic authors for elucidation of the Hebrew in its simple sense. In the Greek Testament, he examines the putative Hebrew original. His hold on the rabbinic literature seems altogether fragile. On Matt. 28:19, concerning baptism *"eis to onoma"* ("in the name of"), he writes: "Since this locution has various meanings in Hebrew usage, I think preferable the one that is the most particularly related to baptism." And so, among other explanations, he cites "MAIMONIDES *de bello capta,*" [in which it is written:] "matbilah be–shem gerut," (Hebrew letters are used) "he shall baptize her according to the name of proselytes, that is, according to that religion that proselytes profess."[117] The text of Maimonides in *Hilkhot Melakhim* 8:5 actually reads the second Hebrew word as "le–shem," meaning 'for the purpose of'; it makes little or no real sense to read it as Grotius transcribed it, or to explain it the way he has.

Regardless of whether Grotius is in error or not, the function of the citation is clear: it is one more "parallel" that will "illustrate" the original. In general, as George Foot Moore pointed out, Grotius's rabbinic glosses on the New Testament were not intended either as historical representations of the Judaism of New Testament times or as points for refutation.[118] They were used by Grotius "in the same way in which [he] and others illustrate the same book and often the same passages by a redundancy of quotations from Greek and Latin authors."

If this tendency vitiates their usefulness, Grotius is, again, no different from anyone else of his day. The premium that was placed on a superabundance of erudition was a product of the utilitarianism of the age and probably one of the causes of its ultimate decline. Indicative of this and of the fact that Grotius viewed himself as a completely integrated person, no part of him being either incongruous or incompatible with any other, is his directive to the reader of his Old Testament commentaries: to read the work "utiliter," he advises, that is, "in a useful way," one must refer to the notes on *De veritate, De jure,* and the *Evangelia.* They were all of a piece, as he saw it: law and theology were part of the same erudition and the result of the same method. Maimonides was the great Jewish authority in the *Annotations* because Grotius had read enough of him by the 1640s to mine him for every conceivable piece of exegesis.

But the basic approach had not changed.

If dogmatics were absent from the commentary as a result of the method chosen, they were still present in Grotius's outlook. His anti–Jewish animus would continue to be intertwined with the supposed needs of scholarship. It will be recalled that Grotius had argued for and felt a need for Jewish teachers, turning this into one of his arguments for the toleration of the Jews. So far as we can tell, he never profited from their having taken up residence in Amsterdam. His own personal contact with Menasseh ben Israel came much later and it was by correspondence only, through the intermediacy of G. J. Vossius. Grotius's sources of Hebrew learning were non–Jews for the most part. It fact, it was probably Junius, in whose house he lived during his Leiden years, who had introduced him to the study of Hebrew and rabbinic interpretation. In a long annotation to the *De veritate* in which he discusses the origins of a series of biblical place names, Grotius credits one or more of these to Franciscus Junius, whom he styles as one "diligent in the interpretation of Scripture," and whom he credits with "not a few of the other observations that we have already made" (ad 1:16). Junius had been the pupil of the converted Jew Immanuel Tremellius (1510–80) and had worked with Tremellius on the Latin Bible translation that soon became the standard among Calvinists. Grotius himself relied on it virtually as an additional primary text for the *Annotations* on the Hebrew Bible.

The *lemmae* appear in Latin, as a matter of fact, and Grotius makes mention of their value for exegesis. It would be improper to underestimate the extent of Grotius's indebtedness to Junius. And it would be equally wrong to assume of Grotius or of any of his contemporaries that the growth in his rabbinic learning or the possible encounter with one or more living Jews did much to change postures and attitudes that had been formed early on in his career.

Johannes Coccejus, the First Hebraist Commentator on the Mishnah: *Sanhedrin* and *Makkot*

What is true of Cunaeus and Grotius applies in even greater measure to Coccejus and l'Empereur, the first Dutch Hebraists who can truly be called rabbinic scholars. Their editions of Mishnaic tractates are landmarks, yet their efforts to promote the conversion of the Jews appear to have been even more vigorous than those of their predecessors. Even more striking is the distinction they set between method and goal or, more correctly, their insistence on scholarly precision as essential to the furtherance of the goal. A virtual, though not a total elimination of polemic and controversy from their commentaries is the remarkable result.

Johannes Coccejus gave his name to Coccejanism, the "Federal Theology" of which is generally accounted to have been the great liberating force of the Dutch Church. Its heyday was during and immediately following the years Coccejus served as professor of theology at Leiden, which position he held from 1650 to his death in 1669. But its roots lie back in his earliest days, when he produced his edition and commentary on the Mishnaic tractates *Sanhedrin* and *Makkot*. The work appeared in 1629 and gained him an immediate following, not only because Jewish jurisprudence, the main theme of these tractates, was popular as the most fundamental part of the study of Jewish antiquities, but because the translation and notes were perceived as a show of great erudition and deserving of study in their own right.

At the background of the work are Coccejus's studies with a Jewish teacher of Hamburg. In 1625, at the age of twenty–two, Coch, as he was still known, left his home town of Bremen to continue his Hebrew training. His reasons for seeking out a Jewish teacher were the usual ones, most notably, the "auctoritas," or "authoritativeness" of the Jews, whose vernacular is Hebrew, in explicating the language of the biblical text:

> . . . nor have Christian interpreters been ashamed to follow the lead of recent Jewish [ones] in expositing the sacred writings. The Jews have truly devoted their whole lives to that one thing, to hammering out the underlying meaning ["mens"] of the sacred text, whether on the basis of biblical usage, the usage of the ancient writers, or on the basis of evidence the ancients themselves provided. Any one who thinks he can understand these matters properly without knowing the ancients and without a great deal of training is mistaken. That is . . . what first moved me to consult the writings of the ancient masters and to learn them from the Jews themselves.
>
> [From his Preface to the Reader]

Indeed, instruction by Jews of his own day seemed indispensable for learning the teachings of the ancient rabbis on Scripture. Coch stayed with this teacher, who is not otherwise identified, a mere nine months, and his view of the results indicates both losses and gains:

> Although I know perfectly well that I have not yet advanced as far as I wanted to, the reason I do not regret my undertaking is that there are not a few other benefits that the Talmud and the writings left by its authors can yield.

His training was apparently such that he was able to find many useful things ("utilitates") in the Talmud; his view is by now familiar.

It was, however, Amama, whose student he became upon arriving at Franeker in September 1626, who proposed, encouraged and supervised the progress of his edition and commentary. Amama gave his impressions of the significance of the work in a preface and commendatory poem he prefixed to the printed edition.

> . . . COCCEJUS, like another Jason,
> with the serpent lulled to sleep, carried away this fleece
> to the bright shining world above. . . . [119]

The opening of rabbinic literature to Christian study was like the activity of Jason among the Scythians: it would help win the kingdom of the talmudists over to Christianity. (The echoes of Ennius,

Lucretius, and Virgil in "in dias luminis oras" indicate Amama's philological training, but are clearly used in the service of Christianity, in the sense of bringing eternal life to those who read the Scriptures in the evangelical sense.) Amama remained a philologist by orientation, however, as we have indicated above, and so did Coch—for the most part. But we must digress for a moment to consider the implications of his subsequent inaugural address at Leiden, which was on the question of "The Incredulity of the Jews and its Causes."

The theme was an outgrowth of his having been charged by the curators, as part of his appointment, to write "against the Jews." The 1650 address, however, is really a summation of his theology as it had developed to then. Its arguments against the Jews consist mainly of commonplaces that serve as vehicles for his own views and hardly reflect any ongoing experience with living Jews. His polemic is really rather tame, in fact, and he really argues more in opposition to certain viewpoints in contemporary Calvinism than against rabbinic Judaism per se. This can be seen in his expressions on the classic issues Sabbath and circumcision, which attack the literalism prevalent in certain Calvinist circles and defend his own spiritual understanding. The views expressed here would attain their full flowering in certain later writings, from 1658 on, where the question of the Sabbath and its observance was debated heatedly. Mention of these debates has already been made in discussing Cunaeus; they need not be examined, though, for they are really part of a long tradition unto itself of deliberations on the question, one that Calvin himself was only a continuator of, and one that is really beyond our purview.

The Jewish positions serve only as examples, then, in this almost bloodless address. Coccejus, as he was by then more widely known, expressed the hope that his listeners will be aware

> how instructive it is for us to look upon the example of another and see both the *type* of our lack of constancy, that we may beware, and the pattern not only of God's sternness, that we may have great fear, but also of His mercy toward us, that we may be have a more burning love for Him, in order to glorify Him and the more solicitously rescue our neighbor for whom sin has been a stumbling block from the fire of hell.

The typology here is the standard variety; it has been seen in Cunaeus and appears even more vividly in others.

It had also been invoked by Coch in his preface to the edition of *Sanhedrin.* His rabbinic studies had had their detractors; Coch came out in defense of their usefulness. How, he asked, are Christians to ward off the wrath of God, that is, the wrath of a kind with which the Jews are beset, unless they know "how great the blindness is in which the [Jews] dwell"? This is is but one of the classic postures to be found here. Other centrally important ones include Coch's expectation of being able to refute the Jews by destroying the "authority" of the Talmud out of the work itself, while at the same time presenting "true and solid explications of the Old Testament" and buttressing them "out of the ancient masters."[120]

Yet it was initially in its overall usefulness for understanding Scripture that he saw the importance of the talmudic literature. And it was primarily as an example of approach and method that he saw his own work, as a first "specimen" for others to follow:

> . . . it is a new thing I am attempting, namely, to show that a knowledge of the Talmud and of the talmudic writers is of extraordinary help in the elucidation of the New Testament.[121]

Before that, though, quoting Grotius's view from the *De jure* that:

> the Hebrew writers can contribute not a little to our understanding of the meaning of the books belonging to the old covenant,

Coch continues by saying that the Talmud, the "Doctrinalis," or the "authorized teaching" of the Jews, as he refers to it at this point, has its usefulness for the understanding of law in all its facets: ceremonial, natural, and that fixed by convention ("positivus").

> Where, but the Jewish Talmud, can the learned traditions handed down by our forefathers be sought? Indeed, these are relevant, whether for a fuller understanding of Mosaic law, ritual as well as judicial and moral; or for an illustration of exotic (?) laws; or for shedding light on accounts of the Jewish commonwealths [e.g., Josephus (?)]; or, what is most important, for confirmation of the account in the Gospels, where there is abundant mention of Jewish custom, law and traditions.

It is at this point, "praeterea," that he introduces his conversionist aims and the hope that, by showing "what the ancients believed about Christ and the kingdom of God,"—Cunaeus had done the same thing in essence—"the obstinacy of the Jews of today will be shattered, by nothing more than the authority of those [ancients]." On the other hand, if the opinions of the ancient Jewish teachers are at variance with Christian views, "unless both their mistake itself and its bases are properly made evident, it can in no way be rooted out." Coccejus's purpose in this edition is the accurate representation of some of these foundations. His view of the entire enterprise of polemic follows from it. He is concerned with

> what must be believed on all those matters where we are in dispute with the Jews. This business is indeed not being carried on in this century as it would be fitting.

Precision is necessary in order for Jewish–Christian controversies to be carried on properly, and it was, in his view and in that of others, a serious failing in his contemporaries that their Hebraism and their knowledge of rabbinic literature was so weak.

Coch goes on from here to speak of the need for an accurate determination of the parallels in rabbinic, not biblical Hebrew, to the putative original Hebrew text behind the Greek Testament; a number of examples are offered of how this might be important. In short, his preface is an amalgam of all the many different arguments of his day for the study of rabbinic literature by Christians. He concludes with several other observations that are both characteristic of the age and possibly also of documentary value. His edition itself came about, he says, despite the many hindrances to these studies, including the Jews' begrudging their instruction and the Christians' own indifference in this area.[122] Perhaps this had been his experience with his Jewish teachers in Hamburg, that they gave of their materials only reluctantly. Perhaps it lies at the background of Amama's vision of Coch as a Jason among the Scythians.

The Mishnah chosen by Coch for translation was *Sanhedrin,* "for it discusses, first and foremost, the nature of the Sanhedrin, its power, jurisdiction, etc." Coch also included *Makkot,* its companion. These were chosen as representative of the order *Nezikin,* which, Coch points out, was viewed by the ancient rabbis as a single tractate, "unicus tractatus." He gives no further reason for his choice, though. The utilitarian arguments for the study of rabbinic literature in general have suddenly given way to scholarly curiosity and detachment and to a philological approach and method.

The commentary, which claims to be almost an *explication de texte,* proves this out. Coch had announced at the very end of his preface to the reader that he would rely on various rabbinic treatments of the Talmud, both early and late, regardless of their genre, "if there are any that appear useful." In this remark, the distinction between goal and method becomes clear. The usefulness of a piece of rabbinic literature for the explication of the Mishnah is of a different nature from the more general "utilitas" of rabbinic studies for biblical exegesis. They are both useful for understanding the text, but the links in the current case are obviously much closer and much more immediately applicable. So Coch has decided to bring the various authorities together, as necessary, in a series of "comments, albeit brief ones." Not all the comments are short, to be sure, but most are fairly narrow in focus. Coch saw it as necessary or useful, for example, to indicate "according to whom the halakhah is, that is, whose opinion is accepted and assented to by all"; the basis for judgment was to be the *Kaf Naḥat* [of the Italian Rabbi Isaac ibn Gabbai], as it appeared "in a Venetian copy" [in the 1614 Venice Mishnah edition, which had the *editio princeps* of that work]. Despite Coch's earlier remark about the invidiousness of the Jews, Hebraists seem to have had little trouble acquiring such editions. We have seen how Drusius and Cunaeus managed; Coch seems to have had no problem either.

Even more heavily than on the *Kaf Naḥat* does Coch rely on such Mishnaic commentaries as Maimonides' and Obadiah Bertinoro's (c. 1450–c. 1510). Coch also quotes the Gemara's discussion of the Mishnah when necessary for comprehension. And he provides a running series of references, paraphrases, or quotations of *Mishneh Torah;* he refers, in fact, to quite a few different books of the code. His comments often summarize or interpret the rabbinic ones; only sometimes, though, does he give his source. For example, on *Sanh.* 11:2 (*Ḥelek*), discussing three kings who have no place in the world to come, he writes: "Not these three alone. Rather, these are intended as examples of the others." And in the next annotation, on the prophet Balaam, who has no place either: "Although he was not an Israelite. For Maimonides says that *ḥaside umot ha–'olam,* the pious of the nations, will have a share of life eternal." Both of the comments are based on Maimonides' commentary, even though only one is identified as such.

To take another case, the penalty for kidnapping a "yisrael" (an Israelite) (*Sanh.* 10:1). Coch stops to examine who falls under this designation; following Bertinoro, he considers the case of a slave. There are, he finds, different degrees of slavery; some slaves have gotten partial freedom, and so on. But "here, when I could not set things in order myself, Maimonides in *Hilkhot 'Avadim*, chapter 7, came to my help. There he says as follows: . . ." Coch proceeds to quote most of Halakhah 4 in translation and then, for further clarification, *Gittin* 4:5 (identical with *'Eduyyot* 1:13, as Coch points out in his citation).

He often adds a brief discussion of the halakhic reasoning or process involved. He examines how the different authorities line up on a given question: "Maimonides approves of this opinion" (ad *Makk.* 2:5). The issue is the murderer by accident who is banished to a city of refuge; the road must be cleared of any obstacles to his swift passage there, and he must be accompanied by two scholars lest the avenger of the deceased kill him *en route.* To the opinion of Rabbi Meir that "the murderer himself may plead with the avenger in his own behalf, as it is said in Deut. 19:4, 've–zeh devar ha–rotseaḥ' (being taken literally to mean 'and this is the word of the murderer')" Coch writes, first quoting the Gemara in Aramaic, then in translation:

> The Gemara adds: " . . . what, then, [are the scholars to speak]? Not a warning to [the avenger] that if he kills [the slayer] he is going to lose his own life as a penalty, but, as it has been taught, they shall speak to him things that are appropriate to him, such as: 'and you shall not act like shedders of blood'; 'he did it inadvertently'."[123] [The accompanying scholars] should calm the avenger's rage with words. For, in the opinion of the majority, the avenger is indeed able to kill [the slayer] with impunity, along the way as the latter flees or is led back or sent back [to the city of refuge]. Their opinion is based on this: that the words " . . . and there is no sentence of death upon him" [refer] to the avenger; moreover, the words "for he did not hate, etc." in Deut. 19:6 apply to the beginning of the verse: "lest [the avenger] pursue." This opinion is approved by Maimonides.

The passage in question from the *Mishneh Torah* is *Hilkhot Rotseaḥ* 5:8. It supports the view that the two scholars do the pleading. The halakhah is not according to R. Meir, of course. What Coch has done is to give the basis of the logic by reference to the scriptural prescriptions; has done so, however, with the help of the rabbinic commentaries, by working out what the Talmud is saying and himself providing a synopsis of that discussion for the reader.

Much in the same way as the rabbinic commentators, Coch will flesh out the argument with just a word or two. In the question of the culpability of the avenger who kills the accidental murderer who had gone beyond the perimeter of the city of refuge, Coch writes: "Per contumaciam. Gem. f. 12, pag. 1." It is only if the murderer had wandered away in *intentional* violation of the law that the avenger is punished for having killed him. Here Coch abstracts the essence of the talmudic discussion from Maimonides' comment on the Mishnah in order to clarify the specifics of the law for the reader, but he also gives a reference to the Talmud because the matter is not that simple.

A case where Coch follows Bertinoro is his explanation of the various types of priests mentioned in *Makk.* 2:6. That passage refers to those prior to Josiah's time, who were anointed, to those who came later, who were invested, and to the disqualified ones. Bertinoro, in fact, had not supplied the name of King Josiah, but the borrowing by Coch is still obvious.

In the preface, Coch had advised his readers to do their own footwork on the more routine words in the text, recommending Buxtorf the Elder's *Lexicon* [*Hebraeo–Chaldaicum*]. In the notes, however, he himself often turns to David de' Pomis (1525–88), an Italian Jewish physician whose *Tsemaḥ David* in Hebrew, Latin, and Italian was popular for its more specialized scientific and historical definitions. Yet, for an audience to whom all of the material must have been quite novel, Coch does stop frequently to provide simple definitions of the working vocabulary of the halakhah. On *Makk.* 2:2, to explain "reshut ha–rabbim," he writes:

> *Reshut* is *exousia* [Gk.], 'facultas', 'potestas' ['means' or 'power']. That is ownership, or what is in each person's control. From this, *reshut hay–yaḥid* is private possession. See *Baal Aruc. Reshut ha–rabbim* is a public place. A *karmelit,* that is, a place that is neither fully public nor fully in the private domain, differs from both of them. *Itstava,* that is *stibas* [Gk.]. See the tractate *Shabbat.*

It is hard to know how the Greek term in the last definition corresponds to the Aramaic other than by sound, but, as for the rest, they are clearly addressed to an audience of novices.

For another of these definitions, he relies on the *Mishneh Torah:*

> *Ger toshav.* Maimonides in *Hilkhot Issure biah* chapter 14 defines him as follows: [the Hebrew is paraphrased] "He is a *Goy* [*sic*] or an alien who has renounced idolatry and taken on the other precepts of the children of Noah, but who is neither circumcised nor baptized. This person is accepted and is one of the righteous of the nations of the world." He is called a *'toshav'* or a 'lodger' because there are no other terms on which he may dwell in the land of Israel. He is contrasted with the *ger tsedek,* that is the 'just immigrant', who is elected ["cooptatur"] into the people of God by *milah u–tevilah,* circumcision & baptism. [Ad *Makk.* 2:3]

These are straightforward, but not overly simplified explanations.

Even more complex, but noteworthy for its conciseness is one that is specifically contextual, though general as well:

> *Goel had–dam* the 'avenger of blood', in Maimonides' definition, is *kol ha–ra'ui lirushah,* that is, 'whoever may enter on the inheritance of the slain.' He is bound by the law to take vengeance on the slayer.

This comment on *Makk.* 2:7 is based on *Hilkhot Rotseaḥ* 1:2.

Sometimes, Coch compares the definitions given by a number of different sources. On "malket," 'pincers' or 'tweezers' of some sort referred to in *Makk.* 3:5, translated by Coch himself in the text as "forpex," which could be 'scissors' or 'tongs', he annotates:

> R. David de' Pomis translates 'forfex' ['shears']. The gloss of *Kaf Naḥat: melkaḥayyim lelakket has–se'ar,* that is, 'volsella' ['pincers'], which is closer to the original language. Yet Maimonides in his comment explains the second word thus: it is an iron instrument that uproots the hair and plucks it out by the root.

Here his purpose is obviously to clarify his own translation, so he presents a variety of explanations, all of which are quite similar, the Maimonidean one standing out, if at all, only as more elaborate. Coch also remarks on his own preference, indicating thereby how he intends his translation to be taken.

Coch's observations are sometimes directed more expressly to "quo sensu hoc capiendum" ['the sense in which this is to be taken'] or to the "ratio" [the 'rationale' or 'principle behind'] or "causa" [the 'reason for'] a Mishnaic statement. These are not always halakhic judgments, and are sometimes his own understandings. On the wicked who [will] stand in judgment in the world to come—the meaning here in *Sanh.* 11:3 is elusive—he writes:

Perhaps there will be reparation for their sins through sufferings endured until *yoma de–dina rabba,* the day of great judgment, so that they may be assigned to the fate of the just. The Jews too have their purgatory.

There is no agreement among the Jewish commentators on the meaning of "'omedin bad–din" here. Coch simplifies while at the same time making a judgment of his own as to the possible meaning.

In one instance, he goes overboard in the other direction. In a comment clearly designed to be a display of erudition (ad *Sanh.* 1:2), he makes a passing mention of intercalation and runs on for quite a few pages on the practice. It is the longest comment he makes, yet it addresses an entirely different topic from that of Mishnah.

In general, though, Coch is almost completely dependent on or aligned with the rabbinic sources. He rarely resorts to the Greco–Roman writers for material. His sensitivity to rabbinic thought is even apparent in the material he chooses to extract from the Jewish commentators. From Maimonides' final comment on *Makkot,* at 3:16, which concludes a discussion of reward and punishment for the avoidance of temptation—the Mishnah says that the many *mitsvot* offer "Israel" the possibility of righteousness—Coch writes:

For if any Israelite, out of love, performs any one of the 613 commandments of the Law as is proper, without any admixture of personal intention, he will inherit eternal life. *Maimonides in his commentary.*

There is, finally, no polemic whatsoever in Coch's commentary. Even in the places one might expect to find some indication of the Christian view, this is lacking. On "epikoros" in *Perek Ḥelek,* for example, he annotates with an etymology and with Maimonides' understanding of the term:

This name, which they consider derived from *pkr,* indicates one who does not believe in the fundamental [principles] of religion, scorns the sages, etc. There are thirteen fundamental [principles]. . . .

Coch proceeds to list the thirteen principles Maimonides had proposed in his introduction to chapter 11; the twelfth principle is listed without comment:

The Messiah will come. Therefore he is to be awaited; but the time of his coming is not to be inquired into.

One other comment is also of interest. On the person "who reads external books," in the same Mishnah, Coch, ignoring the example of Aristotle chosen by Bertinoro (and by others), writes:

> Among them he reckons even Ben Sira, for whose proverbs we have the elucidations of the prince of sacred philology, the illustrious Drusius. Their reading is not prohibited altogether; (Why, then, would [the rabbis] themselves have included maxims of his, maxims that they surely find the greatest fault with, in [the Talmud]?) But it is prohibited to read them with such esteem that you prefer them to the study of the divine word.

More important, though, than the question of why the rabbis would have written Ben Sira's opinions down if they had forbidden them altogether is the style in which his question is couched. It shows a penetrating philological insight, one based, perhaps, on some comment by Drusius in his edition. But Coch's comment also gives us occasion to comment on the tradition in which he saw himself when studying rabbinic literature, i.e., the philological one begun at Franeker by Drusius. It is clear that Coch's interest in and expectation of the conversion of the Jews did not entirely recede before his philological mode of learning and of evaluating both this tractate and the many other works that went into the makeup of his commentary. An interesting irony presents itself, as a result. In the edition of Coch's complete works that his son brought out after his death, it was still necessary for the son to defend Coch against a charge that he had overindulged in "Jewish–talmudic exegesis." The study of rabbinics continued to have its detractors, and no amount of either detachment or utilitarianism, even for an application of it in polemics, could seem to sway public opinion in favor of the discipline.

Constantine l'Empereur, Professor of Jewish Controversies: His Commentaries on Mishnah and His *Clavis Talmudica*

The task of moulding public opinion was thrust even more forcefully, however, on l'Empereur. The professorship of Jewish controversies (his title: "Controversiarum Judaicarum Professor") was created especially for him. He was to defend Christianity against the Jews and convert the Jews to Christianity by familiarizing Christians with the modes of rabbinic dialectic and with Jewish thought and writing in general. He was also to instruct his students and readers specifically in the techniques of Jewish controversy. Though both the title and the goals were characteristic enough for the day, the position that l'Empereur held was virtually the first chair in rabbinic literature in any university.

Constantijn l'Empereur van Oppijck (1591–1648) was a native of Bremen (as was Coch), whither his family had fled from Opwick, in Brabant, on account of religious persecution. He was a product of Leiden and Franeker, coming to Leiden in May 1607 under the Faculty of Letters. It may be presumed that he encountered Scaliger before the latter's death in 1609. He may also have heard Arminius, who died that same year, even if he inclined himself, as it appears he did, to the Gomarist position. (L'Empereur's doctoral degree at Franeker in 1617 would be for a dissertation *de Originis Peccato,* but he does not seem to have been an active participant in the Remonstrant disputes.)

L'Empereur's first Hebrew teacher was Rudolf Snell (1546–1613). Though Snell's regular appointment was in mathematics, he had, for a short while after Drusius's departure in the mid–1580s, been charged with the public teaching of Hebrew as well.[124] Even during the 1587–97 tenureship of the Hebrew chair by Franciscus Raphelengius (1539–97), the grammarian of Plantijn Press fame, and even, subsequently, during the period when Junius and, after his death, his student Guilelmus Coddaeus (1575–c. 1625) were charged with the task (1599–1602 and 1602–10 respectively), Snell appears to have continued tutoring the language "informally." From Coddaeus's dismissal in 1610 till his own death in 1613, Snell appears to have been even more active, but he was never officially reappointed to his former post.

Rather, the vacancy was let stand, as Thomas Erpenius, the founder of modern Arabic studies,[125] added Hebrew to his duties in 1612. Erpenius was essentially a grammarian and a linguist, though he had had an undisguised missionary motive in his pursuit of Arabic.[126] L'Empereur studied with Erpenius until April of 1614, when he went off to Franeker to continue in theology, and, more particularly, in Oriental languages and Jewish antiquities. He would become Erpenius's successor upon his return to Leiden in 1627 as professor of Hebrew.

There were certainly other important figures whom l'Empereur came to know during his first Leiden period. Both Grotius and

Vossius were already established, and the latter would, indeed, praise l'Empereur as Erpenius's star pupil in a funeral oration on the death of the famous Arabist. Presumably this was from first-hand acquaintance and not just on the basis of reputation.

At Franeker, l'Empereur undoubtedly came to know Drusius and Amama, even though his degree from that institution was in theology. Nothing is known of his relationship with them, however. As for the rest of his career: from 1619 until he was called to Leiden in 1627, l'Empereur was professor of Hebrew and theology at Harderwijk (founded 1600), in Gelderland. In 1633 at Leiden, the professorship of controversies was added to his Hebrew appointment; in 1646, two years before his death, he would succeed to the chair of theology there. In sum, l'Empereur was exposed widely to the major scholars of his day and to their methods. His own *curriculum vitae* followed naturally from his training.

L'Empereur's inaugural lecture at Leiden in 1627 already shows his approach in scholarship. His theme, "De linguae Hebraeae dignitate ac utilitate," "On the Worth and Usefulness of the Hebrew Language," makes the study of Hebrew a part of humanist erudition in its use of "dignitas" and a part of theology in its address to "utilitas." Drusius would probably have been appalled at the utilitarian aspects of the presentation, but times were changing. On the other hand, Scaliger would probably have applauded his opening remark, that religious controversies are more easily solved with a knowledge of Hebrew. Scaliger's opinion, "Non aliunde dissidia in religione pendent, quam ab ignoratione grammaticae" ("Disputes in religion derive from nothing other than an ignorance of philology"),[127] was well known, but l'Empereur makes no mention of it. Yet he adopts the position and its implications and begins with some of the traditional gibes. He maligns the Jews for the veil over their eyes that keeps them from perceiving the light of Scripture, despite their knowledge of Hebrew. He impugns the "Talmud, Midrashim and other commentaries" for their "old wives' tales" ("aniles istas fabulas") and he cites a few examples, all *loci classici* such as Genesis 49:10, of how the Jews have misunderstood and misconstrued Scripture. His treatment of these is not original and may be passed over here.

At the end of his address, however, l'Empereur turns to place himself in the tradition of the great Reuchlin, of whom he says:

"He was the first to take up the Hebrew language after it had long lain buried. We must give him the credit for all our progress and advancement." This estimate was undoubtedly widely shared, for Reuchlin's activity in other areas was well known. Indeed, l'Empereur goes on, Reuchlin always kept up his Hebrew, no matter what his political concerns. Now the audience on this occasion reflected a broad spectrum of society and included many nonacademicians and many public figures; the address was a defense of Hebrew studies among precisely this group, all of whom could be expected to have pretensions to learning. But l'Empereur certainly was not blind to the further implications of his invocation of Reuchlin. Reuchlin had defended the Talmud, of course, against the attacks of a Jewish apostate, Pfefferkorn. Though Reuchlin lost little love on the Jews as a group and always continued to hope for their conversion, he was a willing defender of the Talmud for its kernel of truth and its benefits for Christian knowledge. If he also defended the Jews in his argumentation, Reuchlin did so on grounds of Roman law; it may be noted in passing that such an appeal represented a shift from the argument based on Christian charity or on other theological reasonings, even if they may still have been underlying issues.[128]

Like l'Empereur, incidentally, Reuchlin too had had Jewish teachers. Among Reuchlin's, one of the most famous was the exegete and philosopher Obadiah Sforno (c. 1470–c. 1550), with whom he studied in Rome in the years 1498–1500. Sforno thought it was an obligation of the Jews to teach all mankind to know and worship God, according to his comment on Ex. 19:6. Reuchlin's interest was Scripture and the kabbalah; Sforno was apparently a very willing instructor. L'Empereur's interest was to be the Talmud, and he would see it as his task to gain an accurate knowledge of talmudic techniques. As a controversialist, moreover, he could hardly be called a defender or a champion of the Jews, as Reuchlin might.

Originally, l'Empereur's humanism and Hebraism, like everyone else's, aimed at a Christian understanding of Scripture. If his address and even his mention of Reuchlin were part of a general appeal to an audience of nonprofessional Hebraists, Hebrew was, therefore, a necessity for all:

Already anyone can say that no one dealing on a higher level with humane letters fails to learn the Greek and Latin languages. Is there any mortal, though, who is not bound to delve into the sacred mysteries of each testament in the most precise fashion? Is not everyone, therefore, also to learn the Hebrew language?

The questions are clearly rhetorical. Though translations had made much more of the relevant literature available to non–Hebraists, Hebraists still considered a knowledge of the language indispensable for an understanding of Scripture. As such, they never ceased advocating its study. Perhaps the reason for their dwelling on this topic time and time again is that the usefulness of Hebrew study never became firmly established as a popular conviction. Not only during l'Empereur's tenure was it orphaned at Leiden, with its instruction often assigned as an added duty to those with other interests and responsibilities, but l'Empereur's successor also had to call attention to such a state of affairs. Johannes Gerhardi Terentius (d. 1677), who filled the chair of Hebrew at Franeker from 1651 (after Coch had departed), had himself studied at Leiden and even had lessons in rabbinica from Menasseh ben Israel in Amsterdam in 1650. He entitled his inaugural lecture at Franeker: "De excellentia, utilitate, jucunditate et necessitate linguae Hebraeae ad rem theologicam." ("On the merit, usefulness, pleasurableness, and necessity of the Hebrew language for the field of theology.")[129] Even in the chair that Drusius had made famous, the need to articulate the premises of Hebrew study continued to exist two generations after his death.

For l'Empereur, though, the consequences of his view were quite specific: scholarship on rabbinic literature for the purpose of illustrating Scripture. In 1630, he brought out an edition of the Mishnaic tractate *Middot* similar in format to Coch's *Sanhedrin,* with which he was familiar and which he regarded highly. L'Empereur here shows the same utilitarianism both he and Coch had shown earlier. Here that utilitarianism is even more applied, though. The dedication to the States of Holland and West Frisia (yet another one to this noble body) captures much of the familiar rhetoric concerning the proper relationship of Church and state in the Netherlands. The dedication is sympathetic to the Calvinist position, of course, and thoroughly orthodox in its views. It begins:

This writing the Hebrews call *Middot* desires eagerly to rush away and come to you from the libraries where for fourteen hundred years and more it has lain concealed, read by few and understood by the utmost few. The book had to rush away and not be hidden any longer, [for] it sheds such important light on sacred things. And, indeed, not only does it elucidate the religious ceremonies of the Old Testament, when it places clearly before our eyes the place and the several areas of that place where those ceremonies were performed, but it also holds up a bright light before the Gospel narratives, when it shows those who until now did not know these things, exactly in which section our Savior did each thing in the Jerusalem Temple, and where therein he taught.

Aside from l'Empereur's somewhat exaggerated claim to having "rediscovered" something previously unknown, his arguments about the need for such a work and about its ability to "illustrate" and "illuminate" the sacred antiquities in a particular way are fairly standard. L'Empereur comes forth here again as the humanist orator, trying to persuade his audience not only about the possibility of historical reconstruction, but, even more, about the links between the intellectual and practical spheres of their own experience. Continuing in this vein, he sees it as his function to produce such a work, "endowed with Latinity" and "rendered clearer with annotations." It is his particular concern to establish a strong nexus between the translation and the commentary, i.e., between form and meaning, for, he claims, the reader who consults the translation along with the annotations will be able to understand the Mishnah more easily. This is obvious, of course, but l'Empereur was apparently concerned that readers might fail to notice how interdependent the translation and the commentary were, and that he considered the translation an integral part of the commentary.

These characteristics and techniques will, in l'Empereur's view, increase the "auctoritas" of the Mishnah at a time of great significance and danger to the Church. The magistrates are like the builders of the Temple and its protectors: "who are building a temple of God that is composed of living stones, restoring one that has collapsed, keeping it intact, . . ." Their careful management is most essential at this moment. "Religio periclitatur," he says, 'religion is in danger'. The heresies of the Arians and Socinians are undermining the unity of the state, and the guardians of the state must protect the [Dutch Reformed] Church.

An explicit historical analogy, based on the use of antitypes, follows, and it is a classic one: "tabernaculum Dei, id est Ecclesia." The Calvinist church is a living tabernacle. It has wandered through Germany and France, just as the tabernacle of the Israelites had wandered through the wilderness; it has now found a home "sub vestris auspiciis" ('under your authority') in the Netherlands, "transmuted, as it were, into an utterly immovable edifice, a temple." The typologies of this period range, of course, from the historical and literal to the allegorical or spiritual. The "type" and "example" of the Puritans[130] is l'Empereur's "exemplum" or "typus & figura," by which he means a prefiguration.

Here is his example for the Netherlands: The choice of religion may not be left to individual conscience. The magistrates, whose control extends over all of civil life and, hence, over religion as well, must remove the enemies of the Church, the "instruments of false religion"; they must coerce and direct the people "to true religion," just as their predecessors did of old. They must curb liberty of worship, for such license opens the way to error. It can destroy the obedience "in the proper observance of the divine cult" that, according to the very word of God, is owed to the magistrates themselves.[131] L'Empereur remarks that, when the Temple in Jerusalem fell into disrepair due to old age and to neglect by the undutiful, the kings saw to its restoration. L'Empereur provides *testimonia* "worthy of attention"; he names names: Joash, Josiah, and so on; he cites verses; he batters away:

> In a similar manner, with [your] very judicious and well–managed support you have stabilized and repaired the living temple that was threatened with disaster, so that all states can regard it as an example to follow in similar circumstances.

The support of the state will enable the Church to grow and flourish; what would destroy one would destroy its partner. And so he summarizes:

> On this account, not only because that Jerusalem sanctuary was, in the unanimous opinion of everyone, the type and figure of a living sanctuary, that is, of the Church, but also because the things that occurred in it represent in every respect the circumstances and condition of this Church that you administer, I assert that it is not absurd to present a sketch of it to you.

Middot, which gives the layout and measurements of the Jerusalem Temple, is, he implies and even states, like a portrait of the history of the Dutch Church. For he appeals to the meaning and moral function of contemporary portraiture directly in calling the Temple the very "effigy" of the Dutch Church:

> Parents often set up portraits of their children in their rooms, it being pleasant for them to gaze upon them, inasmuch as they are images of the offspring that has been entrusted to them by God and nature. By the same reckoning, in this book that I willingly and deservedly present and dedicate to you, the heads of State and of Church, you will look upon an agreeable representation of the likeness and image (*effigies ac imago*) of that offspring, that is, of the Church, depicted and portrayed with its characteristic features in that Temple of Jerusalem.

L'Empereur goes on and on in this vein. We may, for a moment, compare the use of Jewish subjects by Rembrandt to this use of Jewish literature by l'Empereur. In having his Jewish neighbors sit for him as models for paintings on biblical themes, Rembrandt drew an implicit link between them and their ancestors, even though his representation was hardly a photographic one of their contemporary life in the Netherlands. Similarly l'Empereur, in using rabbinic literature and Jewish teachers, draws the same inference about the continuity of past and present.

L'Empereur saw his work as a benefit to the University of Leiden. It was, after all, his colleague Heinsius, who, he said, "had thoroughly mastered all disciplines and fields of knowledge," and whom others referred to as "little Scaliger," who had encouraged him "to render the Mishnah into Latin and embellish it with notes." Heinsius was one to know the utilitarian and academic applications of such works. So was Vossius, who had also spurred l'Empereur on. Their own works follow a similar philological methodology and present the same arguments. What distinguishes them, however—and to this l'Empereur failed to address himself—is that they categorically reject controversies as a part of scholarly commentary. In their work, even if the apologetic function is sometimes evident in the body of the work, whatever polemic there is is confined to the dedication. L'Empereur would be less cautious.

It is also useful to compare Heinsius's stated principles; these would not be articulated until his famous *Sacrarum Exercitationum ad Novum Testamentum Libri XX* of 1639, but they were widely shared by others even before hand. In Jonge's admirable summary, they are as follows:

1. Elucidation ("illustrare") of difficult passages;
2. Testing the exegesis of the Fathers;
3. Adducing parallels or illustrative material ("quae maxime accommodata videbantur") from early Christian and other literature, pagan and Jewish;
4. Comparison with Old Testament parallels;
5. Supplying linguistic information ("linguarum ope usi sumus") by elucidation of the Hellenistic idiom and above all by comparison of translations;
6. Avoidance of allegorical interpretation and a search for the "sensus literae" or "sensus historicus" [the 'literary' or 'historical' sense];
7. Avoidance of "controversiae."[132]

Even Heinsius, though, was concerned with "inner meanings"; he invokes Jerome (about annunciations of the New Testament in the Old) and Athanasius: "propter spiritum literam non tollimus, sed vim spiritus per literam servamus" (Heinsius's translation) ["We do not abolish the letter on account of the spirit, but we preserve the force of the spirit through the letter"]. Among those whom Heinsius mentions as having been of the greatest assistance to him in preparing his massive work is l'Empereur, "with whom, on the advice of the greatest experts in [rabbinic literature], we have shared and discussed our observations on the New Testament." If Heinsius was helped by the comparisons with rabbinic literature that l'Empereur suggested, l'Empereur undoubtedly owed something to the encounter as a help in the formation of his own commentaries.

L'Empereur's commentaries are "illustrative" by design. "Illustration" implies a fair number of things, more than merely the citation of other sources in parallel or as amplification of the text under scrutiny. It is elucidation in the largest sense and includes: the definition of words and terms; the analysis of grammatical, lexical, or etymological forms; the clarification of the author's "mens," his meaning or basic idea, or his "phrasis," his mode of expression ("loquendi modus"). In the "illustrative" commentary, moreover, processes or the *realia* are described; the various "sententiae" ('opinions' or 'views') explained; the rationale ("ratio") or reason for a statement ("quia . . .") given. The larger context is also kept in the foreground: the continuity of the discussion is followed, discrepancies and contrary views or explanations are weighed, often with an attempt to reconcile the different materials. There is also a frequent comparative evaluation of textual readings in the several editions.

The intent of all this is to shed light in the broadest possible fashion. Much of this was thought to be accomplished by the amassing of "testimonia" of all kinds. L'Empereur was no exception on this score; if he was guilty, as a result, of obfuscating rather than elucidating or shedding light, he is hardly to be blamed for following the conventions of the time.

"Testimonia" are not merely 'proofs' or demonstrations that either the author or the commentator has spoken the truth. They are corresponding examples from other sources that might have dealt with the same issue or used the same phraseology in clearer fashion. They are, to be sure, also demonstrations of the commentator's having read widely, i.e., being erudite and able to collect the material from a variegated group of authorities. "Authorities" and "authority" itself are very much a matter of fashion and taste, often determined by criteria other than intrinsic worth or probability of truth. "Auctoritas" is not invoked only as a defense for something otherwise impossible or at least impossibly difficult of demonstration by other means. That is to say, the ancients have the veneration of age and so do many of the latter–day scholars and teachers; their words are considered to express what must be said or argued by the commentator in much more persuasive fashion than he could possibly articulate them alone.

For l'Empereur, the authorities he relied on most for his *testimonia* and "for the correct understanding of the Mishnah" were the Talmud and its commentaries, preferably the earliest possible sources. But he did not exclude the later ones; he made use of Maimonides' *Commentary on the Mishnah* and of the *Mishneh Torah* as well. Though he sometimes finds that a rabbinic explanation "hallucinatur" ('is deluded', or 'is idle talk') this criticism is levelled at any author who seems to be grossly in error; it is not a gibe reserved for the rabbis. The general usefulness of rabbinic literature is taken almost for granted.

One of l'Empereur's comments will make this clearer. It refers to a piece of exegesis by Isaac Abravanel (1437–1508), the biblical commentator also known as a philosopher and statesman. The substance of Abravanel's comment is of no consequence here. According to l'Empereur, though, it is

> useful for a much better understanding of several *testimonia* of the New Testament to pay attention to it. For that reason, I am not unwilling to include Abravanel's view; all the more willing, even, in order thereby to render that author the more commended to all, for many additional things . . . can be learned from him, inasmuch as he explains the rather obscure things in the sacred writings fully and felicitously (except when he goes along with his own [fellow Jews] and resists Christian truth). [Ad 5:2]

When Jewish literature does not clash with Christian truth, its views shed light in a felicitous way on obscure places. Its pronouncements are a help in understanding the *testimonia* of the New Testament (and obviously those of the Old Testament as well).

As for his use of rabbinic sources, his recourse to the *Mishneh Torah* was largely to *Sefer 'Avodah,* which describes the Temple and its service. Yet he also drew on the commentators on Maimonides' code, including Joseph Karo (1488–1575), the famous author of a code of his own, the *Shulḥan 'Arukh* (1565), but whose *Kesef Mishneh* on the *Mishneh Torah* had first appeared in the 1574 Venice edition. In general, it may be assumed that l'Empereur was familiar with other rabbinic works.

The prime use to which he put these works and their views and interpretations was the advancement and substantiation of his own, Christian argumentation. If this usage is not novel, the method itself is. A notable example of his technique is to be found in his use of R. Moses Alshekh's commentary on Latter Prophets. Dating from the sixteenth century, this work is heavy with spiritual and allegorical interpretations. In discussing Zech. 6:14, which is cited in *Middot* 3:8 and speaks of the attire of the high priests, l'Empereur digresses to remark that the high priest "was the type of that priest whose name was *germen* (Lat.)." The word "germen," 'seed' or 'shoot' ('tsemaḥ' in Heb.) is found in Zech. 6:12 and was often interpreted by both Christians and Jews as a foreshadowing of the Messiah. L'Empereur develops this line of thought and applies it to some of the ideas he had expressed in his preface:

> . . . and that may be the reason he is called *'germen'* (just as the sign and what is signified are here and there said of each other in turn). By this procedure, God once portrayed the royal priesthood of Christ in the

ancient church of the Jews: and that is the reason both offices, the royal and the priestly, are linked in v. 13; and it is on that account, perhaps, that that *consilium pacis* ['peace and understanding'] (as the text reads there) may have had to be mentioned. Those crowns [v. 14] were thus set aside as a remembrance [*mnemosynon* (Gk.)] of a future event: as R. Alshech explains in v. 14, . . . where . . . he comments on [the phrase] *'in memoriale'* ['as a remembrance']: [it refers to] that which will be in future times in the temple of God.

Alshekh uses these verses homiletically as part of an overall exhortation to repentance that looks to a messianic redemption. He takes the expression "le–zikkaron," 'as a remembrance' not in its usual sense of reference to the past, but as an indication of the future. L'Empereur sees this as license for a specific application elsewhere:

These crowns that were placed on the type of Christ, that is, on Joshua the high priest, were afterwards a sign of a future [fore]shadowed event, in particular for those persons by whose generosity they were furnished: and for that reason they were set aside in the [Temple] as a perpetual memory of the event.

This is but one of a number of such Christian interpretations that l'Empereur advances, usually out of context. Another is his view of Haggai, chapter 2, for the understanding of which he again has recourse to Alshekh. It is in l'Empereur's discussion of the vine that stood at the entrance to the Temple; it follows immediately upon the above. First l'Empereur establishes the presence of such a vine by quoting Josephus. Then he continues:

The Hebrews comment on why this portal was adorned with vine–sprigs, namely, that the assemblage of Israel is likened to a vine, as in Is., ch. 5, and Ps. 80:9, and passim elsewhere. Moreover, just as this vine represented the Jewish church, just so even the Temple referred to the Church. Whence R. Alshekh observes several times that the Israelites are [equated with] and are called 'temple'. (Consult his commentary on Haggai at the beginning of ch. 2.) Whence it can be seen in passing that the promises of God about the Temple, and, in the same exact manner, about the land of Canaan and the life that was to be led there are not always to be taken, as they say, *ad literam* ('literally'), not even by the Jewish expositors.

L'Empereur does introduce the spiritual interpretation that he advances with an "obiter." But it appears to be an essential part of his presentation nonetheless. He had referred to the same passage in Haggai and to Alshekh's interpretation in his preface, as well as in his comment on *Middot* 3:1 (s.f., s.v. "fundamentum," on the "yesod"). The concept should already have been familiar, but l'Empereur reinforces it with further citations from Abravanel and from Maimonides, the latter a reference to the *locus classicus* in *Hilkhot Teshuvah* 8:1–2. Of this he writes, not altogether inaccurately: "Insofar as the land of Canaan is concerned, however, Maimonides affirms that those promises designate a future life, but one that is spiritual." (3:8, n. 3) In this passage, Maimonides offers a vision of the world–to–come as incorporeal; there is a difference, however, between incorporeality and the understanding of the prophecies in a spiritual sense.

Not only does l'Empereur resort to spiritual interpretations, he also discounts rabbinic interpretations in other ways. On rabbinic statements about things missing in the Second Temple as compared with the First, he says (3:1, n. 13) that this does not accord with the claim of Haggai 2:1 that the Second Temple will be the greater, its greatness resulting from the presence in it of the Messiah "God and man." In the same note, he also advances the standard Christian view of Gen. 49:10, on the scepter of Judah having been removed from the Jews with the advent of the Messiah; he shows a number of Jewish exegetes "admitting" that the Jews are destitute of power:

> . . . the power that Jacob had said would endure till Messiah has clearly, by the evidence of the Jews themselves, already been done away with. Nay, Kimchi even confirms this expressly, that they have been deprived of this power, and therefore live under the power of others: " . . . We are under the power of the nations and the power of their kings."

The foregoing are but snippets of several extensive digressions on Christian themes. At the end of this last one, he sends the reader to his *Systema Theologicum* (1626) for an even fuller treatment of them. This work consisted of dissertations or disputations between himself and his students at Harderwijk; it was clearly not a new undertaking for l'Empereur to present such views at Leiden. But it was definitely irrelevant to the Mishnaic discussion of the base of the altar—and even to the fact of the placement of the altar on the boundary between the tribes of Benjamin and Judah—to have introduced them, and l'Empereur knew this.

There were other digressions, to be sure, yet of a slightly different quality. In discussing the Chamber of Hewn Stones where the Sanhedrin met (5:3, n. 5), L'Empereur had talked at length of idolatry and the worship of Peor (3:4, n. 8), and on the trial of Jesus. On the Sanhedrin itself, though, he writes: "Since my friend Rev. J. Coch, a man distinguished and remarkable for his wonderful erudition, dealt with these things fully in his *Sanhedrin,* I refrain from dealing with them." Yet he then proceeds to quote a long extract from the Gemara that Coch had not included in his edition! Nonetheless, some of the ironic tone and even the general thrust of the work is indicated in this brief aside on the hermeneutic rule *gezerah shavah:*

> Consider, please, readers, the logic of the rabbis, which elsewhere is even more absurd: so much so even, that it is no wonder that, with their foolish logic, they elicit from Scripture, as true as it is, opinions as false as those are.

Though he thought that his edition would show to the not unsophisticated that "the usefulness of the talmudic and rabbinic writers in sacred things is not slight" (5:3, n. 6, s.f.), he had, in other respects, already provided a clear indication of what was to come in his future work.

The controversialist dimension does not predominate here, to be sure. L'Empereur saw himself as a public functionary who, by elucidating the Mishnah, was advancing the cause of the proper management of the state. He surely had no wish therefore to destroy the authority of the Mishnah by adopting as a general approach the combatting of the "erroneous" interpretations of the rabbis. It was only where he found them specifically in error that he felt he had to reprove them. On the other hand, he did often find occasion to digress from his philological investigations to address those errors.

The digressions become the central focus of his *Clavis Talmudica* of 1634. This translation of *Halikhot 'Olam,* a handbook of talmudic methodology by Yeshu'ah ben Joseph Halevi, a late–fifteenth–century talmudist, has a specifically conversionist aim and is the direct outgrowth of his appointment to the chair of Jewish controversies. In his "Dissertatio ad Lectorem," l'Empereur minimizes the importance of "Jewish antiquities" and of other pursuits characteristic of Hebraists, suggesting that the study of rabbinic hermeneutical methods was of far greater importance. "It is remarkable what great power and authority the ancient Jewish [writers] hold [over contemporary Jews], power in which [these Jews] glory." On that basis, he proposes, those ancient authorities should be invoked and made use of for the purpose of "refuting the enemies of the Gospels and stopping up their impudent mouths."

One must, in other words, learn how to confute the Jews out of their own literature. (The classic dual approach is asserted yet again.) That "power" and those "strengths" ("vires") had to be dealt with directly, through Talmud study, that is to say, only with the proper weapons. Christians would then be able "to show the glory of their Savior more clearly before the [Jews], with whom they live, not only elsewhere, but here also. They would be able to defend their beliefs more solidly . . . and in this way make their faith more and more firm, and resist and respond to the artifices [of the Jews] that much more skillfully." Inasmuch as Jews were present "here also," in the Netherlands, he praises the curators of the University of Leiden, to whom he dedicates the work, for having shown exemplary concern for the Jews in their miserable state of ruin. The curators were right in thinking that "not by force of arms, but by instruction and a demonstration of the truth was that people to be led on the road to salvation." L'Empereur's function was to make that possible.

Previous attempts to work from the literature of the Talmud have not, says l'Empereur, been successful; this was because Christians lacked a knowledge of the methods of talmudic dialectic. Now the curators had set aside funds for the acquisition of books and manuscripts that could demonstrate the rabbinic modes of argumentation. Christians must know and understand the weapons of the Jews before they find them wielded against them "unexpectedly" and are overcome by "sophistic arguments" and "deceptions." It would no longer suffice to draw arguments or "testimonia" at random.

It is interesting that, despite this insistence on a knowledge of dialectic and of the rules or "canons" of halakhic decision making, the specimen of proper controversial method that l'Empereur gives as the "Dissertatio ad Lectorem" is hardly novel and hardly relies on this kind of new skill. It is largely a demonstration of how talmudic statements agree with Christian expositions of various biblical passages. His example is Isaiah 53, on the suffering servant, and he quotes, along with Rashi's comment, the passage from *Sanhedrin* 98a on the Messiah sitting in misery among the poor. He further invokes the passage from *Sukkah* 52a that speaks of the death of "Messiah the son of Joseph" and concludes with Zech. 12:10: "They shall look on him (*rather* me) whom they have pierced through." On this he writes: "Who does not see Christ here, that is, the pierced–through Messiah?" One other major concern of l'Empereur's in this introduction is the question of the abrogation of the ceremonial law; he advances no new arguments, however, on this issue and topic of long standing.

Of greater interest, to return to the dedication, is l'Empereur's account of his personal experience in dealing with the Jews. They have books, he says, in which are described the methods of devising difficulties for Christian disputants. These treatises they restrict to themselves, he says, refusing to allow others to examine them. Somehow, though, he had himself secured a "manuscriptus codex" containing a chapter on the doubts or anxieties ("scrupuli") with which Christians are to be made to waver. By using the word "codex," he seems to think that this is a book of laws of some sort; he must be referring, however, to one of the numerous anti–Christian polemical treatises of the period. These were really intended for internal use, mostly against wavering members of the Jewish community, and then for honing Jewish skills against outsiders. They existed, of course, almost exclusively in manuscript. The reluctance of Jews at this period to engage in overt disputations and to advance their own position too boldly is well known. The era of the "friendly disputation" is not yet at hand; it is only the second half of the century when it becomes a real possibility. It was, then, such writings as these manuscript treatises that had stimulated the authorities to appoint l'Empereur.

He continues by remarking that this particular chapter is apparently snipped out when, by chance, the "codex" is given to Christians, lest they become able to prepare themselves and have things thought out by the time they come together (the word he uses is "congrederentur," signifying: 'in disputation') with the Jews. Moreover, what was true of polemical literature was true, he thought, of the remainder: there was internal Jewish censorship. The Jews, he says, "prefer to conceal from us in equal measure the [passages] in the Talmud or its commentaries and [the passages] in their other books that respond to the testimonies we cite, and [to conceal] as well the way they expound those passages."

Nonetheless, the Jews were compelled to carry on these disputations, or so it would appear. L'Empereur recalls his own involvement in them and the consequences that accrued:

Memini ubi olim in ipsorum synagoga & privatis aedibus cum ipsis conferrem, jam tum ulteriorem in Talmudicis, similibusque libris profectum mihi invidisse: praeceptori meo à synagogae *parnassim* [Hebrew letters are used] praefectis vocato interdictum, ne in ista opera mihi navanda pergeret; ut quem non lateret, quorsum ista studia tractarem.

To translate:

I remember when I formerly used to debate with Jews in the synagogue and in private homes. Even then they begrudged me further progress in my study of the Talmud and related literature. My teacher was summoned by the leadership of the community and prohibited from rendering me further assistance in these works, since my purpose in pursuing these studies was not unknown to him.

To l'Empereur's mind, all this was due to one thing: the Jews knew themselves to be unequal to the Christians and tried therefore to catch them unawares with their "strophae," their tricky arguments.

What happened to l'Empereur is clear, even though no date or specific locale can be assigned to the events with certainty and even though l'Empereur writes "olim," as of a distant past. The *Mahamad,* the governing council of the community—l'Empereur's "parnassim" are the individual members of the board, its administrators—had clamped down on a member of that community, preventing him from teaching a Christian whose purpose was more than routinely hostile. There is also a suggestion that the teacher himself should have known better. Few communities, if any, however, were categorically opposed to any and all instruction of non-Jews. Amsterdam was not one of these; there can be almost no doubt that Amsterdam was where this encounter took place.

There had been a series of debates there as early as 1605–8, between Hugh Broughton, the Middelburg pastor and an opponent of Jewish settlement in his town, and David Farrar (d. 1624), a somewhat outspoken member of the Jewish community. Amsterdam may have had a synagogue as early as 1602 and a second one from 1608; other places in the United Provinces still lagged behind. (Haarlem, despite Scaliger's hopes for it after the Jewish community was chartered in 1605, was still dormant; Rotterdam had had debates forbidden there by the charter of 1610, though that in itself is not decisive; it seems remote, though, as a place to go and carry on such a debate, in view of l'Empereur's general odyssey, as does Alkmaar, which had been chartered in 1604, the first Dutch municipality to have granted the Jews a charter.) By 1606, though, Amsterdam may already have had some 200 Jews, as Scaliger reports.[133] It was the most likely place for l'Empereur to have gone in pursuit of his goals.

Whenever it was, then, the community was determined to frustrate him. We can see now that his aims and his methods were only superficially detached; this had obviously been clear to his contemporaries from a very early period, and they perceived him as a threat, much as he did them. His method was not "biblical antiquities" with a Christian bias, it was the demonstration of "the errors of the Jews." His great erudition made him an even greater threat; but the power of the community was such that they could take measures against one of their members who might be likely to compromise their position, and this is what had apparently happened here.

The perceptions of the community must have been further substantiated and reinforced by l'Empereur's 1637 edition and commentary on the Mishnaic tractate *Baba Kamma* (*De legibus Ebraeorum forensibus;* Leiden, 1637). Once again there is the subtle mixture of utilitarianism and apologetics. It should be stressed that the utilitarianism is not just a vehicle for antirabbinic, even anti–Jewish argumentation, but also an important component in its own right. The study of the Mishnah is important, he tells us here again, for the understanding of Scripture and for the light shed on the New Testament, "even though from time to time traces of Jewish blindness may be found in it." And so, he asserts,

> that is the reason I have translated several such tractates and illustrated them with commentaries; a few of these are already published and more, God willing, are to be [in future]. From this group I have, for the present, taken this one out of the order Nesikim [*sic*] and with the same goal and purpose that I have prepared the others.

It is the fruitfulness of this tractate, says l'Empereur, for an understanding of biblical law that has prompted him here; in a digression, he then expatiates on the law with regard to its several "species," those handed down by the "great lawgiver" Moses to the "summo . . . Ebraeorum magistratui," the "heads of the Jewish state." Though he adds nothing new, this is how he defines the three species:

> The first was that of general restrictions; the second, limitations that aimed at a goal, namely, the observance of the divine law; the third, [the kind] that prescribes a way, method, and means by which an act enjoined by divine commandment can be most easily performed.

Yet, even though the method of commentary is more scholarly here than in *Middot* and less beclouded by polemics, focusing on the ways in which Jewish law had developed (with the above guidelines in mind—surely the notes deserve a more elaborate study than we intend here) and, for example, on "analogies" to Roman law (ad 3:8, s.f.), this edition is still part of l'Empereur's overall efforts at getting the Jews to recognize, as he says in the final lines of his commentary, both "their spiritual wretchedness," and also, consequently, the truth that is not passed over even in the Talmud itself.

If any change might be suspected to have taken place in l'Empereur's approach because of his willingness to treat Jewish law as an independent subject of study, strong apologetic currents still underlie his writing and come to the surface from time to time.[134] Characteristic comments are to be found first in the dedication, and they are worthy of historians' attention. The addressee is one Caspar van Vosbergen, possibly identical with a certain diplomat from Zeeland (fl. 1623–37); l'Empereur addresses him, though, as "Dominus," that is to say, as a "Dominee," or a Calvinist pastor or "Reverend." Whether or not he was a practising clergyman, van Vosbergen had apparently undertaken special efforts with regard to the Jews:

> And so, since you have shown such great kindness to the Jews, and have taken them into your tutelage in this way, I have no doubt that you will welcome this book of the Jews with similar good will and approve of this small present [of my dedication].

Of course, no specific information can be extracted from this, but we can be certain that the "benignitas" and "tutela," the kindness and care, were like the solicitousness displayed by curators of

Leiden to whom the *Clavis Talmudica* had been dedicated. There was a clear movement afoot to bring about the Jews' conversion: one can assume nothing less.

In passing, note may be taken of one of l'Empereur's own asides, one that resembles a remark in the *Middot* edition. It too is a general condemnation; it is found in the final annotation:

> You see, reader, that it was with perfect justice that our Savior censured those doctors [sc. of the Talmud]: on the grounds that they permitted vengeance, anger, and enmity, if anyone should, with words or deeds, detract from their honor.

This is possibly a disparagement of the method of debate common in the Talmud. Earlier, l'Empereur had criticized the logic of the Talmud for drawing false inferences from Scripture. The pattern here is the same, indicating the basic entrenchment of his goals and modes of thought.

Ironically, though, in the same way as with Coch, theologians among l'Empereur's colleagues were concerned that the professor of Jewish controversies tended to teach too much "out of the rabbis." Despite all the motivations he professed, despite his public function in the university and all his antirabbinic statements, which hardly can be considered show, his interest in rabbinic literature was seen to have a momentum of its own. And it probably did have that momentum in fact. His works, then, with respect to the erudition that went into them and the illumination it produced, were, indeed, forerunners of the more detached observations of the eighteenth century.

One final observation on this group of scholars is in order. Regardless of their own methodological dispositions, they all saw themselves as part of the same enterprise. Vossius and Heinsius contributed commendatory poems to l'Empereur's *Middot;* Coch presented a long one for the *Clavis Talmudica.* In this poem, Coch rhapsodized on l'Empereur's dispelling the darkness of the Jews, concluding with:

> Oh, let the blind see the true light uncovered!
> Let him shudder, oh, who sees their minds sunken in darkness!
> Great, in God's praise, will your glory be, L'EMPEREUR:
> When there will be noble offspring from your child.[135]

Despite his general and striking difference in method, Coch

shared the hopes of his friend l'Empereur. These productions would bear fruit when they brought about the goal of the Leiden appointment: when they brought about the conversion of the Jews.

Buxtorf's Translation of the *Guide*

All this may be compared with the remarks of the 1629 translator of Maimonides' *Guide of the Perplexed.* For it was not only in the Netherlands that such attitudes persisted, but all over Europe; there could be no better comparison on the question of rabbinic literature and, in particular, on Maimonides than Johann Buxtorf the Younger (1599–1664), of Basel, himself a Calvinist. The Buxtorfii not only shared the same dual attitude to rabbinic literature as the rest of the European Hebraists, but were themselves more hostile than many to Judaism, even though they had worked with Jews and used the services of Jews for their own benefit. The elder Buxtorf's *Judenschül* (Latin tr. *Synagoga Judaica*) had given ample evidence of that in 1603. His son's *Doctor perplexorum* was a badly needed new translation and appeared in the year of his father's death. In the preface, the younger Buxtorf shows the same tendency as l'Empereur by writing with glee of Maimonides himself:

> He was a noted Doctor of Theology in his religion and faith, and (this praise must be granted him) given over very little to talmudic fables and traditions. For he writes as follows in a letter to his disciple R. Joseph [ibn Aknin]: "Beware lest you waste your time in exposition and painstaking reflection on the Gemara. For I lost much time in those things and derived little benefit [from them]."[136]

As for Maimonides the jurist, the overtones are similar:

> That no one was more adept at Jewish jurisprudence than he is evidenced by the fact that he not only adorned the whole *corpus juris* of the Hebrews with glosses [Buxtorf may be referring here to the *Commentary on the Mishnah*], but also, out of a confused and very entangled order, out of a vile and varied language, forced the [rabbinic] sayings into a perspicuousness, into a fixed order, with a pure Hebrew language, and in a facile and elegant style. [This must refer to the *Mishneh Torah.*]

This hardly differs from the views of Ainsworth, for example, or from those of others who may have expressed it differently. Buxtorf, incidentally, shows an understanding of some of the criticism of the *Mishneh Torah* by Jews:

It is censured (invidiously no doubt) by some, and, certainly, most of all on this ground, that it assumes the role of the Talmud, teaches many things that disagree with it, and suppresses the names of the sages under whose names the traditions are preserved in the Talmud.

This awareness was probably not unusual either, especially since most of these Hebraists seem to have been familiar with the commentaries on the work. Yet Buxtorf infers this from the "Letter of Self–Defense" that Maimonides wrote to R. Pineḥas ben Meshullam of Alexandria and that Buxtorf himself was translating as an appendix to the *Guide*. Buxtorf's range was really quite broad, and his whole introduction, which offers a general survey of Maimonides' life and works, is of great interest.

"G. N.": An Englishman's *On Repentance*

In sum, matters stood approximately the same elsewhere in Europe. And in 1631 in England, where John Selden was by then a past master at accumulating quotations from Maimonides, an anonymous translation, under the initials "G. N." and the title *Canones Poenitentiae*, was made of *Hilkhot Teshuvah*. The Cambridge translator had this, among other things, to say about the Jewish view of penitence and Maimonides' presentation of it:

The things that we have in common with them, though they are not requisite for confirming our teachings, will nonetheless not be useless for elucidating them. The pious Christian will, without any warning [being necessary], avoid those that are peculiar to Judaism.

As his defense for exposing the unwary reader to danger, as it were, G. N. notes that, in the marginalia throughout his translation, Buxtorf had warned his readers of possible "errors," e.g., on the question of free will (an issue here too). He quotes Buxtorf: "'the author, out of the common error of his nation, declares that [there is] free choice.'" He then calls the reader's attention to his own frontispiece, which is a clever and playful use of Homer *Odyssey* 4. 230. It is based in part on the original context, of which the erudite reader will have been aware. The lines there speak of a woman

> Of Egypt, where the fertile earth produces the greatest number
> Of medicines, many good in mixture, many malignant,
> And every man is a doctor there and more understanding
> Than men elsewhere. [tr. Lattimore]

The *Hilkhot Teshuvah* of Maimonides, "Rabbi Moses of Egypt," a physician by profession, even though G. N. may not have been aware of this, was a book about repentance, healing of a sort; but some non–Jews may find some of its medicine too hard to swallow, even poisonous. To wit: the censors who reviewed the work, who found much "for elucidating the principle of penitence," but who—and the overtones are specifically Calvinist—took exception to Maimonides' treatment of free will:

> But in the fifth and sixth chapters, hypothesizing that our nature was not in the least injured through Adam's fall, he declares, in the manner of Pelagius, that each person can, solely by means of free choice, incline equally to good and evil; in like manner, he teaches throughout the work that penitence and turning toward God are not a gift of God, but [derive] from human choice alone. It is no wonder that a Jewish man should fall into deceptions of this kind.

Such was the use of rabbinic literature that its doctrines, though understood to be characteristic and representative, were viewed specifically in light of the current Christian agenda and discountenanced accordingly, even while other aspects of the same work were being looked upon more positively for their usefulness in increasing Christian understandings of the issues at hand. In England at this date, there was no living Jewish community for which such comments would have immediate repercussions. In the Netherlands, though, this utilitarianism had a more direct application, moving outside the scholarly recesses of literary analysis.

Millenarianism and Hebraism

From one perspective however, the Jews and their role were live issues both on the continent and in England. This perspective was the millenarian one, and here too the impact of rabbinic literature can be felt. The incipient messianism that affected all Christians to a greater or lesser degree at this period as one of the great leavening forces of the age made its mark on Christian Hebraists as well.

Coch, for example, manifested only the germ of this outlook. Many others who more properly deserve the designation of millenarians, though, and who demonstrated the same or a similar mixture of attitudes to the Jews were also Hebraists. It has even been contended that the overall development of eschatological ideas at this period was partially due to Hebrew studies in Protestant universities.[137] The English apocalypticist, Nathaniel Homes, a correspondent of Menasseh ben Israel in the Netherlands, even "justified his millenarian ideas by printing several hundred pages of excerpts from early Christian and Jewish writers."[138] This interest was often coupled with an interest in Jewish law,[139] as "the theory of the elect nation [i.e., the true Israel] fused with millenarism."[140] If all this was usually attended with a hope for the conversion of the Jews, it may even be that "Hebrew studies," rather than muting the expression of such hopes was probably the one most important force in enhancing them.

Indeed, not only were such views common all over Europe, as some have said,[141] but millenarism became more and more normal for the period.[142] Johann Alsted, a widely respected German Calvinist academic (and Hebraist) who had been one of the foreign observers at Dort in 1618, made apocalyptic predictions already in the 1620s. These early ones were characterized by restraint, but even he predicted that the conversion of the Jews might take place as soon as 1636 or 1642.[143] His views became widely known in the Netherlands. And English chiliasm in general, which was suppressed at home prior to 1640, had been preached in less restrictive Amsterdam in the 1630s.[144] Grotius himself had been interested in millenarian trends; he looked with anticipation at a growing church unity as a sign of the millennium, and he saw this era preceded by the conversion of the Jews.[145]

Calvinist thinking on the way in which the conversion of the Jews would come about ranged from a rather spiritual eschatology on one side to an apocalyptic one concerning "Israel in the flesh" on the other.[146] Moreover, the hopes for Jewish conversion ranged from the traditional expectations of an eventual one to the chiliastic sense of an impending one. While Arminians were less preoccupied with the question of Jewish conversion as an imminent reality than other groups—theirs was primarily a spiritual eschatology, with the kingdom of God largely a matter of "the inner renewal of human life," rather than "an aspect of the drama of history"—they had "certain expectations" with regard to the

Jews.[147] One of Menasseh ben Israel's Amsterdam friends, Simon Episcopius, the rector of the Remonstrant Seminary and a most representative Arminian, gave voice to some of these. Essentially cautious, he made no predictions about the way in which the Jews would achieve grace. Only God knew that, he felt.[148]

All of these men have several points in common. They all share the traditional attitude that rabbinic literature contains both Christian truth—or that it at least sheds light on that truth—and Jewish errors, which may be dangerous for Christian consumption. With regard to the Jews themselves, the text of Romans 9–11 serves as their basic guideline: the Jews are an example of imperfect faith; the conversion of the Jews in spirit is to be looked forward to because it will mean the ultimate unity of the church, all men having then been converted. (The Jews themselves were interested in trends toward unification in the churches, which they too looked upon in messianic terms.) Third, contact with living Jews among the foregoing individuals, that is to say, among a good number of them, was minimal; they give little indication in their writings of having had any personal encounter with Jews: this was true of all of them for the majority of their careers, even if they had once had a Jewish teacher or interlocutor. If they had any attitude to the Jews as Jews then, it, too, was a twofold one: they wished both to have them as teachers and to exclude them from membership or participation in the larger society.

Baron has remarked that, "among liberal scholars, the study of Hebrew often did serve as an argument for Judeo–Christian coexistence."[149] It is hard to see that the word "often" applies here. Even Baron admits that a "knowledge of Hebrew, to be sure, did not make a man a Jewish sympathizer." This was true of both "liberals" and "precisians." Toleration of the Jews has many roots, but very few of them lie in Jewish literature alone. More often, it was personal experience that made the difference. Instruction by Jewish teachers may have made a few inroads, but it was usually dealings with Jews in the marketplace as either rivals or partners that made the greatest difference. The exiles of the Sephardic diaspora, making their way northward and westward in increasing numbers as the century progressed, provided that experience of a living Jewish community. Even then, deep–seated attitudes persevered, being altered only rarely and being shattered almost never. Yet it was on the banks of the Amstel that the first great encounter between Jews without all the previous disabilities of medieval Europe and Christians, some of whom at least made a pretense of wishing to have Jews living among them, took place. If Jewish Amsterdam could justly be called the Dutch Jerusalem, moreover, it was in great part the rabbinic leadership of the community that made this possible. In fact, it was this rabbinic élite who were among its most important spokesmen to the world at large, that is to say, who became the most significant apologists for Judaism and the rights of the Jewish people in the entrepôt of Western Europe.

II

The Portuguese Nation on the Amstel and Its Rabbis: *"Veritas è terra orietur"* ("Truth Will Arise from the Earth")

The Instruction of Christian Hebraists in the Setting of the Amsterdam Jewish Community and in Light of Its Major Concerns

In the midst of a newly independent Dutch nation trying to establish its religious and political identity, a group of Spanish and Portuguese Jews newly arrived from the Peninsula was trying to reclaim its patrimony and, with it, their identities as rabbinic Jews.[1] They faced enormous difficulties from within and without. There was often, at very least, their own Christian upbringing that they were trying to cast off; for many, there was an extreme difficulty in becoming accommodated to life under a regimen that they had not yet come to understand fully. This regimen involved both standards of practice and principles of doctrine, and there was frequent internal dissension on these questions. From without, as we have seen, there was the full panoply of prejudices against the Jews and Judaism that had existed since before the Christian era. Though some moderation was visible, a newly developed or refined emphasis on rabbinic literature both for a better understanding of Christianity and as a stronger defense against Judaism was equally apparent. In other words, the attitudes of Christian scholars toward rabbinic literature bore no relation to and often specifically militated against any real toleration for the living representatives of that literature, the new Jewish residents of the United Provinces. Concern with the "errors" of the Jews was rife, and it turned Christians toward the Jewish community with either distrust or, at best, compassion. Regardless of any putative advantages that the Jewish presence in the Netherlands might confer, the religious question remained a stumbling block for both theoreticians and even the general public.

Coccejus, for example, rendered the opinion that, since the Jews have the same "principium fidei" as Christians and were not "heretics," they were to be admitted to residence. But, he felt, they were also to be missionized, out of love, humanity, gratitude, and the respect due them as the people from whom the founder of Christianity came.[2] Yet, Scaliger had also spoken volumes in his taciturn comment: "They are not to be expelled, they bring profit, then we learn from them."[3] Many Jews relied primarily on such utilitarian arguments, regardless of the complex of sentiments that lay behind them. Others coupled a basic reliance on arguments of the usefulness of the Jews with a flow of apologetics, missionizing in their own self–defense, as it were. If this was not particularly new as a phenomenon, the necessity for such activities seemed to have grown. For there were distinct cultural similarities between the Dutch Calvinists and the many Portuguese whose basic value system had been formed under Christian auspices. While indebted more heavily to the Northern European Renaissance and to the Reformation, the world view and erudition of the Calvinists nevertheless had a certain cultural background in common with the Portuguese, aside from their own experience of Spanish domination. Despite the differences between the Spanish and the Dutch schools of thought, many of the fashions and conventions of the two groups, in literary style and method, in the topics or questions for discussion, and even in the basic conception of what constituted erudition, were remarkably close. This made relations between the two groups, as both were trying to adapt to their new circumstances, fraught with tension.[4]

Some Christians appeared rather accommodating, to be sure. In February 1633, Gerardus Joannes Vossius sent his friend Aelius Everardus Vorstius, the famous professor of medicine at Leiden, a recommendation for one David de Haro, a Jew. De Haro, already a physician for a least a decade, had completed his preliminary training at Leiden and was long since known to Vorstius. He now sought to continue at Leiden to the "medicinae supremum gradum," that is, the highest degree obtainable. Vossius was willing to support de Haro, as the young man had hoped, "as an old friend and acquaintance of [my] children." Of de Haro's aims, character, and background, Vossius offered the following assessment: "His requests were proper; I found his character and morals acceptable. If I am unable to love his religion, inasmuch as it deviates from the Christian one, I approve of his unassuming conduct, and, on that account, did not think I ought to refuse him." Though the field of medicine was not one of those closed to Jews, the quality of Vossius's statement reflects the delicate position of the Jews even in such areas.[5]

For not everyone was convinced of the "modestia" of the Jews. They were often accused of being too bold and reproached for their "stoutichheden," or "boldnesses."[6] Jews were suspected, for example, of recruiting Christians to Judaism; calls for the banishment of the Jews were the result. Despite the generally few specific disabilities under which they labored, though, their status was not nearly that of full citizens or even of free men in a free society. While Menasseh ben Israel could tell Prince Frederick Henry in 1642, "We live safely and make use of liberty like the others," this, as Bloom says, "must be taken *cum grano salis*."[7] The Jews were able to be excluded from some of the guilds, for example. More than the purely religious element was at work here, of course; there was undoubtedly a strong fear of competition that prevented intrusion by an easily identifiable group. But some members of the petit bourgeoisie turned their Calvinist views to account by warning merchants against the Jews and calling for their exclusion as unbelievers. Abraham Coster's 1608 *Historie der Joden* is one such appeal and has been seen as a classic of anti–Jewish propaganda.[8]

If some Jews advocated keeping a low profile on issues of religion, this was hardly possible. For one thing, they were asked from time to time to engage in religious disputations. While this does not mean that they were forced to submit to them, the pressure was undoubtedly great. One incident tells of Henry Ainsworth, who had found a diamond apparently belonging to a Jew, refusing to accept monetary compensation for returning it, insisting instead on the opportunity to debate the rabbis on the prophecies concerning the Messiah.[9] There were also such tracts as the one by J. H. J. van der Ley (c. 1566–post 1630), a former admiral turned theologian, on *Hidden Features in Scripture, as in a sealed Book . . . [that] need to be known for the upbuilding of the Temple of Peace, for Heathens, Jews, Christians, and Mohammedans. Addressed to the Reverend Rabbis of the Synagogue of this City of Amsterdam* (1626, in Dutch). This pamphlet, an exposition of various disputed biblical passages—it also includes a mention of the *Zohar*—has the appearance of a conversionist sermon, even though the only indication of its original context is that it was "Actum ['delivered' at] Leeuwarden, den 24 Martij 1626." It is more probably, though, merely an epistle after the model of one that van der Ley quotes in passing, from Antonio de Guevara (c. 1490–1544) to the Jews of Naples, "On the Great Mystery of the Trinity." The author here, van der Ley, however, is one of the proponents of an ultimate Christian–Jewish–Islamic unity who would become increasingly numerous over the next few decades and would even include some of Menasseh ben Israel's most famous interlocutors.[10]

The Jews were also subject to the likes of Gisbertus Voetius (1588–1676), the professor of theology and Hebrew at Utrecht. This most orthodox of theologians can be called l'Empereur's arch–rival and was certainly Coccejus's arch–enemy. He was violently anti–Jewish, accusing the Jews of everything from avarice and injustice to atheism and "odium Dei."[11] In his 1637 *De Judaismo,* he suggests ways to promote the conversion of the Jews, avoiding both the intolerance of the Inquisition and too great an intimacy with the perfidious Jews. Aside from "prayers, a pious life, [and] a living faith" on the part of Christians who looked forward to the conversion of the Jews as a part of the *eschaton,* he advocated

> sympathy and beneficence toward the Jews, a sound interpretation of the Scriptures, a demonstration of the perfidy of the Jews and of their desperate state, either in public or in private colloquies, and the furtherance of the studies of Oriental languages and of Jewish controversies.[12]

To his *Exercitationes et Bibliotheca Studiosi Theologiae* of 1644, Voetius adds an "Apparatus ad controversias Judaicas" as but one aid in pursuing his goal. It contains both works by Jews that are useful for study, including: the Talmud; the classic polemical treatise *Nitsaḥon,* of which he writes, "See same. An edition of it with a refutation has been promised by the most distinguished [student] of Jewish literature, our friend, Rev. Constantine l'Empereur. We await it eagerly."; Maimonides, [who], "in the *Moreh Nevukhim,* and the *Yad Ḥazakah* [note this title for the *Mishneh Torah,* indicating familiarity], contrived not a few things against the truths of Christian theology"; and "of the most recent writers, several things of R. Menasseh ben Israel, although he cannot be called a disputant, except quite homonymously."[13] These and others are listed "On the side of heterodoxy." "On the side of orthodoxy," he adds to a previously published list works by Broughton (his "Epistola ad R. Abraham Reuben" and his commentary on Daniel that had been translated by Borelius, as well as his "Collatio cum R. Farrar") and l'Empereur (the "Animadversiones ad Abarbanel in cap. 53 Iesaiae"), not to mention several others.[14] In the mid–1630s in general, Voetius, who also attempted to have the books of the Jews censored, was probably behind much of the anti–Jewish agitation, even though the actual task of argumentation may have been put into the mouths of others.[15]

Of course, some Jews welcomed the opportunity to engage in disputations. David Farrar, a bit of a maverick, to be sure, is said to have been the instigator of that 1608 debate with Broughton, following it up with a Latin tract trying to confute Broughton's opinions on the Fourth Monarchy.[16] On the other hand, some invitations to the rabbis were turned down, as with Jan Beelthouwer in the 1640s.[17] In general, such requests for disputation were not looked upon with favor by the rabbis, who seem to have preferred producing their own literary polemics in languages closed to the general public, that is to say, Spanish, Portuguese, or Hebrew. A veritable flood gushed forth from the pens of such leaders as Saul Levi Morteira (c. 1590–1660), Moses Raphael d'Aguilar (d. 1679), and Abraham Israel Pereyra (d. 1699). Many of their writings were Janus–faced, of course, trying to prove to such Christians as could read them, but more to their compatriots as former Christians, that Judaism was meaningful, if not superior. These works were more for internal than external consumption. But apologetics vis–à–vis the outside were much in evidence as well, and the works of Menasseh ben Israel, who, as Voetius recognized, was not a "disputant" per se, were largely of such a type and character.

Many in Amsterdam perceived such polemical activity as dangerous, even in its milder forms. In 1616, the Amsterdam municipal council had passed a resolution that "the Jews must refrain from speaking or writing ill about Christian religion."[18] And Hugo Grotius in the *Remonstrantie* had proposed not only that a declaration of faith be made mandatory (this never came to pass), but also that the Jews not be permitted to induce any Christians to become Jews.[19] This was certainly violated in the letter, if not in the spirit, when Menasseh and others tried to proselytize visitors from Spain suspected or known to be of New Christian origin to induce them to return to Judaism. (The Calvinists probably had little concern with these Catholics, whose religion they considered idolatry anyway.)

In 1639, though, at the merger of the three congregations Bet Yahacob, Neve Shalom, and Bet Yisrael, one of the agreements or regulations forbade the discussion of matters of religion with the specific intention of winning converts. This was probably in response to charges by the Church to a certain extent, but it was also a general precautionary measure. These "Ascamot" carried all the weight of the *Mahamad*'s authority, which was considerable; even the rabbis of the community were subject to it. The regulation in question (#38) states that

> No one may discuss matters of religion with a non–Jew in order that he may come out to our Holy Law, nor may one speak scandalously of his faith to him; this would be contrary [to our interests and] disturb the liberty which we enjoy and make us hated for something that is neither a law nor an obligation.[20]

The Parnassim also reconfirmed the precensorship established in May 1632 over publications by Jews, the earlier version perhaps having had something to do with the impending publication of Menasseh ben Israel's *Conciliator*.[21] All this was part of the larger attempt to ward off any possible threats to the safety of the "Nation."

An interesting perspective on both the accomplishments of the Portuguese and their possible treachery is provided by none other than G. J. Vossius in a 1640 letter to Grotius. It is the well–known letter in which Vossius lets Grotius know of Menasseh's impending departure for Brazil. The substance of Vossius's remarks about the community has never been taken note of. Writes Vossius:

> Clearly . . . Menasseh is thinking about something other than his studies, since the Portuguese, on account of the synagogue's moderate circumstances, are not at all giving their teacher his due. Indeed, if the Jews

[can] be trusted (and it seems to me that they do tell the truth), it would be easy for our people to investigate and learn all their skills and stratagems, good and bad. [For] the [Jews] have been accepted into the city, employ our people as their servants, [and] are even often in business together with us. But we either sit immobile or have them as patrons and friends. Therefore, if any danger should arise, either here or in the Spanish lands even, leaving them mired in difficulty or rather in a deep morass, it would not be difficult for them to extricate themselves with the help of those, both here and in other countries, who have more influence.[22]

Vossius's letter, which gave rise to Grotius's even better known reply,[23] is not merely critical of such "friendships" between Christians and Jews (Vossius himself comes in for implicit criticism), but even downright suspicious of the international connections of the Portuguese Nation.[24]

Considering the impression of the Jewish community held by non–Jews such as Vossius, who could be counted among the friends of the rabbis, the wariness of the *Mahamad* was not surprising. But the Parnassim obviously did not forbid such contacts entirely. Indeed, over and above contact there was even instruction, and Menasseh, Isaac Aboab (1605–93, who became the Haham of the community, its chief rabbi, for much of the second half of the century), Aguilar (Aboab's closest associate), and even Morteira were all engaged in one form or another in the instruction of Christians.[25] The *Mahamad,* from what we know of the case of l'Empereur, obviously gave its consent to their activities.

There is little specific indication of what motivated these particular rabbis to their teaching of Christians. Their thoughts must be reconstructed almost completely, sometimes from external evidence. Yet, since the phenomenon of the Jewish tutoring of Christians was fairly widespread throughout this period, any one of a number of general standpoints may have found its echo in Amsterdam.

It may have been the kind of thinking that had formed Sforno's approach in his teaching of Reuchlin about 1500. His view was that the Jews had a duty to teach all mankind to know and worship God.[26] Other sixteenth–century views are also worthy of note. In 1538, Elias Levita wrote of the profit that accrued to the Jews from the study of Hebrew by non–Jews:

I solemnly declare that all the Christians whom I know, and whom I or others have instructed, are all of them good and upright men, and with all their power have acted kindly toward Israel; so that the very knowledge of our language among Christians has actually been to our advantage.[27]

If his remarks had ever been true of Levita's Italy, they were certainly untrue of seventeenth–century Holland, even if some Dutch rabbis obviously looked for positive results from their teaching.

Some undoubtedly held to the position of Yosef Shlomo Delmedigo (1591–1655), who came to Amsterdam in 1626, serving as rabbi of Bet Yisrael from 1626 to 1629. Menasseh published Delmedigo's *Sefer Elim* in 1628–29 and helped secure approbations from Venice for the work.[28] Delmedigo, it is said, looked upon the pursuit of secular and scientific non–Jewish learning and culture by Jews as "the best means to safeguard a Jew's standing and honor in a foreign milieu." We find his view supported in the approbations of Jacob le–Vet hal–Levi, Leone Modena (himself a teacher of Christians), and Simone Luzzatto, who looks forward to a Latin translation to "set honor and glory upon us" and "gag the mouths of those who say, with arrogance and scorn, that we lack wisdom and that we have rejected all philosophy" ("ve–khol tushiyyah nidḥah mimmennu").[29] Menasseh, who was dismayed by Delmedigo's attitude to kabbalah, was nonetheless imbued with much of the same mentality as his wandering friend, forever putting his own wide erudition on display as he sought to win friends for the Jewish people. His rabbinic colleagues were hardly less cultured than he, it might be added. His and their instruction of Christians would be a natural outgrowth of such views, a demonstration of their own and the rabbis' wealth of learning. The thought even comes to mind that Menasseh's search after translators for his works may have been stimulated by Luzzatto's hopes for Delmedigo.

These rabbis clearly had the same "incredible faith in the power of the word"[30] as non–Jewish Renaissance humanists and their Dutch successors. The rabbis most probably shared the view of some earlier colleagues that Hebrew at its source and Jewish literature read in the original had a great power to render null and void the intentions with which Christians had turned to that language and literature in the first place.[31] And they also obviously had faith in the power of personal contact. While Vossius had looked askance on Christian–Jewish friendships, he had also welcomed Menasseh into his home. Menasseh, moreover, and the other rabbis were hardly unaware of the various motivations of the Christian students, but that did not deter them from maintaining their contacts. Especially in view of the religious polemics that were still very much in the air, they must have realized that the explication of Jewish texts by Jews was a necessary antidote to the explication of those texts by Christian polemicists. Since the Calvinists especially made no secret of their reluctance to have Jewish texts read without a proper accompanying refutation, the rabbis surely looked to their own propagandizing via instruction as a form of more positive, though still, naturally, defensive apologetics. What instruction did do, to be sure, was provide a contrast and a supplement to the ordinarily more aggressive argumentation found in direct polemics. Though both approaches were part of the rather modest offensives on which certain members of the Portuguese community set out, the inculcation of normative, nonpolemical texts was clearly designed to be less salient an approach and less likely to incur odium. The rabbis undoubtedly considered instruction no less pointed or powerful a presentation of Jewish thinking on important questions of common interest than either their own literary works or the enterprise of polemics; they, therefore, engaged in it with great frequency. In sum, even if personal friendship might be had across the bounds of religious differences and was either the stimulus to or outgrowth of such instruction, the amity between the rabbis and the Christian Hebraists of Amsterdam, widely heralded as an indication of a growing liberalization, still had a strong apologetic character.

At the background of Jewish apologetics also lay the strong conflicts of both a political and doctrinal nature that existed both within the Jewish community and among Christians as well. The debates of the 1630s covered such points as whether punishment for past sins was eternal, a matter of great concern to a group of former *conversos*; whether the soul was immortal; and whether the dead (and who among them) would be resurrected. Moreover, the very legitimacy of the Oral Torah came into question. Some Jews felt constrained to show a surrounding society, itself, like the Jewish community and perhaps as its model, much concerned with doctrinal uniformity, that all was right in the newly reconstructed Jewish house. If such internal dissension gave rise to the various milder forms of apologetics, such as the translation into Latin of a number of Spanish essays by Menasseh on these subjects and such as the continued private instruction of Christians on these topics and others, this strife certainly saw its most formidable denouement in the excommunication of several notable "heretics," beginning with Uriel da Costa and culminating in Baruch Spinoza. This pattern of action was hardly distinctive for the day; the secular authorities in the republic had countenanced similar measures against the likes of Grotius and John Oldenbarnevelt, the Grand Pensionary, imprisoning the former and, after his escape, forcing him to remain an exile, and beheading the latter directly, for a complex of political and religious reasons. The Jewish community could imprison da Costa and even get the authorities' support in banishing him, but, since there was nominally freedom of religion and no inquisition, and since the authorities probably did not want to see a repeat of the Oldenbarnevelt affair, the Jews were not permitted to impose the death penalty, as they seem to have wished. All of this was of a piece. While there is a risk of interpreting "instruction" too broadly, one can see its usefulness, even in the narrow sense, in such a charged situation.[32]

Last, but hardly least, in this consideration of ulterior motivations to the instruction of Christians are the eschatological presuppositions of the age. Menasseh, Aboab, and Aguilar all would become involved in messianic speculations, Menasseh through kabbalists and other visionaries both Christian and Jewish, Aboab and Aguilar also through kabbalah, the two of them becoming the most enthusiastic Amsterdam supporters of Shabbetai Tsevi, the messianic pretender, in 1665–66. Commonly associated with Jewish eschatological thinking in the sixteenth and seventeenth centuries was a hope that the general spread of the knowledge of Torah, via both the Reformation and the activities of Christian missionaries in the newly discovered lands, was a harbinger of the Messiah. Sforno's view that it is the duty of Jews to teach the Torah to gentiles is to be distinguished by its nonactivist millenarian posture from that of others who developed the idea of a *praeparatio legis* [as the late H. H. Ben-Sasson referred to it, distinguishing it from the Christian *praeparatio evangelica*] to a new point of refinement. It is hardly surprising, then, that even those who might otherwise have been rather isolationist and even bitter toward an increasingly hostile surrounding society praised Christians for spreading this knowledge. One of them, Judah del Bene, an Italian rabbi writing in 1646, stated in hopeful tones that "as a result of the work of Christian missionaries, [the peoples of the New World] will also learn about the 'Torah, prophets, and other writings,' and thus be prepared 'for the anticipated day.'"[33]

These sentiments are little different from those expressed at the height of the Reformation a century earlier, and they have the same Maimonidean ring to them. In the censored portion of chapter 11 of *Hilkhot Melakhim,* Maimonides had expressed the view that Islam and Christianity had been of benefit in spreading the knowledge of Torah to the world at large:

> . . . And everything that came about in respect to Jesus and the Ishmaelite who arose after him only did so to smooth the way for the Messianic King and to prepare the whole world to worship God together, as it is said, "For then will I turn to the peoples a pure language that they may all call upon the name of the Lord to serve Him with one consent" [Zeph. 3:9]. How [is this so]? The world has already become full of talk about the Messiah and about the Torah and about the commandments, and this has spread into far islands and among many uncircumcised peoples. And they are discussing these things and the commandments of the Torah. Some say, these commandments were true but they have become null and void at the present time and were not binding for all generations; others say, there are mysteries in them and they are not [to be interpreted] according to their literal meaning, and the Messianic King has already come and revealed their secret sense. But, when the Messianic King will arise in truth and be successful and be exalted and lifted up, they will immediately reconsider and know that their fathers inherited falsehood, and that their prophets and Fathers deceived them.[34]

Not only were the motivations of the Christians in studying Jewish literature not closed to the Amsterdam rabbis, who had certainly heard all the arguments against Jewish interpretations, they themselves would hear these Maimonidean sentiments expressed in kabbalistic garb right in their own midst, in circumstances very much intertwined with Menasseh's own.

There are two other considerations; these involve the texts chosen for study and the purposes of promoting translations into Latin. Both are somewhat speculative judgments, to be sure.

The fact that the pupils of these rabbis chose portions of *Sefer ham–Madda'*, the book devoted to doctrinal matters and related issues, for translation and comment is easily understood. If Christians were also interested in law, they still had just as great a preoccupation with theory and doctrine. They may also have had a greater familiarity with *Madda'* to begin with, inasmuch as there were those Hebraists, like Vossius the Elder, who both knew of and were able to read and make independent use of the *Mishneh Torah* before ever coming into contact with the rabbis.[35] But *Madda'* was also prominent in the curriculum of the Jewish primary school, probably for its précislike character (which also made it of interest to Christians). Any Christian, therefore, trained inside the Jewish community, would surely have been exposed more than casually to *Madda'*. Dionysius Vossius, for establishing his own text, relied primarily on the 1614 Venice edition of the *Mishneh Torah,* one intended in some respects as a school edition and comprising only the first three books of the code, *Madda', Ahavah,* and *Zemanim.* We can be fairly certain that Menasseh helped secure the volume for him, possibly from copies on hand for use in the school, though, perhaps, from his own store—Vossius had used Menasseh precisely for the purpose of acquiring books. In short, *Sefer ham–Madda'* seems to have been used for the primary training of both Jews and non–Jews; while many of the leading scholars of the day already had more than a passing familiarity with the *Mishneh Torah,* there was a group of younger Hebraists who derived particular benefit from the presence of the *Book of Knowledge* in the Jewish school curriculum.[36]

There is one other closely related possibility as to the stimulus to translation. Baron has suggested that the translation of the prayerbook into Latin by non–Jews was encouraged by the rabbis with a Latin–reading audience of ex–Marranos also in mind. We may be tempted to think that these translations of parts of *Sefer ham–Madda'* were encouraged for similar reasons. Since they preceded David Cohen de Lara's (c. 1602–74) Spanish translations of two sections of *Madda'* by fourteen and twenty–two years respectively, there was probably a need for them. Yet the presence of Gentius's translation of *De'ot* in Aboab's library proves nothing—Aboab had contributed a sonnet to the edition—and even the presence of other Hebraist translations in Aboab's library hardly demonstrates that the broader Jewish public would have the same interest as the rabbinic *littérateurs*. Moreover, though Menasseh's works were originally in Spanish for the most part and thus open to the members of his "Nation" by and large (unlike many works originally in Hebrew), and his pupils' translations of the Spanish works could therefore only have been directed at non–Jews (possibly unlike these translations of Maimonides), still, there is no evidence to suggest, and it would be difficult even in theory to defend the view that the rabbis had Jewish readers in mind when supporting the translations of *Sefer ham–Madda'*. Though the commentators did not always show an anti–Jewish bias or even a consistent one, the aims of the rabbis were related much more to their own desire to propagandize for Judaism among the gentiles.[37]

The Intellectual and Moral Concerns of the Rabbinic Leadership

Isaac Aboab da Fonseca, Kabbalist and Preacher

Menasseh ben Israel, Isaac Aboab, and Moshe Rephael d'Aguilar were, for Christian Hebraists, the three most prominent rabbis and teachers in Amsterdam. Yet in the memory of the Sephardic community of that city, Haham Aboab, whose life spanned eighty–eight years and who was behind the construction of the Great Portuguese Synagogue, the Esnoga, in 1675, probably has the greatest reputation. That undertaking came at the height of his career, after a long period as one among a group of leaders and largely in their shadow. It came after a sojourn in Brazil from 1641 to 1654 and after the débâcle of the Sabbatian movement.[38] Born in Castro d'Aire, Portugal, in 1605, he arrived in Amsterdam at the age of seven. He became a pupil of the kabbalist Isaac Uziel; in the 1650s, probably while still in Brazil, he would translate two works of another kabbalist, Abraham Cohen de Herrera (ca. 1570–1635 or 1639), from Spanish into Hebrew. (Herrera, a former *converso,* was a pupil of the Lurianic kabbalist Israel Sarug and had come to Amsterdam early in the 1630s; in his will, he had designated Aboab as his translator.)[39] In the 1620s and afterwards, Aboab was involved in a variety of endeavors: as the rabbi of Neve Shalom, a teacher in the schools of the community, and a member of the Bet–Din (along with Morteira, Menasseh, and David

Pardo).[40] After his return from Brazil, one of his positions was as the leader of the Yeshivah Torah–Or, founded in 1656 for the study of, among other things, Maimonides.[41]

Of his personal life and sentiments, little can be known with certainty. It is possible, however, to glean several personal references from his writings. For example, in the poems of thanksgiving he wrote in Brazil after having been saved from the Portuguese attack of 1645–46, Aboab manifests a virtual guilt complex for certain misdeeds in his past and views them as being responsible for his present suffering. He speaks of "following foreign ideas . . . , criticizing Jewish law and its practitioners; I loved the flatterer and the evil one and bowed to their worshippers." This is probably a reference to his childhood as a Catholic in Portugal, which must have been starkly recalled to him in the face of this attack from which he had been saved. His feelings of guilt had probably been reinforced, though, even earlier, in the conflict of 1635–36 over the duration of punishment for past sins, even if his own position had been the more lenient.[42]

Aboab's personal library shows the man's diversity and his easy accommodation of a broad range of interests. A catalogue of the library was compiled when it was auctioned on his death in 1693. In itself, it is a bibliographic rarity, but, even more so for its remarkable contents, it merits closer study than has hitherto been given it. There were 373 Hebrew books, 19 Hebrew manuscripts, 49 books in Spanish and Portuguese, and 114 titles of works in Greek and Latin, many in multiple volumes. Also sold were several copies of Aboab's own *Parafrasis,* several lexicons, a Hebrew map of the Holy Land, and his organ and clavichord.[43]

Among the works in the vernacular languages are political, moral, historical, and theological treatises by various authors, including Menasseh ben Israel, the sole Jewish one. The rest are either Renaissance and later Spanish and Portuguese writers or a Homer, Virgil, or Velleius Paterculus in Spanish. The only other translations of classical works in the catalogue are of several Greek authors, who appear with a Latin translation as well, and Hebrew manuscript translations of Aristotle's *De Anima* and *Metaphysica.* The rest of the classical collection is remarkably comprehensive, including both major and minor authors down to the *Scriptores Historiae Augustae,* Vitruvius on architecture, the Greek and Latin poets, each in its own corpus, and a Cornutus *De Natura Deorum.* All the major authors are there; the sixteenth– or seventeenth–century editions that Aboab continued to acquire till late in life show only Plato as the one major absentee. Among later authors, there is again a full panoply, from Justin Martyr to Jean Bodin to G. J. Vossius and to the *Scaligerana* of 1668. There are two volumes of Lope de Vega, one of them the *Jerusalem Conquistada,* Polydore Virgil, and Machiavelli and Montaigne, each in the original. There is Thomas Hobbes, in Sorbière's 1652 French translation. Even an Arabic grammar and a Syriac New Testament are to be found. From the dates of the editions, it would appear that it was only the advent of blindness toward the end of his life that put an end to Aboab's activity as a bibliophile.

Needless to say, there was also a treasure of Hebrew material, one that offers an almost complete panorama of rabbinic creativity. There are two editions of the *Mishneh Torah,* and a separate edition of Abraham de Boton's *Leḥem Mishneh,* which had appeared in 1609, and thus was not included in the 1524 or 1574 Venice editions that Aboab possessed. This is but a trifle, though, considering the large number of biblical commentaries and supercommentaries, homiletics, philosophical works, talmudic commentaries, and, of course, the immense selection of kabbalistic literature: from the *Bahir* or Gikatilla's *Sha'are Orah* (two copies of the latter) to local treasures such as Sasportas's edition of Moses Albaz's *Hekhal hak–Kodesh* (Amsterdam, 1653), a commentary on the prayerbook, or foreign ones like Samuel ben Moses Heida's *Zikkukin de–Nura* on *Tanna de–Ve Eliyahu* (Prague, 1676). In the Hebrew list are also found the Gospels in four languages, the Psalms with a Dutch translation, Gentius's *De'ot,* and l'Empereur's Benjamin of Tudela in Hebrew and Latin (1633).

There are omissions, to be sure. While belles–lettres are not lacking in the vernacular or classical languages, they are nowhere in evidence among Hebrew works. And there is a total absence of polemical literature, probably due to a certain precensorship by the sellers of the library. Even as late as 1693, even after the publication of a work such as Wagenseil's *Tela Ignea Satanae* in 1684, with its extensive collection of anti–Christian polemics, and surely even long after 1693, a need was still sensed for circumspection in this area. Yet there can be no doubt whatsoever that this literature was there during the Haham's lifetime. Its complete absence from the catalogue makes this a certainty, since such literature existed in numerous manuscripts and even in Spanish printed works dating from the seventeenth century and published in Amsterdam—Isaac Troki's *Ḥizzuk ha–Emunah,* for example, had been published there as early as 1621 in a Spanish translation. And so, to sum up, there can be no doubt of Aboab's erudition. It was as great as Menasseh's, even if it was channeled more often into other activities and genres than apologetics.[44]

Aboab's own compositions were few, but they had quite an importance. Apart from the aforementioned translations and the poems of thanksgiving composed in Brazil that made him, as many have suggested, the first Jewish historian of the Americas, several other poems of a liturgical or complimentary nature, as well as the approbations he wrote (as a function of both his office and his wide range of friendships), constitute his lesser works. His 1681 *Parafrasis commentado sobre el Pentateuco* and his *Nishmat Ḥayyim* of 1636 stand out from these, the latter for its value in illuminating his conflict with the eternalists, the former as both his own magnum opus and as the standard Spanish Jewish running commentary on the Pentateuch. It was the Hertz Pentateuch of its day, very much the work of the Chief Rabbi. Its character and contents deserve greater scrutiny than can be given it here. For it reflects the capacities and concerns of the Amsterdam community just after the dedication of their new synagogue, one that stands to this day and was the model for Spanish and Portuguese synagogues everywhere. Both the Esnoga and the *Parafrasis* were the summation of Aboab's lifework.

Under the milestones of Aboab's life, David Franco Mendes (1713–92), the Hebrew poet who was also the chronicler of his native Amsterdam Jewry, mentions a "Parafrasis" dating to the Haham's thirty–first year, but to the calendar year 1626. Whichever of the two numbers must be modified—Aboab was only twenty–one years old in 1626—it would appear that the preparation of his final published work spanned many years.[45] In his own 1681 dedication, Aboab himself speaks of his fifty–five years of service to the community, of his desire that the work appear "with all possible perfection," and of his gratitude to the community "for giving me time to make it possible to publish it." Aboab's was no great original mind; his work was "drawn," as he himself says, "from the most famous authors that my library comprised." Nonetheless, he has, he thinks, improved on Josephus: "In his *Antiquities*, . . . he wrote as if ("como") for the Romans; I am writing as if for my Jewish brethren." Josephus wrote History ("lo Historico"); "I am writing History and Law" ["yo escrivo Historico, y Legal"]. By this, he refers, undoubtedly, to 'Torah'. If the latter distinction was a defense for his lack of rhetorical flourish, based on the requirement of fidelity to the original text of Scripture, the former was directed at an audience that may have been weary of apologetics and anxious for a straightforward general exposition.

As its title suggests, the work is a sort of 'Targum', a mixture of translation and homiletics, with a compendious amount of the latter. For example, in the verse, "Let us make man in Our image," (Gen. 1:26, but the verses in the *Parafrasis* are neither numbered nor distinguished one from the next), Aboab writes: "Let there be a microcosm, a condensed world, with our image as to form, an intellectual and eternal substance; a similarity with us: let its deeds imitate those of the *Espiritus* [i.e., 'spirits' or 'souls'], acting with reason and understanding." This is popular philosophy and preaching of the period. Aboab was a renowned preacher, and did leave a number of his sermons in manuscript as well; the *Parafrasis* may well be a general summary of these. Accordingly, while he does quote the remarks of others from time to time, he more often paraphrases their views and identifies them as either "Theologos" or "Sabios," the 'Sages'. The homogenized quality of his presentation shows this work intended neither as a scholarly commentary nor as a bold statement of unusual views or opinions. If he ever intended such works, and, in the preface to the *Parafrasis,* he does promise his readers a "Philosophia Legal," one containing "things necessary to know to attain happiness in this life and glory in the other," neither this nor any other was completed. Moreover, though he continued to acquire kabbalistic treatises almost to the end of his life, there is no evidence that he ever composed one of his own after the *Nishmat Ḥayyim* of 1636.[46]

This very short work is Aboab's contribution to the discussion of whether there was eternal punishment for sinners who died without repenting, his position being non–eternalist.[47] Aside from their concern with the potential impact of their views on prospective returnees to Judaism among the *conversos* of the Spanish peninsula, both Aboab and his opponent were also concerned about the impact of their views in the Calvinist Netherlands. The editor of the treatise and its companion pieces, Alexander Altmann, has argued, more or less, that the more lenient position taken by Aboab was the result of his kabbalistic leanings and that it aligns him with the opponents of orthodoxy in the Calvinist church.[48] We may point out that Menasseh ben Israel, who undoubtedly was on the side of Aboab's opponents, if he was not, in fact, the major figure of the opposition, was himself both a kabbalist and an eternalist. In addition, Menasseh, who was in close contact with the liberal Remonstrants, was condemned by their opponents. Aboab's adversary, whoever he was,[49] saw danger in the probable reaction of the Christians to the non–eternalist position: "Why should the Gentiles say . . . , Surely, this is a nation trusting in its good fortune, the righteous and the wicked being alike, 'and now nothing will be withholden from them, which they purpose to do' (Gen. 11:6), for the fear of God is not before their eyes."[50]

The echo here is just as much that of the Remonstrant voice as that of the orthodox Calvinists: Vossius's suggestion of possible Jewish treachery expressed in his letter to Grotius about Menasseh, a letter that dates from January 1640, is not all that different really from what the eternalists feared. In other words, in the midst of an "amity" between such liberals as Vossius and such eternalists as Menasseh, even Remonstrants show themselves as hardly more accommodating toward the Jewish community at large than do the orthodox Calvinists. Perhaps it was for that reason and, also, because the views of the non–eternalists seemed closer to those of the liberal Calvinist group, that Menasseh (or Morteira, or both) thought that the party of Aboab was playing too fast and loose.

The protest of the eternalists takes on added significance in light of their adversaries' charge that, "by believing in the eternality of sin and punishment, we support the religion of the Christians who say that Adam's sin was eternal and that, on this account, only God, who is eternal, could make atonement for it by his incarnation and death."[51] This must have stung the eternalists deeply. For the charge applies not merely to the hold of Christianity on the New Christians of Spain, but equally to the Calvinists of Amsterdam. The non–eternalists were thus arguing, perhaps, that it was important for Jews to ally themselves with the Dutch liberals as a way of opposing the more orthodox Calvinists. But Menasseh ben Israel, one who had the support of the liberals, knew from personal experience that their support could go only so far. There was a conflict here between two friends, Menasseh and Aboab, over political issues, over and above the specifically doctrinal one at their center.

We must see Aboab and Menasseh as friends as well as "rivals." Aboab had been the corrector for Menasseh's *Pene Rabbah* in 1628 and had written a complimentary poem for the work; he would, furthermore, contribute a poem to the Spanish edition of *De la resurrección de los muertos* in 1636. This latter poem was undoubtedly a signal of something, perhaps Aboab's having reconciled himself to Menasseh's view, or, at least, a patching up of their differences—Menasseh's work was, after all, on the very same topic as the dispute.[52]

But *De la resurrección* is a product of the da Costa affair, and Aboab can hardly have been unaffected by that *cause célèbre* at this point in time. Aboab's statements in the last section of *Nishmat Ḥayyim* on who is a heretic were definitely related to the storm around da Costa. So Aboab considers the question of whether non–eternalists were to be labelled "heretics" and comes, of course, to a negative conclusion.[53] The issues that are raised in passing have direct bearing on Aboab's attitudes to the instruction of gentiles. The term, Aboab says, applies only to those who contradict an interpretation in the Oral Torah. For example, if one criticizes the *sefirot,* which, according to Aboab (after Cordovero), were a part of Oral Torah, and he does so specifically from having been too caught up in "secular learning" ("ki hurgelu be–ḥokhmot ḥitsoniyyot") and because "they considered the children of gentiles sufficient" ("u–ve–yalde nokhrim yaspiku"), i.e., if one gains much of his knowledge of Judaism from non–Jewish sources, then, argues Aboab, despite the fact that he is in general a believer with regard to his overall "theology," such a person is termed a "heretic." Now this is obviously not a condemnation *in toto* of secular learning, considering Aboab's personal breadth and interests. The statement concerns those former *conversos* whose theological views are in accord with Jewish ones, even though the majority of their early learning came out of non–Jewish sources, but whose point of view on questions of Oral Torah is at variance with the correct Jewish one.[54] Da Costa was, of course, a much more thoroughgoing critic of Judaism than the figure posited here. Moreover, Aboab clearly does not side with those who fail to repent or those who have not fully emerged to Judaism; he walks a narrow line, arguing that secular learning is misleading if not coupled with Jewish piety.

According to his opponent, however, Aboab also believed that, "at the end of days, even the gentiles who did not know God will have a share in the world to come."[55] Yet Menasseh's eschatological presuppositions were based on the Maimonidean (and kabbalistic) expectation of a knowledge of God spreading to the gentiles. Aboab undoubtedly shared these views, even though they find no expression here or anywhere else in quite these terms. In the *Parafrasis,* we may note, under a consideration of the causes of the Jewish dispersion and of the meaning of Jewish preservation through the ages, he would articulate the view that it was through the Jews that the knowledge of God would become manifest in the world.[56] Here, though, there is a greater immediate concern with the absorption of returnees to the Jewish fold: if some gentiles, who may even lack a knowledge of God, could be assured of a measure of salvation, former *conversos* with an imperfect knowledge of Judaism—as long as they do not strike at basic tenets—could also be assured of a share in the world to come. Yet the following also emerges: just as instruction in Jewish piety was necessary for former *conversos,* it was important for non–Jewish scholars that Judaism be presented within the context of Jewish piety. (Though Aboab also argues that the mysteries of the kabbalah cannot be understood except by the initiated, that is more circumscribed in its application.) While we are by no means claiming that Aboab has here articulated his view of the value of the instruction of gentiles by Jews, it will become clear that the conclusion drawn from these remarks is consonant with his actual views. For, in his poem for Gentius's 1640 version of *Hilkhot De'ot,* Aboab would suggest quite openly, as would Aguilar in a poem of his own on the opposite page, that Jewish teachers are indispensable for a sympathetic understanding of Jewish works.

Moshe Rephael d'Aguilar, Hebraist and Teacher

Aguilar was, in fact, Aboab's closest colleague, one who collaborated with him from the 1630s down to 1679, when he died. The two emigrated to Brazil together as well, though Aguilar always remained in a lesser capacity both at home and abroad. Still, Aguilar too was possessed of a fine library, including at least 50 manuscripts;[57] the catalogue of the auction came to forty–eight pages, as a matter of fact, while Aboab's comprises only about half that. Aguilar has been described as "many–sided" ("een veelzijdig ontwikkeld geleerde"), with general philosophical as well as purely Jewish interests.[58] He, too, was probably of Portuguese birth; though the date is uncertain, it was probably between 1615 and 1620, as he already was teaching in the Ets Ḥayyim Seminary in Amsterdam by 1637 and he already had at least one daughter before his departure for Brazil in 1641. His published works are two: an *Epitome da Grammatica hebrayca* (Leiden, 1660) (it is interesting to note the place of publication), based on his own instructional method—he is reported to have conversed in Hebrew with his pupils—and including, in the second edition (Amsterdam: David Tartas, 1661), a few pages on Hebrew metrics; and a posthumously published work on ritual slaughter (Amsterdam, 1681). Aguilar was on good enough terms with Morteira to be asked by his senior colleague to edit or collect several of his works: "On the divinity and eternity of the Law of Moses" and, in a Spanish translation out of the Portuguese original, a group of writings, perhaps of a polemical character, coming to some four hundred and twenty pages.[59] (The two may be identical compilations with different titles in the register.) Aguilar himself was the author of quite a few polemics, among many works of his that still exist in manuscript only.[60]

These manuscripts deserve mention as an indication of the scope of his interests. The longest among them is an index by topic to the Babylonian as well as the Jerusalem Talmud and to the Midrashim; this runs to more than 350 folios. Aguilar also wrote on the fifty–third chapter of Isaiah, on Is. 9:5–6, and other biblical loci. He covered issues of concern to former *conversos* in two responses (responsa?) to Isaac Orobio de Castro (1620–87), the famous physician and philosopher who was also the author of apologetic works himself and participated in an "amica collatio," as his opponent, Philip van Limborch, the Arminian professor, called it, *De veritatis religionis Christianae,* (*'On the Truth of the Christian Religion'*).[61] The questions addressed by Aguilar were: 1) "whether an Israelite who has been born and been a believer among the Gentiles [i.e., one born a Christian in Portugal] or [who] does not have his family origin [among those] obligated to observe the divine law, and [who] lived and died in this manner, acting like a gentile—will he be saved or not?" and 2) "Whether, in order to save oneself with the observance of the seven laws given to Noah, it is necessary that one observe them as God's commandments to Noah as manifested through Moses our Teacher, or is it sufficient to keep them as dictates of natural reason and to teach such an understanding of them?" Aguilar's answer to the latter question is emphatic. Philosophers who, like Aristotle, relied solely on natural reason, to the exclusion of revelation, would not gain "the eternal reward of glory and salvation."[62] Depending on the individual, to be sure, non–Catholic Christian Hebraists who led a moral life would almost certainly have proven an exception in Aguilar's estimation. In any case, though, the continued currency of such issues in Amsterdam, even in the second half of the century, when these responses must have been written, cannot be underestimated.

Aguilar was also very much concerned with issues prompted by Dutch Calvinism. He wrote a "Brief Discourse against Calvin's Doctrine" and a brief comment "on Adam's state before and after his sin." In another composition, he discussed the nature of Divine compassion or grace ("como se compadeceu a sabedoria de D[eu]s") and whether it was by divine decree or human free will. This work, he added, was intended "to correct the doctrines of the author of the *Obrigação dos corações*" [a translation of Baḥya ibn Pakuda's *Ḥovot hal–Levavot* by Samuel Abas (Amsterdam, 1670)], but it must also have tried to counter the influence of Calvinist theology. Also found among Aguilar's works is a ten–page opinion on the permissibility of representational art ("on the use of the painters"); given the anti–iconographic views of the Calvinist divines and the prevalence of such a tradition in Judaism as well, despite many deviations from it, we see here that this was not a settled issue. After all, Dutch culture lived, almost, by portraiture.

Worth mentioning among other works of Aguilar's are: responsa to Bayonne, Antwerp, and even Venice; some texts prepared for teaching, on logic; and a collection of "notable things" from Sixtus of Siena's *Bibliotheca Sancta.*

The responsa have a fair measure of historical interest. They document further the ambivalence in *converso* attitudes toward Judaism and the great reluctance among many emigrants from the peninsula to France and even to Amsterdam to resume open Jewish practice in all its details. Here again Aguilar's approach is unequivocal. One must rejoin the Jewish community if possible, says he, considering how easy it is to leave France for places where the practice of Judaism is not forbidden. One cannot automatically claim persecution as a substitute for open practice or economic necessity as an obstacle to emigration. Indeed, Aguilar even takes the view that it is only due to "religion and the Torah" that the enemies of the Jews hate them. In other words, the economic arguments advanced elsewhere are only a "pretext," and religious and not economic exigencies ought to be the most decisive determinants of a Jew's response to hostility. Persecution, in short, was based on hostility to Judaism. On this reasoning, the instruction of Christians on the character and literature of Judaism, an instruction that Aguilar strongly advocated and engaged in, was a direct corollary, and one of the most appropriate responses, even in the Calvinist Netherlands, to the hostility that many still felt.[63]

Two other works deserve special mention. The denial of the immortality of the soul by da Costa and others brought forth a ten–page treatise that was published by Jong in Coimbra in 1934. According to Jong, the work is distinguished by no special philosophical originality, being rather "Aristotelian and scholastic"; Aguilar himself saw it as based on "rational proofs." These consist of thirty–six "syllogisms" (§37) and constitute sufficient demonstration, "placing aside the infallible proof provided by the true faith and tradition we have about its certainty, [a proof] the origin of which is God himself and his teaching ["dotrina"], confirmed and repeated in so many passages of Sacred Scripture."

The treatise speaks of the parts of the soul and its mortal and immortal aspects, the senses and reason respectively, the possibility of free will, the virtues, and so on. Its conclusions seem closely related to some of Maimonides' in *Hilkhot De'ot.* Aguilar argues

(§28) that it is "not only according to Scripture that man is made in the image of God, but also the nations who had never had its light believed and taught the same, taking for granted the fact that the sovereign maker did not abstain from engraving his portrait on his principal work; it may be said that this is one of the things the knowledge of which is common to all mankind." But then Aguilar goes on to say (§32) that "every Israelite is bound by a command to sanctify and not to profane God's sacred name, by refusing to transgress His holy Law and giving up his life so as not to do so; all those who profess Religion defend this view and claim to perceive [its truth]." Throughout the work there is a stress on the agreement of revelation and reason, between the conventions and convictions of rational men everywhere and those of the Jews. Certainly the kabbalist in Aguilar is very little in evidence here. Rather, it is the individual able to move between two cultures with ease. He has relied, he says (§34), on "all the philosophers and historians, sacred and profane, being full of examples." This, he concludes, should suffice to insure anyone firm guidance ("derezão") (§37).

All this does not make Aguilar any less a defender of Judaism. That is clear from his other works and, especially, from the "Reposta a certas propostas contra a tradição" ("A rejoinder to certain propositions against tradition"), dating from 1639. This is one of a series and is judged by Gebhardt to be directed specifically at da Costa. The *Tratado da immortalidade da alma* (*Tractate on the Immortality of the Soul*), says Gebhardt, "was given rise to by da Costa, but did not engage him in a polemic."[64] It is an "apologia et defença" of the Oral Torah and all the institutions of the sages. Oral Torah, in Aguilar's view, has its proofs from the wisdom of the ancients being greater than that of the moderns, and from other such fairly standard sounding arguments. There was little to persuade da Costa in them, but they obviously persuaded Aguilar himself, who considered the authority of tradition to have great weight.

One last point is to be made about Aguilar's view of the art of persuasion, however. In his posthumously published *Dinim de Sehitá e Bedicá,* a work on ritual slaughter, Aguilar tells his readers that the treatise "cannot be understood perfectly without the help of a teacher who can explain [the laws] *viva voce*" ("com viva boz") and that practical application would be even better. While this handbook is devoted to a narrow sphere of ritual practice, Aguilar's entire professional life surely was based on the same general principle: the indispensability of a living teacher.[65] Moreover, if his own written works appear to have been guided by this view, so must his teaching of Christians have been predicated on the assumption that Jewish works can be best understood under the tutelage of a living Jew. Aguilar's defense of Oral Torah to his fellow former *conversos,* his attacks on Calvinism (for internal consumption), and his oral expositions of Judaism for non–Jews all derive, in theory and, apparently, even in method, from a basic belief in the compatibility of Judaism and secular knowledge, provided piety and learning are conjoined in their instruction. The foregoing is the sum of the background of the man who encouraged Gentius. That is to say, almost the sum, for of his fervent kabbalism, the specifics of which might help explain something more of his ultimate goals, Aguilar has left us no testament. He lives in the Sabbatian movement solely as an associate of Aboab's. Still, in view of the standard eschatological hopes and expectations of the age, his motivations toward the instruction of Christians were probably shared with Aboab and Menasseh as well.

Menasseh ben Israel, Defender of His People in Person and in Print: Millenarian Goals and Temporal Controversies

Menasseh ben Israel sought to share his presuppositions and his hopes with everyone. That was, in fact, a major goal of his life. He was by far the most complex of the three rabbis under discussion here and, perhaps, at once the most and the least understood of his colleagues. We have not undertaken a biography of the man. Yet there is so much of him that is intertwined with his instruction of Christians that, perforce, our discussion of Menasseh will be the longest and most detailed of the group.

Menasseh has been the subject of numerous studies. By some, he has been considered orthodox—he was, after all, an eternalist—by others, a free thinker, under the influence of Delmedigo.[66] Neither of these two perceptions claims that Menasseh went to an extreme in either direction, of course. Most recently, he has been summed up (following Roth, Menasseh's biographer) as one who "succeeded in being an apostle of Judaism without being a detractor of Christianity."[67] If his success, many would counter, was hardly unqualified, he still remains, in most people's minds, "the first Jewish scholar who wrote largely, if not predominantly, for non–Jews."[68] It is probably fair to point out that Menasseh saw himself, first and foremost, as a spokesman to and for his people. If he was "an apostle to the gentiles,"[69] it was only for the honor of his nation.

There were, in fact, four guiding principles to Menasseh's work. First was his instruction of his community and his undying efforts to attract as many New Christians as possible back to the Jewish fold. His advocacy of the rights and privileges of Jews everywhere, that they might be entitled to their own beliefs and to freedom of worship and, in general, that they might live in security was second. This he pursued by asserting repeatedly that many beliefs and tenets were held by Judaism in common with Christianity and, secondly, by constantly putting forth the "Jewish view" on issues of the day. His purpose was to show that the Jews were neither idolators, nor heretics, nor blasphemers, nor intent on destroying Christian society. Such was the third principle of his work. And the fourth, by association, was a promotion of the knowledge of God (though not necessarily the conversion of Christians to Judaism) as a prerequisite and a hastening of the advent of the messianic age. If, at that point in time, the nations that had oppressed the Jewish people would be destroyed, this did not apply in the same manner to those that had befriended and aided them, and Menasseh undertakes to convince the nations of that as well. In short, Menasseh was a kabbalist with political aspirations, a teacher who saw the world as his classroom.

If Menasseh the author was an apologist, Menasseh the man was an entrepreneur by temperament. Born at Madeira in 1604 and brought to Amsterdam soon thereafter, he came to hold various rabbinical posts and to be regarded by some as the foremost Jewish preacher in the city. Also by profession and even more out of financial need, his major preoccupation was the printing trade: he is known as the first Jewish printer in Amsterdam. Menasseh became involved in other business ventures as well. Some of these got him into a good deal of trouble, and one even resulted in his being placed under the ban for a short period. He had hoped to go to Brazil to pursue some financial undertaking, but he saw Aboab and Aguilar go instead. He did travel, though: to Antwerp in 1654 to see the ex–queen Christina, whose financial backing he had been seeking for several years through Isaac Vossius, the son of G. J. Vossius; and, in diplomatic garb, with visionary dreams and utilitarian arguments, to England in 1655, to intercede with Cromwell in behalf of Jewish resettlement. This trip was his last. He was received favorably by Cromwell, though not so by Parliament en masse; moreover, he quarreled with members of the Jewish community that was being established there without his help. When he left, it was as a broken man, not having secured the legal confirmation he had hoped for, yet having lost his one remaining son, who had accompanied him to London. Menasseh departed England in 1657 to inter his child back home, but, having reached only Middelburg, in Zeeland, he died and was himself buried there as well.[70]

Menasseh as Literary Apologist

The first work of Menasseh's to appear in print may not be entirely his own, but it already indicates the direction in which he was moving. The *Pene Rabbah* of 1628 is an index to the midrashim in *Midrash Rabbah* on each verse of the Pentateuch. In the preface, Menasseh speaks of his difficulty in finding references to many verses that "masked their faces from the first author, . . . whose work I possessed on a scroll"; in the procedure that must have laid the groundwork for the *Conciliator,* Menasseh claims to have gone over the midrashim time and time again and added "countless verses" to the original manuscript. Whose work this was is impossible to tell, but it served Menasseh well. It began the series of reconciliations between scriptural verses and rabbinic statements that, despite the announced aim of his *Conciliator,* would really be its true one.

For it was already from this early period that Menasseh's contact with non–Jewish scholars dated. Delmedigo, in his preface to *Sefer Elim* in 1629, wrote of Menasseh, "the ornament of scholars and the glorious diadem of our people in the eyes of the nations, who writes learned works, the likes of which have never been seen in any lands or peoples; and their theologians consult him daily to hear his learning . . ."[71] Though these scholars are not named by Delmedigo, and while it is unlikely that we can identify them with certainty, there is at least a remote possibility that one of them was Constantijn l'Empereur, and that Menasseh was actually the individual in question who had been forbidden by the Parnassim to continue with his instruction.[72]

The Conciliator

By the beginning of the 1630s, Menasseh's work on the *Conciliator* had surely begun. In his prefatory remarks to the Latin translation of 1633, Menasseh states that he had been at work on his book for several years.[73] It had first been published in 1632 in Spanish, with preparations for the Latin version by Dionysius Vossius already in hand. The Vossii had only arrived in Amsterdam at the beginning of 1632, though; we may assume that either the reputations of both author and translator preceded them to their encounter or that they had already met at an earlier date. While there is no mention of Menasseh in G. J. Vossius's letters prior to 1633, that signifies little. Chances are that Vossius and his children had already had some dealings with Menasseh while they were still in Leiden.

Menasseh announced his purpose as follows: it was to reconcile the seeming contradictions in Scripture. It was, he said, "a new work, never before undertaken by any one of our nation." And it was prompted, though he nowhere says so explicitly, by the questioning of wavering former *conversos*.[74] In the dedication to the Latin translation, however, Menasseh advances two additional reasons for collecting these "loca" and finding out the "opinions of the ancient rabbis" (which he had already done, to repeat, in preparing the *Pene Rabbah,* even though that appears to be only an index). It was his intention, he wrote, partly to rouse ("ut accenderem") the rest of his "nation" to follow his example and partly to render useful assistance to society at large ("ut . . . utilem orbi operam navarem"). This was necessary "so that those who lacked either the leisure or the willingness to learn Hebrew would have a one volume compendium of what had been written over so many centuries by "doctissimi nostrae nationis viri," 'the most learned men of our nation'. This explanation is found only in the dedication of the Latin translation published a year after the Spanish original, yet it is not just a retrospective rationale for Menasseh's having composed the work. It also emerges from the original preface, though not as straightforwardly. Menasseh wished to be of service not only to ex-*conversos* who lacked a knowledge of Hebrew, but also to Dutch Christian students of Scripture with a similar lack of knowledge.

For the "reconciliation of seeming contradictions" was a regular pursuit among non-Jewish scholars of the age as well, and even, one would imagine, among a broader reading public. The translator would also indicate as much in his preface. Menasseh's approach and technique was probably suited to both audiences. He assembled all the discussions of major (and minor) problems (and related issues) he could find, "having searched diligently the works and sayings of the ancient and modern sages." Now Menasseh states that he assembled "reconciliations," implying that they were laid out already before him, yet it is really Menasseh himself who was the "conciliator." For many of the remarks quoted are only tangentially related to the actual reconciliation, and it was Menasseh who put them all together under a series of "Questions," i.e., juxtapositions of two or more verses seemingly at variance.

The writings consulted by Menasseh were many and varied, Jewish and non-Jewish; he placed them side by side without distinguishing between their authority. All was grist for the mill of Menasseh's mind, and all, in his view, served to extricate him from his supposed difficulties. Included among the authorities (a list of both the Jewish and the non-Jewish ones is appended to the Spanish edition; in the Latin edition, the non-Jewish ones are omitted) are church fathers, medieval and later scholastics, and, of course, the broad range of classical authors.[75] These he illustrates, compares, corroborates and interprets, "leaving it, however, to the reader's judgment to select the one [conciliation] he likes best." This is Menasseh's standard pose: he wishes to appear accommodating. He does not intend, he says, to give a verdict, approving some views and condemning others: "tastes differ."

But, "the Bible being true in the highest degree, it cannot contain any text . . . contradictory of another," and, by implication, rabbinic views also being true, they can be brought in to demonstrate this best. Menasseh did exercise some principle of selectivity and he clearly removed any interpretations that appeared to conflict with those that he deemed most suitable. He would advance, he says, those interpretations "más conformes á la letra" ('that accord most with the letter', with the significance of "letter" unspecified). The Latin translator renders the phrase rather ambiguously as "quae maxime Scripturae menti accedere videbantur" ('that appeared to come closest to the meaning of Scripture'), but he still takes the literal sense to be the one "that comes closest." Menasseh himself had pointed out, though, that one of the reasons the "contradictions" seemed to exist was that some texts were being taken literally when they should be taken metaphorically, and he himself hardly avoids homiletical or midrashic interpretations.

Nevertheless, Menasseh was not only certain that a proper "reconciliation" would emerge from his assemblage of sources, because "todas podrian quadrar" ("all the interpretations could be squared"), but also confident that "the doubts [could be] eased in a variety of ways." Thus he hopes that his work and, it goes without saying, especially the part compiled from the Jewish "doctissimi" would be "accepto" (Sp.) ["gratus" (Lat.)] to all "doctos," in other words, that there would be a meeting of minds between "learned men" of all denominations. But then Menasseh goes on to say: "We find, if we examine the Talmud well, that this kind of study was . . . held in esteem even [by] several gentile princes, [who] raised [such] doubts to the ancients among our fellow [Jews]. These [Jewish sages] alone, as the disciples of the prophets, could find a way out and a solution for many passages that, on account of their difficulty, would remain completely unintelligible." Clearly, Menasseh intends his work to be, first and foremost, an exhibition of Jewish commentaries on passages of the greatest interest either because of their difficulty or because of disagreement over their interpretation. Accordingly, he expects, that (in a line omitted by Vossius) from this enterprise "no poca honra se siguira á la nacion Hebrea, y a los sabios de Israel; pues claramente por esto se vera, el ingenio Divino, y sciencia que tuvieron." ("No little honor will accrue from it to the Hebrew nation and the sages of Israel, as the knowledge and intelligence they possessed will clearly be seen from this.")

Here Menasseh the defender of his people emerges; here is a defense through literature given by a Jewish teacher. The translator, probably deeming it something that would fall hard on the ears of his audience, omitted it from his abbreviated version of the preface. And, in another passage naturally omitted from the Latin, Menasseh remarks that he had written in Spanish seeking to be of benefit "á los señores de mi nacion Española (á quien dedico esta obra)," ["to the men of my Spanish nation, (to whom I dedicate this work)"], most of whom do not know Hebrew, and also hoping "that it will soon be extended into other languages." Menasseh mentions the Latin translation specifically, "que también saldrá presto," that is, 'is also immediately forthcoming', as well as other works he has "in hand." (These are not identified here.) "For it has always been our intent to direct our works," he says, "á la utilidad comun, y aprovechar á todos" ("to be of benefit to everyone").

Whatever Menasseh's wishes and hopes, though, Jewish precensorship had just been reinstituted several months earlier, perhaps as much in expectation of Menasseh's work as with an eye to other impending publications.[76] In any case, Menasseh had to secure approbations and he did so, from Herrera and from Daniel de Caceres, a legal scholar.[77] In addition, he sought and received Hebrew approbations from the rabbinate of Frankfurt am Main, the "av bet din" and the leader of which was Shabbetai Sheftel Horowitz (c. 1592–1660), the son of Isaiah Horowitz, the noted moralist, who had himself served as the rabbi of Frankfurt until 1614. Shabbetai Horowitz had only arrived in Frankfurt in 1632, though, and his approbation was merely one of four. The rabbinical Synod of Frankfurt in 1603 had established a requirement that any book printed anywhere in Germany must have the approbations of a least three rabbis; it is not clear what the extra one implies other than perhaps an honoring of the author and his work. It is clear, though, that, insofar as Menasseh was concerned, this double set of approbations was mandated for two reasons.[78] First, he needed the consent of the Parnassim of the community in which he lived if he was to be employed by them in the future. Second, since he could not be certain from the outset that he would receive that consent, he thought it better to publish the work abroad, where he felt certain he would secure approval.[79]

There is much of interest in the various approbations. Herrera, for one, found nothing discordant with "Holy Writ, the sages . . . or pious and good customs," i.e., tradition. (This is formulated according to the letter of the statute on precensorship.) Accordingly, Herrera advised "los Señores dela nacion Portuguesa" to rush out and get their copies, especially if they did not know Hebrew. Daniel de Caceres found the work suitable "para se poder publicar a los de nuestra nacion Hebraea," to be able to be published or revealed to the members of the Hebrew nation. These are the judgments that Menasseh had hoped for. But he had also looked to the Frankfurt rabbinate to support him, and they came out enthusiastically in his behalf. Though none of them appears to have seen more than a portion of the work, probably while it was still in manuscript—several of them speak of a "kuntres" (implying a 'pamphlet' or some sheets of paper) read to them by a translator—they all perceived it as something intended "le–zakkot et ha–rabbim," that is, 'to cause the many to be righteous', and therefore worthy of publication. They also mention Menasseh's reputation as a factor in their decision.

Yet each of these men wrote his own opinion and each has different, often novel touches in his statement. Horowitz noted only that Menasseh "meir be–ḥokhmato li–vene 'iro," that he enlightens the people of his city with his wisdom; this may be an oblique reference to Menasseh's contacts with non–Jews. Aaron ben Samuel Düdelsheim (d. 1639) adds nothing to Horowitz's remarks; his is the briefest of the approbations. But Joseph Hahn–Nördlingen (1570–1637), certainly a more important figure in the history of Frankfurt Jewry than this colleague and probably even more important than Horowitz the younger, did add. Hahn was a new adherent of Lurianic kabbalah. He had, just two years earlier, completed his *Yosef Omets,* a guide to religious observance. In it, there are, among other things, some remarkable proposals for educational reform and an insistence that those qualified study kabbalah. Hahn, in his approbation, dismisses any criticism that might arise from Menasseh's book being in a foreign script and language (the term is "mesorasim")—in his book, Hahn himself had advocated the use of the vernacular. He recognizes that "our brethren, the Portuguese House of Israel," had appointed Menasseh to guide them in the correct way and that he was their "melits," their 'interpreter', to teach them the Jewish books ("le–lammedam sefer"). Menasseh's aim, as Hahn understood it, was to be an effective teacher to his nation ("le–lammedam le–ho'il"), "so it was necessary to compose [the work] in a language they know well."[80]

At this point, Hahn shifts into another vein: those, he says, who make the many righteous, such as Menasseh, will become one of those who greet the Messiah: when the wellsprings of truth emanate from his book to the multitude, Menasseh will gain this eternal reward. To be sure, no concrete sense of immediacy is imparted by Hahn's comment, but his invocation of the figure of shepherd and princes from Micah 5:4 seems to suggest, especially in light of the kabbalistic views Hahn expresses elsewhere, that he considers Menasseh's work both a defense of the Jews and a harbinger of the Messiah's coming. This might appear a bit farfetched, were it not for the intermingling here of a play on Daniel 12:3 and for the last of the four approbations from Frankfurt, the one by Hahn's colleague Simeon ben Jacob Günzburg.

Little information on Günzburg is available. He died in Frankfurt about two months after he had given this *imprimatur,* having served earlier as a rabbi in Hildesheim. He was remembered by a later chronicler as "a leader in communal affairs and a rabbinic judge" ("parnas u–manhig ve–ḥad mid–dayyane hay–yeshivah"). And he was the grandfather of a fervent kabbalist, David Grünhut (fl. 1682–1712). From his approbation, it is clear that he was also one himself.[81]

Günzburg picked up on several of the points Menasseh had made in his prefaces and turned them into a messianic vision. In simple terms, at the outset, he saw Menasseh's activity as teaching "in the language of his followers in order that they may understand and see where it is that the light of Torah dwells and distinguish between the light of our tradition [kabbalah] out of the mouths of the sages of Israel and the darkness in which the translators, who do not know to exercise caution where they might go astray, walk." Menasseh is, by intention, in Günzburg's view, a defender of Judaism to a people without a knowledge of the tradition who may easily be drawn astray by Christian interpretations. But Günzburg also saw a much greater merit to Menasseh's work. The remainder of his pronouncement, which both reflected and further stimulated a good deal of Menasseh's thinking and action in the area of Jewish–Gentile relations, must therefore be quoted in full. Günzburg continues with a judgment on the entire enterprise:

This sage, Menasseh ben Joseph ben Israel, entered and stood in the breach to strengthen the foundations of our Torah, the Torah of Moses, and the words of the prophets in one accord. This is certainly a correct and meritorious way. Because in this manner the wisdom of the sages of Israel will become recognized in the eyes of the nations and the understanding of its wise men will become known among a broad public, and all the nations of the earth will see that God has named us as His own. For this is a sign of the truth: that there will not be found in her [the Torah's] parts things that contradict one another. And, in this way, honor, esteem, and respect for our holy Torah will be magnified, and it will become public knowledge that we are her children, her believing children, and that we have the true kabbalah and that "they shall become one" through us [var. on Ezek. 37:17]. And, on this and the like, Daniel said that "at the time of the end many will [search out truth] hither and yon, and knowledge will increase" [12:4], and that "those who are wise will make the many to understand" [11:33 & 12:10]. I apply to this sage the following verse: "thine ointments have a goodly fragrance; thy name is as ointment poured forth; therefore do maidens love thee" [Cant. 1:3], according to the midrash of our sages, of blessed memory [this refers to *Shir hash–Shirim Rabbah* 1:21–22]. Therefore I too am among those who consent to the printing of this book, because, without doubt, many will follow its light and will say: "O people of Jacob, come, let us walk in the light of the Lord [Is. 2:5], and the Lord will be your everlasting light and ours" [vars. on Is. 60:19–20 (see Is. 60:3 in *Shir hash–Shirim Rabbah* 1:21)]. And all the nations will have pure language [*safah berurah*] to serve the Lord with one consent [vars. on Zeph. 3:9]. And in our days Judah will be delivered and Israel will dwell in safety. The kingdom of the house of David will be revealed on [lit.: will spring forth from] earth and the language of truth [*sefat emet*] will stand firm for ever [vars. on Ps. 85:12 & Prov. 12:19].

Some of this was anticipated by Maimonides in *Hilkhot Melakhim:* the connection is almost certain.[82] Now it is specifically applied to Menasseh, who had referred to his own unpublished Hebrew grammar, *Safah Berurah,* in the preface to the *Conciliator.* The immediacy of Günzburg's expectations are startling, even for a kabbalist. Moreover, while Lurianic kabbalah had already been reinforced in Amsterdam with the arrival of Herrera, it is not Herrera, but this Frankfurt rabbi who offers the propagandistic statement just quoted. We can perceive in its agenda another, hitherto undocumented, influence on Menasseh's and, possibly, all

Amsterdam's thinking. The spread of Lurianic kabbalah among Ashkenazim in western Germany before 1630 through emissaries from Safed[83] appears to have had an impact on Amsterdam Sephardic thinking also.

In Menasseh at least, Günzburg found a sympathetic response. For six works published by him between 1635 and 1638 (including his own *De creatione* of 1635 and the two versions of *De resurrectione mortuorum* of 1636, as well as the 1638 Hebrew *Shevet Yehudah* of Ibn Verga), Menasseh adopted one of the phrases from Günzburg's closing sentence as his printer's mark.[84] Under the Latin line "Veritas è terra orietur" [Ps. 85:12], that is, "Truth will be revealed in the land," Menasseh inserted the Hebrew original, "emet me–erets titsmaḥ," into a nine–box anagram reading the same across and down.[85] In this way, Menasseh identified his own thinking with Günzburg's.

This Frankfurt authority had, in effect, more than merely agreed to the printing of Menasseh's work. He had agreed with Menasseh's contention that from such presentations of Jewish thinking as the *Conciliator,* which vindicates the truth of the Torah, honor would accrue to the Torah, and that respect for the Jewish people would follow. Yet Günzburg also expected that the spread of the knowledge of Torah would unify mankind under the leadership of the Jewish people. Furthermore, he claimed, the demonstration that the true kabbalah was in the hands of the Jewish people would be a prelude to the messianic era. It is clear that Günzburg intended to specify the esoteric "tradition" in preference to, if not necessarily to the exclusion of, the normative, exoteric one.[86] To be sure, the motifs of light and darkness, for example, are to be found even in the *Shir hash–Shirim Rabbah* passage that Günzburg appeals to. Also, the *Conciliator,* though the work of a kabbalist, is hardly a kabbalistic book. Finally, Günzburg does not appear to be articulating any specifically Lurianic doctrine or mythology. Nevertheless, it is hard to escape the conclusion that his hope, "ve–titparsem le–'ene hash–shemesh ki anu baneha bene maaminehah u–ve–yadenu hak–kabbalah ha–amitit ve–hayu la–aḥadim be–yadenu," 'that it will become public knowledge that we are her children, her believing children, and that we have the true kabbalah and that "they shall become one" through us [lit., in our hands]', is anything other than the sympathetic response of one kabbalist (a fellow believer, or "ben maamin") to another well–known one, i.e., Menasseh. Günzburg's colleagues, Horowitz and Hahn, were, as we have said, both kabbalists. Moreover, among the four Frankfurt authorities, Günzburg is the one in whose pronouncement is to be found the most explicit and expressive vision of the messianic era. Even more than Joseph Hahn, he had a phenomenal impact on Menasseh's thinking.

In physical proximity to Amsterdam, Frankfurt was the nearest major Jewish community. Menasseh now had the support of at least two of its leading rabbis in pursuing his immediate and temporal, as well as his eschatological goals. Menasseh clearly understood the verses surrounding the half of verse 12 that he later quoted, and even the whole of Psalm 85, in messianic terms. Delmedigo's assessment of Menasseh in 1629 as "the ornament of our people in the eyes of the nations" was coming to have an even more specific application in Menasseh's mind than had probably been conceived by his friend.

There were several other preliminary contributions to the *Conciliator.* Two were by Jewish physicians of some renown, Joseph Bueno (d. 1641) and Abraham Zacuto (1575–1642), better known as Zacutus Lusitanus. Bueno mistakenly foresees no possible calumny against the work; he even looks forward to further works from Menasseh's pen to the honor, adornment, and edification of "nuestro Lusitano destierro," that is, 'of the Portuguese nation in exile'.

Zacuto's contribution was the only preliminary compliment or approbation retained in the Latin translation. It was itself the only piece of preliminary matter that was originally in Latin, which, in part, explains its having been the only one carried over. Moreover, it may have been felt that the obligation to print approbations had been satisfied with the Spanish original. But, among non–Jewish audiences, Zacuto's name was also probably the best known of any of the contributors,[87] and that too would have been a factor in its retention, for the added stature it might confer on the work. Zacuto added a few lines to his letter, but omitted nothing, when he renewed the compliment for the Latin edition, a year to the day after he had signed the original one. In both versions, Zacuto praises Menasseh for his erudition and claims primacy for him in all areas, linguistic, biblical, talmudic, and kabbalistic. His address to Menasseh is amplified, however, for the new audience: "For you . . . are a most worthy teacher of the holy tongue, born of noble stock, most learned in kabbalistic speculation, [and] for many years a distinguished preacher [among] the Hebrews."[88] In truth, Menasseh became known in precisely this fashion, as a preacher, a kabbalist, and, especially, as a teacher of Hebrew, to his non–Jewish friends. Zacuto had made reference to the students of Scripture for whom the work is necessary. In the Latin version, he adds the idea of its usefulness and expands the group to include students "living all over the world, where[ever] divine Scripture is held in high honor."[89] One last variant, probably the most interesting. Zacuto had originally made casual reference to certain additional works that the public might look forward to from Menasseh. In the 1633 revision, he adds a specific mention of one "on the resurrection of the dead, a work filled by you with the sweetest nectar and ambrosia." Thus, a 1633 date can be assigned to the inception, and probably the composition of much of the *De la Resurrección de los muertos,* not to be published until 1636. The translation by Antonius Zilius (c. 1605–1655) must have waited until the work was complete, sometime in 1635, before being made, in view of the references in it to the *De Creatione,* published that year.

There were more than literary or editorial reasons for the delay in publishing the *De resurrectione* and its Spanish original. The years 1633–36 had seen Menasseh rebuffed at every turn by gentiles, not only by the Calvinists, with whom he seems to have had little personal contact, but even by the Remonstrants. The story has been reviewed frequently, but never with all the available documents, and it includes the rejection of Menasseh's dedication by the States–General, the rejection of Menasseh's bid to teach at the Athenaeum, a Remonstrant institution, and the involvement of the Vossius family and of Caspar Barlaeus (1584–1648), Menasseh's most ardent non–Jewish supporter. What has escaped the notice of historians to date, largely because of its survival in possibly only one copy, is Menasseh's dedication and its companionate piece, the translator's preface to the Latin version. These shed new light on all the other circumstances of the mid–1630s.

Menasseh had dedicated the Latin translation to none other than the Magistrates of Holland and West Frisia, the body his Christian Hebraist counterparts had so frequently dedicated their works to. He had the support of Vossius, Sr. and Barlaeus, the two leading professors of the Amsterdam Athenaeum. Menasseh aimed high because he felt something important was at stake, the welfare of his people. His goal was to help his "nation," long exiles from their fatherland—and here he means the Land of Israel—to be able, by the gift of the rulers, to live in peace and safety under a jurisdiction and rule not their own. That is what they hoped for most, says Menasseh:

> Indeed, so long as we continue, [as] hitherto, tossing about in exile from the dominion of our ancestors on account of our sins, what more can we hope for than that, by the grace of those under whom we live, we are afforded the possibility of passing our lives quietly and inoffensively.[90]

It was not, however, merely that Menasseh did not wish to cause offense. For it is, he continues, the responsibility of the Jews under Dutch rule to devote themselves to the most useful things possible, to producing works such as the *Conciliator,* a compendium of Judaism in one volume. But there is also a measure of self–effacement here. He did not, Menasseh assures the magistrates, intend to compare his own writings with those of the greatest authors, when he inserted his own views. It was only "studio veritatis adstruendae adversus eos, qui divino verbo nefarie abuntur," 'to add to the truth against those who impiously abuse the divine word', that he did so. With this remark, Menasseh begins the other half of his apologia, proceeding to disarm his critics, or so he thought:

> To be sure, I am not unaware that it is a difficult thing to search out and determine the hidden senses of Sacred Scripture; and for that reason this subject matter ought to have been left to people with greater genius. But again and again it came to mind that where there is piety and the desire to serve the public well, labor of any kind is approved by good men. I can say this, that I have tried here neither to injure anyone nor to speak against the religion of those who differ with us.[91]

He did not intend, he was not out to offend anyone or to speak against Christianity ("the religion of those who differ with us"). This is not an intentional misrepresentation; Menasseh did not wish to appear openly hostile to Christianity, even if his interpretations were clearly Jewish ones. That is in part what he means when he says that works of any kind can be approved by good men, as long as there is piety and public spiritedness present in those works. That is to say, piety is not a commodity limited to Christians.

But the possibility of attacks on Christianity by Jews had been a matter of concern to the Dutch authorities, secular and religious, for almost four decades, ever since professing Jews had reemerged in the Netherlands. With this dedication, Menasseh, in effect, assures the Dutch authorities of his own and his coreligionists' common interest with their Christian neighbors against those who try to use the more perplexing ("intricatiora") and seemingly contradictory *loca* in Scripture in order "omnem tollere religionem & Majestatis divinae contemtum invehere," 'to destroy all religion and to bring contempt on the divine majesty'. Menasseh proclaims himself a loyal citizen and a devoted one, a nonheretic. His dedication is dated 23 August 1633; he has now formally entered the lists as an apologist. This was a direct approach to the authorities and a venture into the world of *shtadlanut,* of intercession on behalf of his fellow Jews, even though a specific request was not made.

Menasseh openly anticipated the difficulties he might face with such a political declaration. On August 26, a mere three days later, he determined to add another dedication, this time to an individual, in case the political one failed. He even decided to insert it into the middle of the volume, between the "Quaestiones in Exodum" and those "in Leviticum." His would–be patron was Cornelius van Campen (1564–c. 1638), a businessman and member of several "Chambers of Rhetoric." Menasseh admits to Campen that he did not know him very well, but, inasmuch as Campen was a man of erudition, favorably disposed toward devotees of study and learning [possessed of an "in studiorum cultores affectus"], he appeared a worthy choice. Even to Campen, though, Menasseh is forced to admit his misgivings. He apologizes for involving Campen in this delicate matter: "Non aegre feres, vir praestantissime, te publice a me compellari," ('Do not take it amiss, most distinguished sir, that I accost you in public'). But, Menasseh reasons, Campen would be able to judge his work equitably at a time when others could not:

> And because it it a familiar thing in this century for even those to be disparaged who write with no offense intended against anyone and with the intent of helping everyone, I thought it prudent, after publicly dedicating this work to the ruling powers, the States–General of Holland and

West Frisia, and the most esteemed burgomasters of this city, to select some private individual also, under whose name my writings might more safely appear in public.[92]

Menasseh distinguishes the private from the public sphere and takes up a second line of defense. He knows that even works such as his were subject to attack, that is to say, even works that do not attack others and, according to his earlier claim, are specifically intended for public benefit. Accordingly, Menasseh deems a second dedication necessary to secure the appearance of his work. Still, and justifiably, he feels the need to assure Campen, as he would subsequently assure and reassure others, that consent to a work's publication and even patronage of it does not necessarily imply or compel agreement with its point of view:

And so, for that reason, I would not want anyone to think that I am so unaware of everything as to think that by [my] dedicating [my work to you] you are obliged to assent to everything that I have written here. I know that there is barely a consensus among those of the same religion. How much less so among those whose differences are not at all insignificant.[93]

Still, Menasseh further urges the idea of the common legacy of Christian and Jew and defends his own responsibility to tell the truth as he sees it, to the best of his ability.

As it turns out, this dedication does not appear anywhere in the 1633 *Conciliator.* Instead, it appears in the 1641 and 1643 printings, the former with the false imprint "Constantinople,"[94] the latter with none at all, and both with the title *Quaestiones in Quinque Libros Mosis.* All this indicates both the popularity and the notoriety of the work. For Menasseh had, it appears, excised even this dedication, when he suffered his first reverse in 1633.

For the magistrates, of whom Menasseh says that God wished them to be "the custodians of the laws and of the realm" ("legum atque imperii custodes"), rejected the writings that would serve "to elucidate the Law of God [i.e., the Torah]," ("ad illustrandam Legem Dei"), writings that he had dedicated to them in recognition of their benefaction. Menasseh had gone to the Hague to present his dedication armed with two things, with the letter of support that G. J. Vossius and Caspar Barlaeus had written for him, and also with a second preface to the reader, this one by the translator, Dionysius Vossius. In the letter, the two professors took up Menasseh's view that a Jew could be of service: "How could a Jewish man be better deserving of Christians than by collecting and putting down in one book everything the Jewish teachers of old wrote [on a given question]?"[95] They further expressed the hope that the rest of the Jews could provide works as useful. Their reason for having come to Menasseh's defense: having written well in an area both "celebrated and venerable," Menasseh appeared to deserve well of Christians ("quia scribendo bene de Christianis meritus videbatur"), especially since "we do not usually look upon Jews with favor" ("homines Judaei minus grati nostris esse solent"). In this latter vein, they remark also that Menasseh "is himself a man of virtuous conduct and far from the maliciousness of others of his religion, inasmuch as he never insults Christians in his work."[96] While this is a show of support for Menasseh's own claims, it is a sign also of a certain underlying malignity on their part and a downright insult to those whom Menasseh had wished to defend.[97]

The States do not appear to have forwarded this recommendation to Leiden for the faculty's consideration, since there is no mention of it in the faculty's response and "advice." There is mention, however, of the translator's remarks, which were bound into the initial printing, appearing on the verso of the second leaf of the dedication. When that dedication was excised from most of the copies of the Amsterdam printing after the States rejected Menasseh's overture, the translator's preface disappeared along with it. I have, however, found one copy of the *Conciliator* that still contains both this preface and Menasseh's dedication, and they appear to be the sole survivors.[98]

The translator's judgment was a cautious one. He was a definite advocate of the usefulness of such studies and of knowing the rabbinic opinions, and he counseled his readers to show moderation in their response.[99] His counsel was completely ineffective. In the faculty's judgment, the work, while it might serve some learned men to be taught "with the Jews," meaning, through the use of the various Jewish opinions and "uytvluchten" (the standard gibe for rabbinic arguments, and meaning 'subterfuges'), "as the translator says," it would also serve, "with inconstant souls, of whom there are all too many to be found in our day, to engender doubt about everything and to concoct new heresies and to give marked offense to other good Christians, who are not so experienced in such disputes, and to impart doubts, if answers to and refutations of these explanations are not added to them."

But, in point of fact, the translator had not used the expression 'uytvluchten' at all, though the first part of the judgment, on the usefulness of the work for learned men, was definitely in keeping with, if not the entire point of, Vossius's sentiments.[100] It was the Leiden faculty who substituted the gibe. They would never have considered Jewish literature of this type to be able to stand alone without comment or confutation. While they agreed that Christians could derive benefit and profit from several conciliations that did not appear to be "vremt," 'alien', just as distinguished Christian writers had previously profited "from these same rabbis," the faculty felt that the "fables," e.g., about the creation of man and woman from the same person (see Question 9, on Gen. 1:27), not only do harm to the Christian religion, but make all the Jewish interpretations suspect. They thus harm the Jews too. Yet there is one feature of Menasseh's work, above all its other characteristics, that places the author "not only against the Reformed, but against the whole Christian religion, though he does not mention it by name: to wit, that in these conciliations he tries, in his explanations, to take away from the Christians the arguments for the Trinity and Christ's divinity that have rightly been brought out of the five books of Moses. He does the same with predictions of Christ's coming in the flesh, of his spiritual kingdom and of his doing away with the ceremonies of the Old Testament, etc."

That was one of Menasseh's purposes, to be sure: to take away the Christian arguments. But he also wishes to stress the usefulness of the Jewish ones, even for Christians. Still, Menasseh's book proved unacceptable to the Contra–Remonstrant faculty of Leiden, who, despite the book's avoidance of any direct attack on Christianity, saw in it all the old anti–Christian biases of the Jews.[101]

There had been a similarity in format between Menasseh's dedication and those of l'Empereur and Coch. That similarity now proves to be highly ironic. For, in Menasseh's case, the position of the Jews is seen to be at stake, over and above the writer and his work's: his utilitarian argument is a defense of the Jews, while l'Empereur's had merely been a defense of his own enterprise as useful for the country. Menasseh, morever, had seen rabbinic literature as a vehicle for gaining the Jews some security; l'Empereur considered rabbinic literature something quite the opposite, a tool for their conversion. In fact, as Prins has shown,[102] l'Empereur's appointment as Controversiarum Judaicarum Professor was probably the Leiden curators' direct response to Menasseh's plea to the States. Though fourteen years had elapsed since the Synod of Dort had proposed such a measure, the establishment of l'Empereur's chair followed the negative "advice" of the theological faculty by a mere two days.

We are now, incidentally, in a better position than previous writers to compose an account of the printing of the *Conciliator.* It appears that, during the first few days of September 1632, Menasseh sent off his Spanish original, its Latin translation just getting underway at Dionysius Vossius's hands, to Frankfurt. It would appear to have been accompanied, at least by Zacuto's letter and also, perhaps, by some of the Spanish contributions aside from Herrera's and Caceres's approbations. Menasseh knew he could count on the support of Frankfurt, but he did not as yet have any guarantee of support from the Amsterdam Parnassim.[103]

The Frankfurt rabbis did not see the whole work, however; they only saw a few sheets of the manuscript. Rather than an argument for the work's having been printed in Amsterdam, this is, in fact, one for a Frankfurt printing: the rabbis, who could not read Spanish, probably wished to hear only a few pages of a work on its way to the press. Hahn wrote: "the translator read me the thrust of one of the pamphlets" ("tokef 'inyane kuntres eḥad mis–sefer hal–lazeh"); perhaps he saw one signature from the volume in press, if not a portion of the manuscript. Hahn also mentioned the language of composition, as noted earlier; this would not have been as much of a problem were the work to have been printed outside Germany. Moreover, Shabbetai Horowitz wrote as follows: "ve–yaday 'imo le–haskim 'al sifro le–havio bi–defus" ("I support him by consenting to his book's being brought into print") "ve–ashre ham–mesayye'im lo 'al kakhah" ("and praised be those who are helping him in this"), which implies that others were engaged in printing the work for Menasseh.

At any rate, approval from Amsterdam came quickly. On September 6, Herrera and Caceres penned their opinions and sent them along. The work appeared in Frankfurt, under a Frankfurt imprint, but at the author's expense: "Auctoris impensis." An Amsterdam printing from the same plates soon followed, success having been guaranteed.

Emboldened, Menasseh printed the first run of the Latin translation himself a year later in Amsterdam. When the dedication was rejected, most of the Amsterdam copies had the dedication to the States and the translator's preface excised. But the work was extremely popular and another run was called for. Menasseh retreated to Frankfurt, but only by way of imprint, most likely; the title page is marked "Francofurti/Auctoris typis & impensis," but the volume has none of the Frankfurt approbations. Having had Frankfurt as the initial place of publication, Menasseh clandestinely changed the title page to suggest it again. At least one of the Amsterdam copies escaped, as we have seen; the rest had their dedications removed. Frankfurt was still willing to support Menasseh, even though Amsterdam was probably too much taken aback by what had happened.

All this was really a defeat for Menasseh. Despite the success of his book and its growing readership, even among counter–Remonstrants, it had, in political terms, succeeded only in bringing a detractor of the Jews into a position of responsibility. Furthermore, with Menasseh's next publication, the anti–Jewish polemicists would come out fighting again.[104]

This time the controversy did not center on Menasseh, however. Rather, it was on Caspar Barlaeus, for his epigrammatic compliment to the *De Creatione* of 1635.[105]

The De Creatione

De Creatione Problemata XXX is the immediate follow–up to the *Conciliator.* Even though it is only a short work, it is a much more general one than its title implies; it may more properly be considered Menasseh's *De Fundamentis Fidei.* It is a defense of Judaism, of course, and hardly claims to be original, relying heavily on the authority and opinions of others. But it is also a defense of revealed religion in general, and that means biblical religion. This defense had already been begun in the *Conciliator.* Again here Menasseh was appealing to Christians on the basis of what Judaism and Christianity have in common, in order to bring Christians around to a purer understanding of God in anticipation of the messianic future. Menasseh claims to advance "rational arguments" to prove his points; it is these elements of proof that, in his view, form the common ground of the two religions. We might term these "arguments" more precisely 'displays of erudition'. In fact, Menasseh begins his whole treatise with a summary and discussion of Maimonides' Thirteen Principles. These he sets up as the basic premises of faith upon which all Jews and, implicitly, all reasonable men agree; from these he proceeds to one authority after another in order to make his points.

Our concern is not entirely with what Menasseh wished to prove, however, but really more with the why and how. He undertook to write this treatise even though the *De Resurrectione* was not yet complete; he published it first as well. He says in a passing reference to the *De Resurrectione* that the reason he kept working on the book was that he wished to provide firmer arguments.[106] But that is not all. In his preface, Menasseh speaks of the many who had, for over a dozen years, approved of his sermons and teaching. There were others, however, who felt otherwise: "Yet I could not say how many, swollen with the sap of envy, have also tried to oppose [me] and, as much as was in their power, to ruin me completely with their deceitful accusations."[107] But this was not the first indication of the "invidia," the 'ill will' or 'unpopularity' under which Menasseh labored among his fellow Jews. Already in November 1632, Vossius could attribute it to Menasseh's willingness to be of service to Christians: "He even tries to be as accommodating as possible to Christians: and so on, account of it, he suffers from considerable ill will, indeed, from his fellow [Jews]"[108]

The idea for *De Creatione* was proposed by several of his friends, presumably some of the Remonstrants (it was "ex consilio hominum quorundam doctissimorum"), probably as a simple way for Menasseh to show common cause with them again after the *Conciliator* débâcle. "If," writes Menasseh, "*De Creatione* is not rejected" ("si non improbabitur"), like the earlier work, "or, rather, if this effort of ours does not appear unuseful, we intend to publish several others as well" ("vel non inutilis videbitur labor hic noster, animus est proferre etiam alia nonnulla"), including "dissertatio nostra de Resurrectione mortuorum." It would appear that the *De Resurrectione* was also being withheld pending the acceptance of something less controversial. The *De Creatione* was a mixture of philosophy and kabbalah discussing the creation and the *sefirot,* and not really part of any raging debate. Still, Menasseh reminds his prospective patron of who he is, asking him, "to read without prejudice and remember that [he] only accedes to the religious truths of the children of Abraham" ("memor sola Abrahamidarum me sacra sequi cum venia hac lege"). Menasseh is seeking again to get a Christian audience to listen to Jewish ideas with some measure of dispassion.[109]

It was this request that was picked up by Barlaeus in his epigram. The cause célèbre that resulted from Barlaeus's contribution has recently been dealt with in enlightening fashion by F. F. Blok, but Blok did not lay enough stress on the associations and allusions that show Barlaeus's poem as a specific response to Menasseh's embattled position. In light of the connection between Menasseh's identification of himself as one who follows the teachings of the "Abrahamidae" and Barlaeus's famous last line: "Sic ego Christiades, sic eris Abramides," the entire second half of the poem takes on a new significance, especially in light of the dedications of the *Conciliator* that we have now discovered, which *had* been rejected and which had had the support of Barlaeus. Here is the final portion of Barlaeus's poem:

Vera placent, placet egregijs conatibus author,
Et pietas fidei disparis ista placet.
Cunctorum est coluisse Deum. Non unius aevi,
Non populi unius credimus, esse pium.
Si sapimus diversa, Deo vivamus amici,
Doctaque mens precio constet ubique suo.
Haec fidei vox summa meae est. Haec crede *Menasse.*
Sic ego Christiades, sic eris Abramides.

Barlaeus picks up Menasseh's challenge to the States that he too was in search of truth and he too, though of a religion that differs from the Christian one, was possessed of a *pietas* toward God, the same God the Creator whom both Christian and Jew worship. It is impossible to judge whether or not Barlaeus was really aiming at a "pietas universalis," as Blok quotes Barlaeus in his later self–defense.[110]

It seems to me that the issue really addressed by Barlaeus is the same one Menasseh had put forth: that each remain true to his own religion and base their amity on their individual uniqueness. Obviously the edges here are fuzzy, as Menasseh also hopes for a spreading of Judaism and for enlightening the eyes of the gentiles. Barlaeus is hardly any more tolerant of religious difference and of the right of the Jews to be themselves than Menasseh really is of Christian beliefs.[111] He insists on a "docta mens" and he applies it (exclusively?) to Menasseh: erudition, he says, will form the common ground. Menasseh had said the same in his *Conciliator,* filling it with what "the most *erudite* men of our religion have written for so many centuries" ("tot saeculis *doctissimi* nostrae religionis viri scripsere" [emphases mine]). Moreover, in the preface to *De Creatione,* Menasseh himself had spoken of the worth of the sages as being equal to that of the prophets:

> . . . this was my plan: to discuss the whole subject diligently, on the basis of the opinion[s] of the wise men of old: inasmuch as they lived not too far away from the times of the prophets, for this reason especially do they deserve to be considered worthy.[112]

The *pretium,* the 'worth' of the rabbinic sages is at issue, and Barlaeus assures Menasseh that their learning, and his, Menasseh's, will guarantee their own friendship, even if "sapimus diversa," that is, even if they have different understandings of things. Let erudition be valued at its worth everywhere, Barlaeus urges, regardless of the identity of its possessor. Barlaeus was thus coming to Menasseh's defense, though not without a certain challenge. His defense can be seen to be an outgrowth and a look backward also at the *Conciliator,* as well as a defense of Menasseh's most recent work.

And so the opposition forces were placed on notice, and they shot back with a vengeance against this so–called "Vorstius redivivus." It is ironic that the person who informed Barlaeus of the mounting furor against his poem was none other than the son of this Vorstius. Conrad Vorstius had been the Remonstrant professor banished from Leiden a generation earlier. His son, Willem Vorstius, the informant, was both Menasseh's pupil and the translator of his *De Creatione.*[113] Now Gisbertus Voetius was the leader of the opposition; the major pamphleteers were his lackeys only. The story of this episode is too well known to require retelling here. It was basically not a conflict over the contents of Menasseh's books, though Voetius appears to have read them. It is an attack on their having been published in the first place and on the fact that non–Jews, and, more specifically, Christians, could see fit to preface those works with panegyrics or offer approval and patronage at all. Voetius was incensed that Menasseh had dared to dedicate his books to Christians and he criticized everyone involved, even to the extent of proposing censorship.[114]

G. J. Vossius, in a 1637 letter to Grotius, summed up the whole business: many have come out against Barlaeus, "for having prefaced to a little work by Menasseh the Jew on creation a poem in which he even recognizes genuine piety in a Jewish man and allows that [the Jew] even serves God."[115] This was the substance of the charge. Vossius, while sympathetic to Barlaeus personally, did not share such a view, and, indeed, Barlaeus himself in his subsequent self–vindication would disclaim any such intent in his writing. Now the thrust of the attacks was based on the premise that "those who do not know Christ, indeed, who blaspheme him, deny God" ("Deum negari ab illis, qui Christum nesciunt, imo blasphemant"). This is how Vossius read Vedelius's sentiments in *De Deo Synagogae,* the major tract put out by the other side. It was probably a correct assessment of the mood of Voetius: there was no common ground of any sort between the extreme Calvinists and the Jews, regardless of what the liberals might say. And the orthodox intended to bring the liberals on the carpet for even daring to consort with the Jews, regardless of the Remonstrants' views on Jewish piety or service of God.

The De Resurrectione Mortuorum *and Other Works of the 1630s*

The net result of the storm was to quiet neither Menasseh nor his Christian friends. Though the Athenaeum backed away from Menasseh's solicitation that he teach Hebrew there—presumably, Menasseh looked to both honor and financial reward—because the *De Creatione* looked too hot to handle, Menasseh proceeded, a month later, in February 1636, to dedicate his *De Resurrectione* to two curators of that same institution.[116] This book, as has long been recognized, was, first and foremost, Menasseh's response to Uriel da Costa. What has not been noticed is the extremely close connection in time between da Costa's second excommunication and the genesis of Menasseh's book. They both date from 1633. If Menasseh's response is filled with standard pieties, it is still a direct response to da Costa's charges. In some ways, that was precisely Menasseh's intention: to show his fellow Jews that commonly accepted truths could be defended, and to show and reassure Christians that normative Judaism still adhered to those truths that were common to both faiths. The main points of da Costa's criticism, all of which were addressed by Menasseh in *De Resurrectione,* had been summarized a decade earlier almost, when the Amsterdam community was seeking advice on the case. Da Costa, it was said, "denies the validity of the whole Oral Torah . . . and denies the basic principles of our belief, i.e., the permanence of the soul and the resurrection of the dead; he defends arrogantly the opinion that there is no difference between man and animal; and he simply denies the many wonders described in the Holy Writ, especially those of the prophets Elijah and Elisha."[117]

The community had been in a bind. There was "freedom of religion" in Holland, and neither da Costa's prospective works nor his public pronouncements were subject to public scrutiny by the ruling powers, "there being no Inquisition." Da Costa's works were burned publicly, however, and he was imprisoned by the community.[118] That had been in the mid–1620s and to little avail. A great deal of *odium* arose on account of da Costa's works and he himself was quite unrepentant; in 1633, he was excommunicated a second time.

Even this, apparently, was not enough. Menasseh was moved to write against him. To be sure, as the work grew, other issues crept in, including the controversy about eternality of punishment. Toward the end of the *De Resurrectione,* Menasseh lays stress on "the martyrs and those who profess my name" ("martyres nominisque mei confessores") who will be resurrected to life: those who have undergone the trials of the Inquisition in Spain will not be damnned for eternity for not having been completely observant, while those, he implies, who failed to express their Jewish yearnings and died "in sin" would be punished "in aeternum." "Non consistent impii in judicio," 'the impious will not stand in the [day of] judgment', quotes Menasseh from Ps. 1:5.[119]

In the Latin translation by Zilius,[120] these things are not omitted; they were matters of interest to Christians. What Menasseh himself changes, though, are the dedications. Since both versions, the Latin and the Spanish, have the famous anagram as their printer's mark, it is clear that Menasseh is undaunted. And undaunted is his appeal to a sense of commonality that he expects Christians to evince. Not merely the entire republic, in Menasseh's claim, but "all religion that has God in view" ("tota erga Deum religio") is based on the "truth" of the immortality of souls—Maimonides' Thirteen Principles are rehearsed here again—and this "truth," itself, is based on both "naturalis argumentibus" and "autoritate sacrarum literarum," 'arguments from nature' and 'the authority of the sacred writings'.[121] Then, at the end of the first dedication (there are three, one for each section), Menasseh addresses his Remonstrant patrons, who were leaders of Amsterdam society and politics, with his boldest proclamation yet: "One God do we [viz., both] worship, to His commandments are we subject, and, after the difficulties of this life, to a better life do we look forward."[122]

The whole aim of his work is based on the principle of commonality, that "everyone may know that, in this doctrine so necessary for all, we are all in complete agreement against the Sadducees, the destroyers of souls and governments." If the Sadducees are those, like da Costa, who called rabbinic Jews Pharisees, then Menasseh is, in effect, asking his patrons and readers to identify themselves with the views of rabbinic Judaism; even more, he is telling them that they already do so.

Menasseh dwells repeatedly on these ideas, promising immortality to those of the nations who follow the Noachide commandments without sinning, and so on. And he continually returns to ask for fair judgment of his work from his readers:

> The goal that I was resolved upon for myself was certainly a good one and does not deserve in the least to be censured: for I have always tried zealously to aim at the truth and make the glory of the divine name more celebrated. Accordingly I also hope that this work of mine will be acceptable to and welcomed by the more fair–minded judges, who know the worth of things.[123]

This is the request of a man who has already been rebuffed more than once. His three separate dedications should be understood in this light as pleadings by someone disheartened but still in need of acceptance. To Joachim Wickefort, a German diplomat resident in the Hague who was a friend of Barlaeus,[124] he writes: "You possess such piety that you will not take it amiss that I also lay claim to that learning that we hold in common." ("Ea [es] pietate, ut non aegre sis laturus, etiam illam doctrinam a me asseri, quam communem habemus"). Even on matters of common agreement, the slogans "pietas" (which might in other contexts mean little more than 'compassion') and "doctrina" (meaning 'erudition') had to be invoked. Menasseh is even more explicit as he continues: "Nec enim non resurgere amant omnes, qui Deum Abrahami, Isaaci, & Iacobi piis animis venerantur": "all who worship the God of Abraham, Isaac, and Jacob with pious souls," he assures Wickefort, "delight in the doctrine of resurrection." (The form of expression is rather bizarre, to be sure.) At any rate, says Menasseh, Wickefort should be able to distinguish "the duties of friendship, by which men bind themselves to each other, from a public acknowledgment of another religion" ("amicitiae, qua mutuum obligantur homines, officia, a religionis diversae professione"). Here again is an appeal for friendship across religious boundaries. What prevents different individuals from living harmoniously together, Menasseh asks, each with separate views and ways of thinking, each abounding in insight, each with a clear conscience before God, each with good will toward all men of good will, regardless of their religious opinions?[125] Accordingly he invites Wickefort to sample the opinions of the Jewish "Fathers." Wickefort may not be able to agree on everything, but he will see that there is value in such association, for the greater knowledge and, hence, understanding that such writings can confer, and even for the sheer refreshment and delight that students and lovers of ancient truth can derive from them.[126] Wickefort was addressed by Menasseh as a "student of Greco–Roman Antiquities"; Menasseh now links up rabbinic truth and places it on the common ground of intellectual interest, careful to distinguish between acquiescence in religious dogmatics, which he does not call for, and a willingness to hear the views of others, which he earnestly entreats.

Again, there were those who came forth to offer their support. Barlaeus, tellingly, signed himself only as "Amicus."[127] Genebrand Anslo, one of Menasseh's favorite pupils—Dionysius Vossius was his fellow student—and a translator of Maimonides' *Hilkhot Teshuvah* into Latin (it remained unpublished), as well as the patron of Vorstius and Gentius, wrote a Hebrew poem "In honorem Autoris, quondam sui Praeceptoris, L[ibens] M[erito]" ('with great pleasure, to someone well—deserving'). Anslo recommends the *De Resurrectione* to all students of religion, especially those who are pious: "ki mib–bene 'ever zaraḥ ve–tsats or lay–yesharim," 'a light for the righteous has shone forth from the Hebrews'.[128] The translator, Zilius, adds his praise also, asking the reader who knows the classics, the ancient religions, the historians, and the philosophers to give consideration ("accipe") to what the "talmudic fathers" have to say on the subject of eternal life. These three contributors provide support for Menasseh's idea that a common ground can be found amid the differences in religion that would be maintained.

And so, in March of 1636 or thereabouts, just as the storm was erupting around the *De Creatione,* the work was published in two editions. The popularity of both works was in the end enhanced by this storm, although Menasseh showed some reserve by giving publication of the second printing over to Jan Janssonius.[129] The *De Resurrectione,* incidentally, gained a different sort of notoriety of its own by being placed on the Roman church's *Index* some twenty years after this.[130]

Menasseh must have shown a rather low profile between mid–1636 and the latter part of 1638. The furor over Barlaeus's poem and over Menasseh's several dedications to non–Jews probably made both the Jewish community rather uncomfortable and Menasseh anxious to avoid trouble. During these years, he continued his work as a printer, publishing no fewer than four new titles, including the *Shevet Yehudah* of Ibn Verga.[131] This was the first Hebrew chronicle to be printed at Amsterdam; a Spanish translation of the work would appear in 1640 and, in 1651, at Menasseh's suggestion, a Latin one by Gentius.

The year 1639 would see the reunification of the community. We may presume that efforts toward that end took up some of Menasseh's attention during the year preceding. Menasseh secured from Barlaeus (and we may also presume that it was through Menasseh's intercession that Barlaeus came to write) an ode in honor of the new synagogue. In it, Barlaeus not only sounds the hopeful theme of security and freedom of worship for the Portuguese Nation on the Amstel, but also advances the idea that only through the construction of this synagogue and its public place in the life of the city can Amsterdam truly be called a city of God: "This people, this city, who could deny that it is of God?"[132] There were those of course, who still did deny this. Menasseh was not one of these, as he continued his work.

In 1638, we find him responding to a query from Vossius the Elder with a long quotation and explanation of a passage from Maimonides' *Hilkhot Sanhedrin.*[133] In fact, by the end of the decade, he had responded to more than 150 letters from various scholars,[134] which must have been a fairly time–consuming process.

One of these letters proved even more challenging than the rest. It came from Johannes Beverovicius (Beverwyck, 1594–1647), professor of medicine at Dort from 1625, on the question of "the term of life." Between late in 1638 and June of 1639, Menasseh composed his little treatise; Beverovicius had asked that the voice of the rabbis be heard in the "Republic of Letters," for which such a work would be "no less pleasing than useful," as Beverovicius foresaw it.[135] Menasseh adopts his standard disclaimer, nonetheless, about the position of the Jews vis–à–vis Christian doctrine:

> I have determined to say nothing here that would impugn the Christian religion. So much the less so, since, in this controversy, most of its doctors did not embrace a different view from that of most of the rabbis.[136]

There is no attack on Christianity here, he says; there are, in fact, many points of agreement.

The claim is repeated again and again by Menasseh. His 1641 dedication of the second part of the *Conciliator* (in Spanish only) to the governors of the West India Company—he was still thinking of a Brazilian venture at this time—assures these gentlemen that "the greatest and most famous men of this and prior centuries have labored not a little on the questions discussed in the volume at hand, and there is no difference [of opinion] between Christians and Jews." He further presents his work as a show of gratitude for the benefits conferred on his "nation" by the States, who have protected these Portuguese from the tyranny of Spain. But the security of the "Portuguese Nation" is further ensured, Menasseh claims, by their literary and theological services to the Dutch

Republic. One might be tempted to consider this mere rhetoric; Menasseh obviously did not. There is a strong personal interest riding here as well, yet it transcends purely selfish motivations.

On Human Frailty, *to Anslo*

Menasseh's last appearance outside his native tongues before his English adventures was the 1642 *De Fragilitate Humana*. The original had been in Spanish, but there is particular interest for us in the Latin version, which is dedicated to Anslo. Menasseh opens up the question of friendship and its nature anew:

> That you are called most erudite by me no one will wonder; that you are called dearest friend, many men will, men both of this religion and of that, for all that both [religions] believe in one and the same God of Israel; since it has become more and more the prevailing view that no friendship can exist except among [those whose] souls have sworn about [the same] divine things.[137]

It is precisely on the same grounds that Barlaeus had trod, the matter of a "docta mens," that Menasseh now proceeds. For he sees many now doubting whether erudition suffices to bring about and sustain friendship, even though, to Menasseh's own mind, and, he hopes, Anslo's, both Christians and Jews believe in the same God of Israel; indeed, many deny that any friendship can exist except among those who have sworn allegiance to the same religious confession.

In some measure, this is a response to criticism from the left as well as to that from the right. Even though da Costa's *Exemplar Humanae Vitae* would not be published until 1687, surely he had, before his suicide in 1640, voiced aloud some of the criticism he levelled against the narrowness of the Jews and their hostility to Christianity. He must have sounded just like his written words: "I ask you, [Pharisee], tell me, if I were a Christian, what would you have said? It is clear, you would have said that I am a most detestable idolator, and that that, with Jesus Christ the teacher of Christians, I will suffer punishment before the true God against whom I had rebelled."[138] This too is what Menasseh comes to confute.

Such views, Menasseh says, are greatly in error and far from the thinking of former generations, who saw man as a "social animal." Now, though, men take delight in putting to the test those they reject, in order to single out the good ones among them: "juvat aversantes experiri, ut seligere bonos liceat." In other words, the surrounding society is only willing to accept a select few, those who are willing to go along with their thinking. The majority find it hard to tolerate the opinions of those who disagree with them. Menasseh is amazed, he says, at this "poison" (the word he uses is "loligo," a 'cuttlefish') that possesses and presses on men's minds; it is contrary to human nature, he argues, to be thus, as it is a slipping into Chaos.

Anslo is thereby singled out by Menasseh for his reciprocity: "You both visit my home and treat me honorably when I enter yours."[139] Menasseh knows he cannot please everyone, though: a sign of a noble and moral disposition, he says, is that one is judged to be to the taste of only a few. This was not the case historically. The greatest personages showed "familiaritas." Aristotle evinced friendship for Simon the High Priest (this legend was considered nothing less than true history by Menasseh), and even Paul the Apostle avoided offending the sensibilities of the Jews. And St. Jerome, "as he himself declares about himself, employed a Hebrew by birth and by religion as a teacher."[140] There is ample precedent for both friendship and instruction, Menasseh assures Anslo. This is a good indication that the *odium* and *invidia* had hardly died down on either the Jewish or the Christian side; many on both sides continued to reject such liaisons. But, Menasseh insists, good will on both sides is all that is necessary to restore man's natural state as a social animal: Men need not be of like minds, but they can enter into fellowship.[141]

There is much on teaching in this dedication; Menasseh reveals quite a bit about his view of the instruction of Christians: "the long way," he says, adducing Seneca, "is through rules; the short and effective one, through examples." We must come to know something about the student in order to teach him; we must have human contact, using all our senses; instruction by example and viva voce too (Aguilar's words as well) is the best method for communicating knowledge.[142] That, in a nutshell, was Menasseh's rationale for instructing Anslo and his friends. The experience of living Jewish teachers is essential to the understanding of Judaism by non–Jews.

From this emerges Menasseh's appeal to his former student:

Let us, most learned Anslo, drawn only by the reward of a good conscience, tread the trail of virtue onwards, and, reluctantly though we might do it, allow ourselves to live each by his own light, in the conviction that we do not utter such [ideas] out of a malicious inclination, but out of a certain human weakness.[143]

Menasseh realizes how each of them is probably unwilling to undertake such a challenge, the reward ("pretium" is perhaps used here with Barlaeus's poem echoing in the background) being so meager, that of a good conscience alone. But that, insists Menasseh, is what constitutes virtue: for each of them to be a public example of how one individual can let another live according to his own convictions, certain at the same time that such views do not emanate from a meanness of spirit, but rather out of a certain human frailty *that all men share.*[144]

Menasseh is thus appealing for more than support; he is imploring Anslo to join his effort in an area of discourse, the subject of sin, predestination, and repentance, that was still a very touchy one in 1642. Compounded with this is the fact that Anslo was a Mennonite, the views of which group were not countenanced in many instances even by the Remonstrants. Menasseh is thus asking Anslo to place himself on the line even more daringly than he, Anslo, did in contributing a poem to the *De Resurrectione.* Menasseh also reminds Anslo that Anslo had chosen him above anyone else to be his teacher, suggesting in turn that this is the reason for his own having chosen Anslo as a patron for what might prove to be his most daring work. Anslo's personal affection for him should overcome his difficulty, Menasseh feels:

It shall be yours, because it is due to your merits [that it has come into being]. It shall be yours, because your affection for me claims it, already from that time, when you employed me, of all people, as your guide in Hebrew and Aramaic letters, and for getting to know the monuments of rabbinic [literature]. In these, you rose to such a level and [showed] such talent and [such] diligence that the teacher himself does not merely delight in you but even glories. May the most learned men, indeed, both on general grounds and also on this one, love you, admire you, yea, even revere you.[145]

Menasseh hopes for plaudits and love for his precious pupil, but he is not entirely optimistic. While he looks for those who have a "docta mens" to recognize it in Anslo's regard for him, Menasseh closes with a prayer also:

> May Almighty God grant that the love successfully endure and remain unshaken in the face of all threatening dangers, however much the throng of the jealous ones bares its fangs. The worth of good men is not judged according to the number of supporters, or determined that way, since they constitute their own reward unto themselves.[146]

The *invidia,* the ill will that Menasseh had felt in the Jewish camp, and the *invidia* that Anslo, and Barlaeus before him, had experienced in the Christian one was still a force to be reckoned with. Menasseh asks Anslo to remain firm in the face of mass disapproval. He hopes that their friendship based on learning can survive and produce results, but he knows that it may end up being its own reward alone.

This dedication was completed about three months after the dedication of the Spanish edition to the Parnassim of the United Community had been given an approbation by that community's representatives. That acceptance, moreover, had come a week after the visit to the synagogue by the Prince of Orange and Queen Henrietta Maria of England, an occasion on which Menasseh himself had given the oration of welcome. (The oration was subsequently appended to the Spanish edition of the work.) Roth considers this occasion to have been "one of the crowning days of Menasseh's life."[147] Menasseh had, only a short while beforehand, as a matter of fact, been restored to his position from having been under the ban and having intended a departure for Brazil.[148] His dedication to the wardens had been most conciliatory, even adulatory, speaking of the lack of contention or dissension in the community that their rule had insured.

It was Menasseh's friends Caceres and Aharon Sarfati who issued the approbation. They praise Menasseh's works, but they also ask the wardens for additional help for him, in order that he might be able to devote himself entirely to his "honrosas exercicios, y muy realsados estudios," that is, "his very outstanding and honored works." The results, as they see it, from this will be "universal provecho y loor, a nuestra esparzida nacion." This is a statement of support for all of Menasseh's announced goals, centering on the hoped for praise and advantage to the Portuguese Nation in exile.

The Parnassim probably did not share Menasseh's enthusiasm, considering the touchy nature of the subject of predestination and grace. It was suitable for publication in Spanish, for in that language it would not offend the Dutch.[149] They most probably disapproved of Menasseh's Latin dedication, even though they let him go ahead with it. So Menasseh turned to Anslo, whom he thought to be his last trustworthy friend. Anslo, who had translated *Hilkhot Teshuvah,* was a likely patron for another reason as well. Menasseh's discussion is in some ways an exhortation to and a eulogy of repentance, and he knew he could find a sympathetic listener and reader in Anslo.

For example, after speaking of how men fell into error of their own volition or ignorance, Menasseh suggests the remedy that is provided by divine goodness:

> That is penitence; for, if we have fallen, [God] reaches out His hand to those drawn to Him through repentance, raises them, and again restores them to His grace in accordance with His mercy, just as parents are wont to [restore] their children [to favor] as soon as they promise to amend their ways.[150]

This was, of course, a thoroughly Jewish and anti–Calvinist statement and potentially an inflammatory one. Hardly surprising, therefore, but certainly worth noting is the total absence from the Latin edition of any panegyrics or commendatory letters or poems. The work came forth bare into the world; no one would risk another confrontation, neither Christian nor Jew.

Even Vossius, whose treatise on Pelagianism was the only contemporary (it dated from 1618) non–Jewish work cited by Menasseh (prominently, at the very close of the book, which had itself begun with a reference to Pelagius), even Vossius kept silent. Menasseh must have felt truly abandoned. Anslo, moreover, would be dead within a year.[151]

As it happened, no outcry resulted. The work may have even had a modest success. Nonetheless, at this point, Menasseh turned away for the most part to internal Jewish matters, over a period of almost eight years.[152] The issues of friendship, commonality, and usefulness to the surrounding society had been articulated over a decade with limited results, despite the claim by Menasseh referred to earlier, i.e., his boast that "we Portuguese live safely and make use of liberty like the others." While he may have told his royal guests that "this [was] a great proof of your virtue and an even greater one of your wisdom,"[153] it is obvious that he himself did not yet fully believe this.

At mid–century, however, Menasseh would return to the forefront of the quest for liberty and security, trying to find fulfillment as a teacher in true political diplomacy. Yet his view of himself and his destiny was clearly shaped to a great extent by his pupils' responses. It is time to turn to these pupils and their work on Maimonides.

III

The Latin *Mishneh Torah* of Amsterdam

The earliest Hebraist commentators on the *Mishneh Torah* were all pupils of Menasseh ben Israel. They were also, however, either children or disciples of the colossi of Arminian learning and scholarship whose disposition toward rabbinic literature has been considered above. No summation of their general posture is more fitting at this point than Grotius's 1638 evaluation of Menasseh's works. The famous jurist first argued that, while some rabbinic works have "not improbable" interpretations, among which those of Ibn Ezra and Maimonides stand out (*excellunt*), "many things present themselves in those writings that show a poverty of judgment (*judicii tenuitatem*)." Of the *Conciliator, De Creatione,* and *De Resurrectione* he said specifically that they contain "not a few worthy things" ("nonnulla . . . digna"), but, then again, "a few . . . rabbinic things, that is, absurd and ridiculous ones" ("quaedam . . . rabbinica, id est, absurda atque ridicula"). Even if Grotius is favorably disposed to one or another odd "worthy" rabbinic statement or viewpoint, he is basically condemning the totality of what Menasseh had come to defend. Even though Grotius saw Menasseh himself as a "vir publico etiam literario non inutilis," 'a man certainly not unuseful to the Republic of Letters', his remarks undermined Menasseh's larger goals.[1] While this kind of attitude was common in the inheritance of the younger group of Arminians, those who came to Menasseh for instruction, their own approaches to rabbinic literature showed that they were not always bound to their legacy. The individual variations provided some of the dynamic that stimulated Menasseh further in his enterprise.

Dionysius Vossius

The Son of Gerhard Johann Vossius; The Scholar in Training

Dionysius Vossius's *De Idololatria,* his translation and commentary on *Hilkhot 'Avodah Zarah,* was published together with his father's *De Theologia Gentili.* It was also intimately bound up with the larger work in other ways as well. The elder Vossius's interests were primary, formative influences on his son's life. Had he lived, Dionysius, by universal acclaim his father's most gifted child, would undoubtedly have become a great luminary in the Republic of Letters and the inheritor of his father's mantle.[2]

As such, his work must first be evaluated in light of his father's writings and interests.[3] Dionysius's commentary on Caesar was a sample of the kind of scholarship his father had tried to stimulate with his *De Historicis Latinis,*[4] annotations that shed new light on the text by illustrating it with other classical sources. The *De Idololatria* stood in what seems to have been an opposite relationship: not merely was it the direct stimulus for the *De Theologia Gentili,* it was also a detailed illustration of some of the historical evidence for the *argumentum* of the larger work.[5] This was very much in keeping with the Vossian conception of history as composed of particulars ("singularia") or illustrations ("exempla"), that is, of specifics that, taken together, become the mirror of divine providence and the parent of moral and civil philosophy.[6]

Gerardus Joannes Vossius was the virtual "legislator" of historical methodology during his own lifetime and down into the eighteenth century, or as long as the antiquarian tendency of his thinking was able to hold its own.[7] Vossius was also the Latin and Greek grammarian whose works remained standard textbooks for generations.[8] Along with Nicholas Heinsius, he was the dramatic theorist par excellence for the Republic of Letters, especially in France,[9] and he exercised a noteworthy influence as well on Vondel, Holland's greatest playwright.[10] His reputation as an authority on classical antiquity was so great that students came from all across the continent of Europe to Amsterdam to meet and consult him.[11] Ultimately, though, Vossius was a theologian; he made all his other efforts subservient to his religious propensities and interests.[12] His major studies merged the sacred and secular: he approached the study of religion on a historical basis, using the historical method as he conceived it to defend and explicate his religious convictions. He wrote on all the leading topics of his day, arguing for the major tenets of the Arminian creed as he did so.[13] His scholarship was uncompromising in its search for factual accuracy; he paid great attention to details and to the truth of his reporting, but history was for him nothing if not useful.[14] His general aim in history was a pragmatic one: the public welfare.[15] By this he often meant, as he did in *De Theologia Gentili,* that history, together with an understanding of nature and of Scripture, could lead humanity to the knowledge, love, and worship of the true God.[16]

Vossius *père* collected literary materials from every available source to "illustrate" his studies, and he did not spurn Maimonides. As noted earlier, he did not, in general, reject the writings or the culture of the Jews out of hand. Hebrew he saw as the mother of all tongues,[17] and he obviously considered the Jews, who had preserved that language,[18] as suitable and even valuable for the instruction of Christians. He used Menasseh ben Israel to train Dionysius, and Dionysius, in turn, taught his brothers.[19] Vossius senior thought that the books of the Jews could be useful; the Talmud he had characterized even before 1620 as "a work containing many things not unworthy of being known."[20] In the same breath, though, he advised his audience to be cautious, "so covered with lies and falsifications was the work." Although he was willing to accept Menasseh ben Israel into his home, since he found him friendly and obliging of Christians, he wished that Menasseh were a Christian;[21] in fact, he regarded most Jews as hostile to Christianity. Vossius too thought Christians should pay greater attention to proselytization among the Jews and saw the study of Oriental languages as a tool to that end:

> I feel utter pity for the Jews. . . . How unremittingly I would rather Christians attended to converting them. . . . In almost all countries now, there is a remarkably small number of men who know how to defend their views against this people (*gentem*)[and] even fewer who seem capable of overcoming them. We justly accuse the Jews of obstinacy, but even we ourselves are not free from [blame], since the literature of the Orient is almost neglected by us, and we often defend a most excellent cause with play arms rather than real ones [see Sen. *Ep.* 117], as if this were something other than proclaiming the truth (*prodere veritatem*). I would not be writing this if I had not too often seen with what a light cloak the Jews evade our weapons; and I have become even more acquainted with this than before, here in the city of Amsterdam.[22]

It will be remembered that Menasseh too was concerned with proclaiming the truth. The two camps were still far apart, it would appear.

How, then, did Maimonides' *Hilkhot 'Akkum* illustrate *De Theologia Gentili?* What did two authors separated by an ocean of doctrinal and religious differences, and by four centuries and more in time, have in common? They shared several viewpoints, even though Maimonides was certainly the more profound and seminal of the two, by far. In general, both writers established the universal knowledge of the true God—Vossius made only casual reference in his work to the specifically Christian—as the ultimate goal. Maimonides was far more intellectualistic—this lies at the core of Maimonidean thinking—in his argumentation, but Vossius appears as a true humanist, in line with much of the thinking of the Italian Renaissance, and more than holds his own: like Maimonides, he too argued that an understanding of the true nature of all things, earthly, human, and spiritual, was the correct path to the knowledge of God. (Vossius's erudition was vast, but he was not a logician or a true metaphysician like Maimonides; he was concerned to amass the historical evidence. Maimonides is said to have had little sympathy for historical writing,[23] but he certainly had a great interest in the nature of history; the first chapter of *'Avodah Zarah* was, after all, an attempt at historical analysis. It was, in truth, highly conjectural, but it did present the kind of historical judgment that Vossius himself was engaged in making.)[24] Both writers lay stress on the interdependence of knowledge and action as the correct road to the worship of God.[25] They also held somewhat similar views on the relationship of tradition to speculative knowledge. In Vossius's view, tradition, divinely preserved, helped keep men on the path to the knowledge of God, but man's intellect penetrates higher and, through "philosophy" and a knowledge of the natural order, leads him to the architect and moderator of all things.[26] The *Mishneh Torah* is a codification of tradition that goads its readers to philosophical speculation as the cardinal method by which God is to be known. Vossius did not lag behind: "By investigating the order of all things," he wrote, "we reach the first cause, immortal God." Then, by considering God's power, wisdom, and goodness, "we are inflamed with a love for Him and a desire to worship Him."[27] These sentiments would have found a responsive chord in Maimonides, even if their formulation might not have been exactly parallel.

Finally, both Maimonides and Vossius preoccupied themselves with those who lose their way in their approach to God and end up worshipping His subordinates: natural phenomena, artifacts, human passions, and men themselves. Vossius wrote that those who go astray move rapidly from impiety to iniquity.[28] Maimonides could hardly have dissented, even if his definition of the terms might have been different. Of all Vossius's attempts to articulate his view of religion—and it was largely a mainstream view—none was more comprehensive or original, despite its reliance on a host of traditional sources, than his *De Theologia Gentili et Physiologia Christiana; sive De Origine ac Progressu Idololatriae; deque Naturae mirandis, quibus Homo Adducitur ad Deum.* In this work, as suggested by the title and specified in the various prefaces, Vossius attempted a critical examination of all things worshipped by men, meaning the gods, the things of the world, and, in general, all the forms of cult. From this he hoped to show the natural order of things and the governance of God Himself and thus, implicitly, to be freed of any suspicion of heresy, impiety, or blasphemy, i.e., *in toto* of the charge of idolatry. Arminianism too, though he does not say so explicitly, would also be vindicated.[29] In specific, though, Vossius had a twofold stated purpose: to demonstrate the falsity of "gentile" religion and theology, and to bring about a correct understanding of the nature of the world. Thus he would bring men to the love of God.[30] (Vossius almost entitled his work *De Natura Deorum et Rerum,* but, in view of the paganism of Cicero and Lucretius whose titles suggested this one, thought the better of it.[31]) Though Maimonides' treatise was only partially responsible for the larger enterprise undertaken by Gerardus Joannes Vossius,[32] there could be no better illustration of his views than Maimonides' detailed description of the many forms of idolatrous worship and cult. Maimonides' "historical" introductory chapter was also valuable as support.

Though the *De Theologia Gentili* inevitably far outstriped the *De Idololatria* in scope and depth, the two works originated in the same group of interests and had a basic ideological and religious affinity. The father's treatise was an outgrowth and continuation of his own earlier work, with which we know the son was familiar, based on citations of it in *De Idololatria.* Yet Dionysius also had a viewpoint of his own. While his work also grew out of his overall *paideia* and out of the history of Christian Hebraism in general, it also showed itself an independent work in many ways.

For, as strong an influence as Gerhard Johann Vossius exercised on his children, he had still seen to it that they all received the best education available. This meant, of course, in addition to the instruction he gave Dionysius, philological training by his colleagues at Leiden, so Dionysius began with these masters even before he entered his teens. He also followed the course in *jus et politica,* that is [Roman] law and political science, in the Leiden tradition established by Justus Lipsius. Aside from his father, Dionysius's teachers included the most noted classicists, orientalists, and theologians of the day, among them Heinsius, Meursius, Erpenius, Golius, and l'Empereur. Grotius (from afar later on), Barlaeus, and numerous others also took an active interest in the young man's work. Dionysius's linguistic accomplishments alone bear witness to his teachers' successes as well as to his own talents. Over and above the standard classical and romance languages, he mastered the major Oriental ones: Hebrew, Aramaic, Syriac, Armenian, and Ethiopic.[33]

The scholars of Albion also played a role in Dionysius's development. He had accompanied his father to Oxford and Cambridge in 1630 and had been introduced to all the luminaries of English scholarship.[34] It was in England, moreover, that he became inflamed with his zeal for the study of religion. His brother Isaac's very dedication[35] of the *De Idololatria* to the two great English universities bespeaks their role in Dionysius's life. But Isaac Vossius also offers some details of their influence on his brother. It was not merely as one of Gerhard Johann Vossius's children, he writes, that Dionysius had drawn the attention of the English. Rather, he had benefited from their "doctrina et humanitas" in his own right. By Dionysius's own estimate, Isaac Vossius continues, the example of English luminaries, alongside that of his father, was crucial: "nec dissimulabat . . . vehementius se accensum ad sacra studia, tantorum virorum, paternoque etiam exemplo, excolenda"; it was they who fired his interest. Further testimony was lent Isaac Vossius on this score by Dionysius's private reading notes on the church fathers ("antiqui ecclesiae doctores"), which dated from this period and thereafter and thus reflected the enhancement of Dionysius's latent interest. Certain individuals were more important in stimulating Dionysius's studies; these included William Laud, John Selden, Edward Pococke, and Méric Casaubon. In the *De Idololatria* proper, Dionysius refers to Selden, for example, as "doctissimus," or, again, as "summus vir,"[36] characterizations with the familiarity of tone he seems to have reserved for those he knew personally. In short, Dionysius's interest in religion followed immediately on his travels to England; as for his interest in rabbinics, though, his encounter with Menasseh ben Israel in Amsterdam brought it to flower. And yet, having commenced work on the *De Idololatria* in October or November 1632, Dionysius received encouragement again from England. He had planned to dedicate his proposed work to Laud, the future Archbishop of Canterbury, who, as Chancellor of Oxford, had brought the Vossii to England. Laud responded positively to the letter in which Dionysius's father had announced the project, commenting "et Author placet & Argumentum."[37] The ultimate dedication, of course, was not to Laud. By 1641, he was already imprisoned in the Tower of London and hardly suitable as a candidate for the honor. At his father's suggestion, Isaac Vossius dedicated Dionysius's work to the two universities. Laud could still be included implicitly, though, even then, and the personal copy that the elder Vossius presented to Laud was accompanied by a private letter reminding the former Chancellor of his role in the genesis of the work.[38]

To return to Dionysius himself, though, the name he made for himself and the erudition he had acquired became even more widely known after the family transferred to Amsterdam in 1631. He was selected as the first librarian of the new Athenaeum Illustre, to which his father had been appointed as professor of history; as a result, Dionysius can be considered the founder of the present–day University of Amsterdam Library. Subsequently, he was offered the professorship of history and rhetoric in the new university founded at Dorpat by King Gustavus Adolphus of Sweden.[39] This position he declined, out of concern for his mother's health, in deference to his father's qualms over his youth, and because of his own sense of incompleted projects at home. Then an appointment in England beckoned; this too he refused. Finally, he had accepted the position of historiographer to Queen Christina, obviously hoping to do for Sweden what Reyd, whose history he had just finished translating into Latin and was hoping to continue also, had done for the United Provinces. Dionysius was planning to proceed to Sweden, learn the language of the country, work through the national archives, and return home to write his history of the realm. Abruptly, as he was about to embark, death cut him down, however, on October 25, 1633. Though specifically a victim of smallpox, his constitution had been weakened previously by what his brother diagnosed as "studia immoderata"; he had regularly worked far into the night, often until three in the morning, on his studies. His death was lamented widely, mention being made repeatedly of the sweetness of his character and the innocence of his life, of his innate genius and his prodigious learning, his good judgment and, especially, his piety. He was eulogized, in brief, as a glory to the Republic of Letters.

Even discounting the hyperbole that inevitably inserts itself into such remarks, it is clear that Dionysius was deemed a young man of special talents. His several literary productions further contributed to his reputation, and they also provide some insight into his makeup. Aside from the *Conciliator* and the *De Idololatria,* his other major works were: a Latin version of the *Historie der Nederlandsche Oorlogen* by Everard Reyd (d. 1602) [first Dutch edition 1626, in Arnhem], rendered as: *Belgarum aliarumque gentium annales* (Leiden, 1633); and the series of annotations on Caesar, published posthumously (Amsterdam, 1697). (There were also some minor occasional pieces, some letters, and a body of unpublished material, ranging from annotations on other classical authors to exercises in mathematics.) All of Dionysius's major works have their background in the same process of intellectual development. All were completed during 1632–33, but all date back in one way or another to his earliest studies.[40]

Vossius began his Hebrew studies almost as early as he did his studies of the classics. First he studied Latin literature and Roman history with his father and with Heinsius. No specific date can be assigned to this, but, by the age of ten, Dionysius was already studying Greek as well, and with Meursius. It is not certain when he began his Hebrew. Yet he progressed so under l'Empereur, his first teacher, that, by the age of fourteen, he had already read the entire Hebrew Scriptures through twice in the original. From that point, he was, in his father's estimation, "literarum Hebraearum studiosus," 'learned in Hebrew letters'. Rabbinic learning came later, in the person of Menasseh ben Israel, an association "not without benefit," despite Dionysius's earlier familiarity with the Hebrew language:[41]

> . . . In order to further Christian scholarship and at great cost, [Dionysius] had already acquired talmudic and rabbinic books for himself, in this making use entirely of the advice and help of Menasseh ben Israel, a Jew, yet of a virtuous [mode of] life and very learned, whom he consulted repeatedly, especially about ancient Jewish practices. All the more easily, therefore, was [Dionysius] induced to translate [Menasseh's] *Conciliador* from Spanish into Latin, an easy task [to begin with]. And his goal was none other than this: that even the authority of the rabbis might be brought to bear in reconciling scriptural passages that seemed to conflict with one another (which is surely not the meanest part of sacred learning); and that, in this way, the Christian teachings about these passages might be more completely confirmed, and the false opinions, in fact, of the rabbis refuted with greater certainty, especially by the expositors of the divine lawgiver's Pentateuch.[42]

Represented here is not Dionysius's, but his father's view[43] of the dual aim of the translation: one, to adduce the authority of the rabbis in an area of Christian concern that was of the greatest importance, the reconciliation of apparent discrepancies in Scripture; and, two, to set rabbinic teachings forth clearly so that, when they become known, the false opinions in them may be the more readily and positively refuted. Rabbinic teachings appear again, in the elder Vossius's view, in their classic twofold character, being sometimes authoritative, sometimes without foundation. Part of the Christian task, accordingly, was to put them forth, so that the reader could distinguish between true *auctoritas* and *falsa opinio*.

Menasseh's *Conciliator*

This duality may have existed in Dionysius's mind; he had expressed it with much greater reserve, however, in his own preface to the reader of the *Conciliator*. While Dionysius does mention the apologetic goal, he does not play it up. On the contrary, the prime thrust of his remarks is the acceptability of rabbinic views where they can be of use. Dionysius remarks several times, in fact, on the overall usefulness ("utilitas") of the enterprise of reconciliation, making particular mention of its value against "athei ac profani." These are the individuals who take advantage of the seeming inconsistencies in Scripture. As a child of his age, like

Menasseh, and of a century that Dionysius himself characterized in this preface as "infelix," surely because of the constant internecine religious warfare both abroad and at home, he was equally troubled by these skeptics and their attacks on scriptural religion. He can only have perceived these attacks as detrimental to the general welfare of society, especially at home. It was, indeed, "solely for the public good" that he had prepared his work, after all.

Now the Vossii were, to be sure, among the rear guard of the defenders of the old standard against the new criticism, certain as they were that the authority of the ancients was still sufficient to all tasks. This authority included that of the rabbis: it was unthinkable, wrote Dionysius, that "tot tantosque Hebraeorum Doctores," so many and so great as they were, "had sweated away in vain at explicating Scripture." Even if there appear from time to time "things that one might not wrongly reject,"[44] there were undoubtedly many excellent observations that could help the expositors of the divine word and remove a great part of the burden from them. The Jews were clearly engaged in the same activity as the Christian expositors. The criticism that had been levelled against "contradictions" by some ex–Marranos in the Jewish community was one root of Menasseh's work; as it had its direct counterpart in the non–Jewish community, Menasseh's contribution to this literature was worth making available to the Latin public.

The other application of the work appears subsidiary as a result. "If the reader likes to dispute with the Jews (. . . si cum ipsis Judaeis disputare libet), it is undeniably necessary first of all to know the opinions they hold." The need to know seems to exist rather independently, however, and to relate directly to the major function of the work: presenting the explanations of all the rabbis, old and new, for the difficult places in the Pentateuch. For, as a further aspect of the enterprise, Vossius considers and dismisses the claim that one has to have a thorough knowledge of Hebrew to engage in these investigations. Even for those who do not have the leisure to learn Hebrew thoroughly, it will be well, he asserts, to have consulted the work.[45]

Vossius is obviously anxious and at pains to disarm any critics who would reject the utility of the work. His primary goal is to defend the possibility and the very idea of the Jews making a contribution in this area. De–emphasizing, therefore, the gulf that separates Jew and Christian, he insists that something is to be learned from Menasseh and rabbinic literature: even though Menasseh's style is very simple, there is grandeur ("majestas") in the material itself: nor is there any dearth of examples ("exempla") of great men who took it upon themselves to comment upon or translate the writings of the Jews. Also, to make the work more acceptable, he announces that he has, "non ignaro Autore," with Menasseh's full awareness, omitted several things too difficult for Christian ears to bear.[46]

It would appear, then, that G. J. Vossius had misplaced the emphasis of his son's remarks and their thrust. For Dionysius, the usefulness of Menasseh's work outweighed all other considerations, and that usefulness was due precisely to the wealth of rabbinic learning it contained.

The usefulness of Menasseh's work had been recognized elsewhere, of course, by Gerhard Johann Vossius, even though he too suggested several dimensions to Dionysius's work. "My son did not waste his efforts on the translation," he wrote Casaubon on October 15, 1633, a mere ten days before Dionysius's sudden death and a mere twenty after the translation had been rejected by the States, "since nothing is more necessary than to show the agreement of seemingly contradictory places in Scripture. This work will be really useful for future commentators on the Books of Moses. We do not approve of everything in this volume. It is the work of a Jew who ministers among his own [people] in this city. Nonetheless," he remarked, "we shall see that those who, henceforth, wish to comment on the Mosaic [writings] will draw on rabbinic books they have not read and procure [*concilient*(!)] love and favor for themselves and attain honor from the ignorant for widespread reading. Indeed, such is life today. Some are erudite, others [only] appear [to be so]."[47]

G. J. Vossius understood full well the abuses to which his son's work could give rise. Yet he also perceived the need it would fill. By associating a thorough knowledge of rabbinic literature with true erudition, he vindicated Menasseh to an extent. He had expressed himself similarly in other letters. To Laud he wrote: "Etenim utile visum est Christianis omnibus quae ad Quaestiones divini operis commentati essent Rabbinorum doctissimi." Though

Dionysius comes out sounding more modest than his father, the general attitude of both father and son made it possible to produce this work "in Christianorum gratiam," 'to please Christians', it being the earliest translation of a Jew's work by a Christian in the lifetime of the author.[48]

Personal friendship played a major role here. The Vossii may already have held rabbinic literature in a certain favor, and this attitude may have led to their contact with Menasseh to begin with, but there was also Menasseh himself, who appears to have understood immediately the uses to which the Vossii could be put. Even though he himself was only a single individual and even though they maintained their overall hostility to Jews, it was through the Vossii that Menasseh got his book out and, with its publication, began that series of his writings addressed to the Latin literary public at large. And so, the rejection of his work by the States did not diminish Menasseh's enthusiasm. He looked directly into the face of hostility and saw specific personal support as an opening for apologetics.

In other words, Menasseh contested one of the announced goals of the Vossius family. To G. J. Vossius's mind, the conversion of the Jews had been Dionysius's specific purpose in taking up rabbinic literature.[49] Now, even if we consider the father's claim exaggerated, in view of the modesty of the son's expressions in his preface to the *Conciliator,* we can only take at face value G. J. Vossius's statements about an anthology his son had had in mind before his death: "an immense volume [drawn] from all the rabbis, whose books he had devoured voraciously, comprising especially [materials] relating to the conversion of the Jews."[50] Or, again, we must take note of the elder Vossius's plaint on his son's unfulfilled promise: "If God had granted him longer life, we would have many things illustrated by him out of the talmudic writings, and no fewer in defense of the Christian religion against the Jews."[51]

There can be no other conclusion: Dionysius was engaged in a dialectic with Judaism. He might use such rabbinic materials as could illustrate or elucidate his studies, but he also hoped to put forth an overall refutation of the legitimacy of rabbinic Judaism. Still, if the *Conciliator* was useful, the *De Idololatria* would be an opportunity for Dionysius to show off his manifold erudition.[52] That was his father's view prior to the actual composition of the work. Though Dionysius himself did not leave any written personal statement about his goal, "he longed passionately," his father recalled after his death, "to share Maimonides' *De Idololatria* . . . with the Republic of Letters." This statement has several implications, aside from the general sense of a young scholar presenting his credentials as a Hebraist to the "literarum principes," as the elder Vossius styles them.[53] Even if there is hardly any such thing as "objective scholarship," works addressed to or produced for the Republic of Letters were presumably meant to be of a predominantly nonpolemical character. They might contain criticisms, of course, but they were meant to be something other than confutations based on dogma or doctrine.[54] It was undoubtedly the scholarly side of Dionysius's personality and erudition that Menasseh wished to encourage, knowing full well that there were theological motivations behind even the best scholarship and that Dionysius's conversionist aims were quite undiminished. While Menasseh's inner thoughts can only be probed by speculation, outwardly he remained a friend of the entire Vossius family. Even Isaac, who elsewhere spoke of Menasseh somewhat disparagingly,[55] allowed the generous characterization of Menasseh in the preface to the *De Idololatria* to stand as testimony to Menasseh's having sanctioned both of Dionysius's Hebraist productions.

Even if we can reconstruct the young man's character only from afar, then, it is clear that Menasseh's acquaintance with Dionysius's personality and scholarly propensities was an intimate one and that Menasseh chose to support Dionysius for cause. This can be borne out by reference to other sources. For, in addition to the material in his father's letters, the body of Dionysius's own writings, including his non–Hebraist productions, can provide substantial insight into his overall makeup.

Reyd's *Annales*

The preface to Reyd's *Annales* shows the aspiring young historian Dionysius's approach to scholarship and knowledge in general. He conceives of the historian as the seeker of truth who has both an exact knowledge ("notitia") of his subject and the vigor to transmit it to posterity. Dionysius saw his own role as the preserver of truth also, for it was he who made the author and his work known to foreign nations. Truth, of course, has a fairly specific connotation in all of this. It refers to three things basically: "res ipsas," the facts themselves, related, no doubt, to "res gestae," the classical expression for history, and meaning "deeds"; "qualis quisque est," the nature of each individual; and "actiones humanae," human actions or what people did. Indeed, history is the "actionum humanarum speculum," the mirror of these actions, and it has a moral function. Through a "nobile argumentum" it transmits "exempla" suitable to enkindle in posterity both an imitation of virtues and an avoidance of vices. For that reason, the virtues and the vices have to be represented accurately, in a style equal to the substance. In order to transmit *notitia,* which has truth as its content, the historian must have both *notitia* (or *scientia*), as well as a talent for writing. The spirit of the presentation has to be at the level of its truth. For the *aestimatio* in which the subject will be held by posterity rests on both *facta* and *dicta.* Excellence in these, along with the *pietas* and *prudentia* necessary to appreciate them, are the true virtues of the historian.

All of this has a higher purpose as well; the honor and glory of God. The events Reyd described were the miracles that God wrought for the Dutch nation. The task of the historian is ultimately, therefore, to give expression to this and thanks to God and thus to make posterity come to recognize the power and the glory of God's name in the truth he, the historian, has discovered and conveyed. The historian, then, is more than the mere narrator or reproducer of events, he is the one who gives expression to them as aspects of truth in a world under the providence of God.

The Commentary on Caesar

Dionysius's concern with *utilitas* and with truth, knowledge, accuracy, and the glory of God, concerns that are manifest as well in his preface to the *Conciliator,* also found their expression in his two commentaries.[56] As such, the genesis and the philologico–historical methodology of the Caesar commentary, which, as noted earlier, was substantially complete when work on Maimonides began, can shed even further light on the background of the *De Idololatria.* Though not published until 1697, Vossius's Caesar was probably the first modern edition with commentary.

While scholia on classical authors, including Caesar, had been produced down through the sixteenth century, the scholiasts confined themselves largely to textual or lexical matters. Toward the end of the sixteenth century, though, Lipsius and Scaliger expanded the range of commentary on classical authors to include political, moral and historical observations, over and above new critical annotations on the classical texts themselves. It was in the aftermath and under the ongoing spell of their having resided in Leiden that Vossius composed his Caesar.[57]

It was also along lines they had established that Vossius wrote. The edition and commentary on Tacitus that Lipsius had published in 1574 gave Lipsius his name and made Tacitus's prose style (followed by Caesar's) the ideal for the entire seventeenth century; Vossius was one of many who found it a suitable model for his own emulation.[58] The *auctoritas* of both Tacitus and Lipsius had been further enhanced by Lipsius's *Politica* (1589), essentially a collection of loci from the great ancient historian. Lipsius had also been an editor of Caesar (1585, repr. 1593), among other classical authors on whom he wrote. In short, Lipsius's impact on education and rhetoric during the first half of the seventeenth century was considerable, and the Vossii, in the Leiden tradition, were heavily indebted to him.

Lipsius's Tacitus contained no real advances in textual criticism, though. It demonstrated instead the wealth of Roman antiquities and the *exempla* and *moralia* that Lipsius deemed so important for his age. In addition to scattered philological or critical comments, the Lipsian commentary was characterized mainly by a series of short monographs on set topics.

Scaliger, on the other hand, had tried first of all to collect manuscripts and, with reference to the best of them, to establish a system of criticism. He chose not to rely on his own ingenuity or on the clever emendation alone, as had more often been the case with his immediate predecessor. Scaliger's prime tendency in his commentaries was to go beyond the elementary explanations of the scholiasts and beyond their paraphrase and to grapple with the meaning of the text itself, avoiding the longer discussions and the tangential questions characteristic of Lipsius. Scaliger too had been an editor of Caesar (1606). Though this edition was not annotated at all, it was still reprinted regularly during the seventeenth century for the supposed soundness of its text.

Vossius's edition was specifically "post Scaligerum ipsum."[59] His text had apparently been intended as a critical revision of Scaliger's; it was based on additional manuscripts and it devoted a good deal of attention to textual cruces. Yet Vossius's commentary was in many ways closer to the Lipsian type, with frequent long disquisitions on matters related only tangentially to the text or its subject matter. The implied function of Vossius's commentary was to render the text clearer or more intelligible. Dionysius's father also thought his son had "explained Caesar more fully (*fecit planiorem*) with his erudite notes," even if Dionysius's erudition often obfuscated rather than clarified. Be that as it may, the comments themselves, whether text–critical in the modern sense or not,[60] whether concise or monographic, gave evidence of one underlying assumption: that both text and substance must be elucidated by illustration, that is to say, corroborated by reference to all accumulated knowledge, be it a corresponding example in classical literature or a presumed etymology based on a Hebrew counterpart. Internal evidence was also to be brought: from Caesar's [intended] meaning ("mens"), such as Vossius judged it, and from the facts ("res") and "ipsa historia," all are looked to for support. At one point, Vossius rejects a certain reading by remarking rather boldly, "Indeed, I do not remember any of the ancients to have said anything like that." Many of Vossius's emendations were based on his own sense of what was proper; his concern with his predecessors' supposed misreadings (regardless of their *auctoritas*) would influence his own successors to devote their commentaries to his lapses.[61]

Following Caesar himself, Vossius showed particular interest in the customs (*mores*) of the Gauls, especially in their religious practices. He was expansive, for example, on the Gallic gods and their equivalents in the Greek and Roman pantheons. He drew parallel loci not only from other classical authors, with their "auctoritas," but even from the practices of his own day ("hodieque": even today such is the case); both parallels were supposed to illuminate Caesar's text "(magna lux Caesari ex [Jordanis] loco . . . ubi describit morem funeris Attilae": Caesar's description of Gallic funeral practices is illuminated by Jordanus's [Dominican, fl. 1321–1330] description of the funeral pyre of Attila the Hun). The stock expressions in this type of comment are numerous: "Nam soliti Galli" or "Germani," "Romani," etc.; "ut et aliae gentes"; "simile exemplum in . . ."; "mos olim"; or "antiquissimum hunc esse morem." These invocations of "example" and "custom" are intended to corroborate as well as explain a given practice.

Such a style of congeries was, of course, extremely fashionable and the mark of an erudite writer. Sometimes, one author is even pitted against another in virtually dialectical fashion, in order to reconcile apparent discrepancies. In other words, the method of juxtaposing differing sources that Menasseh employed in the *Conciliator* has its counterpart in Vossius's commentary on a classic of ancient pagan literature. Still, if this is supposed to enhance the attractiveness, scope, and authority of the original work, the end result is here too merely a virtuoso display of knowledge. The likelihood is, therefore, that Vossius designed his commentary on Caesar for those who were already conversant with the writer, rather than for those who were approaching Caesar for the first time. It may even be fair to say that the commentary is designed for other virtuosi, for those who knew the issues and the cruces. For example, Vossius does not elaborate on or explain Caesar's description of the Gallic view of man, neither discussing its doctrines nor even summarizing them, while he devotes a great deal of space to such technical details as the title *Commentarius* or the authorship of the *Civil War.*

In many ways, Vossius's approach left Caesar as open as possible to the individual reader's interpretation, understanding and appreciation. The commentator had posed an implicit challenge: that the reader himself consider, investigate and help choose the most accurate textual reading and thus become aware of the customs and other realia behind Caesar's reporting. Even if the commentator, Vossius, betrays certain preferences and a certain conception of Caesar's style and interests, Caesar's history remains almost intact as the commentary veers off into the tangential. Inevitably, some light is shed on the history. The reader need only beware lest he become bedazzled by the illumination itself.

While Vossius had fairly clear–cut goals and interests, then, he manifested no obvious biases. His goal was accuracy, illumination, and independence from his predecessors. If some of his comments seem superfluous, these were often due to youthful exuberance; they may be accounted, at worst, transparent displays of erudition. They all have their counterpart in the *De Idololatria* which, if it manifests greater erudition than the Caesar commentary, is still very much of a piece with it, both in attempting such a display and in its interest in the customs of the ancients, and in many other ways as well.

Maimonides' *On Idolatry*

The Canon of Translation

To turn now to *De Idololatria* itself, an exact canon of translation can be said to have existed in Dionysius's mind. He had given some indication of this in his Reyd. The preface that G. J. Vossius composed for the *De Idololatria* under his son Isaac's name offers this account of Dionysius's *modus operandi* in the earlier work:

> In this translation, he took care especially, as befitting a faithful translator, not to omit anything Reyd had said, or to say anything [Reyd] had not; but a most closely related concern was, insofar as a translator might be permitted, to imitate at the same time both the clarity (*puritas*) of Caesar and the grandeur (*semnotes* [Gk.]) of Tacitus; these two among prose writers, in addition to Tully, he had [previously] almost restored to life and vigor.[62]

Faithfulness and correct Latinity had been the guiding principles of most translators since the Renaissance, and Vossius was no exception. Though proper models of Latin style may appear to be aspects of rhetoric, the issue of style is also a substantive one; it is intimately tied to the concern for faithfulness and precision.[63] Vossius himself had written in his preface to the *Conciliator,* "I did not think that an embellishment of style was to be aimed at in matters that, although conveyed in the simplest manner, have sufficient majesty." In other words, he preferred to let the material speak for itself, fully aware as he was of the distinctions between a simple, clear style (like Caesar's *puritas*) and the more august variety (as in the diction of Tacitus).

Dionysius himself corroborates this in his notes on Maimonides. The "interpretatio," the 'meaning' or 'translation' must, he remarks on a certain passage, be "apta" (p. 46). Not just any equivalent would do, but only one that suited the "genuine sense" (p. 172) of the passage or context. Accordingly, Vossius several times makes the distinction between "ad verbum" (also "kata lexin" [Gk.], i.e., 'word for word' [p. 174] or "proprie" [e.g., pp. 32, 108, 109]) and "ad sensum" renderings. He was intensely conscious of the process of translation and of conveying the meaning of the original, remarking in one instance "ita enim haec transferenda sunt" (p. 92), where a euphemism had to be restated in order for it to make sense, or, in another, that a given word "vertendum est secundum Rabbinos . . ." (p. 170), where the scriptural meaning was at variance with later usage. Finally, Vossius weighs equivalent choices and states a preference for one, "quia simplicius videtur" (p. 152). The simpler of two meanings refers here to more than a question of style, really. It is, again, a substantive issue, and Vossius expresses here an overall preference that he often hints at elsewhere: for simplicity and clarity, but never at the expense of the variegated strength and grandeur of the Tacitean style.

In conveying the sense of the original, Vossius employed a vast reserve of vocabulary. He brought in extra words as the sense required and substituted a variety of particles for the simple connective in the Hebrew, giving expression to the different nuances contained therein. If he deemed his rendering open to dispute, he regularly took pains to supply the authority for a given translation. And yet, he regularly used alternative choices of vocabulary or different forms of expression when a previously used Hebrew word or phrase recurred. Even the simplest terms appear in multiple forms in Latin. *Mitsvah,* commandment, can be "praeceptum," "mandatum," "in mandatis est," or, in a periphrasis, "jubemur" (8:1, p. 85f.). Such conscious resorting to a variety of expression must be understood as more than a mere stylistic device. It did not destroy the clarity and faithfulness that Vossius strove for; it may even have enhanced it. Now one might object that, in a legal text such as this, a one–to–one correspondence in vocabulary between the original and the Latin might reasonably be expected. Yet the original was to appear on the printed page alongside the translation, and the edition was obviously intended for those with at least some knowledge of Hebrew—the quantity of Hebrew in the annotations helps reinforce this view. Also, this variety does not appear to have conflicted with Vossius's ideal of simplicity; it was simplicity for which his translation of Reyd's history had been praised, and it was undoubtedly simplicity to which he was referring when he wrote, in true humanist fashion, "aequanda factis dicta," that the style and the substance must be of the same order. If such variegation, then, in the texture of the translation was seen to be the Latin form or style of diction best suited to a noble style in the Hebrew original—and Vossius had also referred in his Reyd preface to its "nobile argumentum"—then such a usage would appear to have gone beyond any routine meaning of the idea of simplicity. It would more nearly approach the idea of clear correspondence in design and in the character of the argumentation or rhetoric, which already begin to be substantive issues. Vossius's concern with understanding the Hebrew text manifests itself in his goal of turning Maimonides' clear, yet elevated prose into a suitably elegant and eloquent Latin.

Contemporary expectations about such translations and the success Vossius was seen to have attained are nowhere better expressed than in a letter Vossius's teacher, l'Empereur, wrote G. J. Vossius upon receiving a copy of the work. Having spoken first of the advantage and satisfaction ("utilitate & fructu") he derived from reading it, l'Empereur then continued:

> There are comparatively young men around who have made an effort and undertaken the same things as your son Dionysius. Is there anyone, though, who does not know the difference between stage money and genuine coins? The late Dionysius preserved and presented those things that somebody might not easily copy or express, when he rendered Maimonides' words and mode of expression with the clearest Latinity and with so much faithfulness that he did not leave out (as the philosophers say rather boldly, and so may we) the secondary meanings or connotations. Those who have undertaken the rendering of Oriental tongues in a "Western" one know how difficult this is. Moreover, he has given all of us a copious demonstration of his great knowledge, in the very learned notes he appended to the individual paragraphs.[64]

Since Maimonides, as the elder Vossius wrote to Laud (and as Cunaeus had noted before him), "ille est, de quo Hebraei vulgatum illud dicere solent, à Mose usque ad Mosen non fuisse similem Mosi" ("is the one about whom the Hebrews commonly say, 'from Moses to Moses there was none like Moses'"),[65] he was the one chosen for Dionysius's first venture. Undoubtedly Menasseh had a hand in this choice, though there is no specific mention of this anywhere.

The method was fitted to Dionysius. His "luculento commentario" (Isaac [read: G. J.] Vossius's phrase) was supposed to "shed light on" or "illustrate" Maimonides, just as the Caesar commentary shed light on that author, with parallel *exempla*, rabbinical, ecclesiastical, or general. Characteristic are such statements as "Illustrantur haec verbis Rasi" (p. 171) or "haec non parum capient lucis ex iis quae disseruit . . . Grotius" (p. 139). Also, just as the stimulus for the *Conciliator* translation had been "ut etiam Rabbinorum accederet auctoritas," 'that the authority of the rabbis be brought to bear' (as G. J. Vossius had then written), so too here, in an area like that of his father's work, "quod inter disciplinas liberales ac theologiam quasi medium intercedit," that is midway between the liberal arts and theology, so to speak. (This last remark is surely Isaac Vossius's, from the preface to the 1700 edition of *De Theologia Gentili.*) All in all, the method was suitable to the goal of illumination. As G. J. Vossius said of his own work, not only "externi scriptores," but even the "theologi antiqui" would be illustrated and illuminated. So too, as a result, would be the "Scripturae Sacrae."[66]

The Sources of the Commentary: Rabbinic and General

Dionysius drew on a broad range of sources in pursuing his goal. The *Conciliator* had been a big help in this regard, not merely enhancing his fund of rabbinic knowledge, but probably giving Dionysius his initial exposure to many of the authors, titles, and themes in the Jewish literary storehouse. This can be seen, for example, in the fact that the only reference Dionysius makes to Joseph Albo's *'Ikkarim* parallels exactly the series of references used by Menasseh in one of his "reconciliations."[67] The contents of his book, the suggestions for building a library, and the general assistance Menasseh provided all led Dionysius to characterize his Jewish adviser as "[vir] in omni Hebraeorum eruditione versatissim[us]" 'a man most versed in all Hebrew learning' (p. 16).

Dionysius had other books at his disposal besides the *Conciliator*, however. To begin with, he must have a rabbinic Bible, one with a selection of rabbinic commentaries. Perhaps it was the elder Buxtorf's edition of 1618–19, one of the most readily available during Vossius's formative years. It may be pointed out, though, that, after the first two editions of the early sixteenth century, and prior to the eighteenth–century Amsterdam edition, all rabbinic Bibles had virtually the same selection of commentators for each of the individual books or parts.

Vossius makes some thirty references to rabbinic exegesis of Scripture, over and above his frequent use of the Targumim. He was most familiar with Rashi, Ibn Ezra, and David Kimḥi. His references to other exegetes are generally to those included in the Buxtorf edition. To take one instance, in considering the "Witch of Endor" passage in 1 Samuel 25, he refers to a comment by Gersonides, one of only three writers included there; the others were Rashi and Kimḥi.

To be sure, Vossius sometimes moves outside the rabbinic Bible. Naḥmanides and Abravanel, whom he invokes half a dozen times each, had a great popularity in separate editions of their own; so too did Baḥya ben Asher, whom Vossius uses twice.[68] Yet one of Vossius's references, to a comment by Naḥmanides on the Decalogue, comes right out of Question 104 of the *Conciliator*, or so it would appear (p. 29). And Abravanel, apart from his general *auctoritas* among Hebraists—compare l'Empereur's comment quoted above—had been the great–grandfather of Rachel Abarbanel, Menasseh ben Israel's wife, Menasseh taking immense personal pride in his connection to such noble lineage. Apart from this personal aspect, though, the *Conciliator* also made constant references to Abravanel. Menasseh's prior citation must have been responsible for at least some of the scriptural passages that Vossius addressed and, consequently, for some of the exegesis by Abravanel and others that he cited.

Yet Vossius could also go beyond the *Conciliator*. Menasseh had associated Gen. 4:26, "Tunc profanatum est in invocando nomine Dei" (or variations on this translation—the substance of Vossius's annotation is a determination of the meaning of the verse) with the opening statement of *Hilkhot 'Avodah Zarah*. So had others before him. Vossius too identified the verse as a possible support for Maimonides' view. Of interest to us is his use of a comment by Eliezer Ashkenazi on this verse. Menasseh had, in Question 21, merely invoked Ashkenazi's name along with those of other exegetes who held a certain view. Yet, while Vossius's sole reference to Ashkenazi is found in this note, his use of Ashkenazi is far more elaborate than Menasseh's. He cites Ashkenazi's disagreement with Rashi and Ashkenazi's criticism of the verse's being read as a reference to idolatry. Menasseh had made no mention of these issues. In fact, Vossius's use of this comment by Ashkenazi was part of a larger criticism of the overall rabbinic position on the origins of idolatry. Their view, says Vossius, had been adopted by "viros quosdam eruditissimos" who were writing about this time ("his annis," 'in recent years'); the question was obviously a live one, and their view of Gen. 4:26 was one to which Vossius did not entirely subscribe ("quibus non accedo"). In sum, Vossius was able to use Menasseh's references for his own purposes.

As for the biblical text itself and translations of it, Vossius was not bound to any one version. When Vossius copies Maimonides' quotation of Gen. 21:33 (1:8, p. 15), he copies Maimonides' error as well. including the name Abram that appears in similar wording in Gen. 13:4, but not in the verse quoted. The translation also follows Maimonides' text, except for the name, which appears in full, as Abraham. This interesting quirk shows to some extent that Vossius was not slavishly dependent on either Maimonides or another biblical version. Vossius was not unaware, however, of the many versions, both Greek and Latin, that existed. He was familiar with Origen's *Hexapla,* calling upon the Septuagint repeatedly and referring also to Aquila and Theodotion. He also examined more than one Latin version: in considering a certain usage in Jeremiah that parallels one of Maimonides' phrases, Vossius gives his own version and then, having mentioned the interpretations of Vatablé and Pagninus, provides the Septuagint version (accompanied by a Latin translation, as is his general procedure with all Greek words or quotations) and the Vulgate's rendering as well (12:1, p. 162). In this same comment, Vossius makes reference also to the interpretations of Lyra, Kimḥi, Rashi, the Targum (Chaldaeus), and to a similar understanding of the particular usage by Jerome. None of the more notable translations, to wit the Complutensian and Antwerp polyglots, the Latin versions of Vatablé, Pagninus, Münster, or even that of Tremellius and (Vossius's kinsman) Junius, corresponds in every instance to Vossius's renderings. The last named of these versions does stand out, however. Vossius was sometimes content to work from the Tremellius and Junius translation. Their Latin is often very sparse and literal, providing a good starting point: indeed, it sometimes reads almost like an interlinear translation. This type of translation would set the biblical quotation off, as it were, from Maimonides' own prose, which Vossius generally renders more *ad sensum* than *ad verbum*. Yet Vossius's rendering of Num. 15:30, "Anima quae commiserit elata manu . . . Iehovam blasphemat" (2:9, p. 31), shows a use of only part of the Tremellius version, the latter portion of the verse having been translated by Vossius to accord with Maimonides' discussion of the blasphemer.

Sometimes, Vossius even goes to the Tremellius version when rendering a biblical idiom that is not actually part of a quotation or proof–text. So, for example, Maimonides' "kevan she–'alah davar zeh 'al libbam" becomes "Postquam ascendit hoc verbum in animos eorum" (1:2 p. 5). In the Vulgate, the idiom "'alah 'al lev" is sometimes rendered "ascendere in cor." Tremellius had rendered the idiom as it appears in 2 Kings 12:5, "venerit in animum," noting in the margin that the literal meaning of the Hebrew is "ascendit in cor." Vossius picks and chooses, then, hardly feeling bound to the phrasing of those on whom he drew.

Moving on to classical literature, we find that Vossius cited more than sixty different writers, in almost every genre, many of them more than once. His wide reading had included poets and philosophers, rhetoricians, grammarians, and historians. He disparaged none of them for having been pagans, even if he does seem to have designated the "gentium scriptores" (p. 47) as a distinct category, alongside Christian and Jewish authors (see also p. 87*n*). Far and away Vossius's greatest favorite was Herodotus; he cites him some fifteen times by name. Virgil, Pliny the Elder, and Cicero among Latin authors, and Plutarch and Strabo among Greek ones are utilized half a dozen times or more each. Lucian's *De Syria Dea* is quoted four different times. Yet the pattern of citation is essentially random with respect to choice and frequency. The selection probably says as much about Vossius's freedom and broad knowledge as it does about his predilections. We should, therefore, not be at all surprised that Caesar and Tacitus are used a mere three times each and Ovid just twice. Vossius's reading was far wider than the individual number of citations shows. He could, therefore, at the end of a certain disquisition and with some assurance, make the generalized claim: "Quod probat satis Romana historia"

(p. 10), or note in passing: "Caesar certe tacet" (p. 7). Still, there are remarkable omissions or near omissions. Josephus appears but once, Lucretius, Catullus, and Juvenal not at all. Neither Plato nor Aristotle among philosophers, nor any of the great Greek dramatists is ever cited or mentioned. Some of this may reflect the predilections of the age. Yet Vossius's own training and interests tended to the historical and philological, where the heaviest emphasis lies. Even though there is a large admixture of poetry in the citations, the preponderance tends toward sources of practical information rather than toward belles–lettres or speculative literature. This emphasis was perfectly well suited to such a treatise as *'Avodah Zarah.* As we have noted earlier, this section of the *Mishneh Torah,* aside from any theoretical function it may have had, was also very much a practical manual, replete with details of ritual, custom, and institution.

Patristic literature is also well represented in the commentary. Vossius seems to have considered "SS. Patres" a distinct category also, lumping them together under this label on one occasion at least (p. 150). These figures were the biblical exegetes, the philosophers, historians, rhetoricians and polemicists of the early Christian church, men whose works often went beyond the confines of any one genre. Vossius moves easily from Clement to Tertullian, from Justin Martyr to Eusebius, and from Jerome to Augustine. In all, he mentions some two dozen writers, elucidating Maimonides via contrast or parallel to the practice or language of those whom he called also "veteres Christiani" (p. 86). As much as Vossius had, initially, considered a knowledge of rabbinic literature essential to the understanding of Christianity, so too did he view references to the Christian sources as indispensable for the explication of rabbinics.

Vossius was conversant with later scholarship as well. We may note in passing his familiarity with José de Acosta's work on the peoples of the Americas, one of the most popular books of the day; he mentions the work thrice. Not only does Vossius use the Arabic language, citing the Koran and the Arabic paraphrase of Scripture, he also cites Elmacinus's *History of the Saracens* (p. 116), the work of a Christian Arab of the thirteenth century that had been edited and translated into Latin by Erpenius, appearing posthumously in Leiden in 1625 in a bilingual edition. Vossius had also read Gonzalez de Mendoza on China and on Chinese religion in particular; this work, first published in 1585 in Valencia, had been translated out of the Spanish into many languages, including Latin, even before 1600.[69]

Vossius's familiarity with the issues of the day has already been suggested. Further evidence appears in his assigning the Hebrew vowel points to a date later than Jerome (3:12, pp. 49–50) and his asking, almost in passing, how those "doctores" who, "like the Jews, maintain that the vowel points came forth together with the Torah, have such self–assurance as to write down many different ones as well, in investigating the senses of Scripture." No real attack on either the rabbinic understanding of the proof–text "You shall not make with Me" (Exod. 20:22) or on Maimonides' use of it here is made by Vossius, though; he merely seems concerned to show how conversant he is with an important scholarly issue. In fact, he even supports the vocalization and cantillation assigned by the Masoretes, saying of the repetition of "Non facietis": "No one is unaware that repetition often adds effectiveness to a discourse." Incidentally, in defending this viewpoint, he had also quoted Ibn Ezra's dictum that any interpretation not according to the cantillation [or punctuation] ("she–eno 'al derekh hat–te'amim") should not be consented to or listened to.

There is ample evidence of Vossius's indebtedness to the great Hebraists of the day, including Scaliger, Selden, l'Empereur, and Coch. The last–named appears as "doctissimus Cochus" (pp. 81, 144, etc.). [On p. 81, incidentally, Vossius varies Coch's translation of a certain line, and, as a result, falls into error: "laterum," the genitive plural for *later,* 'brick', is switched to "ferentium," as if the root for *tollo* was at work here. This is undoubtedly the inadvertent product of a hasty transcription, for Vossius had included the original Aramaic text from *Sanhedrin* along with the word 'livna'.] On Coch's "eruditissimas . . . notas" (p. 33) Vossius drew heavily, though not uncritically. (See, e.g., pp. 57 & 171, for exceptions to Coch's views or scholarship.) Indeed, Coch's work had probably been central to Vossius's development. It had come into the Vossius household almost immediately upon publication, and Dionysius himself is reported to have borne a personal affection for the author.[70]

Several examples showing Vossius's use of Coch's *Sanhedrin* are in order. Vossius's version of the directive by the *musat* (the individual instigated to idolatry) to the *mesit* (the instigator) that the latter repeat what he had previously said to the *musat* in private, "emor mah she–amarta li be–yiḥud" (5:5, p. 67) [unbeknownst to the *mesit,* he was within earshot of concealed witnesses], is a case of partial indebtedness. The original locus of Maimonides' usage is *Sanhedrin* 7:10, "unde," Vossius comments, "haec, & priora omnia, ad verbum prope transcripsit autor [i.e., Maimonides]." The directive, says Vossius, had been reproduced verbatim from the Mishnah by Maimonides. In the overall account of the procedure, though, there is one discrepancy, and Vossius takes note of it; Maimonides places the witness "be–makom afel," 'in a dimly lit place', while the Mishnah has them "*aḥore hag–gader,* post parietem." The Latin in this rendering is Coch's. Yet Vossius's translation of the directive itself is entirely different from Coch's, except in one crucial respect. Both Coch and Vossius construe the adverbial "be–yiḥud" as belonging specifically to the main clause, whereas the Hebrew seems to leave the word dangling. The two translations are as follows:

Coch:

> Tum, qui ab ipso ad idololatriam invitatus fuerat, jubet eum repetere in secreto, quod ei dixerat. [p. 56]

Vossius:

> Deinde seductori, inquiet: *Dic age hîc seorsim mihi, quod ante retulisti.*

For "be–yiḥud," Coch uses "in secreto" to mean 'in private, without witnesses'; Vossius uses "hîc seorsim" as 'here separately' or 'in private', i.e., "Come tell me here in private what you proposed before." Both of these interpretations accord with those of Jewish Mishnaic commentators. Vossius's "ante" sounds close to the "kevar" in Bertinoro's paraphrase. (Coch also gives an alternative explanation: "Expressiùs, clariùs, apertiùs. . . . *be–verur*" [p. 65]. This too is found in the Jewish commentators, but Vossius does not pick it up.) Here, then, Vossius shows that he is not completely bound to Coch; rather, he determinedly shows his independence.

Sometimes Vossius calls specific attention to his use of Coch, if only to associate his own work with one so well received. From his remarks, though, the latent processes of his thinking become clear.

Vossius defends his choice of "gymnasium" for "yeshivah" (1:9, p. 17) by annotating (he uses Hebrew letters, not transliteration): "*yeshivah* Hebraeis est *makom she–yesh sham marbitse torah ve–talmidim rabbim, locus in quo sunt doctores legis & discipuli multi,* id est, Academia, aut gymnasium" (p. 18). This is followed by some speculation on the origin of the term: "The name undoubtedly arose out of a custom of the Orient, where, even today, they are wont to teach and learn sitting down together on the ground; from this the Arabs [take their term] *maqāmat, 'consessus'* ('assemblies, sittings down together'). . . ." Here Vossius cites Hariri's famous work as an example of the use of the term in Arabic. Regardless of the merits of the etymology, it is part of Vossius's fascination with the term, and this derives from Coch. For Vossius continues with a Hebrew parallel that he would develop further in another annotation later on: "ba'al hay–yeshivah & rosh hay–yeshivah, 'teacher' [*doctor*], whom the *Hebraei* also call *marbitse torah,* in a phrase derived from the same custom, because *they make* (sc. people) *recline to listen to the law.*" It is this view of the origin of *marbitse torah* that is partly indebted to Coch, "cui multum linguae hujus studiosi debent," and partly to de' Pomis (3:9, p. 46). In this latter note, Vossius cites both of these in his attempt to explain the term *'merabets'*, which Maimonides took from *Sanh.* 7:6, as Vossius notes. Coch, writes Vossius, had rendered this "*collocat,* id est, ponit in loco iis destinato: respiciens credo ad Hebraeum *rvts,* quod *cubare* (i.e., 'to lie down') est, aut [ad] usum Rabbinicum ejus vocabuli: quo doctores legem praelegentes, vocantur *marbitse torah.* Sed illa interpretatio huic loco minus videtur apta." Vossius understood exactly what Coch had done. Coch had confused the several uses of *rvts.* But Vossius himself was caught up by Coch's definition. Even though in this instance ("huic loco") Vossius "preferred" to translate "*aquam effundit;* praeeunte Davide de Pomis, qui *rvts* interpretatur, *pizzer mayim bab–bayit* [:] *effudit aquam per domum,*" his derivation of *marbitse torah* should also have had recourse to de' Pomis's basic definition. Vossius had gotten one up on Coch, but, in the process, had also been led astray.

For the most part, though, his understandings are his own and are the result of his own efforts after leaving the original source behind. Maimonides had stated (4:9, p. 60): "If a caravan that travels from place to place passed through a seduced city and was seduced with it, if [the caravan] remained thirty days, they are killed by the sword and their property is confiscated. And if not [Vossius: "Sin tantam in ea moram non traxerint"], they are stoned and their property passes to their heirs." For the Hebrew "sheyarah," the group as a whole, Vossius substitutes "peregrinantes," the persons, i.e., the individual wanderers, foreigners, or sojourners. In his note, Vossius first comments that, "ad verbum," the translation is "turba iter facientium." He then remarks on the military sense, 'convoy', that de' Pomis had given, on the Chaldaean equivalent, and even on the Arabic "caravana."[71] Yet Maimonides, he continues, "is interpreting 'the ass–drivers and camel–drivers who move from place to place save [the seduced city from destruction]'." This is a quotation of *Sanh.* 11:5, with part of Coch's version retranslated. Now the *Kesef Mishneh* had quoted this source also, along with Rashi's interpretation of it to the effect that the caravan helps constitute a majority so that the seduced persons are judged as individuals. Vossius cites none of the rabbinic commentators by name, though he expands on them considerably. As for Coch, his note here had been extremely brief; he commented that, if the travellers had remained in the city thirty days, they are accounted inhabitants. Vossius first explains that, if they stay thirty days and are thus accounted inhabitants, they can be of sufficient help to free the city from destruction—this is already more than Coch had said—because they then contribute to the creation of a new majority of righteous inhabitants; this parallels Rashi's explanation. Then Vossius goes on: "Verum alia est quaestio, de qua Maimonides hic agit." The issue is one of seduced travelers (not of those who are righteous): "Loquitur enim de peregrinantibus seductis." Vossius's goal here is to show the simple meaning of the halakhah, as Maimonides had stated it, not to encumber it with other issues. He therefore explicitly distinguishes the halakhah from its source in *Sanhedrin* in this way, and concludes with a straightforward restatement of the Maimonidean text. Though Vossius had derived some of his information from others, he showed himself able to see through the smokescreen they had unwittingly put up.

To turn to other authorities on whom Vossius drew, l'Empereur, who taught him Hebrew, rates mention as "vir ut genere, animi integritate, doctrinaque egregius, ita praeclare de Hebraeis literis meritus" (p. 85). Surely this says something about Vossius's own aspirations also, considering what we have seen of l'Empereur's tendencies, even though the tone of Vossius's commentary was far different from his teacher's and much closer to Coch's. As for Grotius, he was, in Dionysius's words and, surely, in the opinion of many, "vir nobilis atque eximium seculi decus," the "pride of the age," and, perhaps as a further measure of Vossius's own aspirations, "divinarum humanarumque literarum scientissimus" (p. 79). And we must, again, not fail to note how crucial G. J. Vossius's works were in giving direction to his son; at one point, Dionysius decides: "Sed potius paterno more premam in isto etiam veterum vestigia" (p. 38). If his father had been a prime stimulus to Dionysius's study of the ancients, Dionysius, in turn, sent the reader to his father's works half a dozen times. Finally, his grandfather Junius's wisdom and piety were also a source of insight for Dionysius. He borrowed from the *Analysis in Genesin* twice, fulfilling thereby, in small measure at least, his father's express hope that their grandfather be a model for his children.[72]

Aside from what could be derived via other Hebraists, Vossius took comparatively little from rabbinic literature directly. Though he showed himself able to handle what he came upon or had recourse to only by chance, there was virtually nothing, in real terms, to which he was able to turn with real ease and independently. There are a mere seven references to the various Midrashim, and two of these are to the hermeneutical rules of R. Ishmael. Of the rest, at least one and probably all five are also mentioned by Menasseh in the *Conciliator;* the story of Abraham's being thrown into the furnace by Nimrod is alluded to by Menasseh in Question 15 with a reference to "Rabot," among other sources for this piece of aggadah. On the other hand, Vossius also searched the story out and gave a fine eighteen–line summary of it, showing his ability to read and comprehend, once put on the right track.

Vossius made only two specific references to halakhic works other than the *Mishneh Torah* itself, though he used the rabbinic commentaries on Maimonides printed in the folio editions and though he paid quite a bit of attention to halakhic matters. The only other works cited by name—the "arms bearers" are never referred to by name or title—are the *Shulḥan 'Arukh,* "Hilkhot Mekaḥ u–Mimkar," probably followed up from a reference to the

Turim in the margin of the 1614 Venice edition (Vossius, p. 90), and the anonymous *Kol Bo,* perhaps via some reference in the *Bet Yosef* on the *Turim* (Vossius, p. 108). Out of the many references in the margin of the 1614 Venice edition, these seem almost gratuitous choices. Among philosophers, aside from the aforementioned citations of Albo, at least the first of two references to Maimonides' *Guide* (Vossius, pp. 29 & 164) also comes from the *Conciliator.* In this instance, Vossius merely reproduces Menasseh's brief paraphrase of an idea from the *Guide* 1:36. This is in Question 104, which is devoted to idolatry, and from which, as we have also seen above,[73] Vossius undoubtedly learned a great deal. The second mention of the *Guide* is in a bibliographic context: it takes note of Maimonides' reference to *Sefer Tomtom.* That Buxtorf's translation of the *Guide* was on the bookshelf in the Vossius home we need not have any doubt; that Dionysius had done more than open the volume seems unlikely, though.

Indeed, Dionysius had hardly dipped into the remainder of the *Mishneh Torah* either. He had probably read *Sefer ham–Madda';* there are three references to *Hilkhot Yesode hat–Torah* and four to *Hilkhot Teshuvah.* The rest of the code seems to have been almost a closed book to him. There are just two cross–references to anything outside of *Sefer ham–Madda'.* One is to *Hilkhot Mekhirah* (Vossius, p. 91) and one (Vossius, p. 14) to *Hilkhot Issure Biah.* The latter appears in tandem with the reference to the *Shulḥan 'Arukh,* but it is taken out of *Kesef Mishneh.* There are, furthermore, two references to Maimonides' *Commentary on the Mishnah;* these, too, could easily have been followed up from references to the Mishnah in Karo's *Kesef Mishneh.* Vossius knew, in other words, how to use the materials to which he had been led, but he seems to have had little independent knowledge of them beforehand.

A great help to him, as it had been to Coch, was David de' Pomis's dictionary *Tsemaḥ David,* published in 1587. Vossius drew on de' Pomis twenty–six times; he drew on the *'Arukh* of Nathan b. Yeḥiel only three times, and, in these instances, the quotations were to be found in the margins of the Venice edition of 1614. We can only assume that Vossius had other lexicons at his disposal also. Buxtorf's *Lexicon Hebraicum et Chaldaicum* had had its third and fourth editions in Basel in 1621 and 1631, and there were numerous other lexicons to be had as well. (In at least one instance [p. 75, on the *ov*], Vossius can be seen not to have used Buxtorf.) To be sure, Vossius makes no reference to anyone besides de' Pomis, though there were many standard works of the day that must have been in his father's possession. Yet the advantage of the de' Pomis dictionary, which had been recommended by Coch, was that Vossius could quote both the Hebrew and the Latin directly. Vossius also used Kimḥi's *Sefer hash–Shorashim* once, contrasting its explanation favorably with one advanced by "Grammaticorum filii," i.e., the epigoni. The usefulness of all these works for someone in Vossius's situation can hardly be underestimated.

Of the greatest importance, though, were the printed editions of the *Mishneh Torah* from which Vossius worked and created his text. The commentators printed alongside the master provided explanations and elaborations of some of the problems internal to the halakhic context of the work. The single most important function they served, though, was as Vossius's guides to Maimonides' use of the Talmud. Vossius makes reference to some sixteen different talmudic tractates, the vast majority of his references having been made previously by one or more of the Jewish commentators. Vossius does not, even once, acknowledge the Jewish commentators. This has already been adverted to and it bears repeating. The single tractate to which Vossius refers most often, some twenty–five times, in fact, is *Sanhedrin*. Even before Menasseh had come on the scene, works such as Coch's had opened the world of the Talmud up before him, making it easier for him to follow the rabbinic commentaries on Maimonides that Menasseh would bring to his attention. Dionysius ultimately felt quite confident in his rabbinic learning, in fact, referring often to "Talmudici," "Hebraei," "Judaei," or "Rabbini," and making generalizations about their views, just as he did about secular subjects. The foregoing designations, by the way, appear to refer to somewhat distinct groups, but the lines often seem blurred.

Vossius does appear to have read some talmudic tractates on his own; he refers extensively to *'Avodah Zarah,* going beyond the Jewish commentators on Maimonides at times, in the detail and even in the specific reference. Vossius also makes four separate references to *Avot.* He even stops to quote (p. 19) [as always, with accompanying translation], a comment of Joseph Ḥayyun's (d. 1497) on *Avot* 1:3 ("Qui coronae servito utitur, peribit, *be–taga ḥalaf*"). In order to explain "Cur Lex *taga,* id est, *corona,* vocetur," Vossius quotes the gist of Ḥayyun's comment: "Just as a mortal king places a crown of gold on his head, so the Law is a crown for the blessed God." Vossius then continues: "I should prefer, following Maimonides' example, if he had called the Law not the crown of God, but of Israel." The lemma here is "Praeceptis coronavit," 'crowned them with the commandments'. This low–keyed, yet adverse reaction to such a close association of the commandments with God is probably a reflection of some reading that Vossius had once done that now came to mind when reading Maimonides. *Avot* may have been one of the earliest rabbinic books he studied, and it seems likely that he did it with Ḥayyun's commentary at hand.[74]

From the Hebrew text printed in the *De Idololatria* it is possible to determine which editions Vossius used in constructing his text and, consequently, which commentaries he had available. First of all, while there is no evidence that Vossius worked with any manuscripts in constructing this text, as he had in his Caesar, and while there is certainly no *apparatus criticus,* it is still clear that Vossius attempted to be a textual critic even here in his Maimonides. He worked from at least three printed editions, it seems, using the 1614 Venice edition as the basic one. Though several variations appear to be his own—Vossius, as we already know about his technique in translation, often sought variety for its own sake, the changes he made often being of no real consequence—most of his readings have prior authority. The paragraphing scheme he used is found in both the Venice 1614 and the Mantua 1565 editions (also the Mantua 1587–92, essentially a reprint of the earlier one); a specific mention of the Venice edition on p. 101, however, and a number of other discrepancies eliminate the Mantua editions as likely sources. Vossius's annotation: "I have filled in a few words from *Veneta major* that were lacking, *typographi culpa,* in *Veneta minor.*" The only Venice edition in which the words in question are lacking is the 1614; like the two Mantua editions, it is a "smaller" one, containing only the first three books of the *Mishneh Torah.* The "larger" edition to which Vossius must be referring is one of the two complete editions in folio published in Venice in 1550–51. Now a 1550–51 edition—it is not certain which one; perhaps it is both—was subsequently referred to by Carpzov, one of Vossius's readers, as "major," even though Carpzov refers to the 1574 edition as "minor," and to both editions as folios.[75] At any rate, in the 1574 edition, part of the text that appears in the 1614 and the 1550 editions is lacking, even though the supplemented words are present. Moreover, the text that Vossius has reconstructed is more complete than any found in a rabbinic edition. Yet some of the other readings in Vossius's text, ones he did not deem worthy of annotation, are peculiar to the two 1550 editions, and there is no significant reading that Vossius's text shares with the 1574 edition. (This latter edition contains an inferior text, in any case, over and above the distortions brought about by the censor.) Vossius showed good judgment, as it were, in rejecting the text of this edition, even though he had it at his disposal; he did have recourse to the *Kesef Mishneh,* we have seen, and this commentary had made its debut in that edition. And so, while the 1614 edition is hardly of a higher textual caliber than its immediate predecessor, Vossius obviously found it convenient to work from in establishing a basic text. Its comments were confined to the margins, the text almost filling the page. This too may have been a factor in Vossius's preference. Most important, though, was probably Menasseh's endorsement of the volume on the basis of its use in the Jewish schools. Yet, finally, Vossius appears to have chosen his readings at random; no general pattern or motive can be discerned in his preferences for one reading or another. If anything, he relied on his own evaluation and understanding of the author's intentions, much as he had done in his Caesar.

At Vossius's disposal, then, both for constructing and understanding the text, were many of the standard commentaries on the *Mishneh Torah.* From the larger editions, Vossius had and used the *Haggahot Maimoniyyot,* the *Migdal 'Oz,* and the *Kesef Mishneh.* He also seems to have had the *Leḥem Mishneh,* which had appeared initially in a separate edition in Venice in 1609. The only credit he gives any of these is as "Hebraei." Though he also had Rabad of Posquières's "Hassagot" available, he does not refer to them even once. Also, if he used the "Mafteaḥ" to the *Mishneh Torah* printed in the 1574 edition, he gives no indication of it.

He did, however, draw directly on the marginalia of the 1614 Venice edition. His discussion of the age at which Abraham came to know God is but one such instance. The marginal note in the Venice edition remarks that Maimonides "struck a compromise (*hittil pesher*) between the opinion of Resh Lakish, who considered it to have taken place when Abraham was three, and that of R. Yoḥanan and R. Ḥanina, who both assigned it to Abraham's forty–eighth year, saying that [Abraham] began to search at the age of three, and at forty–eight—all the texts at Vossius's disposal read "forty–eight," except for the 1574 Venice, which reads "forty"—he verified the matter and came to know the truth with certainty." Vossius abbreviates this, distinguishing the position of Resh Lakish from that of "alii," but then he continues: "Yet our Maimonides reconciles these views. For, at the beginning of this section, he declares that Abraham, when he was very little, began to waver in the faith of his elders and, more and more, to hold idolatry in suspicion. But, at the end of the section, he informs [us] that Abraham was wholly confirmed in the correct belief (*in fide recta*) in such a way that, from then on, he always clung to the true God alone." To this point, Vossius's elaboration on the marginal comment in the Venice 1614.[76] (It should be noted that there is no source reference in this edition to the talmudic discussion at *Nedarim* 32; Vossius cites this source, though, as "in Gemara Nedarim sub finem," following through *Haggahot Maimoniyyot*'s reference to "shilhe Nedarim.") Now Vossius continues, in a way characteristic of his mode of thought, asking where the rabbis had figured out ("exsculpserint") that this happened when Abraham was forty–eight, "since Scripture nowhere says [this]." And he answers that "there is no better place this can be learned than from Isaac Abravanel's *Commentary on the Law.*" He finds Abravanel's chronological reckoning, which dated Abraham's forty–eighth year to the confusion of tongues at the Tower of Babel, most satisfactory, even though he recognizes that other chronologers came to different conclusions. Vossius is also convinced by the idea that the miracle at Babel confirmed Abraham's belief, but he says that "this is not the place to calculate out (*disputare*) whether the confusion of tongues happened in Abraham's forty–eighth year." He leaves matters at a standstill, therefore, but it is clear that the original stimulus to his deliberation on this question was the marginal note in the 1614 Venice edition.

He used this edition in other ways as well. He drew on its citations of the *'Arukh,* on its scriptural and talmudic references, and, perhaps, on the abundant references in the margins to the *Turim,* though he never refers to this code by name. Yet he was also capable of suggesting sources other than those indicated in these marginalia. For Abraham's transmission of his teaching to Isaac and Jacob, he offers (1:9, p. 18) Gen. 13:19, which, if it seems obvious, is not mentioned by any of the Hebrew commentators. Vossius quotes it, incidentally, in the Tremellius version, except that he substituted "Domini" for "Jehovae." He states that "Maimonides . . . appears to have inferred what he says" from this verse, suggesting that the source reference was probably his own surmise and specifically directed at his non–Jewish audience to help promote their understanding of Maimonides.

Vossius did not have to contend with any censor in establishing his text. While he used the phrase *'Avodat Kokhavim u–Mazzalot* as the general term for idolatry, he also used *'Avodah Zarah* almost interchangeably with it. The 1550 editions have the latter term, while the subsequent ones, including the 1614, have the former, the one mandated by censorship. Vossius knew that the latter form was the title of the talmudic tractate, yet he deemed the term *'Akkum* to be more precise, because the Jews had attributed the origins of idolatry to the worship of stars and planets (p. 2, the note on the title). Vossius also used the term *goy,* which he often translated as "gentilis," rather than any of its substitutes; he never used *kuti,* the reading imposed in the 1614 edition, and only rarely did he substitute *'akkum* as an alternative term for 'gentile'. He never used *mumar;* the term for an apostate was always *meshummad,* the noncensored form, though in one cross–reference to *Hilkhot Teshuvah* 3:17, he used *'avaryan,* while other editions varied (p. 30). Vossius used *yerid,* the expurgated form, never *tarfut,* though both his translation, by expressing the sense of the original as "nundinae idololatrarum" (p. 135) [more frequently it was "nundinae gentilium" (pp. 133, 136)], and his comment here, with its description of a *yerid* (p. 133), appear to be in defense of his textual reading. He alternated randomly between *komer* and *kohen.* Though he most often used *min* and *minut* for 'heretic' and 'heresy,' he sometimes resorted to *epikoros,* devoting a long note, in fact, to the meaning and legitimacy of the term (p. 26f.; see below). Lastly, Vossius omits the famous passage at 9:4, which, in unexpurgated editions, specified that *Edomim* (a euphemism: most of the manuscripts actually read "Notsrim," 'Christians'), whose holiday is Sunday, are idolators and that business should not be carried on with them on the three days prior. This paragraph appears in the 1550 editions, but not in subsequent ones. Vossius may have omitted it as not fitting in with the enumeration of the paragraphs that he had carried over from the 1614 Venice edition, or his editors, that is to say, his brother Isaac, who, along with his father, submitted it for publication, may have done so, having been offended by the statement. Most probably, Dionysius himself omitted it deliberately, in consonance with his policy in the *Conciliator* of omitting things too painful for Christian ears. Even if he himself may have been able to exercise detachment and dismiss the remarks more casually, he was undoubtedly inclined to be wary in his readers' behalf, in order to insure the credibility and acceptability of the work. This one paragraph could change the character and implications of the entire treatise in the minds of Christian readers. Dionysius obviously considered the work informative and authoritative. Wishing to impart this conception to his readers, he chose not to include this halakhah in his edition, despite his having seen it in earlier ones. Ironically enough, though, the *De Idololatria* still found its way into the *Index Librorum Prohibitorum,* probably because of Vossius's having used the term *'Avodah Zarah,* which the Roman censors themselves identified as a reference to Christianity.[77]

This, then, is the text Vossius translated and commented upon, linking the translation and the commentary in a tight nexus. There are quite a few different types of comment, ranging from the lexical to the homiletic and covering topics legal, philosophical, historical, and religious. Often the comments bring support for Maimonides' statements; from time to time, they criticize rabbinic teaching, but this is not widespread. Vossius offers explanations for novices and displays his own erudition for the cognoscenti. Still, even if he regularly makes personal judgments, his commentary is, by design, an illustrative rather than a polemical one. Having described the genesis of the commentary, we now turn to an examination of the work itself as it exists. Vossius's dispassionate treatment of Maimonides is what probably earned him Menasseh's support, and it is this that we wish to demonstrate as we proceed.

Lexical Annotations

The most basic type of comment Vossius makes is the lexical one where he defines specific terms. Not all such explanations are advanced in the notes, though, or are even seen to require annotation; they can often be derived directly from the translation. This is true especially for *termini technici.* "Gufe torah" are rendered "potissima legis capita" (2:8 p. 29); "safek sefekah," in the line "safek 'avodat kum asur; safek sefekah muttar" (8:14, p. 97), becomes "Ea, quae suspicio est ad idololatricum cultum pertinere, prohibita sunt. Sed licita, de quibus suspicio est, ea ad illud pertinere, de quo suspicio est." Vossius leaves this translation unannotated. "Ha–avanim ham–mefutsalot" (8:9 & 11, p. 83) are "lapidibus glabris, effigiem nullam habentibus" (Halakhah 11 has this in the singular). Though this enters into the specifics of the halakhic issue, Vossius makes no comment here either. But, when he finds a piece of medical terminology such as "'ad she–yippol nikhpeh" (6:3, p. 77) not used in its actual clinical sense by Maimonides, he translates "donec fiat mente commotus," following this with a note to the effect that, while he understands (via David de' Pomis) that the basic meaning of 'nikhpeh' is 'epilepsy', "*morbus . . . quo cadit homo in terram cum furore* . . . Hic tamen pro *mania* (Gk. is used) seu *furore vatum* accipio; unde & *manteis* (Gk.) Graecis nuncupati sunt." The connection to prophecy is thus emphasized and Vossius has had an opportunity to display his familiarity with the classical institutions.

Vossius also pays attention to the "phrasis," the idiomatic expression. He renders the hermeneutical principle "kal va–ḥomer" as "quanto minus" (p. 141) and annotates with the observation that the Hebrew corresponds ("respondet") to that Latin "phrasis," even though the words are literally to be rendered "*leve, & grave.*" He further explains the meaning of the Hebrew as designating an "argumentum à minori ad majus, aut contra."

In yet another instance, after rendering the idiomatic "ve–en tsarikh lomar" verbatim as "nec dicere opus," Vossius notes that this is a "phrasis rabbinica, quam Latinè expresseris: *Manifestius est, quam ut admoneri oporteat:* vel, *Hinc, utut non dicatur, sequi quisque videt,* & c." (p. 94).

Differences between cultures in patterns of expression and implications of terms are sometimes bridged not by Hebraizing the Latin, but by Romanizing the context instead. Having used *dijudico* for *la–dun* (2:5, p. 26), but *disputo* for the expression "la–'arokh din" (1:7, p. 14), Vossius feels the need to clarify further: "Et disputare cum iis. *'arakh din* Hebraeis est *disputare, litem movere. ba'ale had–din partes quae contendunt.* at *'orekhe had–dayyanim advocati*" (p. 14*n*). This definition points both to the juridical context and implications of the original Hebrew and to the juridical nuance intended by "disputare." But Vossius does not always maintain consistency. When the expression "la–'arokh din" recurs in a later chapter (5:9, p. 70) as "la–'arokh din u–teshuvah," Vossius uses only *disputo* by itself, masking the fact that, in the former instance, where the whole had read, "le–hashiv teshuvot 'al bene ur kasdim ve–la'arokh din 'immahem," he had translated the first phrase "reddere responsa," an expression with both a juridical significance of its own and an application in Roman law. In the latter case, which specifically recalls the former, Vossius did not translate the additional word "teshuvah" at all. (Compare also "respondere" for "le–hashiv teshuvah" [2:8, p. 29].) Sometimes, then, even if Vossius's annotation seems to stress the specific function of a word or phrase, his translation of other, later appearances of that word or phrase is rather casual.

Still, Vossius devotes much space to distinguishing between several meanings or implications of Hebrew words, especially when he has resorted to variety in his translation. Let us take, for example, his treatment of "le–hishtaḥavot," 'to bow down'. Maimonides' initial use of the term contrasts physical with verbal adoration; Vossius employs "se incurvare" (1:2, p. 6; see also 3:3–4, p. 40). Subsequently, where it is a question of idolators having made an idol "kede le–hishtaḥavot lah kol ha–'am," Vossius translates "quod ab omnibus adoraretur" (1:3, p. 7); later, though, when the sense may require it, he also uses *adoro* again or *se prosterno.* All these differences exist, Vossius's note (p. 6) implies, because of differences between the respective types and stages of "cultus": "Is fuit adoratio, quam Hebraei voce *hishtaḥavah* designant . . . maximus *hishtaḥavayah* id est, *proskynesis* & minor, osculatio manus." He firms this up with a reference to Herodotus: "Tradit, ni fallor, Herodotus, Orientis morem fuisse, ut aequales in occursu invicem osculum darent; qui humillimi, *sese incurvarent* [italics mine]." There were various kinds of obeisance, and the verbal distinctions between them had an importance for Vossius. Vossius was expressly interested, in fact, in how Maimonides used words: "Nam verbi *'avad* natura apud Hebraeos tam late extenditur, quam apud Graecos *douleuein* & *latreuein:* utrumque enim & generatim pro honore, etiam civili, & adstricta magis notione pro divino sumitur. . . . Maimonides sua definitione non tantum sese complecti ait eos, qui creaturis cultum exhibent ut Deo; verum & qui iis supplicant ut ministris Dei" (2:1, p. 20). These remarks contribute to the definition of both word and topic as a whole.

Vossius also comments on such things as: the euphemism "barekh" (p. 32), giving corresponding examples from elsewhere; the term "zakhah" (p. 60): "est *mereri, dignum esse, axion einai.* Utuntur autem hac voce, quia laudabile videtur studium ejus, qui mox à lata sententia irruit in facultates eorum qui apostatae esse credebantur," showing that the annotations were not to be seen as merely attempts at lexicography, but as part of the entire process of elucidation.

He demonstrates this more clearly in applying the Talmud's definition of "mesit" and "madiaḥ" (5:1, p. 65) to explain the terms both as they appear in Maimonides and as he, Vossius, has translated them, the one term as "seductor," the second as "impulsor." The translation of the following halakhah puts this into perspective: "Qui seducit majorem civitatis partem, ille est MADIACH, sive impulsor; neque vocatur MESSIT, sive seductor." This is what Vossius must have meant when he annotated the first halakhah by saying: "Quod planius ex sequentibus fiet."

Sometimes, Vossius adds etymological investigations to such discussions. Maimonides himself had distinguished between the two different kinds of altars (8:19, pp. 120–21). These are, respectively, a "mizbeaḥ" and a "bimos." The words are used independently by Maimonides, though, before he makes his distinction. At that point, Vossius translates: "misbeah sive altare . . . bimos, sive ara." Then he translates the distinction itself: "Qualis verò *bimos?* quale item *misbeah? Bimos* est unius lapidis: *misbeah* est lapidum multorum." Vossius obviously felt that the distinction between *'altare'* and *'ara'* in Latin was not strong enough in this context. Moreover, in his note, Vossius restates what Maimonides had said, conjecturing that *bimos* "is undoubtedly of Greek origin out of *bomos,*" and expressing surprise that this was the word used to denote an altar of one stone ("aram ex uno saxo factam"), "although I would not deny that the gentiles had such altars" ("aras"). The etymology having created a problem, Vossius resorts to de' Pomis's definition of the word *'bimos': "even nigzar la–'asot elil o mizbaḥ elilim* Lapidem incusum ad faciendum idolum, aut aram idolorum." Vossius can now remark on the halakhic meaning of the distinction: "for that reason, an altar (*ara*) of one stone is permitted, if shattered (*disrupta* [the Hebrew is: "she–nifgam," 'damaged']), because it is thus defined; but an altar (*altare*) of many stones remains an altar, unless the greater part of the stones has been forcibly torn away." The etymology and the pagan practice are part of the cultural information that Vossius wishes to convey. The fact that that stone was expressly cut for idolatry is significant for understanding the halakhah.

The weight often comes to rest on display, though. On "matrin u–me'idin" (4:6, p. 57), part of the discussion of the admonition given to the citizens of a seduced city, the etymology is hardly integrated; it appears to be more an opportunity for Vossius to counter Coch's view that *hitrah* comes from *torah* with the suggestion that it comes from *raah*—whether or not this is correct is beside the point—and that it is more closely associated with *hatraah*.

Vossius can make effective use, though, of the study of word origins as a clue to the root of a practice, and that, after all, was his prime interest. On the opening halakhah of chapter 9, Vossius begins (p. 123) by listing the "festa gentilium idola colentium" as per Mishnah *'Avodah Zarah* 1:3. The phrase in question is *yom genusia*. Vossius cites the opinion of R. Judah that it is the day of the king's investiture. "I do not accept this," he continues, "unless *genusia* and *kenusia* are the same, and denote a gathering." For Maimonides, he says, in Halakhah 4 of this chapter, considered a "dies inauguralis" to be *"dies, quo congregatur ad creandum Regem,"* which would tend to support the association of the two words. But Vossius adopts an independent stance here too: "Mihi tamen haec vox merè Graeca videtur, nam *genesia* diem notant natalitium. . . ." This creates problems, as Vossius recognizes: "Quod si quis quaerat, cur mox subjungatur *yom hal–ledah, dies natalis:* dixero, prius accipiendum videri de genethliis principis; alterum de privatorum quae privatim celebrantur." There is a link between etymology and interpretation in Vossius's mind, even though he himself would probably have deemed his own conclusions suppositious from time to time. He betrays, as a matter of fact, a certain modesty: "Interea metuo, nequid horum vera sit nominis causa" (11:11, p. 155). He did not regard his judgments as infallible.

Generally, these etymologies are subordinated to the larger effort or aim, *explication de texte.* Vossius's restatements of Maimonides' words appear under numerous headings, including: "mens" (the 'meaning' or 'view'), "sententia" (the 'thought' or 'purport', as well as the 'opinion'), "significatio," "interpretatio," and so on, all of which deal with the basic "intelligentia" or 'understanding' of the specific words of the passage ("quae ad intelligentiam hujus paragraphi pertinent" [3:13, p. 51]). This is reflected most simply in Vossius's remark that *Idololatria* is the "vis verborum," the 'force of the words' "'avodat kokhavim u–mazzalot," which, if translated precisely ("kata poda" [Gk.]) mean ("sonent") *cultus stellarum ac planetarum* (p. 2). This is only the beginning of a much larger comment on title and usage.

More integrated, though, is the following, on the phrase "harḥakah yeterah hi" (6:13, pp. 84–85). The issue here is the prohibition of a wooden portico in the temple, even though it is clear that this would not be a planted tree like an *asherah.* Vossius's note distinguishes between the literal meaning of the words and the thought ("mens") behind them, concluding with the observation that all this was so that one might not come to do something illicit. Therefore, he says, the *Hebraei* order people to abstain even from some things that are "per se licita," in accordance with the dictum in *Avot,* "sepem facite pro lege," by which, he says, they mean "traditionibus . . . quae legis transgressione hominem arcent."

Even in this kind of context, Vossius manages to take issue with Coch. On the examination of a witness (2:11, p. 33), Vossius notes that the source of the Maimonidean statement is *Sanh.* [7]:5. "Quo loco eruditissimus Cochus vertit, *Toto die.* Malim ex mente Maimonidae *singulis diebus.*" The text in *Sanhedrin* reads merely "be–khol yom"; in Maimonides it reads "be–khol yom va–yom." Though Vossius says he "prefers" to translate "according to Maimonides' understanding" of the procedure. he continues: "*badak* explorare, pervestigare, quid differat à *ḥikker* & *darash,* vide nunquam satis laudatas Cochi notas ad eundem locum." Vossius's praise is clearly at variance with his criticism. It is obviously also his own understanding of what took place in this procedure, and not Maimonides' alone that the young Vossius is explicating here.

His criticism of Coch is, again, a demonstration of his proficiency for his audience. Elsewhere, incidentally, Vossius is even more straightforward (p. 171): "Ut proinde minus videtur assecutus Hebraeorum mentem doctissimus Cochus, quando vertit . . ."

Vossius uses his notes to specify Maimonides' meaning, even if he does not always see the basis on which the halakhah rests: "I am not discussing whether or not this has any substance. It is undoubtedly, however, Maimonides' meaning." ("Solidene hoc dicatur, an minus, non disputo. Mentem quidem eam esse Maimonidae, minime dubitandum" [3:11, p. 48].) The issue here was the interpretation of a biblical proof–text, but this is the total extent of the criticism.

Somewhat of a different perspective is offered by Vossius's comment on the phrase "mish–shum evah," "odii caussa" (9:13, p. 135). Maimonides has specified that Jewish women may be midwives for hire to non–Jewish women, "on account of hatred." Vossius asks the meaning of this:

> Why may she be a midwife out of hatred? Is it because she will thus have the opportunity of destroying the foetus, or even the woman in childbirth, or the one in labor? I can hardly be convinced that Maimonides would have prescribed anything so detestable. Accordingly, the correct interpretation is that she can act as midwife on account of hatred, that is, in order to escape hatred. Or, lest hatred grow; yet, preferably, let her counter those who, if this service were denied, would hate [the Jews] more and do greater harm. I am not saying this as a favor to Maimonides; this is really what he meant (*sed re vera hanc ejus fuisse sententiam*); this is evident from the second section of the next chapter, where he states clearly that, if someone is afraid of those whose religion is different (*qui religionis sunt disparis* [Menasseh's use of this phrase will be recalled]), he may lend a helping hand medically in order to avoid hatred; not gratis however, but for payment.

Vossius defends Maimonides; the potential for suspicion of Maimonides' motivation lies not in Vossius, but in his readers, and Vossius heads it off with his claim that one must be fair to what was both said and implied or intended.

Indeed, comments such as "mens Maimonidae est" and "scriptoris nostri sententia est" abound; the foregoing are but a few unusual examples of them.

"Rationales" and the Line of Maimonides' Argumentation

Equally plentiful are the rationales Vossius offers for the various Maimonidean rulings and for the many practices and procedures he describes. The goal of such remarks is more homiletical, but they are invariably grounded in philology. Such devices as "ratio est," "causa," or "quia" (meaning 'the reason is', 'because', 'on account of') lead into either an explanation of Maimonides' reasoning or a justification for a given practice.

To explain why the judges are required to stand up when the words the blasphemer had uttered are repeated by him in testimony, Vossius says that this is for the judges to testify to their bristling indignation or, perhaps, out of respect at hearing the divine name (2:11, pp. 33–34). Or, to justify the prohibition against shaving off one's sideburns (12:1, p. 162), Vossius first specifies the nature of the pagan practice, with help from Herodotus and Jer. 9:26 (and the Jewish commentators thereon [compare Cunaeus's treatment of this verse]), and concludes: "The reason God forbade this is that he knew that the Israelites were prone to idolatry, and, the more they had in common with gentiles, the more easily they would go over to their practices (*tanto faciliùs in eorum instituta transituros*)." To explain Maimonides' having followed the more stringent opinion in requiring all the inhabitants of a town that had been condemned for idolatry ('led astray'), including its children and its animals, to be destroyed, Vossius reasons: "because the transgression of abandoning one's religion is so grave that God wants all memory of it to be abolished in order that it will come before others as an example and an object of dread" (4:6, p. 58). This explanation of Maimonides' preference for the view of R. Eliezer over that of R. Akiva is Vossius's own, though his citation of the source of the disagreement between the two Tannaim is probably indebted to the *Migdal 'Oz.*

Though none of these can be called particularly revolutionary in its interpretation, all are sympathetic understandings of the procedures or rulings and are specifically designed to defend Maimonides against criticism or to introduce readers to the rabbinic mode of thought. Even in commenting on the reason an idol of an Israelite is not prohibited until he has worshipped it, Vossius lets this come across: "The reason is because, as the author says, the [non–Jew] makes it his god immediately [when he creates an idol]; the Israelite not so. For he may be moved by repentance before worshipping it." An appreciation of "poenitentia" is crucial for any understanding of this treatise (considering the fact that it is followed in the Maimonidean order by one on this subject); Vossius calls attention to the concept, but by no means does he dwell on it.

Vossius's rationales are, in most cases, the result of his own ratiocination. They are also linked from time to time with corresponding examples in the issues of his own day. It was necessary for the members of the Sanhedrin to be well versed in the details of idolatrous practices, writes Vossius,

> lest they prosecute those who have delved too deeply into the secrets of nature on the charge of sorcery and impiety, as has happened too often in our century and earlier ones. The talmudists say: "'You shall not learn to perform the abominations of those nations' (Deut. 18:9). It is not permitted to learn in order that you may do; it is, in order that you may know."
>
> [3:2, pp. 39–40]

This paraphrase of a passage from TB *'Avodah Zarah* 18a (it appears elsewhere as well, including *Sanh.* 68a, which is not among the talmudic extracts Coch included in his edition of the Mishnah; the reference, in any case, is not identified by Vossius) is not invoked by any of the Jewish commentators. The only source reference, as a matter of fact, that Vossius provides here is one to "Gemara I. Cap. Sanhedrin" (corresponding to *Sanh.* 17a), on the qualifications for membership in the Sanhedrin: "Ait R. Iochanan, non adscisci in Synedrium, nisi praestantes statura, sapientia, forma, senectute, magiae, & septuaginta linguarum peritos." This source reference too, is Vossius's own, apparently (it is also cited by Saul Lieberman in the recent critical variorum edition); drawing a connection between expertise in "magia," 'sorcery', and the passage in TB *'Avodah Zarah,* he reveals something of his own consciousness as a member of a persecuted minority.

Criticism of Maimonides' rulings does crop up in this type of annotation, though, as well. Maimonides had written (7:16, p. 99) that it was permissible to sit in the shade of the leaves and branches of a tree under which an *asherah* had been placed, but that it was impermissible to sit in the shade of its trunk. Vossius traces this to

TB *'Avodah Zarah* 48b, most likely following the lead of the *Kesef Mishneh* and the *Migdal 'Oz.* He judges, though, that the prohibition "does not appear to rest on any weighty rationale." In light of the earlier statement by Maimonides that a flame lit in honor of an idol was permissible "*she–en bah mammash, quia substantia caret,* how much more, therefore, [should] the use of shade be permitted!" For shade, argues Vossius, unlike flame, has no bodily substance, but is merely a privation of light. This he supports with Virgil's words: "Prensantem nequicquam umbras" (*G.* 4. 501). It is a semiscientific disquisition, one that draws no polemical inferences. It is, at root, just as philological as any comment on Caesar.

In fact, this judgment is really just another in a series of comments that keeps the general line of Maimonides' argument before the reader by bringing all the various parts of the text to bear on one another. Vossius repeatedly calls attention to discrepancies and possible antitheses, and also to points of continuity. In order to clear up any apparent discrepancy between the halakhah prohibiting the reading of books on idolatry (2:3, pp. 24–25) and the (aforementioned) obligation of the members of the Sanhedrin to learn the details of idolatry, Vossius suggests that "Maimonides' words are to be [taken in a] restricted [sense]"; he quotes the latter requirement to show that the prohibition actually applies only to private individuals. Here, too, the cross–reference is Vossius's own.

Another one of his own is a comment on the halakhah (8:4, p. 109) that, if an Israelite set up a stone slab in order to worship it and then did not do so, and a gentile came and did, one may not derive any benefit, inasmuch as its having been erected was itself a [significant] act. [Vossius translated this last phrase "quoniam erectio ipsa opus est malum," adding a bit of interpretation himself.] The cross–references:

> Above, at 7:4, we have seen that the idols of the gentiles are said to be prohibited as soon as they have been finished, yet those of Israelites not before they have been worshipped. It may thus be asked, since the author has said in [Halakhah] 2 of this chapter that no one has the power to turn someone else's property from permitted [into] prohibited, why in this passage is a stone erected by an Israelite nonetheless said to be prohibited, even if only a gentile has worshipped it? The reason is that the Israelite appears to demonstrate to the gentile by the very act of erection that it was his will that [the stone] be worshipped.

This is Vossius at his most casuistic, attempting to reconcile discrepancies.

As for Vossius's concern with the general thrust of Maimonides' remarks, when Maimonides at his most intellectualistic prohibits all speculation on idolatry (2:4–5, pp. 25–26), lest it lead to doubt about certain fundamental propositions, such as the unity of God or the truth of prophecy or the Torah's having been revealed from Heaven, Vossius comments:

> Before this, the author was speaking about idolatry alone; now he passes on to the general commandment about impious thoughts of any kind and shows by what useless musings curious men are preoccupied. To wit: what is above the angels, what beneath the earth; what was before the world, and what will be after it. Since men cannot discover this (*comprehendere nequeant*), they often fall into a denial of God (*atheoteta* [Gk.]) or doubting of all things.

This too is a subtle manifestation of Vossius's sympathy with Maimonides' concerns, as much as it appears to be just a summation of the general principles behind the treatise as it proceeds.

There are other generalizations also: "Maimonides posits two genera of conjuring" (11:16, p. 159), with corresponding examples; "Maimonides is here enumerating signs (*colligit . . . indicia*) whereby one may determine whether [certain] images have been made for cultic purposes or only for ornamentation." These are aids to the unskilled reader, but they are also followed in most cases with more extensive philological disquisitions. In the second of the two instances just mentioned (7:8, p. 85), Vossius considers the idol or figurine with a "virga" ('wand') in hand. This example is brought by Maimonides, and Vossius tries to explain its significance by referring back to TB *'Avodah Zarah* 41a. This page had been cited by both the *Migdal 'Oz* and the *Kesef Mishneh,* but Vossius selects a different line from that page than the one they had used. He refers to the "wand that dominates the whole world like a scepter," following it up with Rashi's explanation of the wording of the Hebrew—he mentions Rashi by name—that, while the Hebrew actually reads "a wand that dominates itself under the whole world," this form of expression is one of disgrace. Vossius himself further explains that it is said "out of contempt for the idol"; for he recognizes that "otherwise this construction would not be concordant enough." In other words, he uses a wide variety of sources to move from the simple to the more detailed kind of explanation, even if there is limited direct application of the details that he discusses. For here too Vossius is trying to show off his erudition, more than he is actually elucidating the Maimonidean text.

Still, he manages to devote a fair amount of space to a running commentary on the text. He does not do this consistently, only in spurts. One such instance in a series of remarks on transactions with those going off to a fair of idolators (9:14, p. 136). The first annotation specifies: "*Cum euntibus.*] Puta idololatris, ut intelligitur ex antithesi Israelitarum, quae subicitur." Then: "*Non licet negotiari.*] Ne idololatras pecunia augeas, qua in nundinis promoveant idololatriam." This is followed by an explanation that business is permitted with those who have returned, since there is no longer any danger of their spending money on idolatry. By comparison, it is permitted to transact business with an Israelite on his way, since "he may change his mind." Vossius reasons: "Certainly when he has seen your civility (*humanitas*), in that, though he is en route to a fair of idolators and throwing himself into danger of worshipping idols, you carry on business with him nonetheless." This is Vossius's own inference; it is not indebted to any of the Jewish commentators. The last comment explains why it is forbidden to transact business with an Israelite on his return; it is already too late to get him to call off his plans; he has already gone and contributed to the growth of idolatry. "Atque haec plus lucis accipient ex §. seq." The next halakhah will elucidate this further, says Vossius, though he himself does not annotate that paragraph in the least.

Cross–References: the Corresponding Example, the "Testimonia"; or, Vossius's Learning Displayed

All Vossius's comments strike a balance between an address to the audience with limited background and one to those who would appreciate his scholarly precision and capabilities. Both groups had reverence for the "authority" of the ancients and for certain other leading figures from later periods. Their credibility could lend support to Vossius's reasoning: the "testimonia" he brought from these authorities were mainstays of his commentary. They were also aids to the explication of one of the greatest of Jewish authorities.

Vossius was especially interested in the frequent diversity of opinion between the various sources and authorities. This was a scholarly interest and not a polemical one; it was not set up to confute one truth by the use of another. Vossius writes: "dissentiunt homines doctissimi" (p. 78); "De hoc ambigunt veteres" (p. 13); "Sed aliter Hebraeorum aliis visum" (p. 148). On the nature of idolatrous practice, though, it was most often for corroboration ("Non unus tamen sic sensisse videtur Maimonides: sed ex nostris etiam Iustinus Martyr . . . ac Clemens Alexandrinus . . . Vide de ea disserentem parentem meam Historiae Pelagianae lib. III . . ." [2:7, p. 29]) and clarity that he introduced these sources. One "testis" ('witness') after another is introduced: "This can be demonstrated out of the ancient authors" ("ex antiquis autoribus probare sit") (p. 9), though Vossius also comments elsewhere: "These things are too well known to require attestation (*testimonia*)" (p. 126); or, "the matter is known and has already been related (*tradita*) by many" (p. 29); and so on.

Vossius sometimes weighs the "auctoritas" of a source that he cites (Judith, p. 13; Philomela, p. 147) and then concludes that there are more certain proofs to be brought from other sources. The authority of a writer is based on his reliability, his having been a witness, or on how learned his opinion appears. Vossius speaks of his sources as if he is summoning aid in a court: "ad partem advocare" (p. 132); or as lending credibility or offering proof: "Fidem de utroque fecerit Herodotus" (p. 112) and "argumento erit Palladis ille peplus, quem Maro, vel alius, in Ciri describit" (p. 95). Even here there is a scholarly aside, but it does not destroy the credibility of the source.

Part of the technique of invoking the ancient authorities or other learned individuals was, of course, criticizing them if necessary. Vossius had received a letter from l'Empereur in which his teacher called attention to several instances in his own work where he had "departed from the weighty opinion of other learned men" ("à virorum doctorum authoritate discedo").[78] Dionysius obviously felt it within his province too to make similar judgments: "Neque ignoro viros quosdam eruditos existimare . . . ; verum sane ut locum haec habeant . . . aliter tamen statuendum" (p. 23). Information could not be used recklessly or without regard for what was probable; other learned opinion was not always infallible. The invoking of authority was often for the purpose of arguing to the contrary, as much as it was for support.

In general, the link between *auctoritas* and *opinio,* or the continuity between them have their place in the *De Idololatria,* just as they do in the works of other seventeenth–century writers. When, in one instance, Maimonides had made a statement that disagreed with what the ancient writers had said, Vossius takes note: "id contra Romanorum Graecorumque opinionem est" (p. 113). Yet he does not appear to disqualify Maimonides' view on that basis. This is not a value judgment on Vossius's part; it is merely an erudite observation.

But Vossius questions Maimonides' faithfulness to his own sources on more than one occasion. On the ruling (2:3, p. 25) that a person who turns to idolatry "be–derekh she–hu 'oseh bo ma'aseh," "ita ut opus aliquod faciat," is flogged, Vossius notes that Maimonides goes contrary to the opinion in *Sanhedrin* that even those who offer cult to an idol with words alone are adjudged guilty. Vossius's cross–reference, to 3:6 (p. 43), gives further development of this theme: there too, Vossius comments on the differences of opinion created by Maimonides' insertion of this phrase. (The *Leḥem Mishneh* had also called attention to this discrepancy, though there is no clear indication that Vossius drew on that work here.) At any rate, Vossius nowhere states that Maimonides is wrong. In other words, even though Vossius notes a discrepancy, he does not resort to condemnation.

Even when Maimonides' descriptions of an idolatrous practice are at variance with those found elsewhere, Vossius does not resort to condemnation. According to Vossius, "Maimonides thinks that the gentiles used the fruits of sacred trees to extract a liquor that they imbibed on their holiday" (8:7, p. 112), but, "you will hardly find this anywhere else," i.e., in any other author. Yet, this too is the extent of the comment; Maimonides' view is not specifically disqualified. For, as Vossius remarks in another connection, "it is easier to refute a false opinion than it is to come upon [or devise] a true one" (3:2, p. 37), even though he himself tries to find one in this instance ("sed tenteremus") by advancing a plethora of sources that might help.[79]

It is mostly the similarities, though, on which Vossius wishes to expatiate, the parallel examples from other sources. He regularly invokes the "simile exemplum" (e.g., p. 58) and remarks that something "fieri solitum apud . . ." (p. 107) or that there was a "simile & huic alterum sortium genus . . ." (p. 149), yet he is sometimes forced to admit "nihil tale reperio" (p. 110). In discussing the addition of utensils and other personal effects to the funeral pyre, a custom encountered in the *Gallic Wars* of Caesar, though that source is not cited here by name, Vossius remarks that the "autores," meaning the ancient writers, are "full of such examples, and none is more widespread among the Romans." Such sumptuousness, he observes, was prohibited by the *Laws of the Twelve Tables* (p. 126).

To return though, to the comment (p. 110) where Vossius found no corresponding example, the whole context of his remark merits some consideration. It is a further instance of the setting up of an idolatrous object for cultic purposes. Vossius, like the *Kesef Mishneh,* cites the source in TB *Ḥullin.* Then he comments:

> Maimonides does not seem to have brought these examples of an egg and a gourd because gentiles worship them: at least I find nothing of this sort; and, for that reason, I think that this is what is called synecdoche of the species: a specific [object] in place of an unspecified [generalization] (*certo posito pro incerto*); as may be inferred from the rest [of the passage]. In the same way, those skilled in the law (*jurisperiti*) repeatedly put forth cases about which you may doubt whether they will ever come to pass.

Even here there is a corresponding example, one of a rather unexpected kind, but one that also comes out of Vossius's manifold erudition.

All of these comments are designed to link the rabbinic statement with something familiar to the reader. Even the explication of the phrase "edehem shel goyim" (Vossius: "festa gentilium") shows this. Part of this annotation has been examined above.[80] Vossius goes through each of the terms and gives the Gemara's explanation. For *kratesin,* it is the day on which Rome took over dominion, "in the days of Queen Cleopatra." Vossius defines further: "This took place first at the Battle of Actium: from this time forth Caesar Augustus held sole power over the *imperium Romanum.*" And so on he goes in this vein, invoking Dionysius Halicarnassus and Livy, linking classical learning with his explication of Maimonides and the Talmud.

This reflects a major point of continuity with his Caesar commentary. So, too, does his interest in the various customs of the ancients, "mos" and "mores." In 1630 even, Dionysius had written one of his correspondents that "when the customs of the nations are unknown, all history is unintelligible."[81] Accordingly, in his Maimonides commentary, he also appears to have seen much of his task as that of recounting the various customs ("morem . . . memorare" [p. 150]). Vossius used the word "mos" to translate "ma'asehem" in the passage (1:10, p. 18) "and they relapsed, to learn the practices of the Egyptians and to worship idols like them" (Vossius: "Illic enim redierunt ac (ad?) discendos illorum mores & idola exemplo eorum colenda . . ."). The translation shows Vossius's conception of the historical background: it was a composite of custom and example. And when he quotes Herodotus on the custom of shaving one's beard: "Toisi alloisi anthropoisi nomos hama kedei," he of course uses the term: "Apud alios homines mos obtinet . . ." (12:5, p. 166), "mos" being virtually identical with the original signification of "nomos." Vossius also draws comparisons: just as the Jews and the Christians considered it forbidden to eat things sacrificed to an idol ("eidolothytois"), so too even gentiles refrained from eating of guilt offerings ("ex hostia piaculari"); they felt the same about [eating from] the [sacrifice] in whose blood an oath had been taken because they believed that the curses [pronounced at that moment] would redound upon the head of him who violated the sanctity of the oath ("religionem jurisjurandi") (7:2. p. 87). Whether or not the parallel holds, it demonstrates Vossius's method of elucidating via comparison.

The Halakhah Understood: Legal Issues

Some parallels come from the subject area of law itself. A person was not considered to have committed idolatry unless he had performed the specific practice appropriate to a given idol and had performed it for that idol (3:2, p. 39). Vossius senses the concern of the rabbis and cites *Sanh.* 4:1, which deals with the interrogation of suspects as to which idol they had worshipped and how they had done so. Then he draws a parallel: "This was the law among the Romans: 'The priests are to determine the sacrifices pleasing and suitable to each god.'" Pliny is brought in for further support, Vossius explaining that it was "contrary to custom" to carry the object in question; rather, it had to be pulled along. Thus, specific prescriptions had to be observed in Roman law too, and Vossius finds the comparison illuminating.

Vossius also draws distinctions, of course: "For, from Herodotus Book 4, it is certain that the Scythians used wands . . . in divination, but in a manner different from that which Maimonides described here" (11:7, p. 152). Vossius even advances support from Matthew 9:23 for the Jews' having drawn and taken over from the gentiles the practice ("mos") of playing the flute while in mourning, "although this is prohibited by the law of God" (9:10, p. 132). He once evaluates contrary bits of information on Molech–worship by asking "what would prevent both of them from obtaining?" Some authorities, he indicates, see the child as merely having been passed through the flames, others see him as having actually been cremated. Vossius:

> To many it seems cruel to offer children as sacrifices. And it truly is. Nothing, however, is more certain than that the gentiles immolated their children. The Egyptians did it, witness Athenaeus. . . . Diodorus . . . and Trogus inform us that the Carthaginians, the colonists of the Phoenicians, took over this custom. Even Ennius [speaks of]
>
> 'Ille suos Divis mos sacrificare puellos.'
>
> 'That notorious custom of theirs
> to sacrifice their children to the Gods.'
>
> Why need I mention other nations? . . . [82]

In this display of virtuosity, Vossius's scholarly curiosity is coupled with his human sensitivity.

But the commentator also put such evidence to use in trying to help the reader understand the halakhic implications of a passage. Sometimes his view of these implications is his own, sometimes it is coordinate with that of one or more of the rabbinic commentators. For example, where Maimonides had stated (7:10, p. 96) that figures on "all other utensils" are licit, Vossius writes:

> He says 'all utensils' except for silver or gold. But what if the same image were on earthenware ones? For even those are used in sacred rites, especially among the ancient Romans. Indeed, in Codex (i.e., Mishnah) *'Avodah Zarah* II:3,[83] among the things it is prohibited to derive benefit

from are found the *ḥeres hadriani* (Heb.), *fictilia Hadriani* (the earthenware pottery of Hadrian): these, I think, were the vessels Hadrian or the Roman Caesars used in making a libation of wine to the gods.

Vossius leaves the practical question unresolved, however; it is not a question addressed, in any case, by the Jewish commentators. Moreover, it was not usually Vossius's aim to resolve halakhic dilemmas as much as it was to offer such displays while elucidating the subject matter for his audience.

Nonetheless, the halakhah, its processes, and its institutions, as well as legal reasoning in general, including the process of source derivation, inference, and formation of opinion are all topics of great interest to Vossius, even if sometimes only as aspects of his erudition. Sometimes, the translation alone gives the clue to this. Maimonides had stated that the accoutrements of idolatry are not forbidden until they are used for idolatry, "'ad she–yishtammeshu bahen la–'avodah zarah" (7:4, p. 89). Vossius made a slight alteration and an addition: "non sunt interdicta, priusquam *in cultu ea more gentium* fuere adhibita" (emphasis mine). This accords with the halakhic understanding of the passage, though the accompanying annotation makes no mention of the halakhic significance of the text.

Vossius often announces his explication of the rabbinic background of the halakhah with the words "volunt Hebraei"; the designation appears to refer to the rabbinic commentators on the *Mishneh Torah,* though there are exceptions to this. For the use of the expression also seems to refer to Vossius's own conception of the halakhic implications or conclusions that the commentators *might* derive from Maimonides' statements.

Again, the translation can be the first indication of the halakhic specifics. Maimonides' "hak–koreaḥ korḥah 'al ham–met lokeh" (12:14, p. 172) is rendered by Vossius as: "Qui ob defunctum, capillos evellendo, uno se loco calvum reddit, vapulat." Vossius emphasizes this even more with his note: "Volunt Hebraei, scripturam, quando ait, *koreaḥ korḥah,* innuere, ob unumquemque locum, qui calvus sit, hominem vapulare," that for each individual place where one creates a bald spot one is punished separately. Other instances of the use of this term are more complex.

As for legal terminology, where Maimonides. in reworking part of Mishnah *Sanh.* 7:6, had specified—we have already encountered this passage—that even a verbal declaration is tantamount to idolatry, Vossius translates "ḥayyav" with "crimen est"; his more standard locution for "ḥayyav" is "reus est." He distinguishes in this way between the capital crime here and the lesser offense of transgressing a prohibition ("transgreditur interdictum"), which Maimonides discusses in 3:9, three halakhot further down, but based on the same Mishnah in *Sanhedrin.* Having quoted the applicable part of this Mishnah in his note on Halakhah 6—the reference is in the *Kesef Mishneh*—he quotes the part applicable to Halakhah 9 in his annotation there (p. 46) and follows it with a discussion of the different degrees of culpability:

> The Hebrews maintain that a person is not flogged until he has violated a precept of God by which such a cultic practice is explicitly forbidden. Whence the talmudists say *lav she–bikhelalot eno lokeh 'alav, Interdictum siquod sub universali contineatur, non vapulat quis ideo.* (No one flogged on account of having violated a prohibition derived from a general rule.) God had said: *Ne iis servias* (You shall not worship them). Also prohibited by these words, generally (*generatim*), but not specifically (*speciatim*), are embracing and kissing an idol. However, if one embraced or kissed [an idol], he was not at all subject to punishment, because neither of these was expressly articulated (i.e., forbidden). [P. 47]

The *Kesef Mishneh* had also used this talmudic dictum, but Vossius expands on its meaning and explains what Karo had only suggested, in a manner suited to Vossius's own nonrabbinic audience.[84]

Sometimes Vossius has recourse to de' Pomis for his halakhic information. Maimonides: "kol hats–tsurot han–nimtsaim bak–kefarim asurim be–hanaah mip–pene she–ḥezkatan shel 'avodat kum hen 'asuyin." ("All the images [i.e., statues] that are found in the country towns are interdicted from use because there is a strong probability that they were created for idolatrous worship.") Vossius:

> On the word *ḥazakah* consult David de' Pomis. It designates jurisdiction and possession, and also customary usage and accepted practice. Whence . . . 'they let a man's word stand on his own customary practice,' i.e., they judge him 'according to the good or bad deeds that he was accustomed [to perform] over a long [period of] time.'[85]

The lexical comment illustrates and elucidates the legal sense of the word.

Vossius introduces a number of rabbinic legal dicta for his audience. As to why the false prophet is killed by strangulation (4:10 p. 71): "Because Scripture says, 'and that prophet shall die.' For the Hebrews say: 'Every "death" spoken of in the Torah without specification is categorically by strangulation.'" This dictum appears in the same talmudic *sugya* as that from which the overall Maimonidean discussion is derived, but no source reference is given at all. The page number had been indicated in both the *Migdal 'Oz* and the *Kesef Mishneh,* but Vossius does not carry it over, even though he obviously followed it through himself.

At any rate, such dicta are regularly quoted to explain procedure. On Maimonides' statement that the person who submits to idolatry out of either attraction or fear (3:8. p. 45), Vossius writes:

> The talmudists ordain that there are three things that a truly God–fearing Jew should not do, even though he is threatened with death; they are idolatry, adultery, homicide. However, R. Moses pronounces [the person] who did any of these under compulsion free from punishment. Since he adds *amore aut metu,* this is not to be taken [to mean] out of love or fear of the idol. Indeed, as we hear Maimonides saying in 1:3, idolators worshipped false gods, because they were convinced that they (sc. the idols) had the power to do them good or ill.

This is only part of Vossius's comment. He goes on to paraphrase the *Kesef Mishneh*'s discussion of the original source in *Sanhedrin* 61b. He recognizes that Maimonides followed Raba's opinion: "Raba absolves such an individual, because he did not worship wholeheartedly; inasmuch as he did not consider the idol a god, so that there was not so much a true worship as there was a simulated one." But Vossius himself was not satisfied. He would not dare to absolve such an individual: "Absolvere ego non ausim, cum ut Iurisconsulti ajunt, coacta etiam voluntas sit voluntas"; even a forced will is still a willingness. "For, indeed, he could have refrained, even though someone was threatening punishment. I would not deny, though, that he is to be punished more lightly." Vossius shows both that he understands human foibles and that he is willing to let them enter the discussion; but he also shows that he is quite familiar with general jurisprudence. His reproduction of the talmudic discussion is more than his own parsing of their legal reasoning: it is also a demonstration of his own qualities as a student of law.

This is not the only place where Vossius stresses his legal training. To support Maimonides' similar contention that an idol nullified by an idolator under compulsion by an Israelite is considered nullified, he writes: "These things . . . , if we follow the *Iuris intelligentes* (masters of law), are considered the same as if they were not forced" (Vossius's "acta" here seems to be equivalent to "coacta") (8:15, p. 118). These are not the Jewish "masters of law" to whom he refers, but, rather, his own instructors in "ius et politica," not to mention their sourcebooks, those that they compiled, and the legal traditions of the day.

Another interesting piece of legal reasoning by Vossius is his judgment (8:20, p. 121) on Maimonides' version of how an *asherah* or sacred grove is rendered null and void:

> What the author says here cannot stand unless the grove is understood to be the domain of a private individual. For no one would say that a grove consecrated by public authority can be rendered profane by its having been violated by a single individual. This would be the same thing as saying that any law or statute of the magistrates would become void because one person or another violates it.

Regardless of what one may think of the quality of the logic here, it will be clear that this is a judgment based on general canons of inference and not specifically on prior rabbinic commentary on this passage of Maimonides.

There is yet another case of Vossius evaluating the halakhah through his own general prism. It is the prohibition against making a gentile swear by the name of his god, so as not to cause the name of a false god to be uttered (5:12, p. 72). Vossius remarks that an oath by [the name of] any other deity would be worth nothing and that such oaths are necessary among partners to a treaty: "Indeed, without such oaths, human society and peace among nations does not endure" (" . . . non consistit generis humani societas & pax terrarum"). For this insight, it is a letter of Augustine's that is invoked, along with the incident between Jacob and Laban in Gen. 31. Vossius concludes: "This evil is not praiseworthy, but, on account of a great good—that good is peace among nations—it is rightfully endured (*toleratur*)."

If the foregoing are meant to show a certain sophistication, other explanations, even of the most basic institutions of Jewish life and practice, also move in this direction. We have encountered

Vossius's treatment of the *yeshivah.* Vossius also described phylacteries (p. 157), using Matthew 22:5 to back up his explanation that they help keep one mindful of the Torah ("proforent ad memoriam Legis melius conservandam"), though not omitting mention of the classic remark about the Scribes and Pharisees widening their phylacteries in order to appear "legis observantiores." But this is not Vossius's main point. Rather, it is this: that the phylacteries were being used with a view to securing physical well–being and warding off disease; this, says Vossius, is what Maimonides teaches us. In his note on the halakhah immediately prior, Vossius claimed that similar measures, such as reading the *Shema'* to ward off disease, were characteristic of the kabbalists: "Ad eas autem [superstitiones illicitas] Iudaeorum maxime proni sunt Cabalistae; quorum regulis praestigiatores in Africa uti . . ." This mention of African sorcerers is not really antikabbalist, as it might seem. It is more an offhand recall of Leo Africanus, whom he cites as his source. It thus falls into the category of a display of knowledge and wide reading.

There are other practices and institutions that Vossius dwells on: the Sanhedrin and its composition (p. 54), with his information surely derived in part from Coch; tithing [*ma'aser rishon* and *sheni*] (p. 64); stripes for rebelliousness [*makkat mardut*] (6:7, p. 84); forgotten sheaves and corners that are set aside [*shikheḥah* and *peah*] (p. 141); business transactions in general [*mekaḥ u–mimkar*] (7:6, pp. 90–91)—this is a rather long disquisition on the different procedures in a sale. While it is based on the *Shulḥan 'Arukh,* it is designed, of course, to make Maimonides' discussion of one such sale clearer. For Vossius subsequently paraphrases Maimonides' statement of the halakhah in this particular instance and offers a rationale for the view. There was fraud, writes Vossius; the buyer bought idolatrous pieces unknowingly and a contract must be free from all deception: "à contractu autem abesse debet omnis dolus; ut testatur Maimonides in Halachut Mechira cap. XV (XIV?)." This is Vossius at virtually his most moralizing, expressing a general principle of law and ethics as it appears to apply to Maimonides' reasoning and to the institution under consideration.

Of special interest insofar as Jewish institutions are concerned is Vossius's distinction between the several kinds of strangers or proselytes to Judaism (10:2, pp. 138–39). While the question of proselytes is ostensibly tangential to the larger subject of idolators and their rights in the Land of Israel, Vossius showed the specific relationship between idolatry and the individual types of *gerim,* lit., 'strangers'. There are those strangers who practice Judaism, having abandoned their former religion: these, he says, are the true proselytes ("*gere tsedek,* peregrini justitiae"). Others observe only the seven Noachide commandments, which he specifies; the "*ger toshav*" (resident alien) comprises the latter category, not being reckoned an idolator. This is determined by cross–reference to Halakhah 7 of the chapter, where Maimonides states that the resident alien may not pass through the land without accepting these commandments (and thus renouncing idolatry).

Much of this is book learning. Vossius may have had a slight acquaintance with what Jews did in actuality, however. Where Maimonides speaks of "names that are not erased" (p. 32) Vossius lists the various names of God that fall into this category. "Of these," he continues, "if any by chance is written in an unsuitable (*alieno*) place, they do not erase it, but they cut it out with a small knife and conceal it in small boxes that they have for this purpose in the synagogues." This information was probably communicated to Dionysius by Menasseh. It has the ring of either actual experience or a *viva voce* explanation, and was probably one of the many things on which Dionysius "consulted" Menasseh.

The History and Nature of Religion

Vossius was also interested in the broad range of issues that emerge from *Hilkhot 'Avodah Zarah,* including the origins and history of idolatry, the knowledge of God, and the subject of religion in general. His approaches to these areas may have been influenced by Menasseh, but Vossius certainly asserts his independent competence as well in these areas. His stance is that of a nonpartisan scholar, however; he avoids controversy of a doctrinal nature almost completely. Yet, from his remark in passing that "all suspicion of idolatry is to be avoided" (p. 107) to his observation that "even today a remnant exists of the superstition of 'divination with keys'" (p. 155), it is clear that Vossius was not just an uninterested bystander. He is forever concerned with the larger implications of the Maimonidean text. He considers the origins of idolatry, the definition of an idolator, the various penalties; his judgments about accuracy and reasonableness are reflections of both his own views and his understanding of Maimonides'.

As for the origins of idolatry, Vossius undertakes (pp. 4–5) an extensive investigation of when this came about, basing himself on the various interpretations of Gen. 4:26, which may be translated in a number of ways. Almost literally, we might render it: "Then it was begun to call in the name of God." Vossius introduces the numerous translations, beginning with the one by "the majority of the Hebraei," which he renders: "tunc profanatum est in invocando nomine Domini." Part of his annotation has already been dealt with,[86] but its scope has not been considered fully. Despite the variations in translation, says Vossius, the meaning ("mens") of Scripture is this:

> At the time of Enos, when the human race had already grown, there began to be public assemblies for calling upon God's name; or, then, at last, at specified hours, [that is to say] surely the beginning of the day and when food was to be partaken of or [when] night began, men were accustomed to take up prayers to God. In fact, the words of Scripture do not accord sufficiently with the view of those who apply them to idolatry.

This is followed by the criticism of the several opinions that has been dealt with above. The series concludes with an extensive quotation of Nicholas of Lyre's criticism of the attribution of idolatry to Enos and his alternative proposal of Cain as the originator; Vossius judges this most credible. He also notes that, even if the supposed exegesis of Gen. 4:26 as speaking of the origins of idolatry were true,

> nonetheless you would be justified in charging Maimonides with carelessness, in that, while tracing idolatry back to the period preceding the flood, he did not have in mind or neglected to write that it began again after the flood for a second time, although it was particularly important to record the time at which it began [again] after the flood. It is believed to have sprung up in the age of Serug or Terah.

If Vossius appears to be carping slightly, it is more by way of flexing his scholarly muscles and demonstrating his prowess as a historian of religion. Though Vossius did take a swipe at those who followed the rabbinic exposition of this verse, he used his annotation more to demonstrate his broad reading and as a springboard for his own thinking.

In his next comment, Vossius examines the reasons that idolatry sprung up. He states his preference for Maimonides' view over Rashi's, approving of Maimonides' reasoning that idolatry began from the worship of the heavenly bodies and discounting Rashi's view that it began with the worship of men. Moreover, he says,

> if idolatry began in the time of Enos, as Maimonides maintained, it is highly probable that men could not have been completely ignorant then of the true God, about whom they undoubtedly learned much from their parents. Along that line of reasoning, they more likely went astray and served [other gods] willfully (*ethelothreskeia* [Gk.]) than out of lack of knowledge [of Him]. But I would rather believe that they went astray out of ignorance. Two things, to be sure, drove them into error: that they did not perceive that most supreme and unseen (*summum* & *aoraton* [Gk.]) God at all; and that those who learned of His miracles from their parents neglected to transmit them to their descendants. Wherefore they immediately turned away to worship the things they could see and those that benefited them the most: the sun, the moon, and other things of this kind.

This is corroborated by a variety of sources, from Gersonides to Caesar to Lucian and Diodorus Siculus, whose remarks show that there was an "ignorance of the true God" and that "divinity was ascribed to the heavenly bodies for no other reason that that the greatest good for men comes forth from them." Such is Vossius's inference from these sources; it is an alternative account to Maimonides', but it is essentially corroborative.

The next annotation (p. 6) examines the manner of idolatrous worship, as it first began.[87] Vossius: "Exposita origine idololatriae, ad modum Autor transit" ('Having expounded on the origin of idolatry, the author passes on to its method'). Not only does this keep the reader abreast of the line of argument, it also affords the commentator an opportunity for a disquisition of his own. He proceeds:

> [Maimonides] makes temples, sacrifices, hymns, adoration the first worship (*primum cultum*). I wish he had a little greater principle of order. For it seems exceedingly improbable that temples were built by men simultaneously with the rise of religion. The simplest mortals also used the simplest form of worship.

At this point, there follows a further disquisition, on the term *'hishtaḥavah'*. Like the earlier comment on Maimonides' possible carelessness, none of this is designed to discredit the writer whom

Vossius several times calls "autor noster." Rather, Vossius is trying to show off his own knowledge before his audience.

As for the significance of idolatry, Vossius understands Maimonides' exposition of the proof–text Num. 15:39, "do not follow your heart and eyes," to restrict its application to "scortatio spiritualis," 'spiritual whoring', "which we call idolatry," and he explains why Maimonides reckoned the prohibition of idolatry equivalent to all the other commandments: "Because the worship of idols destroys the knowledge of the true God." This is probably the sole indication of any interest on Vossius's part in the intellectualistic dimensions of the treatise, and it is a very bare indication at that. Incidentally, both Vossius's comparison in this note between the halakhah under discussion and Maimonides' comment at *Guide* 1:36 that an idolator is properly called a hater of God and Vossius's remark that Naḥmanides understands the punishment of children for the sins of their fathers to apply only to idolators appear to have their source in Question 104 of the *Conciliator* (on Ex. 20:5) and offer little evidence of any really independent thought on Vossius's part.[88]

And yet, under the lemma "Magnum hoc fundamentum" (1:9, p. 17), Vossius draws a comparison with the opening of *Hilkhot Yesode hat–Torah,* translating it as follows: "Fundamentum fundamentorum & columna sapientiae est, scire quod est ens aliquod primum, existere faciens omnia existentia," and with another passage from the first chapter of that section where Maimonides says that "he who believes that there are more Gods than one, negat fundamentum maximum, a quo cuncta pendent." This is not just a citation of a parallel usage or phrase; it attests to the link in Vossius's mind as well, one based on an understanding of the way *"ikkar'* is used and of its virtual interchangeability with *'yesod'*.

Nor does he leave the phrase "columna sapientiae" without comment. In his note on the designation of Abraham the Patriarch as "columna mundi" (*'ammudo shel 'olam*), Vossius also makes reference to the phrase in *Yesode hat–Torah* 1:1. Though Vossius was probably unaware of this, Maimonides had adopted the appellation for Abraham from *Exodus Rabbah* 2. But Vossius is concerned to show the appropriateness of both the metaphor and his own rendering of the Hebrew. He writes:

[Maimonides] calls Abraham thus, because the world leans on the just as on pillars, since for their sake the world endures. [And] then [also] because [Abraham] taught true religion and the knowledge of God, which our author calls "'*ammud ha–ḥokhmot,* columnam sapientiae" ['the pillar of wisdom'] in *Hilkhot Yesode hat–Torah*, chapter 1.

[1:5, p. 11]

Here, Vossius himself turns homilist, making the metaphor a starting point for his own thoughts.[89]

Elsewhere as well in the commentary there may be found observations of a very mature sort on wisdom and philosophy, but they are quite scattered. "Wise men," writes Vossius (1:3, p. 8), consider the various images of birds, serpents, and other animals "symbols of the gods, while common minds worship them as actual divinities." Or, in commenting upon the prohibition against even looking at idols (2:3, p. 25), he invokes (following the *Migdal 'Oz* probably) the talmudic dictum, "If you turn toward them, you make them gods," moralizing: "To be sure [you do], because such a base curiosity commonly sprouts evil fruit; and it is unworthy of man, created in the image of God, to occupy himself with vanities of this kind." Vossius also picks up on Maimonides' statement (the source in *Ḥullin* 5b is not cited) that whoever renounces idolatry is like one who admits to the whole Torah: "A remarkable conclusion! In this way, all the philosophers of the nations, who ridicule the cult of statues and think God invisible, are to be said to have accepted the law of Moses and the oracles of the prophets" (2:7, p. 29). While this is little more than a paraphrase of Maimonides' text, it is revealed to be a defense of him also, by the corroboration brought in from Justin Martyr, Clement of Alexandria, and Vossius's own father.[90]

As it happens, some of Vossius's familiarity with the very midrashic background of Maimonides' reasoning is derived from such Christian writers. On Abraham's coming to know God:

It is likely that, at least in his first years, [Abraham] followed the customs of his father and worshipped idols. Afterwards, as he grew older, [and], taught by his elders, [i.e.,], by Shem and others, or, perhaps, by God's providence, led to the knowledge of Him in some other way, he gave up his impious superstitions.

[1:6, p. 14]

This comes from Augustine's *City of God* 16:12, as excerpted by

Eucherius, Bishop of Lyons (d. 450–55). Such are the sources Vossius cites.

There is little more that he has to say specifically on the knowledge of God. He does, however, evince some understanding of religious devotion in general and the service of God. Quoting Ps.–Ambrose that "the servants of God should have no part of soothsaying," that is, they should neither consult a soothsayer [*me'onen*] (translated as '*mathematicus*') nor concern themselves with "auspicious" or "inauspicious" days, he also invokes Ps.–Ambrose's rationale:

> "For if God is loved wholeheartedly, there need be no fear or any regard for these things [i.e., the 'proper' times for doing things]. It is certainly possible for whatever is done straightforwardly, in devotion to God, to come to pass according to one's wishes (*prosperè enim potest cedere*)."
>
> [Ad 11:9, p. 153]

Clearly this is Vossius's own credo as well. Elsewhere, he makes the observation that "those who intend that God be worshipped as devoutly as possible say: 'worship him out of both love and fear'" (3:8, p. 45). This is in the context of the discussion of the person who worships an idol under one form of duress or another.[91] Vossius picked this quotation up from Coch (Coch, p. 62). But Vossius relates it to the issue at hand by commenting further that Maimonides understands fear to mean fear of someone who either offers a reward or threatens punishment, not fear or love of the supposed deity. The quality of his own religious posture and its mixture of rationalism and reverence emerges from these comments.

Indeed, on the "sermons" pronounced by the first false prophets to convince those assembled that a "particular figure conferred benefits and inflicted harm and that it is proper to worship and fear it" (1:3, pp. 7–9), Vossius contends that Maimonides

> is justified in using these words, because nothing drives men to a new religion more easily that hope and fear. This is where Petronius got the following idea from: "Primus in orbe Deos fecit timor" ('the first thing that made gods in the world was fear'). Hence religion itself is called *deisidaimonia* [Gk.] (fear of a *daimon*), and a God or *daimon* is called a *yirah* by the rabbis. *Sanhedrin* chapter 7, no. 10 introduces the seducer (i.e., the *mesit*) [as] one who incites another to idolatry with the following formula: 'there is a *yirah* in a certain place [who is worshipped with] such

and such food and drink and who helps and harms in such and such a way.'

This mix too is characteristic of Vossius: rationale, etymology, and cross–reference, the rationale being based on a general personal observation rather than on anything internal to the text.

Also among Vossius's observations are a comment on the political dimension of religion. In his note on the next halakhah (1:4. p. 10), where Maimonides had described the succeeding stage of idolatry as one where men began to claim direct revelation from a given star or angel and to introduce rituals and laws on that basis, Vossius writes:

These events are perhaps to be deferred to a later period. For those fabrications about speaking with gods did not begin, I should think, until after men began to form social alliances. These superstitions were invented by rulers (*rectores*) for binding [men] together in submission. We have an example in Minos who pretended that he had received the laws from Zeus in a cave. Similarly among the Romans, in Numa with the nymph Egeria [his wife and teacher]. From this I would judge that rites and various ceremonies were not so much the contrivances of men of religion as those of politicians. There is sufficient proof of this in Roman history.

This is Vossius the historian of religion dissenting mildly from, but, more so, adding to Maimonides' account.

In fact, Vossius had just previously corroborated the Maimonidean version: "Recte Maimonides simulachra in templis non statim reposita observavit" (1:3, p. 8), he wrote, following this with half a dozen *testimonia.* He concluded that statues and other stones for worship existed long before temples and that, at first, they were placed in sacred groves, "quod ostendunt vel soli veterum Germanorum mores (as the customs of the ancient Germans alone demonstrate)."

Homiletics, Animadversions, and the Defense of Maimonides

Sometimes, Vossius's observations on religion do tend to border on preaching. Witnesses to blasphemy (2:11, p. 33) were required to substitute the name "Yosé" for the tetragrammaton when they gave evidence. Vossius does not account for the origins of the name, but he takes note of the implications of the substitution:

From this may be seen the scrupulous reverence (*religio*) of the people, not uttering the name of God except truly in dread and of necessity in an actual court of law. Would that some of this quality had been drawn upon by those who today rashly and in the most rotten affairs so often employ the name of God.

But comments that smack of homiletics are not limited to this instance. The philological method adopted by Vossius seems to allow for them, too. When they are based on midrashim, they are quite congruent with the philological approach, as evidenced by the following: Vossius translated Maimonides' description of Abraham's early activity, "ve–hayah mehallekh ve–kore," to read "ibatque praedicans" (1:8, p. 15). In this, he attempted to capture the tradition on Abraham's proselytizing. This is confirmed by the annotation on that lemma: "*kara* (in Hebrew letters)[:] *clamare, vociferari, publice profiteri ac praedicare,*" which defends the translation by showing both the general and the specific meanings that were possible. In his previous note, though, Vossius had made reference to Question 40 (Span. ed., Q. 43) of the *Conciliator,* where Menasseh had referred to other tales about Abraham—the tale about Abraham's preaching is mentioned in passing in Q. 41 (Span.), incidentally. Vossius had also cited the midrash about Nimrod's throwing Abraham into the furnace, referring to it as a "communis Hebraeorum opinio."[92]

All this is the background of his annotation on the proof–text in 1:8, "Vocavit ibi Abraham." There Vossius wrote that Maimonides had meant Abraham's "conciones," his 'discourses', in which he "proclaimed" or "preached" ("annuntiasse") that "God is the creator of the world." Vossius must have been moved by this, for he goes on to cite Naḥmanides and Baḥya (ben Asher?)[93] and even Josephus—this is Vossius's sole use of the ancient Jewish historian—on the theme of Abraham's message being God's governance of the world. Baḥya in particular is quoted on how Abraham "led men back into the path of truth," a phrase pregnant with meaning. None of these writers had been cited in this context by Menasseh. Vossius went beyond the *Conciliator,* then, for his choice of messages, though there is always the possibility that Menasseh had suggested these sources personally. Yet this could still be Vossius's own pursuit of the Hebrew commentators. The *Kesef Mishneh* had distinguished between the private instruction that Shem and

Eber had given and the public preaching that Abraham engaged in. Vossius limits his remarks to Abraham's public activity, but the idea may have suggested itself to him in the *Kesef Mishneh.*

The Talmud gives rise to other homiletic remarks. On the culpability of the person who, albeit in scorn, performs an idolatrous rite in the correct manner (3:7, pp. 44–45), Vossius writes: "[He is certainly culpable.] Because his intention is not known to everyone, and someone may suppose that [his action] arose out of religious scruples." Then, having summarized the talmudic sources in *Sanhedrin* and *'Avodah Zarah* (the references are found in the Hebrew commentators also) and having reasoned that the prohibition against setting out on a road that leads only to a city of idolators exists so that others may not interpret the action as a religious observance, Vossius continues:

> And, indeed, offenses to morality (*scandala*) are to be avoided on account of *ḥillul hash–shem,* [which is] *profanationem nominis divini.* On account of this, R. Yoḥanan says in *Pirke Avot* 4: "It comes to the same thing whether one profanes the name of God through error or deliberately." This is not to be taken as if it makes no difference whether you transgress in error or in spite, but because, in the minds of men who do not know your own, scandal springs up nonetheless.

The maxim in *Avot* is not one invoked by the Hebrew commentators here, incidentally. There is probably no specific preachment or admonition intended here by Vossius. There is, though, certainly a sense of concern with public appearances in the matter of religion. Moreover, Vossius obviously attached no scandal to his own association with Menasseh or to his own study of rabbinics. His purpose was to advance Christianity, but, unlike l'Empereur and Coch, he hardly seems ill–at–ease here or elsewhere in drawing on rabbinic dicta and Jewish learning. The separation of the two dimensions of his work probably helped endear him to Menasseh.

This is not to say that Dionysius Vossius's commentary is entirely without hint of animus, nor is it to argue that every criticism is harsh or doctrinaire. There are a few odd instances of the standard gibes: some rabbinic expositions are labelled "subterfuges" (pp. 21, 164) or "fictions" ("commenta") (p. 95); also, Vossius declares at one point that the midrashic tales ("traditiones Hebraeorum") are, for the most part, worthless ("futiles"). These are chance comments, though, and they are quite offset by Vossius's actual reliance on the midrashim in other instances.

Yet several of the annotations discussed earlier have been seen to contain polemical or semipolemical asides, even if other aspects of Vossius's criticism appear, for the most part, as scholarly disagreements. The moderation Vossius evinced, though, is well reflected in his comment on Maimonides' summary remark, "ve–khol ha–harḥakah haz–zot mip–pene 'akkum hu" ("and all of this *harḥakah* [i.e., separation] is on account of idolatry"). This is translated by Vossius to read: "Hoc autem intervalli statuitur idololatriae ergo," and it gives a good indication of Vossius's personal position on contact between Jews and non–Jews in general. The passage in Maimonides refers to the several precautionary measures limiting feasting with gentiles. Aside from Vossius's "statuitur," which gives added legal tenor to the line and may be translated: "is established," it is the partitive genitive that gives definition to Vossius's view. He read "harḥakah" as a clear–cut, almost measurable 'space between' or 'distance', that is to say, more as an actual '*harḥek*' than as a merely 'precautionary measure'.[94]

But he understood exactly what was at issue here: his note on the halakhah itself—the *lemma* consists of the opening words, "Si gentilis . . . convivium instituerit, nefas est uti cibis ejus" ("If a gentile fixes a banquet, it is forbidden to partake of his food") — confirms this with two "exempla." The first *exemplum* is meant to be Dan. 1:8. Vossius cites it but does not quote it; it refers to Daniel's abstention from the food and drink of Nebuchadnezzar's table. The second *exemplum,* notes Vossius, "minus rigidus est," is less stringent. It is from 1 Corinthians (10:27f.)—this is one of a mere ten references to the Christian Scriptures that Vossius makes—and it permits partaking at the table of unbelievers, except when one is advised that the food has been offered in sacrifice; then one should abstain. "Verum," Vossius remarks, "Iudaeis non videtur tantum licuisse, quos vetuerat Deus communionem habere cum gentilibus" (p. 135*n*); that is to say, the Jews are not permitted even this much: they may not accept the invitation in the first place. Vossius used '*intervallum*', then, because he understood the issue as entirely one of non–'*communio*'. There was to be a complete avoidance of 'mutual intercourse'. Vossius's comment is not angry or hostile at all. It merely reflects his image of the Jews—that is, the "Iudaei" of his annotation—and his understanding of Maimonides' treatise: with the possible exception of Menasseh ben Israel, the Jews, at God's commandment, i.e., as Vossius understood the interpretation of the Torah that was being put forth in in Maimonides' treatise, actually did keep their distance from gentiles.

This was a case of Vossius's experience dictating his view of the text, or so it would appear. There are also a few instances where Maimonides' view may seem to impinge on certain aspects of Christian dogma. In only one case, though, the veneration of angels as intermediaries, did Vossius advance the Christian view over and against the Jewish one.

The annotation (ad 2:1, pp. 21–23)—it is long one—merits full consideration. From the citation of the Albo passages here, it seems likely that the Jewish position on angels had been bothering Vossius ever since he encountered Menasseh's treatment of it in the *Conciliator;* perhaps it was even earlier.

It would be helpful to study Vossius's previous annotation for a moment, before examining the one on angels. In that comment (pp. 20–21), on the words "Nequis serviat ulli rerum creatarum" ("Let no one serve any of the created things"), which Maimonides had defined as the "essence of the commandment on idolatry," Vossius had considered the implications of Maimonides' view of the idolator as one "who venerates any creature": this comprises "not only those who venerate creatures as being God, but even those who make supplication to them as His ministers." He had also examined the range of meaning in *'avad* as including both civil and divine honors.[95] Following up the *Kesef Mishneh*'s cross–reference to *Hilkhot Teshuvah* 3:12–13, he quoted the categories of heretics listed there, took special notice of those heretics who worship a star so that it will be an intermediary between them and God, and recapitulated some of Albo's view expressed in *'Ikkarim* 3:18 that the origins of idolatry lay in the veneration of an intermediary.[96]

All this sets the stage for the annotation of "Non angelo." Vossius begins by reproducing Albo's distinction from *'Ikkarim* 2:28. Where an angel represents God ("cum Dei personam gerit"), he may be worshipped, so to speak, as God's messenger, but not as a being possessing a power of his own. "Obviously," comments this Christian Hebraist,

> this [distinction] had to be established by those who deny the divinity of our Savior, whom the most ancient Fathers, and above all Justin Martyr, have copiously shown to be called by the name of angel and Jehovah in various places in Scripture. Thus, in Gen. 18:13–14, Jehovah is none other than Christ, inasmuch as Abraham there calls him the judge of heaven and earth.[97] Nor will anyone of a more rational mind be moved by that subterfuge of the rabbis, who say that in fact three angels were sent by God, but that, besides them, God himself stood near Abraham. For the words of Scripture prove patently otherwise.

The argumentation and the biblical citations that now follow attempt to show that "angel" is often used as a designation for "Christ."[98] Gen. 32:30 (Hebrew Bible 32:31)—the previous verse had also been cited by Albo—"should suffice," says Vossius, "for refuting the Hebrews." While Vossius's argument is of neither rhetorical nor substantive merit, insofar as Maimonides' statements are concerned, and while this particular remark is at variance with the tenor of the commentary as a whole, it gives away the specific goals Vossius had in this annotation: to show his competence in debating a matter of Christian theology. For, while he goes on to admit that there are other instances in Scripture where angels are worshipped, he makes a different distinction from that of the "Hebraei"; he returns to the distinction between civil honors and divine worship and dismisses theirs, which allowed an angel to be worshipped when he acted the part of God ("personam Dei sustineret"). Yet Vossius also defends his distinction and the legitimacy of civil honors for certain angels against "viros quosdam eruditos," certain non–Jewish scholars (whose position was closer to Maimonides'), who considered both religious and civil honors for angels to be unacceptable, the former as impiety, the latter as foolishness. Vossius argues that civil honors may reasonably be paid to certain angels, depending on their mission. In effect, though, he is arguing even more for his own exegesis of the various verses he had cited. If civil honors were rendered to some angels, and other angels were worshipped as divine, this would enable the several types of *proskynesis* or 'bowing down' that are mentioned in Scripture to be sorted out, and it would thus defend the Christian distinction over against the Jewish one.[99]

Almost lost in all this is Maimonides' simple and straightforward halakhah. Not entirely, however. It stood in fundamental opposition to the Christian position, even if its stance differed slightly from Albo's. Maimonides had ruled that no angel was to be worshipped. He made no exception. This was so much at variance with what Christian exegesis had aimed at that Vossius could not let it pass unnoticed. Yet he does not attack Maimonides directly so as not to destroy his credibility in other areas. It is remarkable that, in this note on "Non angelo," no mention whatsoever is made of Maimonides or his work. Instead, Vossius attacks the Jewish position through Albo, and in really a rather mild way at that.

In fact, Vossius often goes in the other direction, not merely trying to impose balance, but even trying to defend Maimonides. This was, of course, one feature of the commentary. One further example is warranted. It is a case where the legal ruling is so startling that it appears almost unreasonable, and Vossius begins, as he did in one example cited above: "Mira conclusio" ('An amazing conclusion'). The case in point is Maimonides' statement that a person who sacrifices all his children is not charged, while the one who sacrifices but one of his in the proper manner actually is. Vossius marvels at this. Paraphrasing the summary of the *Sefer Mitsvot Gadol* (a codification of law by R. Moses of Coucy (13th c.) that was heavily indebted to Maimonides[100]) in the margin of Venice 1614, he writes:

> The *Hebraei* say [the law] was established [thus] because, if anyone only offered up one son, he would atone for that crime with his death. But, if he offered up all of them, the offense is greater than can be atoned for by death. Therefore that man escapes punishment here certainly; but he is deprived of eternal life by God.
>
> [6:6, p. 80]

This is but one of the explanations Vossius gives. He also offers the rationalistic theory of "others" (they are not identified; maybe they were his Jewish teachers) that "one" was consonant with the custom in this cult, "all" was not. Vossius finds Abravanel's exegesis of "miz–zar'o" more satisfactory. The preposition "min," 'of', was used, said Abravanel, because it was unlikely that anyone would either offer his whole offspring to Molech or be immune from punishment for having done so. Vossius follows this with a response to the question posed in the *Kesef Mishneh,* though, of course, he does not identify it as having come from there: what if the Molech–worshipper had only one son? The answer: Though he had only one in actuality, he had more *in potentia.* In short, Vossius intercedes here, as he did elsewhere, to defend the reasonableness of Maimonides' and others' views on an abstract, but ethically puzzling problem.

As we have seen, though, Vossius did not always defend Maimonides. One last instance points this up most vividly, inasmuch as it also emerges from here that Vossius actually tries to do so and does not succeed. In the annotation at the beginning of chapter 10 (pp. 137–38), the biblical source reference Vossius gives for the ruling that no peace treaty shall be concluded with idolators is Ex. 13:2. This must be a misprint for Ex. 23:32, "You shall make no covenant with them and their gods." At any rate, Vossius's intentions are clear. He writes:

> the prohibition . . . applies only to the seven nations of the land of Canaan. To extend it to all gentiles or idolators, though, would be quite cruel. Therefore, because this commandment does not apply [to non–Canaanites], another one does; it is taught not only by Scripture, but even by reason. This is it: "You shall not kill." For he kills, who, when he is able to help someone in distress, does not concern himself to do so. I don't see sufficiently how to exculpate Maimonides here. That he did not speak of the peoples of Canaan alone is even substantiated by the beginning of the following paragraph, where he says, [as] of an overall class (*generatim*), "These things are said about idolators."

Vossius wished to make Maimonides' ruling less harsh than it is. (A later commentator, a rabbinic one, Judah Rosanes, had similar doubts about the appropriateness of this ruling, as the editor of his commentary *Mishneh lam–Melekh* pointed out.) Indeed, the mildness here too is further proof of Vossius's balanced approach to the text. We may even remark in passing that Vossius refrained from editorializing when mentioning "Jews converted to Christ" (p. 87), when it could have been so routinely expected for him to have inserted some wishful thinking or some hope for the conversion of his Jewish contemporaries. His father dropped such an "utinam Christianus" in speaking of Menasseh, and Dionysius himself was said to have devoutly wished the same. The fact that he did not do so here or anywhere in the commentary is further substantiation of a less than polemical approach.

As a final demonstration of Vossius's characteristics, one example of overexuberant erudition is most suitable. It is his disquisition on the "epikoros," a comment given rise to by his choice of textual reading, in preference to "minut," which he uses elsewhere. Vossius examines Maimonides' definition of an "epikoros" in *Hilkhot Teshuvah* 3:14 [i.e., 3:8], as it relates to Epicureanism. The annotation (2:5, pp. 26–27) is innocuous enough on the whole. In it, though, Vossius states that Maimonides was "mistaken" in using the term 'Epicurean' as the appellation for a person who denies that the prophecy of Moses is from God. "No one," he writes, "who had merely read his magnificent little book *On Providence* would call Seneca an Epicurean." There is more, but we need not go into it. Suffice it to say that Vossius's obliviousness of standard rabbinic usage enabled him to show off his wide reading. Most often, however, it was his familiarity with that usage that was the generating force in his commentary, as it enabled him to bring the wealth of his knowledge to the fore in display.

If there is any single coordinated focus or point of view, though, it is hard to find. The commentary is the result of the interests of the Vossius family and an opening to rabbinic learning for others. Regardless of any ulterior motivation, Dionysius tried to keep it, first, foremost and most fundamentally, a straightforward presentation of and guide to the treasures in Maimonides' treatise.

Vossius and John Spencer: Vossius and his Readership

Among later readers who derived immense help from *De Idololatria*—and there were numerous students of Judaism, many of them without Hebrew, who used Vossius's work—was John Spencer. The use to which he put Maimonides could hardly have been anticipated by Vossius. Spencer's *De legibus Hebraeorum* (*On the Laws of the Hebrews*), which first appeared in 1685, has been seen as one of the progenitors of the secularist Deist critique of religion of the eighteenth century.[101] None of the elements of this critique can really be found in Vossius's commentary. While Vossius and Spencer both have frequent recourse to comparisons, Vossius appears to use them mainly for purposes of elucidation, while Spencer definitely sees in them a pattern of derivation. Religious ideas, in Spencer's view, flowed from one culture to another.

A few earlier comparatists, from the period between Vossius and Spencer, had spoken of derivations, viewing all other ancient cultures as having been derived from the Hebrew, the most noble. To Spencer's mind, though, the points of comparison, judging from the rationales for certain practices given in rabbinic literature and from the calumnies against the Hebrews expressed in all of ancient literature, the Bible included, [where they are referred to repeatedly as "a stiff–necked people,"] actually proved the reverse: many of the customs recorded in the Bible had originated with and been derived from other nations, principally the Egyptians, and were allowed the Israelites as a concession to their essentially debased character. It was, moreover, these comments on the character of the Israelites that were quoted by the later Deists and, having been thus quoted, helped shape the negative views of some members of the French Enlightenment toward the Jews.

The secularist critique that Spencer helped begin was, on all counts, foreign to Vossius's perspective; he can hardly be said either to have been responsible for it or to have promoted it. Yet, some of Vossius's subtle alternative reconstructions of the history of idolatry may have been a foreshadowing of the critique of Judaism, even though Vossius still respected the basic foundation on which the Jewish views rested. Vossius and Maimonides would have stood aghast at the widespread negativism toward Jewish culture and the new overall skepticism vis–à–vis the Bible and religion that came in Spencer's wake. Vossius was probably, though, one of the many unwitting accomplices in bringing about this change; the building blocks that Spencer used are present in his commentary.

Vossius the Scholar: Some Judgments

Dionysius Vossius's most distinguishing characteristic was perhaps the lively, self–aware posture he maintained throughout his work: witness his many comments in the first person and his judgments "recte," "vere," and so on. These are also intended as scholarly judgments. If the various corroborations are sometimes far–fetched or seemingly irrelevant with respect to Maimonides' text, it is because they are also intended as guides to other available knowledge on idolatry. Moreover, if the rabbis were intentionally precise for halakhic reasons, Vossius's precision was to be a demonstration of his competence. Finally, it must have been because he did not prove doctrinaire in his approach that he earned the respect and support of Menasseh.

Yet no record exists of Menasseh's view of Dionysius. We can only extrapolate from Menasseh's views on other Hebraists, that is to say, Anslo in particular, as to how Menasseh might have regarded the *De Idololatria.* It is obvious that Dionysius had tried to integrate rabbinic and secular learning, and Menasseh considered that a hopeful sign. If, as Roth has written, Dionysius actually made his translation and wrote his commentary "under Menasseh's direction,"[102] —and the evidence to support this statement in the way it is couched is rather thin—it is likely that Menasseh would have looked upon the *De Idololatria* with extreme satisfaction. As we know, though, Dionysius's sudden and premature death cut him off before his work was published, and Menasseh's hopes, whatever they were, had to be lavished elsewhere.

Guglielmus Vorstius, *On the Fundamental Principles of the Torah:* The Polemicist

Willem Hendrik Voorst (d. 1652), or Guglielmus Vorstius, was a Remonstrant pastor, first at Leiden, then at Warmond. As noted earlier,[103] he was the translator of Menasseh's *De Creatione,* and there is no reason to doubt that he had been a pupil of Menasseh's as well. The son of Conrad Vorstius (1569–1622), and suspected himself of Socinianism, he would appear to have been at least a member of the more liberal circle in Amsterdam, if not one of its leaders. His date and place of birth are not known with certainty. He was granted his diploma in theology at Leiden in 1640, but had already been studying Hebrew for a while in 1634; we may perhaps place his birth date about 1615. During his lifetime, he seems to have been hounded from just about everywhere he attempted to settle (his father had also been an outcast, of course); after his death, his work would be torn to shreds by critics for its inaccuracies.

Little is available to complete his biography. He was on friendly terms with Barlaeus, and Anslo, too, had been his supporter and patron. In fact, his first literary production, the translation and commentary on *Hilkhot Yesode hat–Torah* [*Constitutiones de Fundamentis Legis* (Amsterdam: Blaeu, 1638)] was gratefully dedicated to the businessman Mennonite. His other works in rabbinics were three: a translation of Abravanel's *Rosh Amanah* [*De Capite Fidei,* published as a companion piece to the Maimonidean treatise]; and translations of *Pirke de R. Eliezer* and David Gans's *Tsemaḥ David,* published together in 1644. The last mentioned, the *Tsemaḥ David* translation, was to be cited by Menasseh in his *Vindiciae Judaeorum* of 1656;[104] like its companion, *Pirke de R. Eliezer,* it was probably known to Menasseh from the 1630s, when it was originally translated. There is no way of telling Menasseh's role in the genesis of Vorstius's work. Vorstius does not mention him even once, nor is there any real evidence of Vorstius having made use of the *Conciliator.* Among his Christian Hebraist contemporaries, the only ones Vorstius mentions are Coch and Amama, the latter having died in 1629. They are cited once each, as are Reuchlin, Drusius, Buxtorf, and the Jewish convert Paulo Riccio. Of earlier writers, Macrobius and Varro are the only classical authors; there are a mere half dozen from other literatures, apart from the rabbinic.

Vorstius shows neither the broad culture nor the overall detachment of Vossius. There are no cross–references from rabbinic literature to other literatures in the manner employed by Vossius, though there was of course less of an opportunity for Vorstius to display any erudition he may have had, given the nature of *Yesode hat–Torah.* What Vorstius does display, in his first published work, is a much broader reading in the rabbinic sources than Vossius. He gives numerous extracts from other sections of the *Mishneh Torah,* makes quotations from quite a few tractates of the Talmud, though the bulk of these is smaller than that of the citations from the *Mishneh Torah,* and makes frequent reference to two works in particular, *'Avodat hak–Kodesh* of Meir ibn Gabbai, a sixteenth–century kabbalist who was fundamentally opposed to the Maimonidean viewpoint, and the *Derashot 'al hat–Torah* of Joshua Ibn Shu'aib, a fourteenth–century preacher and kabbalist. There are scattered references to Maimonides' *Guide* and to the *Kuzari* of Judah hal–Levi. Far and away the single work invoked most frequently is Albo's *'Ikkarim.* The citation of this work is often for displaying the differences of opinion among the rabbis that Vorstius thought would discredit their position. The same reason was given by Vorstius for his use of Abravanel's work as a companion piece; it is probable that the works of Ibn Shu'aib and, especially, Ibn Gabbai were brought in for similar purposes.

Vorstius was a polemicist. Over and above the few illustrative features of his commentary: the several explanations of a word or a phrase; the indication of a possible rationale; the cross reference[105] to Talmud or the Midrashim or some biblical exegete, one can feel his adversary stance at each turn and see it manifested broadly at certain important junctures. Though he had and used the same rabbinic editions of the *Mishneh Torah* as Vossius—his basic text is the Venice 1614, and he also had the 1550–51, for he compares the readings of the two at one point (p. 83, n. 12)—he relies on the commentators therein far less than his predecessor, so busy is he with confutation.

There are hardly more than two or three comments where he seems specifically to approve of the rabbinic position or viewpoint. His comment on the use of amulets is perhaps the only wholehearted one. There he writes, having described how scrupulously the rabbis tried to keep the people away from any appearance of worshipping idols (he cites passages from *Shemot Rabba;* the *Bet Yosef* on *Tur* 'Yoreh De'ah', 'Avodat Elilim; and TB *Pesaḥim*), that there are many similar things in the writings of the *Hebraei* and that these should justly strike a sense of shame into the many who, to the disgrace of the Christian religion, use all kinds of charms in all sorts of ways to ward off disease (p. 63, n. 14).

Even this, though, is indicative of Vorstius's true aim. The indication is that, if the Jews can act in such a manner, the Christians should all the more so. This is, in and of itself, hardly scandalous, but it is found in a commentary the avowed purpose of which is to discredit the Jewish position. For, among the topics addressed by Vorstius are the perpetuity of the ritual law, the character and function of the prophet, and the period of his coming. In fact, the only places in his edition of the Abravanel treatise where Vorstius inserted any commentary are at the ends of chapters 13 and 14, where he attacked the philosopher's position on the question of the eternity and immutability of the oral law and on the period of the Messiah's coming. And, throughout the commentary on Maimonides, there are the traditional epithets and name calling. The rabbinic statements are, routinely, said to be trifles, vanities, falsehoods, and fabrications; at one point, in considering a certain view of Ibn Shu'aib's, he assails the "thick stupidity of [that] Jewish fellow" ("En crassam hominis Judaei stupiditatem!") (p. 46, n. 5), and, a few lines further down, refers to other Jewish writers who held the same view as "Iudaeastri." The topic is of little importance. Neither is the general run of such remarks, by comparison to the more general critiques that Vorstius mounts for the purpose of destroying the credibility of the rabbis. While Vorstius hoped to bring men to the knowledge of God, the way he went about it was by trying to show that the law could and should be dispensed with. He spends a whole chapter discussing the law and whether and how it can continue, invoking Albo both in support of the view that the law is not absolutely immutable and also against the supreme elevation of Moses by comparison to the other prophets.[106]

Greater detail is warranted as to the elements of Vorstius's critique. First of all, this commentary is clearly not a case in point of the traditional attempt to prove the truth of Christianity out of Jewish sources that supposedly contain Christian truths. It is, rather, intended to show Christians that the disagreements between the various Jewish authorities invalidate Judaism. It is also aimed at getting Christians to renounce any insistence they might have on the perpetuation of ritual. Here, perhaps, Vorstius might have been giving vent to some of his Socinian leanings, though, of course, he does not indicate this in the commentary. His goal, speaking generally, is for the truth of Christianity to be asserted.

His introduction is almost misleading. On the one hand, he shows an interest in knowing the fundamentals of rabbinic Judaism. It is the proper beginning, he argues, for a young Hebraist: one should deal with the more obvious elements of the Jewish religion first, rather than entering the more arcane areas too precipitously. This is the gist of his apologia to Anslo, his Maecenas, to whom he also expresses the hope: "May He who munificently bestows wisdom enhance your extraordinary genius through the abundant grace of His favoring Spirit and make your talents long endure for us in the fuller propagation of the firm knowledge of His glorious name." This is the perspective through which Vorstius viewed the activities of others as well.

Moreover, his interest in the fundamentals of Judaism is based on a certain assumption about consensus in religion. It is a dreadful thing, he says in his preface to the reader, and a sheer calamity for a religion not to rest on principles held in common and derived to the greatest possible extent from pure revelation, that is to say, with the smallest possible admixture of human invention.

Sefer ham–Madda‘, he continues, is the book dealing with the precepts—vestiges of revelation, he had called them a moment earlier—concerning men's intellect or mind in order to engender a pure and correct understanding of God and his majesty. But, he argues, there is no consensus among rabbinic authorities as to what the number and order of these precepts or basic principles is: the volume by Abravanel that is appended will demonstrate this readily.

> The consensus . . . must be recognized as lacking. If any, this race of men (*hominum genus*) must be deemed the most contentious; you may often see a mob of [their] doctors disputing, with great effort and in an uproar, over trifles in the talmudic chaos.

Now many accuse Christians of the same lack of consensus, he goes on, and many others find this deplorable. That is to say, there is much criticism of those who spend their time pointing out and examining the areas of disagreement among Christians. Among those who are the most active in making these accusations are the Hebraists, who, "mutatâ adversarii personâ," changing the adversary, prefer sharpening their swords on the "Messiae cultores," those who worship the Messiah, to "opening the door, for the errant [Jews], to communion with the king, whom they have longed for in vain for so many centuries." In this latter way, says Vorstius, the "knowledge of the truth" would be spread better.

Of course, Menasseh too was concerned with spreading truth. Here was the confrontation of adversaries. Vorstius urges that the Hebraists turn instead to promoting the honor of God ("ducis et capitis sui," as he puts it). Vorstius's approach is reminiscent of l'Empereur's: to know the Jewish sources and arguments in order the better to preach Christianity. He makes some comments on the authority of the writers, Maimonides and Abravanel, on the Hebrew text having been omitted in the second work, and on the translation, which, he claims is quite literal. (Others criticized it roundly for its sloppiness, however.) He then concludes by warning his readers not to be offended by any anti–Christian remarks they may come across: "mitiora si quis ab hostibus sibi polliceatur, toto caelo errat (one would be grossly in error to expect anything milder from one's enemies)." And yet one must not remain silent: those who are fair judges will not need any more elaborate admonition, nor are they to fear the Jewish refusal to debate ("nec . . . ab iis metuendum esse diverbium istud *shetok ve–tinnatsel*[:] *Sile, ac tutus eris*").

Indeed, we are publishing this youthful exercise for no other purpose than to arouse others to the pursuit of the same truth in order thereby that strangers may be invited [to share in] the community of a single kingdom and that the Sun of justice spread the rays of his light more broadly.

This expresses hopes as visionary as Menasseh's; it is, in truth, rather restrained and universalist at the end. Nonetheless, it is ultimately an expression of the view that the study of Hebrew was part of the endeavor to promote the knowledge of God through the expansion of the Christian faith. This is, of course, hardly revolutionary, in either concept or manner of presentation. What is of interest is its application here. Vorstius had argued that all the utterances of the rabbis are made to conform to certain norms of belief as to a touchstone: that was his rationale for undertaking the study of this kind of work before delving deeper. And yet he subsequently steps back from this supposition, claiming that there is much disagreement among the rabbinic authorities and that this shows the bankruptcy of their position. In short, it is by no means clear that Vorstius considers the treatise he is working on to be useful in and of itself to convey any truths about the knowledge of God or to lead men to it. Statements such as this, which we might have expected, are lacking; the thrust is entirely polemical.

A measure of the differences between Vossius and Vorstius is the latter's treatment of the terms *min* and *epikoros* (6:10 pp. 83–84, n. 12). Vorstius quotes the same passage from *Hilkhot Teshuvah* as Vossius had at the beginning of chapter 2 of *De Idololatria* (p. 20). (Both translations, incidentally, are rather faithful, if completely different one from the other.) While Vossius's purpose had been to lead into the discussion of angels, and thus by degrees to his single mention of Christian doctrine, Vorstius turns rather sharply to a discussion of the *min* himself. Though the nature of heresy is only of tangential interest to the explication of the Maimonidean text here—the issue is the disposal of a Torah scroll written by such a person—Vorstius proceeds to the investigation of the identity of the heretic. He quotes Rashi (perhaps after the citation of the passage in the *Haggahot Maimoniyyot*), who, he says, "nulla cum veri specie," 'with not a semblance of truth', included in the group "the disciples of Jesus of Nazareth, who perverted for evil the words of the living God." (The text is not the censored one, obviously, which eliminates the name of Jesus and substitutes *minim.*)

This brings Vorstius to a defense of Christianity. Not only, he argues, do Christians recognize the one and invisible God and should, insofar as the recognition of intermediaries is concerned, not be included in the category of heretics, but,

> as for our confession of Christ as mediator, if [the Jews] are indignant at this, then let them reproach the testament and command (*voluntas ac jussum*) of God himself, who confirms this high office of our Messiah in word and in documents able to withstand any objection (*omni exceptione majoribus*). That [the Jews] do not embrace these for any reason other than their inveterate hatred of our Jesus and their absolutely total blindness has been shown more than enough by [Christians], so that there is by no means any further need of proofs.

In other words, since Christianity, in Vorstius's view, is truly in accord with the biblical truth and faith, there can be no question that the Christian Messiah merits acceptance by the Jews. As for the hatred shown him, it is a charge Vorstius repeats elsewhere and is one of the cornerstones of his view of the Jews. He writes (8:1, p. 110, n. 1) that the Jews, "nugacissimi mortalium," 'the most frivolous of mortals', will go to any extreme "lest they be forced to recognize that our Jesus performed his miracles at the direction and by virtue of the order of God himself and that these were all such that they accrued to His glory alone . . ." Vorstius is here attempting to discredit Maimonides' position on the value of miracles or, rather, on the insufficiency of miracles as a determinant of whether an individual is or is not a true prophet.

Vorstius's attempts to discredit Maimonides' and, more generally, the Jewish position on miracles, if there is, in fact, a general Jewish position, become clearer in the annotation that follows (8:1, pp. 110–114, n. 2). Quoting Albo, Vorstius posits a difference between the two religions as to the number and weight of their miracles; Vorstius judges Christianity to come out far ahead in the race. He then reviews the various miracles said to have been performed by Moses, not to detract from the divinity of Moses' miracles, he says—"longissime exulet talis cogitatio," 'let any such thought be banished as far as possible'—but rather to show how incongruous is the Jewish rule that neither the truth of prophecy nor its divinity is confirmed by miracles.

Be that as it may, Vorstius's larger purpose here is to consider the question of the law: the commandments and the rituals and their temporary abrogation and the implication of such an action by certain prophets for the possibility of a more permanent nullification. In the course of his lucubrations, he lets it be known what his purpose is, in terms even more explicit than before:

> that we may assert the wonderful teaching of our Jesus against the obstinate incredulity of these mortals: for virtually everything that is alleged in this chapter is directed at weakening the force of the most divine works of our Messiah, . . . [107]

If Maimonides' remarks are an attempt to minimize the divinity of Jesus' works, Vorstius wishes to minimize those remarks by trying to disprove Maimonides' contentions about the immutability of the law.

Vorstius had dealt with Moses before this as well, and that had formed some of the background of this comment. At 7:6 (pp. 98–100, n. 14), he makes an extensive quotation and translation of a passage from *Numbers Rabbah* (14:34) comparing the prophetic qualities of Moses with those of Balaam. Vorstius's purpose is to show the inconsistency of the sources about Moses, an inconsistency that appears to Vorstius as making the rabbis deprive Moses and even the law itself of "all authority." ("Ipsi omnem autoritatem, non dico tantum Mosis, sed totius legis eversum eunt.") Who could rely on such an individual, he wonders, one whose prowess and powers appeared superior to Balaam's in some respects, yet inferior in others:

> It would indeed not only have been absurd long ago but it would even be absurd now for the Jews to have confidence in a messenger of such a sort that he himself does not know by whom he has been sent [according to this midrash, among the features that distinguished the prophecy of Moses from that of Balaam was that Moses did not know who was speak-

ing with him, while Balaam did]: [the Jews] will now find Christians fairer judges of Mosaic prophecy.[108]

This can be seen, he says, in the freedom with which aggadic statements are treated by the rabbis. He cites Naḥmanides' words at Barcelona to the effect that, as Vorstius puts it, "it is not unsuitable to reject the statements of the talmudists from time to time." This supposed inconsistency is said to make any and all rabbinic statements about Moses unreliable, by contrast to the Christian view of Moses, which recognizes but does not exaggerate his qualities.

And yet, in another context (9:3, pp. 125–26, n. 6), Vorstius argues that Jesus' miracles are superior and that Deut. 13:15, "The Lord your God will raise up for you a prophet from among your own people, like myself; him shall you heed," was fulfilled in Jesus. (Vorstius also dismisses any suggestion that Mal. 3:22, "Remember the Torah of my servant Moses . . ." [Vorstius's tr.: "Mementote legis Mosis servi mei"], used as a proof–text by Maimonides, has any bearing on the immutability of the law.) The same issues crop up again and again in the commentary.

The last and most explicit statement Vorstius makes about his own goals is contained in an annotation on Maimonides' ruling that every prophet must prove himself not by a miraculous sign but rather by foretelling something and actually having it come to pass. Vorstius takes this as yet another opportunity to defend Jesus; here we can see better than anywhere else Vorstius taking a statement by Maimonides as proof of the truth of Christianity. For Vorstius does not, as we have said earlier, make use of this line of argument to the great extent that earlier writers and others among his contemporaries did.

Vorstius contends that the sufferings of Christians on behalf of their Messiah—the types of trials and tribulations are considered at length—should suffice to convince any fair judge of the true divinity and uprightness of Christianity ("ut verè caelestem ac innocentem pronunciat Christi religionem"). Moreover, he continues,

> One will see [in Christianity] a clear image of true wisdom and happiness, one the Jew is still so anxiously searching for in vain through aggadah or halakhah.[109]

After this "demonstration," Vorstius turns, in the same annotation, to the argument that there is no excuse for either the crucifixion of old or the contemporary Jewish commendation of it as a great deed of their ancestors. Regardless of whether Vorstius is or is not justified in understanding the Jewish view in this manner, he proceeds with a series of examples designed to show that nothing Jesus did warranted such a punishment, pausing at the question of Jesus' having abolished the ceremonial law and stating that this was authorized by God himself. This leads into the point that he has been working toward all along: that the most suitable way, as he sees it, for leading all the inhabitants of the world to the knowledge and veneration of the true God of Israel is by destroying the fence of ritual ("septum illud rituum"):

> With this [fence] standing, the approach of the rest of the nations to the worship of that divinity is blocked. There is nothing surprising about this: for this [continues to] produce and foment hatred and aversion between Jews and foreigners, to the extent that, as long as this quarrel over ritual continues, neither party will easily renounce its hostile feelings.

Vorstius admits that the sacrifices had their purpose at one time, citing the *Guide* and Albo to show the view that they were instituted to keep the people from idolatry; of this he approves.

> And so, finally, let the Jews recognize not only that the goodness of God, in spreading the light of His truth to foreign nations even, is to be hallowed with eternal praises, but also that one must strive in admiration to imitate the image of His wisdom as, with this glue of worship, it joins together hearts estranged by almost native enmities, so that, in this way, all mortals may unite their hearts and voices [lit. 'tongues'] in harmony in the recognition of a now common Father and in the pursuit of their mutual salvation.

As noble as these sentiments of Vorstius sound—they hark back also to the "Preface to the Reader"—they are essentially antagonistic to the preservation of the Jews as Jews. Vorstius sees the Jews as part of the larger scheme of the spread of the knowledge of God; Menasseh had looked forward to that as well, but with the preservation of the identity of the Jews. Not only is there no quarter for that in Vorstius's scheme, the whole thrust of his remarks argues against it.

Vorstius's purpose in translating even the *De Creatione* must have been this from the first: to use the work of a Jewish writer, even without commenting upon it, specifically to counter that writer's goals. Menasseh had one conception of what his work might accomplish, Vorstius another. Even though Menasseh was able to put Vorstius to use in 1635 to serve his own needs, we can be almost certain that, after 1638, when the translation of *Hilkhot Yesode hat–Torah* was published, Vorstius was *persona non grata* in the Jewish community. Menasseh may even have been admonished to avoid giving Vorstius further counsel, the same injunction issued in the case of l'Empereur.

Not only did Menasseh not succeed in winning over Vorstius's sympathies, he did not dissuade Anslo from accepting Vorstius's dedication. Moreover, Anslo urged Vorstius to publish his earlier translations also. Though he was dead by the time it appeared, it was Anslo's encouragement of the *Tsemaḥ David*'s being brought to light that was primarily responsible for its appearance. The abbreviated translation of this work that Vorstius had made in the 1630s was published in 1644, coupled with 130 pages of "Observationes" (We might call them "confutationes") that he added while the translation was in the press.

In these "Observationes," Vorstius's hostility appears undiminished. He takes Gans's rationale and hope in writing his work, the hope that the reader would be moved to pray earnestly to God for the coming of the Messiah, "the champion of Jewish liberty,"—there were other hopes and purposes as well, which Vorstius only mentions—as a springboard for his own tirade against the various calculations the Jews have made concerning the date of the messianic coming. Listing a few and ridiculing them, he comes to the conclusion:

> But these mortals, utterly blinded by hatred and prejudice, prefer feeding themselves and their kind on vain hope to putting on the yoke of the kingdom of the true Messiah.[110]

The line of thought he had followed in his edition of Maimonides is maintained here.

But this was not the half of it. Vorstius now announces that he has collected the blasphemies against Jesus from the Talmud and more recent Jewish writers, "not that the reader may derive pleasure therefrom, but rather, that he learn to hate the mad views of the Jews and thus firm up his own religious convictions."[111] A major purpose of his publishing Gans's book was as a vehicle for anti–Jewish argument. It is not surprising, then, that, at this point, Vorstius invokes l'Empereur, "most knowledgeable in rabbinic science" ("rabbinicâ scientiâ excultissimus"), as he describes him. L'Empereur's translation and "refutation" of the classic polemical treatise *Sefer Nitsaḥon* was still in preparation, Vorstius notes, expressing his hope for its successful completion and appearance. Vorstius reveals his identity now even more sharply than he had earlier. Raising, as he had in his preface to *De Fundamentis Legis,* the specter of internal Christian disagreement and quarreling, he states his purpose directly: "Sat hactenus rixarum Christianam vexavit orbem, tandem vertamus arma in Messiae nostri hostes." Enough of quarreling, he cries: "let us turn our arms against the enemies of our Messiah!" Not only had he willfully castrated Gans's chronicle by omitting much of the second book, i.e., the "profana" portions of the *Chronologia Sacra–Profana,* and by barely summarizing the prefaces by Gans that he had omitted from the translation, he had used Gans's history in order to promote the conversion of the Jews.[112]

We may close our discussion of Vorstius with a brief notice of his *Pirke de R. Eliezer* translation. This is the only work in which Vorstius suggests there may be something of value. "From time to time," he allows, "it contains plausible expositions that can serve either for illustrating sacred history or for explaining the rites and traditions of the Hebrews."[113] Yet he also asserts that the messianic calculations of the Jews are deceptive, and that, as a result, the truth of the Gospel is confirmed.

There are a few other elements, but, on the whole, this is the approach that Vorstius took. The illustrative elements of his commentaries are far less important in his scheme than his confutations, all of which had his scholarship turned to a conversionist aim.

The context of Menasseh's *Vindiciae Judaeorum* citation of Vorstius reflects this, as it turns out. Menasseh considered Vorstius's observation on the frequent omission from the "'Alenu" prayer of the line "humbling themselves to things of no worth and vanity," which condemns the gentiles' worship of vain gods—Vorstius, both according to Menasseh and in point of fact, had seen the line as spoken "against Christ" (*Chronologia*, p. 269)—Menasseh saw this as unfounded. He himself considered the prayer to have been composed many years before the Christian era. Menasseh's citation of Vorstius together with Buxtorf and John Hoornbeck, the Calvinist controversialist and apocalyptic visionary (1617–66), who in 1655 had published his *Teshuvat Yehudah sive, Pro convincendis, et convertendis Judaeis* at Leiden, shows, however, where he ultimately came to class Vorstius, if he had not, in fact, done so quite early. Menasseh was anxious to blunt the force of Vorstius's and the others' criticism and he argued that the line not only did not refer to Jesus, but that its omission was due to the Jews' "desire to . . . avoid the least occasion of scandall, and offence." The view of Vorstius and the others was, he implies, itself calumny. Menasseh asks "the unprejudiced and unbiased reader"—the Hebraists themselves, including even Vorstius in other circumstances, often[114] appeal to "aequiores aestimatores," 'more fair–minded judges'—Menasseh asks these readers to judge how just Vorstius's interpretation of the circumstances of the passage was. He must have been quite distressed at his lack of success with Vorstius, even if he had not been deceived by Vorstius's aims. Menasseh always hoped for the best.

Georgius Gentius, *On the Principles of Ethics:* In Praise of Maimonides

Georg Gentze (1618–87), styled Georgius Gentius, was also a pupil of Menasseh's. Seemingly, he was of a different sort. A favorite of the Amsterdam rabbis and even of those in Constantinople, he translated *Hilkhot De'ot* with the approval of Aboab and Aguilar, as well as under the patronage and with the encouragement of Anslo. As a result, most likely, of the attitude he manifests in this edition, which appeared in Amsterdam in 1640 under the title *Canones Ethici* and was published, like the two editions previously considered, by Blaeu, Menasseh would subsequently charge Gentius with completing a translation of Ibn Verga's *Shevet Yehudah* that he himself had begun.

A Lutheran and a native of Dhame in Saxony, he began to master the Oriental languages at an early age. He moved to Halle in 1635, then to Schleswig, Hamburg, and Bremen, arriving finally in Leiden, one of many Germans to do so, in 1638. He came to study with the greats: Heinsius, de Dieu, Golius, and, especially, l'Empereur. Along the way, he had stopped in Amsterdam to receive a letter of introduction to l'Empereur from G. J. Vossius, to whom he had been introduced by his German professors. Vossius considered him deserving. Moreover, during his three years or so at Leiden, he returned to Amsterdam for private lessons from Menasseh. Perhaps Vossius had introduced the young foreigner to the rabbi. At any rate, Gentius's biographer has it that Menasseh drew Gentius in to be his student in order that he might thereafter praise his instruction publicly as often as he could.[115]

Gentius's first product was his *Canones Ethici,* the edition of *De'ot.* While there is no specific praise of Menasseh, there is adulation of Anslo. The work is dedicated to the "mercator sapiens," 'the merchant philosopher', as Gentius calls him, undoubtedly after the title of Barlaeus's inaugural address at the Amsterdam Athenaeum in 1632; Anslo, he says, had treated him like a son. Anslo's coupling of Apollo and Mercury, as he puts it, had set an example for readers as one who knew that erudition should have as its purpose the control and regulation of wealth and power. The secular and the scholarly were to go hand in hand, with erudition as a guide and commercial ventures as the support of learning. Anslo is praised as a qualified Hebraist, one who could appreciate the need for such a work.

The need for the work was clear to Gentius. He felt he lived in an age when ethics and morality had vanished. Maimonides' treatise was suitable for bringing men back to the right path via a discussion of the vices and virtues to which men are subject. But it was not as simple as that. His choice of treatise had to be defended further, he felt. The arguments are familiar: there is no reason why learned men, who admit that many of the pagan traditions have value and who, in general, are prepared to entertain whatever pious and learned traditions might be of public benefit, there is no reason these "doctissimi" should be averse to accepting the thinking of Maimonides, "the wisest of the Jews." Gentius continues: "I don't think anyone is foolish (*ineptus*) enough to be deterred from reading a most excellent author just because he knows that the author is a Jew." Gentius identifies Maimonides for his audience as "a man incomparable with respect to every form of learning, who has been esteemed among [the Hebrews] and will be esteemed among even the esteemed [among them]." In life, he continues, Maimonides shone so brightly as to enlighten minds covered over with the darkness of too many fables—this is a bit of a gibe, to be sure—and in death he left behind that which can be of use for every age.[116] Gentius specifically feels the need to state outright who it is that his own work is directed to, that is to say, for whom it can be useful: it is submitted to the judgment of pious individuals, those with "candida & proba ingenia," those of an upright and honest character. In other words, piety is not limited to Christians; clear and unbiased minds will see the value of this work.

There is much extravagant praise for the work itself. It should not be considered of lesser worth for having escaped the notice of Western readers for so long, he writes, also quoting an unidentified Arab poet to the effect that the greatest pearls lie in the deepest waters of the sea. Maimonides' work affected him so, he states, that, having read it three and four times, he wanted to read it yet again. Not only was its style elegant, it was itself of value for its contents and also of maximum usefulness to the Republic of Letters. He identified so totally with Maimonides' viewpoint, in fact, that he not only mentions the usefulness of the work for Christians and says they will find acceptable things in it, but also suggests that some of the things even some Jews consider too fanatical and reject are actually virtues. These virtues are exemplified by the admonition of others over their errors and are said to be a kind of *imitatio Dei.* As Gentius views it, they raise man to a superhuman state and make him come to resemble the divine nature very closely.

All this is part of a very long preface in which Gentius engages in a general kind of moralizing, based both on an Aristotelian ethical scheme of a coordination between virtues, dispositions, and humors on the one hand, and biblical morality, as explained in rabbinic literature, on the other. His thinking will be much more fully developed in the virtual monograph on the several vices and virtues, twenty in number, that serves as a set of "general annotations" on Maimonides' treatise and is intended as a summary of the rabbinic conceptions of the individual ethical dispositions, though not of rabbinic ethics in general. (There is also a set of "specific annotations.")

Yet there is also a second preface to the edition, this one in Hebrew. It is to some extent an exercise in composition, but it also comes to stress Gentius's background in Hebraism as well as direct the reader to what he may be expected to come away with. This preface is even more munificent in its praise of the work than the Latin preface; perhaps it was written in Hebrew so that more casual readers would not so readily scorn Gentius's extremely sympathetic characterizations of the work:

> After I entered into the inner chambers of the Hebrew language, I saw things I never imagined, never having conceived that a people humbled and despised by the whole world such as the Jews was wise and understanding. I saw that they were.

This is what Menasseh had been striving for, looking for the study of rabbinic literature to be the stimulus to such a view. Gentius further reveals that he had started Hebrew in order to study the Scriptures, but, he says, "I found more than I asked for." He again mentions the several times he read the work and the usefulness he found in it

> on account of the wisdom and morality it contains, all [Maimonides'] words being just, none of them perverse or twisted, all of them straightforward for a person of understanding and pleasing to those who wish for knowledge; in general, all [Maimonides' words] are appropriate for all classes of the multitude of men.

This is the most wholehearted praise for any Jewish work that we have yet encountered in our study. Moreover, Gentius's purposes in making the translation, as he articulates them in this Hebrew preface, are even more in line with what Menasseh had hoped. The translation would be "le–to'elet ha–'olam," 'for the benefit of the world', bringing men back to the right path and away from folly and dissolution, moulding character traits and restoring men sick in body and spirit. It is a work "yakar u–mo'il le–khol ha–'olam," he repeats, valuable and useful for the whole world.

This is not all, though. There is wisdom to be gained from the treatise, according to Gentius, not wisdom that gets written down and forgotten, but wisdom that lives in the heart and mind—Gentius takes his reference from what Socrates said to Timaeus—and brings men to the rank of the pious ("el madregat ha–ḥasidut"). Again Gentius is emphasizing piety; the piety of a Jewish author's view and the piety of Christians can be one and the same, according to this line of argument. (He had also said that he knew that "wise men will praise and confirm" Maimonides' statements.) He expects, therefore, that the reader will come to love and become beloved of God and blessed of God as well; the conclusion dwells on the ample personal reward that the reader will derive from following this treatise.

In all of this, there is no mention at all of Christianity. Though Gentius's closing wish, that the reader come to be among the pious in the graciousness of God ("ve–tihyeh . . . beyn ha–ḥasidim be–no'am hash–shem") probably has the idea of "salvation" behind it, no explicitly Christological interpretation is introduced. True, Gentius would mention his "Messiah" in the course of his "General Annotations" in a passing reference to Ps. 22:7 ("But I am a worm, and no man, a reproach of men, and despised of the people") under the chapter *De Humilitate* (p. 80). He would even validate a rabbinic position by remarking, "Imo, ut nos Christus docet," 'Yea, as Christ teaches us' (p. 123). But this is the extent of the references to Christianity. Though Gentius was a committed Christian, he was trying here to minimize the differences between the wisdom of a Jewish author and what would be valid for Christians. As such, this work is the first fully ripe fruit of Menasseh's efforts to have his pupils demonstrate that there were principles common to Christianity and Judaism upon which the two sides could agree. Nonetheless, it is highly unlikely that Gentius, in view of his references to both Vossius and Vorstius and to their works (p. [viii]), considered himself any different in approach from his predecessors. It was most probably the subject matter itself that was the prime factor in his writing as he did, even if his personality may have been more congenial than Vorstius's.

In the meantime, though, Gentius manifests a positive attitude to Maimonides' treatise, hoping that his readers would learn from it (p. 141). He felt that his edition was designed to uncover the truth without embellishing it, to let the text speak for itself so that the reader could proceed directly "ad res ipsas" ('to the matter itself') (pp. [ix–x]). This implies that nothing had to be eliminated or censured, that the text as it stood was of value. Moreover, though Gentius characterized his commentary as an "illustratio" along the standard lines, that elucidation, he said, was to come directly out of the rabbinic sources, with only an occasional input from Greco–Roman literature (p. 129). If Aristotle or Plato are mentioned—and they are the only two classical writers mentioned at all (pp. 84, 88, 111)—it is as corroboration for the talmudic view.

Gentius's seventy–page monograph, replete with tables and charts of the twenty dispositions and their relationships to the several humors (pp. 70–73), is intended as a summation of the views of the "Hebraei" on morality and ethics. The sources on which Gentius drew must have included the more than one dozen tractates of the Talmud that he mentions by name and the Hebrew commentators on the *Mishneh Torah* included in the Venice 1574 edition. Not only is Gentius's paragraphing a clue to his choice of edition—the Venice 1574, incidentally, has a superior text for *Hilkhot De'ot*—the many source references to the Talmud that he gives in his "Notae speciales" are those given by the Hebrew commentators included in that edition. Gentius refers by name to the one comment of Rabad of Posquières on *De'ot* (pp. 144–45) and concludes a detailed explanation of what Rabad had in mind (he calls Rabad the "aemulus," the one who 'vies with' "our author") by citing what "autoris nostri vindices," 'the defenders of Maimonides', meaning the *Kesef Mishneh* and the *Migdal 'Oz,* responded to Rabad. The specifics are of minimal importance for us; suffice it to say that Gentius shows an ability to work with these sources. The only other works Gentius cites by name are the *Guide of the Perplexed* and the *Regimen sanitatis* of Maimonides (pp. 129 and 149 respectively).

Despite the apparent dearth of source references, Gentius does draw freely on rabbinic literature. In his monograph, he tells one story after another from the aggadah, without giving source references, in illustration of the different vices and virtues. In the margin, these stories are sometimes indicated with the words "lepidae historiae," 'witty tales'. (See pp. 81, 86, 89, etc., etc.) For example, to show Hillel's "humilitas," his meekness, Gentius narrates at length the story from *Avot de–Rabbi Natan* 15 about the calmness with which Hillel responded to the questioning of two querulous individuals who wished to prove a point by angering him. His rendering amounts to a virtual translation. In the chapter *De con-*

fidentia (pp. 117–21), Gentius presents a long disquisition on why the righteous suffer and the wicked prosper. In this latter case, though, the talmudic material is somewhat reorganized; Gentius gives the standard explanations, but cites some biblical verses of his own choosing as well. Elsewhere, Gentius reproduces the aggadah, found in a number of rabbinic sources, about God's mercies: clothing the naked, visiting the sick, comforting the bereaved, and so on (ad 1:5 and 7, pp. 131–34). These he identifies as deriving from the Hebrew commentators on Scripture, but he quotes them, he says, in order to incite his readers to follow the example, for it "thus also behooves men to imitate God in this class of duties, which is of the utmost necessity, . . ."[117] Such exhortation on the "duties of piety" is found in almost every chapter of the brief monograph, Gentius stressing over and over the need for virtue and for attention to one's fellow man (see also, e.g., p. 97, for another piece of eloquent sermonizing).

Gentius seems to have been quite fond of Mishnah *Avot* in particular. Many of his references include citations from that tractate, often with his own elaboration as well. On *De'ot* 2:4, for example, he gives a six–page running commentary on *Avot* 6:6, which lists the forty–eight ways in which the "Hebrew wise men of old ordained that wisdom, i.e., the law, is to be acquired" (pp. 136–41).

There is criticism of Maimonides only for the purpose of coming to his defense. Once Gentius posits some disagreement between Maimonides and Scripture and then goes on to argue that, on closer examination, the disagreement vanishes (p. 130). Elsewhere, he discusses a minor discrepancy between Maimonides and TB *Bava metsi'a* on whether movement after eating is appropriate (on 4:3, p. 156). Gentius concludes by coming out in favor of Maimonides. These are the only two cases where there is any suggestion of disagreement, and they are truly insignificant.

Gentius, like the other commentators, is concerned with the overall structure of the treatise and with the author's intention. Let one example suffice. On the opening paragraph of the work, Gentius writes:

> It is not the author's intention only to restore to health those who are suffering from a disease of the body and, after that, to let them live each in their own way, but even to show the reason they were wretched and

miserable, and, what is more, to teach them those things from which they should abstain. [P. 130]

Virtually all of Gentius's observations and comments are of such a nondoctrinaire variety. He often waxes enthusiastic, in fact. He quotes with satisfaction, for example (ad 4:3, p. 152), the "elegantissimum proverbium" of the *Hebraei,* "mah she–ha–av shokheaḥ hab–ben meshabeaḥ," though the context he had established was merely a discussion of certain maladies and their treatment, this one being the strengthening of the memory. Chapter 4, in general, is about medical matters, and Gentius, who had an interest in medicine—witness his correspondence with A. E. Vorstius, the Leiden professor of medicine[118] —gathers quite a few corresponding pieces of information from the Talmud on the subjects of drugs and healing (see pp. 146–57 passim).

In sum, though the three young commentators on Maimonides shared a number of approaches and techniques, the one who was most favorable in his overall demeanor was Gentius.[119] The panegyrics prefixed by Aboab and Aguilar stand testimony to this.

The Commendatory Poems

Gifts of poetry to an author were a routine, though almost indispensable feature of seventeenth–century editions. Such contributions did not have the force of the formal approbation, the *haskamah,* but they were still eagerly sought after for the more welcome reception and, perhaps, wider circulation they promised a work.[120] More to the point, they embodied the mutual encouragement of authors characteristic of the period[121] and they gave expression to friendship and mutual esteem.[122] A substantial number of these compliments in verse were offered graciously, and many demonstrated abiding affection and profound respect. To be sure, most of the poems contained only superficial or *pro forma* praise, some of them, no doubt, having been contributed less than enthusiastically.

All these panegyrics, however, are useful as documents, even if they are not of uniform value. One cannot be too cautious in assessing the measure of exaggeration, whether careless or intentional, that inevitably went into their makeup. In the case of the two poems for Gentius, though, they provide the major documentation for his relationship with the rabbis and Jewish community of Amsterdam.[123]

We may note, first of all, that neither of the panegyrists, neither Aboab nor Aguilar, identifies Gentius as his pupil. As we have already noted, Gentius was said by his biographer to have been Menasseh's student. Yet, in the year 1640, as we know, Menasseh's influence within the Jewish community was in eclipse, with that of Aboab and Aguilar on the ascendant. Still, they seem to have known Gentius quite well themselves. Moreover, while Aboab and Aguilar would appear together again several times to offer panegyrics to Jewish writers,[124] these are the only two commendatory poems for the work of a Christian that we have by them or by any other Dutch rabbi of this century.

The poems are addressed to Gentius, not to his audience, and are obviously meant to encourage him to a new and higher level of support for rabbinic literature and for the Jews. Though the poetic value of these verses is minimal, there are a number of points of interest in them.

Aboab's poem (see Figure I, overleaf) is a typical hendecasyllabic *ottava rima* of the period. Aboab begins, however, with a piece of literary expropriation. He telescopes the first few lines of a paean of thanks by Israel Najara (1555–1628) in the latter's *Meme Yisrael* of 1599.[125] Though this was probably an unknown or obscure work as far as Christian audiences were concerned, and, as such, the added praise implicit in the actual borrowing would have escaped the audience, Aboab may have alerted Gentius to its significance. Such expropriation from an address to Najara's Jewish friend, a man of great wisdom and talent, indicates quite a bit about Aboab's feelings for Gentius and his conception of Gentius's stature. The addressee in Najara's poem was apparently David Onkeneira, his dear friend, "dodi." As such Najara refers to Onkeneira, and as such Aboab addresses Gentius.[126] Though there seems to have been some friction between Najara and Onkeneira, traces of which are evident in Najara's poem, there is no trace of either cloud or shadow in Aboab's praise of Gentius. Aboab's sense of pleasure, not only in Gentius's achievement, but in the moral value of Gentius's work and in Gentius's apparent integrity as a person and in his moral purity is genuine and hard to escape.

Figure I: Aboab's Panegyric

יוֹם נִגְלְתָה קֶשֶׁת בְּבוֹר כַּפֶּךָ,
אַצְתִּי תְּשׁוּרָתִי וְגַם מִנְחָתִי,
כִּי אֶחְשְׁבָהּ, דוֹדִי, לְהוֹד תָּקְפֶּךָ,
אִישׁ זָר יְגַלֶּה, תּוֹךְ עֲדָתִי, דָּתִי.
לָכֵן בְּהִלּוּלִים לְמוּל סִפֶּיךָ
אָבֹא, וְלֹא אֶדּוֹם עֲדֵי מִלָּתִי
תִּפְתַּח דְּלָתֶיהָ בְּשִׁיר עוּגָבִים
לָרוּם תְּהִלָּתְךָ עֲלֵי כּוֹכָבִים.

יצחק אבואב

3 דפוס: להור. 8 דפוס: כוככים.

Figure II: Aguilar's Panegyric

אַחֲרֵי רְאוֹתִי, אֲהוּבִי, אֶת שְׁלֵמוּתְךָ בְּחָכְמָה
וּבַחֲסִידוּת, וְעַתָּה אֶת סִפְרְךָ הַמֵּעִיד עָלֶיהָ, לֹא עָצַרְתִּי כֹּחַ
מִלְּסַפֵּר בְּשִׁיר יְדִידוֹת מְעַט שְׁבָחֶיךָ, וָאֶשָּׂא מְשָׁלִי
(אֲנִי הַצָּעִיר מֹשֶׁה מֵאֲגִילְאַר)
וָאוֹמַר:

אִם, הֵן, בְּכָל אוּמִים מְאוֹד נֶחְכָּמוּ,
נִתְחַסְּדוּ רַבִּים וְגַם צָדְקוּ,
יַעַן יְמוֹתֵיהֶם בְּטוּב נָמַקּוּ
וּלְהַר אֱלֹהִים עִם חָכְמָתָם קָמוּ,

אַתָּה לְבַדְּךָ, עֲלֵי חֻכְּמוּ;
נָאֶה לְךָ כָּבוֹד בְּכָל אוּמֶּךָ,
כִּי, בִּהְיוֹתְךָ בִּבְחוּרוֹתֶיךָ,
יָדַעְתָּ לְשׁוֹנוֹת אֲשֶׁר יַחְכִּימוּ.

עוֹד, גַּם בְּכָל צֶדֶק, עֲדֵי חֲסִידִים
הוֹשַׁבְתָּ לְךָ מִשְׁכַּן קִנֶּךָ
וּבַל לְבַדְּךָ, אֲשֶׁר בִּקַּשְׁתָּ

עוֹלָם לְהֵישִׁיר עִם סְפָרִים בָּרִים.
מַה תַּעֲשֶׂה, אִם כֵּן, בְּתוֹךְ יָמֶיךָ,
שֶׁמֶשׁ אֲשֶׁר חַמְתָּ בְּעוֹד יָצָאתָ?

Figure I: Aboab's Panegyric

The day a bow appeared in the palm of your pure hand,
I rushed my gift and my tribute.
For I thought it a splendrous display of your power, dear friend,
A stranger interpreting my religion amid my congregation.
Therefore I shall come opposite your threshold 4
With praises, and not be still till my words
Open its doors in a lyrical song,
To raise your fame above the stars. 8

Figure II: Aguilar's Panegyric

After seeing your perfection in wisdom and piety, beloved friend, and, now, [seeing] your book, which bears witness to [that perfection], I could not resist telling a few of your merits in a song of friendship, and I (the young one, Moshe me–Aguilar), took up my theme and said:

Though, surely, in all nations [men] have become very wise,
Many have made themselves pious and have even been just.
For they consumed their days in goodness 4
And rose toward a spiritual height in their wisdom;

You [stand] alone, above those who have become wise:
Honor becomes you among all your nation, 8
Because, while still a young man,
You knew languages that make [men] wise.

Moreover, you even, with all righteousness, set
Your dwelling place near the truly pious 11
And not in isolation, you who sought

To guide the world to righteousness with pure books.
What will you do, then, in the midday of your life,
O sun, who spread warmth with your very appearance? 14

Yet Gentius was and remained an outsider, a stranger, and to this Aboab also makes explicit reference. While Gentius possessed all the virtues praised by contemporary rhetoricians—compare Najara's virtual equation of wisdom with rhetorical power in Onkeneira (who, like Gentius, is now a forgotten figure)—Gentius had achieved something all the more spectacular, being an outsider. He had overcome the disability of being an "ish zar," a stranger within the community, and had even come to be called "dodi," 'dear friend'.[127] Aboab implies that the appearance of such a book by this Hebraist, who had studied, worked, and "uncovered" ("yegalleh") or "interpreted" Judaism in the midst of the Jewish community ("tokh 'adati")—which circumstance in and of itself lent Gentius some authoritativeness—had revealed for his readers something previously hidden from most Christians. Aboab must have had in mind Gentius's remark about his realizing how wise and useful Jewish literature was. And so, because Gentius's purpose was the dissemination of accurate information about Judaism, Aboab "came opposite [his] threshold with praises" to open the book for readers and doors for Gentius. If such hyperbole was not uncommon, Aboab's solicitousness for Gentius's future well–being had a specific goal in mind: that Gentius would not only become a famous and authoritative expositor of Jewish literature, but that he might be of direct benefit to the Jews.

That this was Aboab's hope becomes even more apparent when Aguilar's poem is considered. Aguilar's sonnet is Petrarchan and hendecasyllabic and is preceded by a prose preamble. It appears in the original on the facing page to Aboab's (see Figure II, pages 256 and 257). Says Aguilar: Gentius is to be distinguished from the mass of theologians, even from those who had studied Judaism and even from others who may have been just in their dealings with Jews.[128] The triad of wisdom, piety, and justice that Aguilar employs in the first stanza and amplifies in the balance of the poem reflects a division into "intellectual, moral, and divine" virtues that was popular at this period.[129] Gentius had transcended basic meritoriousness; he was now proceeding to apply these categories of perfection for the benefit of others besides himself. Aguilar considered Gentius to have displayed perfect righteousness in taking his wisdom and settling with it near "hasidim" (as opposed to "mitḥassedim"; Aguilar's understanding of "ḥasidim" is clearly a challenge to Gentius), seeking out the company of the truly pious rather than contenting himself with the society of those who had never quite attained perfection. Moreover, Gentius had chosen not to remain a solitary individual, content with personal achievement, but had been anxious both to demonstrate complete righteousness and to spread the ideal. (Compare the two uses of "levadekha" in lines 5 and 11.) The "ḥasidim" among whom Gentius had dwelt were not and could not be the other members of the circle of Hebraists, as Gentius might have thought. The "ḥasidim" were his Jewish teachers, men whose knowledge and sympathy for Judaism and whose very aims for the spread of a knowledge of Torah among non–Jews as a herald of the messianic age could best bolster Gentius's goal of providing moral guidance for the world. Aguilar clearly mistrusted cold, albeit pure scholarship produced in isolation, as much as he did controversialist literature.[130] He was more than pleased, then, that Gentius, with all his good intentions, had specifically come to the Jews for assistance.

Aguilar concludes with yet another challenge, therefore. In the fashion of his day, he praises Gentius metaphorically as a "sun" whose rising or first appearance in print had spread the warmth of knowledge. Menasseh had addressed Grotius in similar fashion and Gentius himself would subsequently appeal to G. J. Vossius in the same way,[131] Will you, asks Aguilar, "in the midst of your days" (as opposed to "in your young manhood"), prove yourself worthy of my praise both by continuing to be just and righteous yourself in your treatment of the Jews and of Jewish literature, as well as by directing the rest of the world, with appropriate pieces of scholarship, toward proper treatment of the Jews themselves, on the one hand, and to ultimate righteousness and the messianic era, on the other? Such was the challenge Aguilar and, presumably, Aboab and Menasseh as well all posed the young man in whom they had such confidence.

IV

Apologetics and Diplomacy on Elbe and Thames: The Outcome of the Rabbis' Instruction

Gentius in Hamburg

Menasseh specifically showed his confidence in Gentius by entrusting to him the translation of *Shevet Yehudah* into Latin. Menasseh had apparently planned to translate the work himself, but, in the year 1641, when Gentius was about to embark for Constantinople, Menasseh was in the midst of his Brazilian turmoil. So Gentius went off, taking the project with him, planning, however, to dedicate the finished product to Anslo.

But Anslo, who further encouraged Gentius, died in 1643, and Gentius was left without a patron. He looked all over, reports Beyer; among those he appealed to for help was G. J. Vossius.[1] Toward the end of the decade, Gentius found some funds and, having also produced a translation of the *Gulistan* of the great Persian writer Sa'di (c. 1184–1292), and with the completed translation of the *Shevet Yehudah,* entitled *Historia Judaica,* in hand, he returned to Western Europe.

Gentius's own needs converged with those of Hamburg Jewry. There was a vacant position in Oriental languages at Hamburg, and Gentius's stopping in the Baltic seaport en route to Amsterdam may have had some connection with that position. Meanwhile, the Jewish situation in Hamburg, a bastion of Lutheranism, was quite precarious.[2] Not only had the Ashkenazim been expelled in 1648, the Sephardim too were subjected to harassment by the Lutheran church. The situation had been volatile throughout the 1640s with limitations on Jewish rights and privileges constantly being called for by the Church. After 1644, with the publication of the *Judenthumb,* a 1500–page duodecimo diatribe by Johannes Müller (1598–1672), the leading pastor in the city, anti–Jewish agitation even increased. Hamburg become known, in fact, as a place especially devoted to Jewish missionizing.[3]

Hamburg was a growing mercantile city with trade connections all over and with particularly strong links to Amsterdam. In his *Humble Addresses* of 1656, Menasseh would twice mention the Jewish settlement there, indicating that the Jews were "protected by the Magistrat, though molested by the people" (p. 9). Menasseh also speaks of the hundred resident families, a number given by the Senate of Hamburg in 1646. While there were not, then, at mid–century, that many Jews in absolute numbers, their presence was felt as a thorn by the Lutheran hierarchy.

It was both this presence and Jewish literature and its supposed anti–Christian blasphemies that prompted Müller to compose his massive tome. (Among other examples of refutations of Christianity and assertions of the "Jüdischen Unglauben," incidentally, Müller mentions the works of Menasseh.) His preface lists five purposes, in fact, and they are: 1) to show the arguments and grounds the Jews advance against us in their books and to show that these arguments are not irrefutable, as some worry; 2) for the Jews to know that we read their books and, not only are we not as uninformed as they think, we describe their errors accurately ("aus den wahren Gründen von ihren Irrthümern handeln"); 3) for those of his readers who come into daily contact with the Jews and have discussions about religion to be able to answer them; 4) to spur others on to add to the work; and 5) to confirm Christians in their religion and bring about the conversion of the Jews.

In short, Müller's goal was to "uncover the blindness of the Jews." He addresses the Jews themselvcs as well with a "friendly" request: not to be angry with him for his book, inasmuch as, "if they exercise their freedom to slander my Savior Christ, they cannot blame me for defending his honor, as I am bound to, owing to my belief, profession, office, and oath" (from the preface). His goal, however, was to ban the free exercise of Judaism completely; elsewhere, he was even more intemperate in this regard. His "Opinion" for the Senate in 1649 included a condemnation of the Jewish rites he saw observed in his city and also of the numerous examples of brazenness and calumnies that the Jews supposedly engaged in, especially their looking for opportunities to engage in disputations with Lutheran ministers.[4]

There is no need to give a long account of the attempts by the Ministerium to control Jewish worship and even to bring "Christian rabbis," that is, learned Christians or Jewish apostates, into the synagogues to interpret the Scriptures and preach the Gospel to the Jewish worshippers. Nor is there any need to dwell on their attempt to forestall the building of synagogues. Reils's account is explicit and detailed enough.[5] It is necessary to point out, however, that the Senate and the Ministerium were often at odds on the Jewish question. While the Senate did submit decisions on religious affairs to the Ministerium and their judgment, they often disregarded the Church's "advice." Nonetheless, while commercial interests may have prompted the Senate to be lenient, the pressure from the Lutheran leaders, who seem to have had the support of the lower classes, was quite intense.

Such was the state of affairs when Gentius passed through on his way to Amsterdam in 1650. In Amsterdam, he dedicated his *Rosarium* of Sa'di to Johann Georg, the Elector of Saxony, his native land, and his *Historia Judaica* to the Senate of Hamburg. Both works received the imprimatur and copyright in early July 1651, signed by, among other authorities, none other than Jacob Cats, here in his official capacity as censor, but best known as the poet who embodied all the traditional Dutch values. Gentius's works were published that same year in Amsterdam, the former work by Blaeu, the *Historia Judaica* by Petrus Niellius.[6]

The dedication of the *Gulistan* translation is a routine appeal to and praise of a potential benefactor. The address to the Senate of Hamburg, however, is somewhat of a vindication of Menasseh's efforts with Gentius. It is a plea for the amelioration of the position of the Jews in that city. The plea is based, though, on Christian charity. Moreover, it contains a negative characterization of the Jew, as contrasted with the Christian. The Jew is depicted as harsh, proud, and exclusionist, the Christian as kind, loving, and mindful of his origin: "He is loving, even if he is not loved; he tolerates, even if he is not tolerated; and shows kindness, even if no kindness is ever done him; . . ." ("amat, etsi non ametur; tolerat, etsi non toleretur; & beneficit, etsi illi nunquam benefiat; . . ."). Gentius considers Christian and Jew as "inter se genere pares," however;

they are equals in terms of descent. Yet this appears in the context of his criticism of the Jew for not being open to outsiders,

> although the law of nature teaches that those equal in descent are to be tolerated (*ferendos*), and the divine laws, the *exempla* of the ancients, order that the welfare [and salvation (?) (*salus*)] of others is to be looked out for with concern and piety, not by force.

To help make his point, Gentius introduces a long tale about Abraham that he says comes from Sa'di.[7] It concerns a guest who turns out to be an idolator and is thrown out by Abraham, whereupon God rebukes Abraham and bids him call the guest back. The end of the tale and its moral is that Abraham showed such consideration, kindness, and courtesy in the end that his example brought the idolator to the worship of the true God. (There is, incidentally, no exact parallel to this tale in rabbinic literature, though each of the elements echoes something familiar.)

While Gentius appears to have intended no irony in his telling of this episode, there is obviously a Christian message here. Gentius urges the Senate to gather the Jews in, "like Christ's lost sheep":

> You too, most noble princes, may you too show equal favor to the nation of the Jews (*Judaeorum gentem*) and, following Abraham's most praiseworthy custom and example, compassionately rescue and protect them, instead of keeping them out with stern discipline, and gather them in like Christ's lost little sheep, rather than put them to flight and scatter them.[8]

While there is no specific call for the Jews' conversion, the parable has some clear overtones. "Gathering the Jews in" and the verb "servare" itself both have the implied hope for the Jews' salvation through eventual conversion. And yet, this is a plea nonetheless for the toleration of the Jews as Jews, for the moment at least. Moreover, Gentius continues with praise for the *Shevet Yehudah* itself and, in a sympathetic tone, links the work with the destiny of the Jewish people, which he is trying to influence himself. He calls the book a faithful description of the history and mores of the Jews, one that will enable the Senate to learn "by what unspeakable evils th[is] unfortunate people are vexed" ("quam infandis misera gens malis laboret"). The actual charge to the Senate, however, is the most revealing; the Latin must be cited to indicate its thrust:

Pergite, optimi Proceres, servare insigni vestra pietate, quos Christus Servator noster servare ipse voluit, nobisque servandos serio praescripsit.

This call to the Senate to proceed, "in your extraordinary *pietas,*" which implies both kindness and devotion to duty, to rescue, protect, save, and so on—all these meanings of "servare" are possible—is really rather ambiguous. We can translate "servare, etc." to mean: 'preserve those whom Christ himself wished to preserve', through your beneficence in allowing them to dwell unmolested in your city. Yet the link with "Servator" (and with "servare" in the tale of Abraham) is too strong to eliminate the likelihood of "servare" really having as its ultimate aim the bringing of salvation in a Christian sense.

All in all, the dedication seems a mixed blessing, even if Gentius was asking the Senate to protect the welfare of the Jews as Jews, making this a preliminary to their conversion and salvation. Further light is shed on his motivation by the preface to the reader, in which Gentius again minimizes the intrinsic worth of the Jewish people. After a brief praise of history as a necessary beacon and visual guide for men to avoid being shipwrecked, and as a source for men to learn from the examples of others, he asserts that the Jews, the subject of the work—it is widely read by the Jews, he notes—that

the Jews were, of old, the noblest people, indeed, but now, as their fate has it, they are the most despised throughout the whole world. Not having done anything outstanding for several centuries prior, they provided the author with only scanty opportunity for praising them.

Certainly this approach does not constitute a real vindication of Jewish rights, as Menasseh and others might have hoped.

Several other remarks in the preface promote further suspicion about Gentius's motives. While he does take note of the "summa . . . scriptoris auctoritas, quam sibi apud omnes Judaeos hoc opere conciliavit," that is, 'the supreme authority that the author gained for himself with this work', this too motivated Gentius to make the translation, he says: to "snatch the author out of the servitude and errors of the Hebrews, and give him over into freedom" ("me rem gratam facturum rebar foro Romano, si autorem ex Hebraeorum servitute & erroribus ereptum, in libertatem transscriberem"). Moreover, while he suggests that the work contains many things "scitu minime indigna, religiones, vitam & mores Iudaeorum spectantia," 'things not at all unworthy of being known regarding the religion, life and mores of the Jews', also attributing the work's extreme popularity to its "consolation of a people tired out with many calamities," he promises, at the same time, a series of annotations, to be forthcoming at a later date, in which he will respond to the Jewish views expressed in this work. For there is "a considerable [number of] things in this work in which the reader can recognize that the author was a Jew."[9]

Though his biographer calls these prefatory remarks a plea for the "conservatio," the 'preservation' of the Jews, it is hardly an unqualified triumph, it appears. Moreover, it seems to have turned to Gentius's disadvantage. As a result of this work and its dedication, he failed to win the chair in Oriental languages that he had been prospecting for. On the other hand, the Senate did accept the dedication, granting him one hundred ducats for his efforts. In Beyer's view, though, he had placed his career on the line with such a dedication and lost,[10] even if he nowhere in his dedication or preface called attention to the implicit arguments that the work contains for the toleration of the Jews in a Christian milieu.

The result of all this came as a shock to Gentius. The stir among the ministers was so great that Gentius even lodged a protest from Amsterdam. What happened is as follows: The book, having been sent to Senior Müller as a matter of course, was circulated by him to the other theologians of the city, who found it to have arrived "inopportunely." The council, reports one M. S. Gross in a letter dated 30 December 1651 that is quoted fully by Beyer,[11] was in the midst of discussing the appointment of an "orthodox" [i.e., Lutheran] professor properly trained in Hebrew and rabbinic commentaries to preach to the "Judaeis hîc receptis," 'the Jews who had been admitted into this city', and demonstrate the truth of Christianity out of sources the Jews find acceptable. Should they then fail to heed and to become converted, "the Senate and citizens of good conscience could attribute this to Jewish hardheartedness." The issue of long standing was at the very forefront of the ministers' consciousness when Gentius's translation arrived.

Gross continues precisely in this vein. Now comes this book, he writes, with the purpose of "permitting the Jews to live by whatever law they wish, wherever they live." Though this was probably not the thrust of Gentius's dedication, it was a not unlikely understanding of the means to the end that Gentius had in mind. Gross, in fact, offers some examples from Ibn Verga of arguments in favor of Jewish settlement, though Gentius had not done so. Then Gross takes his attack a step further, charging that views such as Ibn Verga's and, by extension, Gentius's, are diametrically opposed to what the Church had hoped for. He makes this claim, he says, especially in light of the "blasphemies" the work contains—he cites several—and of the fact that the author praises Jewish virtues, etc. and harps on the crimes of the Christians against innocent Jews.[12]

The ministers deemed the book, as Gross recorded the opinion, "deserving of the censure of men."[13] Gross himself objected to Gentius's designation of the Jews as the "lost lambs of Christ," since they had never recognized him: "Hirci sunt, non oves Christi"; they are foul billy goats. In short, Gross did not see the tenor of Gentius's remarks as being sufficiently pro-Christian. Gross was by no means a subtle individual or reader, it seems. He also criticizes Gentius for not having stated in the story about Abraham that the "Senatus . . . bene meriturus esse, si eos [sc. Judaeos] paulatim ad Christianam Religionem perduceret," that is, the Senate should have been advised that such winning the Jews over to Christianity would be meritorious; this, in Gross's view should have been explicit. Gross also found fault with Gentius's failure to supply the annotations in answer to this "anti-Christian book," as he had promised. In short, the dialectic that Gentius probably had in mind was not expressly stated in a fashion pleasing to these churchmen. But there was one more factor. The reason Gross was so dismayed was that the Jews were rejoicing ("Judaei hic loci exultant") at the thought that "the attempt by our minister to have the Jews instructed in another manner will be ruined before the Senate by this book." In other words, their attempt to have the Jews instructed in Christianity was about to be quashed by this dedication. The effect that the dedication had, then, could not necessarily have been anticipated from an examination of the preface. Gentius, though himself a Lutheran, had been surprised by the vehemence of the reaction from the Lutheran extremists.

It is clear now what Gentius had in mind when he wrote his dedication. Not that he no longer hoped for the conversion of the Jews to Christianity; rather, he did not think that subjecting the

Jews to conversionist preaching and instruction was the most suitable manner of achieving this. The church hierarchy obviously disagreed and could not see that Gentius's arguments in favor of the book were not necessarily arguments in favor of the Jews. Nevertheless, Gentius's address was to the Senate, not to the Ministerium, and the body of ministers was proven to be without absolute power. This is what the Jews had hoped for. The next year, moreover, in 1652, the Portuguese Jews were granted further privileges, were given the right to build a synagogue, and, lastly, appear to have been exempted from having to listen to conversionist sermons.

One final indication of the fact that Gentius's motives were not all that pure is the proposal he sent John Selden from Amsterdam in 1654. He asked that Selden collaborate in bringing out a second edition of the work. Gentius speaks explicitly in his letter to Selden of his hopes for Jewish conversion and he suggests that the book could easily be edited in such a way—Selden was approached as the best man for that job—as to make it an aid for propagandizing and converting Jews.[14] Selden, it appears, did not accede to Gentius's request, recognizing first of all that what Gentius had forwarded as the proposed second edition was little more than a second printing.

Gentius's designs were what they were. Menasseh's, Aboab's, and Aguilar's designs on him bore only unexpected fruit. Gentius himself had a bit of a diplomatic career hereafter, but his scholarly career was finished. He soon fell into obscure poverty, and other works that he had promised, including versions of other sections of the *Mishneh Torah,* never appeared.

Menasseh in London

Menasseh, on the other hand, pursued his goals during the 1650s in a manner that brought him everlasting fame, if not immediate success. His literary works from this period are direct continuations of his earlier attempts to win favor for the Portuguese Nation through their own merits and achievements, to show that Judaism was of a character equal to that of Christianity and with many similar concerns. We can also see in these works how Menasseh's ideal of spreading knowledge of Torah and Judaism among the nations remained strong in his mind, despite the reception accorded Gentius's work by the Lutheran ministers. We may speculate that the acceptance of the dedication by the Hamburg Senate further strengthened Menasseh in his resolve to put the Jewish case before the highest tribunals in England, even though his first efforts toward that goal had begun before Gentius's initiative had been entered upon.

When we left Menasseh in the mid–1640s, he was in a period of turning his attention directly to the inward concerns of his community. In 1645–47, he produced his multivolume *Thesouro dos Dinim,* which became a standard work for Portuguese Jews. He also engaged in certain business ventures and suffered the loss of one of his sons: perhaps it was as a result of this loss that he set about turning his *De resurrectione* into the expanded Hebrew version, which he entitled *Nishmat Ḥayyim* and published in 1651. He also continued working as a printer, of course.

Nor was he forgotten by his non–Jewish friends. From far and wide they still came to see him and consult with him and to propose all sorts of schemes. From this period begin his encounters, either in person or through literary challenges, with such visionaries as Isaac de la Peyrère, Antonio Vieira, Antonio (Aaron Levi) Montezinos, and, eventually, Paul Felgenhauer.[15] Each of these, except Montezinos, sought, in his own way, to convince Menasseh of certain Christian truths. Even Samuel Sorbière, his French Catholic guest about 1644, came as an interlocutor to find out what was keeping Menasseh from becoming a Catholic. Menasseh's responses, as reported by Sorbière, included the continuing authority of the law, the election of Israel, the preservation of the Jews in the midst of their enemies like the burning bush, and the Jewish hope for the future day when they themselves would rule.[16] Sorbière adds, though Menasseh could hardly have been likely to formulate his remarks in exactly the way Sorbière represents them, given similar comments elsewhere, that the Jews hope for the day when the nations in whose midst they live will be given over to utter destruction. These were, then, some of the basic understandings of Menasseh's and other Jewish thinking as mid–century approached, and these were some of the presuppositions Menasseh set out to explain or to counter in his final diplomatic efforts.

Moreover, there is the link, in many of these submissions and proposals by Menasseh, to some of Menasseh's as yet largely unarticulated, but long since deeply felt messianic dreams. Until the decade was out, Menasseh appears to have been too preoccupied with other matters to respond to these currents and undercurrents. While the full story of his ultimate response is too long and too broad in scope to be told completely again, basic to any understanding of that response are Menasseh's dealings with his Hebraist pupils. It was, in the end, via literary diplomacy as well that Menasseh made his mark, and that diplomacy, as it related to Menasseh's international concerns in the 1650s, was a final playing out of so many of his earlier efforts.

The *Hope of Israel* has been seen as either a plea for the readmission of the Jews to England or a work of consolation for Menasseh's fellow Jews, the English connection coming only after the fact. In truth, it is some of each of these and some of neither. Menasseh's argumentation, regardless of his goal for the moment, was based on messianism, and the immediate reason for his having written was a challenge from certain English millenarists.[17] On this, almost everyone is agreed. The Spanish edition, which appeared first, was in part an attempt to forestall criticism by the Parnassim; an English edition, though it appeared only toward the end of 1650 and was translated from an unrevised Latin version, had certainly been projected almost from the very outset.[18] Menasseh's messianic rhetoric, which does not take its cue from the "relation" of Aaron Montezinos about certain "Jewish" Indians in the mountains of South America that Menasseh prefixed to the work, this rhetoric is basically Menasseh's 1650 view of what constituted a pragmatic argument. For Menasseh was not merely claiming that the messianic era had arrived, since he was also undertaking to defend his people—the immediate present was seen to anticipate their future redemption. The actual and specific defense coalesced in his mind only after the work was in progress, when Menasseh, after adding a second part unrelated to the first, came to give a title to what he had written. As it turns out, neither is the title dealt with nor is its significance reviewed in the body of the work at all. Yet Menasseh's diplomacy begins with both the title and the dedication of the translation to the English Parliament.

Menasseh's own goal was stated in his original dedication, that is the dedication of the Spanish edition to the "Deputies and Parnassim of the Talmud Torah congregation" on 15 January 1650. He writes:

I have titled it *Mikveh Yisrael,* The Hope of Israel, deriving the name from chapter 14, verse 8 of Jeremiah, "the hope of Israel, its redeemer." For the only end to which it is directed is to show that this hope in the coming of the Messiah, in which we live, is a difficult though certain reward for the future, because it is based on the absolute promise of the blessed Lord.[19]

Why does Menasseh point to the chapter and verse in this way, rather than by citation alone? Because he wishes his readers to take note of the rest of the verse as well and even of the one that follows:

O hope of Israel, its redeemer in time of trouble, why must you be like a stranger in the land or a guest lodging for the night? Why must you be like a man abashed, like a warrior without power to redeem us in whose midst you are and upon whom your name is called? Do not forsake us!

Menasseh calls upon God to show that the Jews are His very own—there are echoes of Günzburg—by guarding them as residents in a land where they have hitherto been merely guests for the night. To be sure, this passage is moved in the translations into the "Preface to the Reader," but that rather increases its importance. Here, in Menasseh's own title, not in his later association of "ketseh ha–arets" with "Angle–terre," is his hope for resettlement. There may be some justification for the recent emphasis on the fact that it is Portugal, not England, that is designated the "end of the earth" by Menasseh (Sect. 31), but the corresponding inference that, at this period, Menasseh had no designs on England is not at all tenable.

For it is not only that Menasseh dedicated the translated versions of his *Esperança* to the English parliament, the dedication and the second section of the work are essentially themselves elaborations of Menasseh's earlier thinking about the future and security of the Jews. In fact, the messianic passages from Daniel, Ezekiel, and so on are confined to the new dedication and to the second part of the work, but are intermingled with other, pragmatic arguments about the benefits the Jews offer. The dedication itself shows Menasseh's aims: he first invokes the standard "publick good." But then he proceeds—and this passage merits full quotation—to intone some of the more familiar modes of his earlier years:

> . . . in my dedicating this Discourse to you, I can truly affirm, that I am induced to it upon no other ground than this, that I may gain your favour and good will to our Nation, now scattered almost all over the earth; neither think that I do this, as if I were ignorant how much you have hitherto favored our Nation: for it is made known to me, and to others of our Nation, by them who are so happy as near at hand, to observe your apprehensions, that you do vouchsafe to help us, not onely by our prayers; yea, this hath compelled me to speak to you publickly, and to give you thanks for that your charitable affection toward us, and not such thanks which come only from the tongue, but as are conceived by a grateful mind.
>
> Give me leave therefore (most renowned Fathers) to supplicate you, that you would stil favor our good, and farther love us. Truly, we men doe draw so much the nearer to Divine nature, when by how much we increase, by so much we cherish, and defend the small, and weak ones: and with how much diligence doe you performe this, most renowned Fathers? who though you seem to be arrived to the highest top of felicity, yet you do not only not despise inferior men, but you so wish well to them, that you seem sensible of their calamity; you knowing how acceptable to God you are by so doing, who loves to do good to them who doe good.

The *Hope of Israel* is hardly a work of consolation. It is Menasseh's plea that the English government render assistance and show favor to the Jews. Menasseh, it is true, is far from explicit on how this help might be offered, but his implicit message about the secret Jewish community in England comes out forthright and resolute. He further bases his hope for good will on the religious truth that his work will show. The Jews, in other words, render valuable service through their literary work, which shows how prosperity is about to accrue to the English.

Menasseh points out here, and again in Section 36, how others shall be punished: "God will give blessings upon them who favour us." This theme had already been articulated in the *Conciliator*, where Menasseh, with reference to the *Zohar* as his source, had written:

> Regibus, omnibus adeo magistratibus, qui justa exercent imperia, & Hebraeos in ditione sua habent, certum in Paradiso gradum esse assignatum; quemadmodum eosdem, si male Hebraeos habeant, poena certa manet. (Deut. Question 2)

(Kings, governors, and magistrates of the nations that do good to Israel, and take them under their protection, will enjoy certain degrees of bliss reserved for them in Paradise; but, on the contrary, those who injure them, will not fail to receive their punishment hereafter.)

The Latin parallels the original Spanish fairly well. Interestingly enough, though, to digress for a moment, Vossius did omit certain crucial phrases and even whole sentences from this portion. Menasseh had written that the Jews are not governed by the astrological signs "but the Lord [raised Israel to that eminence, that he] placed them under his sole government." The bracketed words were omitted from the Latin. This is representative of Vossius's general softening of Menasseh's tone in a way that would make Menasseh's statements more acceptable. Even Vossius's excision of Menasseh's conclusion betrays the same tendency. Menasseh had written that the stars and planets were given by God to the other nations "to enlighten them according to their benevolent or malevolent aspect." At this point, Vossius concludes: "Haec mens verborum Scripturae est," 'this is the meaning of the words of Scripture'. But Menasseh had continued as follows:

It also serves to exhort Israel, that seeing the Lord had made that distinction between them and other nations by taking them under his own immediate protection, they should not forsake him, and adopt any other worship.

Thus, early on in his career, Menasseh had presented two countenances to the world, one for his Jewish audience, the second for his Christian one. His defense of his fellow Jews both internally and vis–à–vis the outside world lies at the root of both faces, however; this must be seen as part of the background of the *Hope of Israel* as well. It is in this same Section 36 of the *Hope of Israel* that Menasseh announces that "the time of redemption is at hand." He bases this on Daniel's words: "'that knowledge shall be encreased'; for then the prophecies shall better be understood." He takes this as his personal task (it will be remembered the Günzburg too had used this verse of Daniel, 12:4) by citing Jeremiah, who, in chapter 30, treats of "the redemption of *Israel,* and *Judah* . . . the Scepter of the Messiah the son of *David,* of the ruine of the nations, of the restoration of *Judah* of holy *Jerusalem,* and of the third Temple," and "makes an abridgment of all things that shall be, [as] it is said in verse 2, 'Write thee all the words which I have spoken to thee in a book.' By this meane making the Prophecie clearer . . ." This, then, is what Menasseh is doing: making the prophecy clearer, as the prophecies for the future involve England. To return to the dedication:

All which things of necessity must be fulfilled, that so *Israel* at last being brought back to his owne place; peace which is promised under the Messiah, may be restored to the world; and concord, which is the only Mother of al good things. These things I handle more largely in this Treatise, which I dedicate to you (most renowned Fathers) you cannot be ignorant, that it is not only not unprofitable, but very useful for States and Statesmen, to fore–see the issue (which yet is ever in Gods hand) of humaine Councells, that so they may observe, and understand from Divine truth, the events of things to come, which God hath determined by his Spirit in his holy Prophets. I know that this my labour will not be unacceptable to you, how mean soever it be, which I trust you will chearfully receive, because that you love our Nation . . .

Menasseh is purposely elliptical here because he really has no specific plan or vision at this point. But he was asking for favor toward the Jews from the Councils of the English State, no matter what form that favor might take, in view of the Jewish position at that moment and their anticipated one in the not too distant future.

There is, however, in Menasseh's remarks, one hint of how he expected all this to work out. Not only did he conceive his own work to be a summary of Divine truth, but, since England was, in his perception, looking for Divine truth, the Jews could offer a specific service. The Jews were renowned for their learning, Menasseh writes, having served all the great princes, a theme he had already introduced in the preface to the *Conciliador.* Now he gives a few examples of those Jews who were learned and those Christians who had Hebrew teachers. This is an argument for the readmission of Jews; Menasseh himself was a splendid example—he perhaps also saw personal gain as a potential result—but he alludes to none of that. Rather, he continues (Sect. 33):

So at this day we see many desirous to learne the Hebrew tongue of our men. Hence may be seene that God hath not left us; for if this Prince treats us ill, another treats us well; if one banisheth us out of his country, another invites us by a thousand priviledges; as divers Princes of *Italy* have done, the most eminent King of *Denmarke,* and the mighty Duke of

Savoy in *Nissa. And doe we not see, that those Republiques doe flourish, and much increase in Trade, which admit the Israelites?*

Not only in the past, but even in the present, he argues, men wish to learn Hebrew from the Jews. Were this not sufficient reason to receive the Jews, the practical advantages are even greater! In short, Hebrew studies are linked up with the highest levels of argumentation, even if, from a pragmatic point of view, the rhetoric stresses self–advantage.

This treatise proves to be a mixture of millenarism and pragmatism, related to a great extent to Menasseh's teaching activity. Menasseh's venture into *Realpolitik* and even into *raison d'état* begins anew right here in this 1650 work with messianic visions. The dedication to Parliament was, indeed, "politically motivated."[20]

That Menasseh was now firmly committed to political activism on a literary basis is clear. His next production was not long to follow. Though David Franco Mendes, the eighteenth–century chronicler of Amsterdam Spanish and Portuguese Jewry, reports in his *Memorias* that Menasseh's *Humble Addresses* were composed in London,[21] it may actually have been as early as 1651 in Amsterdam that this next venture into literary diplomacy with the English was drafted.[22] And, even if the "Dedication" and "Declaration" were not added until just prior to the English printing in late 1655—this had been preceded earlier the same year by a Dutch printing—the substance of the work is probably of a much earlier date.

As of late 1655 in London, Menasseh claimed that he had been an England–watcher for "some yeares since."[23] In that "Encyclical" to Jews the world over sent off on the day he finally set sail, September 2, 1655, he wrote that it was "notorious to all of our nations how . . . I have labored for a long time past in order that there should be conceded to us in . . . England the right of public exercise of our religion."[24] In other words, Menasseh's intentions were no secret, and neither was the thrust of his efforts, even in Hamburg and Italy, which he singles out in the address of this letter.[25]

Now Roth points to a certain "disfavor with which Menasseh's self–appointed mission was regarded in official circles in his own country." There has been repeated indication of this hitherto. But Menasseh's ultimate reasons for finally deciding to go to England were his personal finances, as it appears from Mendes's account of how Menasseh was induced to stay home in 1652 by a new financial accommodation and given leave to depart in 1654, after "there were neither sufficient honors nor financial gain to detain him." There is no specific evidence at these particular junctures, that is, when the *Mahamad* first persuaded Menasseh to stay and then, subsequently, when they allowed him to embark, of any official favor or disfavor for any reasons that might be considered political, rather than either financial or related to the internal harmony of the community. (Menasseh had quarreled with Morteira, perhaps about their respective functions and duties.) In short, Menasseh had prepared his *Humble Addresses* in an effort at diplomacy from afar and in response to the St. John Commission, but without any hope of going to pursue his mission on the scene; this hope, raised in 1652, is what caused the whole project to jell.

The preambles to the *Humble Addresses* contain compelling new requests, even if Menasseh could hardly state outright that he had decided to move from Amsterdam to London for financial gain. His "Declaration . . . showing the motives of his coming into England" was necessary not only because, to this point, he had pursued his goals through the medium of the word alone, but also because of his personal stake. While Menasseh advanced no rationales that he had not already advanced elsewhere, he now makes specific new requests. Though he tells Cromwell that Christians and Jews "adore the same onely God of Israel," that he had said earlier. But when he also tells the Lord Protector that "none was ever a Benefactor to that people, and cherished them in their countries, who thereupon hath not presently begun very much to flourish" (Wolf, p. 76), this is something new. For if, in the body of the text, he quotes again from the *Zohar* the classic line about the reward of nations for protecting the Jewish people and the punishment of others for failing to do so, i.e., the same line he had used in the *Conciliator,* the new rhetoric of the surrounding text that speaks of the faithfulness of the Jews to those who protect them is now the foundation for specific pleas and requests. And it is now placed in the prefatory declaration, and no longer hidden in the body of the work, as it had been in the *Hope of Israel.* Already in mid–1652, Menasseh had come to the decision to accompany his petition in person. In late 1655, though, he argues explicitly for that "free & publick synagogue" that he had only hinted at before in general terms.

The pragmatism and the *raison d'état* approach in the body of the work still has at its root religious convictions that come out of rabbinic teachings and are supported by rabbinic teachings. But these teachings fade into the background as the specific arguments of the other variety come and displace them. Earlier, arguments based on religious faith were the substance of Menasseh's *Realpolitik;* now they appear as appendages that show only the religious origins of Menasseh's thought. If Menasseh asks, "What Law, either Humain or Divine, National or Modern, can bear, that the souls of men (which the Most High hath created free) be forced to believe what they believe not, and to love what they hate?" (p. 19), this is now an argument on overtly secular grounds. If Menasseh is still a millenarian and assumes that the English too "expect . . . *the hope of Israel* to be revealed [soon]" (from the preface [Declaration]) and even stresses the need for the dispersion to be completed in order that the redemption of Israel might come about, if these are his motives for coming, they are only secondary arguments at this point. The only reference to the Messiah in the body of the work is a summation, deriving from the *Conciliator,* of how the Jews are profitable:

> So that if one Prince, ill advised, driveth them out of his Land, yet another invites them to his; & shows them favour; wherein we may see the prophecy of Iacob fulfilled in the letter: 'The staffe (to support him) shall not depart from Iacob, untill Messias shall come.' [P. 9]

Of course this quotation of Genesis 49:10 was a risky business, given the long history of the use of this verse in disputation, but the subject was really tangential to the major arguments being put forth by Menasseh at this juncture. Still, the continuity of Menasseh's efforts was unbroken. His absolute faith in the power of the word and in personal intercession were now coupled again in a new way, as Menasseh the teacher is transformed even more into Menasseh the diplomat.

There had been traces of this, we may note, even toward the end of 1651, in the dedication of the *Nishmat Ḥayyim* to the Holy Roman Emperor, Ferdinand III. The fact that this dedication does not appear in all copies of the work may indicate that the dedication was rejected. We cannot know for sure, but it may have been something about the rejection of such a work that made Menasseh's arguments in the work that would follow, the *Humble Addresses,* shy away from religious and cultural affinities. Menasseh praises Ferdinand for his services to the Jews of his realm. (Ferdinand had granted them a charter in 1648, under favorable conditions:

> You defend and protect our Jewish people with your patronage, [and] indeed, go forth with your imperial [power] in our defense with the free asylum you [grant] us.

allowing them to reside in all the royal cities and to pursue all trades except arms manufacture.)[26] The Jews, says Menasseh, pray daily for Ferdinand's welfare. Then, continuing in a familiar vein, Menasseh asserts that his work is necessary in an age of heresy where many have doubts about religion and the immortality of the soul, and that it would be useful for all learned men; this was meant to flatter the emperor, who prided himself on his broad culture.

Menasseh stresses his own being "religione a vobis diverso," 'of a different religion from you', but he claims that his work is "quoad religionem omnibus pariter . . . utile": its usefulness in matters of religion transcends the boundaries between individual faiths. Though the element of self–interest and the prospect of material gain as a motivation is more pronounced here than in other works of Menasseh's, here too his conception of the link between Jewish literature and the Jews themselves is clear; the acceptance of one should entrain the acceptance of the other. For Menasseh also mentions the emperor's concern for the public welfare and makes this, along with his beneficence to the Jews, one of the two main causes of the dedication. The fact that the dedication was not accepted may have set Menasseh thinking again and led him to the kinds of arguments he mounts in the *Humble Addresses.*

Before leaving the *Nishmat Ḥayyim,* it is worth taking note of the Hebrew preface to the reader, which can shed further light on Menasseh's mood at this time. Not only was this work addressed to "all nations," it was prepared under the guidance of a guardian angel, and its function was to counter claims against Judaism and the Torah. Now it is true that much of this criticism had come from within the Jewish family, but the impression Menasseh conveys is that there were attacks from without as well. A personal tutelary angel or "maggid"—Menasseh does not use this term specifically—was often alluded to or mentioned outright by Jewish mystics. Menasseh quotes this angel as reminding him that it was he, the angel, who was responsible for Menasseh's *Hope of Israel* and for providing the purpose for that work: "In your book that you wrote about the ten tribes, I have given you for a light unto the gentiles, to settle barren tracts, to say 'go forth' to the prisoners and 'appear' to those in darkness." This pastiche of verses from Is. 49:6–9 comes from the same passage as the phrase "li–heyot yeshu'ati 'ad ketseh ha–arets," ('that My salvation may be unto the end of the earth'). The element of messianism is in Menasseh's mind even at this point. (The angel, incidentally, claims responsibility for much of Menasseh's work.)

Having linked the Jewish destiny and that of his own work only tenuously here and having dedicated the *Piedra Gloriosa* of 1655, a theological discussion of a famous contended passage in Daniel, to Isaac Vossius, both of these being essentially a search for patronage, Menasseh had gone to England with his *Humble Addresses* in hand. It did not achieve the results Menasseh had intended. Instead, a storm began to brew, due to other tracts that began to circulate against the Jews. On April 10, 1656, Menasseh let forth a riposte to the various calumnies. The *Vindiciae Judaeorum* is Menasseh's most eloquent work, bringing together for the last time all the components of his thought. Menasseh may have felt that arguments from *raison d'état* were not as powerful as he had been led to expect. He certainly realized, though, that certain conceptions about Judaism had intruded on whatever potential might have existed for the formal admission of Jews. The Jews' Judaism was still a stumbling block for many.

After dealing with the blood libel at some length, during which discussion Menasseh makes reference to the "abundance of good correspondency, many interchanges of brotherly affection, and sundry things of reciprocall love" that he had seen between Christian and Jew at home in Amsterdam (p. 3), he turns to the charge of idolatry and remarks on the scrupulousness of Jews in avoiding any hint of reverence for images. His Hebraist pupils had remarked on this as well. For support here, Menasseh adduces the Maimonidean treatise on the subject, just as, elsewhere in this work, he introduces other portions of the *Mishneh Torah*. The tone is such that Menasseh seems to be relying on the authority of the work in the eyes of his readers; he even calls upon *Yesode hat–Torah* by English title (p. 4) for its authority, despite the use to which Vorstius had put that treatise. Thus, he is arguing in effect that Jewish literature confirms that everything the Jews do is above suspicion and is in no way designed "to give an offence to the Christians, or cause scandall," [as his arguments against Vorstius over the "'Alenu" prayer also show (pp. 27, 28–30)].

The link is made here again between the Jews and their literature and the personal activity of Menasseh in conveying a correct representation of Judaism to others. This time it is made because that link was suspect. In order to demonstrate that the Jews do not proselytize, Menasseh recalls his own "friendly discourses" with "many great men." He turns to the Jewish "rituall books" for support (p. 31) and, to further counter the charge, stresses that "we . . . avoid disputing with men concerning religion, . . . that we may as farre as it is possible, avoid scandal and hate." This echoes, of course, the statute in the merger regulations of the Amsterdam community; it also was a charge that Müller had made.

The note on which Menasseh closes this treatise highlights the goal toward which he had been moving for so many years. He exhorts his readers: "read over my arguments impartially, without prejudice, and devoid of all passion." He looks forward to their accepting his work with "grace and favor." Finally, he invokes the verse from Zephaniah that Günzburg had invoked a quarter of a century earlier. He beseeches God to hasten the time when all men shall serve Him "with one consent," viewing his own efforts as the harbinger of the messianic era.

The Hebraists and their training had been an integral part of Menasseh's messianic hopes. If some in Amsterdam, such as the newly arrived Jacob Sasportas, who would both accompany Menasseh to England, having served as the proofreader for the *Nishmat Ḥayyim,* and later become the arch–opponent of Sabbatian messianism, had their reservations about the instruction and edification of gentiles,[27] Menasseh seems to have been undaunted by their scruples. Even though he recognized the extent of the hostility around him, he thought he could argue on principles upon which all could agree. Moreover, he continued to believe to the very end that Jewish literature would sway his audience.

His appeal did not work out as he had hoped. If any successes were attained by those who wished to bring English Jewry out into the open, Menasseh had a limited role in their genesis. If anything, it was his personal diplomacy that swayed Cromwell to refrain from taking action to repress the fledgling community. Moreover, the Lord Protector of England, the Senate of Hamburg, and even the States of the United Provinces all acted more out of self–interest, most likely, than in response to any literary apologias. And yet, in at least one of the instances, a piece of Jewish literature was a catalyst of sorts. Perhaps it proved to be the final blow against the Lutheran hierarchy; perhaps it induced the Senate not to alter a previously established course. Was Menasseh responsible for this? Not entirely, it appears.

For, in terms of ultimate goals, the attitudes of the Hebraists whom Menasseh taught and became friends with did not change as a result of their studies. Their hopes for the conversion of the Jews never left them, regardless of what they studied or how they treated the literature. Styles of scholarship, whether polemical or philological, failed to reflect completely what the commentator or student really had in mind. In fact, the reverse of what might be expected is proven: that, with all that can be learned about the writer from his commentary and scholarship, even the most seemingly detached or even positively disposed writers, Vossius and Gentius respectively, never came to a position were they would absolutely and unqualifiedly tolerate the Jews as Jews on a permanent basis. And Anslo, whom Menasseh considered one of his staunchest supporters, was also a staunch supporter of Vorstius.

Harbingers of the Neutral Society: Some Conclusions

The unity of all thought that the *eruditi* of the age believed in was one thing, the acceptance of the Jews without ulterior motive another. Menasseh too had his illusions, and the rhetoric of the day stimulated them even further. Of this we can be sure. But Menasseh was not completely deceived. He walked through the midst of hostility arguing his case in the rhetoric of the day and knowing full well that the hostility around him was not about to evanesce. He believed, though, as much as the Christians to whose works and arguments he responded, in the absolute truth of his message and in its power to persuade. Though many Christian Hebraists thought that their own lack of subtlety and lack of preparedness in Oriental languages was the major stumbling block to their being able to convert the Jews, Menasseh, and, undoubtedly, others, like Aboab and Aguilar, were sure it was the superiority of their own message that kept them as Jews. And then, there were also the Hebraists who saw their studies more as a tool for the promotion of Christianity from within on a sound scholarly and historical basis. Menasseh surely expected that these types too would come to recognize the virtue of the Jewish position.

The two sides continued far apart in their conceptions of the value of rabbinic studies by and for Christians. Down through the eighteenth century, Christian candidates at the various European universities continued to study Maimonides, and in a variety of different ways. Maimonides remained the sourcebook par excellence for the study of rabbinic Judaism.[28] If Jewish observers of this phenomenon saw this as contributing to the honor and prestige of the Jewish Nation, surely the Christian students themselves understood it as a reinforcement of their Christianity. The numbers of philo–Semites among these students was, indeed, not very large.[29]

If anything, then, the study of rabbinic literature tended to correspond to and even reinforce previously held positions. We may take note of the perspective held on all this by Moritz Steinschneider. He began his still basic bibliography of the Christian Hebraists and their rabbinic studies with the following apologia:

> The attitude of Christian scholars to Hebrew literature deserves special consideration for several reasons. It produced, among other things, the point of view from which Christian theologians, the chief advocates of Hebrew study, and the Christian world at large under their guidance and misguidance, judged, treated, or in part maltreated Judaism and the Jews. It formed the very basis on which they tried to support and even to justify this judgment and treatment.[30]

According to Steinschneider, the fruits of Hebraist scholarship formed the basis and the argumentation for whatever attitude or treatment an individual or a society at large wished to display toward Judaism and the Jews. This viewpoint is certainly comprehensible, given Steinschneider's place in the *Wissenschaft des Judentums* of nineteenth–century Germany.

Yet Hebraist scholarship is more than a collection or reflection of attitudes, and the fruits of that scholarship by no means an *a priori* determinant of those attitudes. The Hebraists were living individuals and their lives were led in the arena of history. Their contacts with Jews were at times epoch–making, their contacts with their fellow Hebraists never without intrinsic interest. No single set of character traits or intellectual interests characterizes them. Each Hebraist may reflect the overall character of the times, with its aspirations toward the reconstitution of biblical Israel and its pretensions to erudition and piety, but none of them fits neatly into any single mold as he fashions and gives expression to his own persona. The main item on the agenda for each one of them was surely the greater glory of the Christian Republic of Letters, but the means to that end differed widely from individual to individual.

From the earliest Hebraist scholars to the most recent, much has been held in common: their scholarship is part of a long tradition of interdependence and also of reliance on Jewish teachers. Their learning and their life often came to be intertwined. While they were often able to function independently and to offer insight and illumination on a broad range of literature, rabbinic and secular, their work always had a practical aim, over and above literary patronage: the amelioration of the contemporary political, social, and religious situation. As a result, their works offer concrete examples of the characteristic interests of the period in time at which they lived.

To be sure, from even before Scaliger, and through the likes of l'Empereur and Grotius to the Vossii and beyond, the increasing familiarity with rabbinic sources could not help but increase the familiarity and contact with Jews, especially insofar as the Netherlands was concerned. None of these men ultimately worked in a vacuum and each of them, and even Coch, had something to say about contemporary Jewry. But they were, primarily, citizens of their own world, not of the Jewish community.

Nevertheless, they were cultivated by the Jewish community. Vossius gave promise of intellectual talent and wide ranging interests. He might well have become the leading scholar of the century had he lived, given his keen eye for detail, his sensitive reading of texts, and, most of all his human sympathy. Given furthermore the personal esteem and universal affection reflected in the eulogies uttered at his death, he would likely have had a large and enthusiastic circle of admirers and disciples. If his voice for moderation, whatever his ultimate aspirations and goals, would have been heeded, Menasseh would indeed have derived satisfaction.

Even Vorstius did not necessarily fit neatly into any category of anti–Jewish writers. His rabbinic learning was perhaps broader than Vossius's; at the same time, his animus was stronger. Still, despite the goal of confutation that he set himself, he had worked with Menasseh in producing a translation of one of Menasseh's own compositions. Neither was Vorstius just a set of attitudes, however basic his hostility was.

We can hardly call Gentius straightforward either. The mixture of enthusiasm for rabbinic literature, eager involvement in practical diplomacy, and even, in the end, enduring malice toward the Jews coupled with Christian charity, these characterize Gentius as an individual and are in no other Hebraist replicated in quite the same way.

It was surely the uniqueness of each one of these men that gave the rabbis hope. For it was, finally, the rabbis' hope that any of these men could be persuaded to support the Jews as Jews that justified these contacts and even made the rabbis draw the Christian scholars near.

If there is any breakthrough to be found, then, in the materials we have covered and examined, it is in Gentius's use of a piece of Jewish literature as a specific tool for promoting the welfare of the Jews. Even if Gentius lost none of his own hopes for the eventual conversion of the Jews, he was persuaded for a brief moment to argue in behalf of their welfare. To this Aboab and Aguilar had looked forward and to this Menasseh had contributed. For other such statements in behalf of the Jews, the rabbis of Amsterdam would have to wait for Pierre Jurieu's half a century later.[31] This did not have the same express hope for the conversion of the Jews accompanying it.

Yet it would probably be closer to the truth to say that the Jews of Europe would have to wait, into the eighteenth century and even beyond, for types who viewed the Jews with greater equanimity. Lessing may well be the first of this kind. It is perhaps not mere chance that he had studied Maimonides, delving into both the *Guide* and the *Mishneh Torah.* Moreover, interestingly enough, when he came out in favor of the Jews, he would employ a parable similar to one used by Ibn Verga. It was the famous parable of the three rings, and with it Lessing would argue, in the age of Moses Mendelssohn, that a Jew could walk the streets of Berlin on an equal footing with a Christian.[32]

Appendix to III: The Publication of *De Idololatria*: The Circumstances

Dionysius Vossius's *De Idololatria* was published in Amsterdam in 1641 at the printing house of Joannes Blaeu. It was republished by Blaeu in 1668, the only changes being in format and in the poorly reset type. In both instances, Dionysius's work was appended to his father, G. J. Vossius's, larger work on idolatry, *De Theologia Gentili*. On the verso of the title page of the second edition of Dionysius's commentary is a note from Blaeu to the reader in which the printer explains the juxtaposition of the two works. He writes that Dionysius's Maimonides was both an opportunity and a pleasurable inducement for G. J. Vossius to memorialize his departed son by writing a short—so he was saying then, comments Blaeu—book of his own on the same subject ("eadem de materia"). In other words, says Blaeu, Maimonides' work, as translated and commented upon by Dionysius, might not inappropriately be called the "mother" of the larger, full-blown work. The connection of the two works is further made clear in Blaeu's assurance to the reader that he decided "not to begrudge [Dionysius's] commentary (*Commentariolus*) the place which it called for in its own right, and not to withhold from you any of those things which may be of service and pleasure in getting to know the kindred work (*consanguinei operis*)," to wit, as the play on words might have it: "the work of [Dionysius's] kinsman," his father's *De Theologia Gentili*.

As for the illustrative method and the appeal to the ancients that the two works share, G. J. Vossius's own remarks are instructive. In the preface to *De Theologia Gentili*, he wrote: "Indeed, I thought that the subject that I was dealing with would thus be explained more fully: and, because those writers often also put forth the reasons for their opinions, I concluded that our views would be more firmly established in this manner, with the arguments and authority of the ancients [for support.]" (1668 edition, p. [viii].) Vossius did not limit his choice of advocates, as he indicates: "for support I cited grammarians, poets, orators, and historians." (Ibid.) It can easily be recognized that Maimonides and Dionysius's commentary on him provided highly suitable *testimonia* for G. J. Vossius's topic and theme.

To return to the statement by Blaeu quoted above, it is, then, extremely plausible. It is quite concordant with our basic assumption of a unity of interests and scholarly efforts between father and son. It must, however, be examined critically. G. J. Vossius's interest in idolatry was already manifest in his 1618 work on Pelagianism. The greater catalyst was probably a different work, though. Selden's *De Diis Syriis* was first published in England in 1617, but it was reprinted in Leiden in 1629 by Vossius's friend Lodewijk de Dieu. Vossius was still in Leiden at that time, of course. Moreover, Vossius refers to Selden's work a number of times in his own treatise, and there is every reason to suppose that it was a key stimulus even before Dionysius prepared his Maimonides. In a 1627 letter to Selden, Vossius mentions that he had read the *De Diis Syriis* three times (1:109, no. 71). And in a 1630 letter to Meursius (1:145, no. 109, Jan. 13, 1630), there is a mention of the Leiden reprint "far longer and decicated to our Heinsius." And, in presenting Selden with a copy of his own work, Vossius wrote of the major role of Selden's work in the creation of his own: "magnum partem eodem pertineat praeclarus tuus de Diis Syriis labor" [*Epistolae,* 1:434, no. 502 (Dec. 1, 1644)]. It is not too much to say that an undeveloped interest in the subject led to Dionysius's choice of extract from Maimonides' *Code* for commentary and study, but there were, to be sure, prior stimuli at work as well in the creation of *De Theologia Gentili.* Yet, we also find Vossius the Elder in 1636 characterizing his own work in progress as a "companion on the same subject" [Jun. 1, 1636, no. 287, (1:289), to Laud]: "Tandem Typographus aggressus est filii Maimonidem de Idololatria. . . . Ne solitarius prodat [prodeat(?)], addam ei comitem de eodem argumento Dissertationem nostram." At the completion of his work, he writes the faculty of Oxford, in his cover letter for the volume, that his own work was "from the same store" as his son's ("de penu proprio") [*Epistolae,* 1:382 (no. 423, Nov. 23, 1641)]. That there were differences he was, of course, well aware:

the work had a similar title and subject, but many of the details were different, he said (*Epistolae,* 1:394, no. 443, Mar. 14, 1642, to Golius).

The actual story of the composition and growth of *De Theologia Gentili* is of interest as well. It is connected with the relations between Vossius and Blaeu—it may help explain some of Blaeu's attitude as expressed in his prefatory note—and it also helps place the relationship of G. J. Vossius's work and his son's Maimonides in proper perspective. Relations between Vossius and Blaeu were regularly strained, as one or the other of them failed to produce what the other had expected. Blaeu was often slow to print what had been given him (Vossius: "Nihil homine illo tardius in exsolvendis promissis" [Grotius, *Briefwisseling,* 9:256 (no. 3558 [May 2, 1638]), but Vossius himself took advantage of the various delays to add material. (Pieter de Groot to his father: "Domini Vossii librum de Idololatria testudineo demum gradu ad vos perveniet, tum ob typographi negligentiam, tum *ob ipsius auctoris quotidiana augmenta* [Italics mine]" [Grotius, *Briefwisseling,* 9:482 (no. 3690 [26 July 1638])]. The progress of the work and its printing is, in truth, almost comic; from March 1636, with Vossius claiming that Dionysius's Maimonides had already been in Blaeu's hands for two years (no mention of his own work) [Grotius, *Briefwisseling,* 7:32 (no. 2512)]; to Vossius's expectation that the Maimonides would be out in a month—the date was then Nov. 30, 1636—and that his own work, then titled *De Origine et Progressu Idololatriae*—this would later become a subtitle— was being printed [Grotius, *Briefwisseling,* 7:542 (no. 2860)]; through January 6, 1638, when Vossius wrote Grotius: "Opus nostrum . . . spisse procedit, partim ob occupationes, quibus vix par sum, partim etiam *quia sub manibus crescit.* . . . Nec video, ut ante tertium abhinc mensem exire in lucem possit." [Grotius, *Briefwisseling,* 9:19 (no. 3414)], and August 29, 1629, when Willem de Groot informed his brother that Vossius was still "sweating away at it" [Grotius, *Briefwisseling,* 10:555f. (no. 4272)]. All the while, we see Hugo Grotius himself regularly inquiring, "Where is it? I can't wait to see it!" [e.g., nos. 2548 (April 1636), 2885 (Dec. 1636) "Tuum . . . librum, simul venerit, avide vorabo (!)," and 3338 (Nov. 1637) [*Briefwisseling,* 7:81; 7:580; 8:716; but passim also]. The *De Idololatria* was clearly ready in 1636, but, "because of the similarity of the subject," the elder Vossius waited to publish his own and his son's work together. (See G. J. Vossius's *Epistolae,* 1:376, no. 412 [Apr. 29, 1641], to Coch): "Id opus jam ante quinquennium prodiit in lucem, sed non [in] manus hominum, quia dum ego aliud opus molior de Theologia Gentili . . . , jacuit apud typographum, expectans duntaxat, ut nostra, ob argumenti similitudinem qualem qualem, prodeant simul." G. J. Vossius had even shown the proofs of his son's work to Golius no later than 1638 (*Epistolae,* 1:393, no. 442). [See also ibid., 1:163–64, no. 128.] Still, it was not until October 1641 that Vossius finally wrote the prefaces, and the two works appeared together before the end of the year.

NOTES

NOTES TO PREFACE

1. On the impact of the *Mishneh Torah* on rabbinic literature and on Jewish life in general, see the concise survey by Twersky in the "Epilogue" to his *Introduction to the Code of Maimonides ("Mishneh Torah")*, pp. 515–37.

2. Altmann, "Wollaston," p. 243. A précis, evaluation, and bibliography of the history of Christian Hebraism and a 'complete' list of Hebraists is Loewe's article in the *Encyclopaedia Judaica* (1971), 8:10–71, s.v. "Hebraists, Christian." Also, generally, on Hebraism in the period of the Renaissance and early Reformation, see Baron, *History,* chapter 57 and notes.

3. Grabois, "The *Hebraica veritas* and Jewish–Christian Intellectual Relations in the Twelfth Century," *Speculum* 50 (1975):613–34.

NOTES TO INTRODUCTION

1. The history of Maimonides' *Guide* in the West was given most notably by David Kaufmann in his "Der 'Führer' Maimûni's in der Weltliteratur," and, a few years thereafter, by Jacob Guttmann in his "Einfluss." See Guttmann, pp. 144–46, 150–52; also, Newman, 107–110. See further Kluxen, "Literargeschichtliches," and "Geschichte." Also, *Jewish Encyclopedia,* s.v. "Guillaume of Auvergne," and, esp., "Alexander of Hales," and Baron, *History,* 9:65 & 69; 271 & 273, nn. 13–14, 19. On William of Auvergne in the Paris disputation of 1240, Baron, 9:80 and 277–78, n. 30.

2. On Christian attitudes to the Talmud in the period 500–1248, see Merḥavyah, *Hat–Talmud bi–rei han–Natsrut.*

3. Moore, "Christian Writers," p. 202.

4. On Yeḥiel of Paris and the 1240 disputation, see Maccoby, *Judaism on Trial,* pp. 19–38; on the above question, ibid., p. 32. The text which corresponds to Maccoby's version is *Vikkuaḥ,* p. 11b; it is unfortunate that Maccoby does not provide any reference for his quotation of the passage in question, despite the general accuracy of his translation, and especially in view of the fact that his own

version of the *Vikkuaḥ,* pp. 153–62, is a paraphrase. Other discussions include Newman, p. 61 and n. 231 and lit. cited there.

5. This incident at Barcelona is reviewed by Maccoby, p. 131, n. Earlier discussion is found in Rankin, pp. 168–69, and Lieberman, *Shkiin,* p. 50. Though no specific reference to any passage in the *Mishneh Torah* would ultimately be made during the disputation, the work would immediately thereafter be subjected to censorship with the intention of having it burned publicly. The passage in question, according to Maccoby, p. 132, n., and he is undoubtedly correct, contra Cohen, is the one in *Hilkhot Melakhim,* 11:4, that supposedly contained a blasphemous reference to Jesus. An English text of the Barcelona debate is also to be found in C. B. Chavel's *Ramban: Writings and Discourses,* New York, 1978. On this passage and its subsequent use among Hebraists, more below.

6. Baer, "Christian Spain," 1:349–50; 2:90–91, 186, 227, 391, and 467, nn. 26 & 29, all related to the use of the *Mishneh Torah.* Martin's references to the *Mishneh Torah* are on pp. 320, 376, 766, 872, and 873, as Lieberman lists them, p. 91. All are to *Hilkhot Melakhim,* chs. 11 & 12, though Lieberman does not specify this fact. As for Martin's Jewish ancestry and other aspects of Jewish–Christian polemic and disputation, including the indebtedness of later writers, including Alfonso de Spina, to Martin or Abner, see Baron, *History,* 9:106–109 and 298–300, nn. 9 & 11; and chs. 38 & 39, passim.

Abner of Burgos's *Mostrador* disquisition on the *Mishneh Torah* is summarized by Baer, 1:349–50. The Latin protocol of the debate at Tortosa also contains scattered references to Maimonides' code by the apostate Joshua hal–Lorki, who conducted the debate. See Pacios's edition, 1:345–57, for a translation of Poznanski's list of hal–Lorki's citations from rabbinic literature; no more than half a dozen are from the *Mishneh Torah.* The one to *Hilkhot Teshuvah* 8:4, for example, can also be arrived at through Maimonides' *Guide* 1:70; the reference would later be used again by Pietro Galatini in his *De Arcanis catholicae veritatis* (1518), p. 176.

7. See Baer, "Christian Spain," cited in the previous note and Rubio y Lluch, *Documents,* 1:309. Also Rubio, 1:404 and 424; 2:xlv, 50, 82 and 246 for related ideas and documents.

8. "Item, in quodam libro quem Judei vocant *Glosas Moysi de Egypto* et actor illius libri intitulavit *Declarationem et reformationem legis,* continentur abusiones et falsitates Thalmuti; item, plures errores et blasfemie contra fidem Christi et specialiter quod omnes illi qui tenent viam et fidem Christi vocant et dicunt hereticos, quod est dictum in hebreo "minim." Item, Christum Jhesum liber ille dicit errasse et contra Deum fecisse et contra Legem et quod plus erravit Jhesus quam Machometus et quod ipse Jhesus posuit majorem partem mundi in errore colendi alium Deum, qui non est unus Deus, et destruendi legem quam Deus dedit; et plures alias blasfemias continet contra Christum." Gui, *Manuel,* p. 18.

9. The perfidy of the Jews was demonstrated first and foremost by their observance of the commandments, said Martin; in their nullification, he said further, and in their allegorical meaning, there would be progress and fulfill-

ment. On this, see R. Bonfil, "The Nature of Judaism in Raymundus Martini's *Pugio Fidei,*" *Tarbiz,* 40 (1971):365.

10. Baron, *History,* 9:68. Bonfil's article, cited in the previous note, is far more pointed, however.

11. See Scholem, "Considérations sur l'histoire des débuts de la Kabbale chrétienne," in *Kabbalistes Chrétiens* (a volume that in general merits notice), pp. 17–46; this is a revised version of his earlier "Zur Geschichte der Anfänge der Christlichen Kabbala," in *Essays presented to Leo Baeck,* pp. 158–193. See also F. Secret, *Kabbalistes Chrétiens,* Blau, *Christian Interpretation,* and Baron, *History,* chapter 57.

12. Pico, *On the Dignity of Man,* tr. Forbes, pp. 252–53. See also, below, n. 14, and lit. cited there.

13. See again the references cited above, Pref., nn. 2 & 3

14. The controversy between Bruni and Manetti over the need for and even appropriateness of Christians knowing Hebrew for their study of the Bible is subjected to a penetrating analysis in Trinkaus, *In Our Image and Likeness: Humanity and Divinity in Italian Humanist Thought,* (pp. 578–601). Though primarily an investigation of the humanists' changing viewpoints on the nature of man, it also examines the evolving scholarly traditions, including Hebraism as an aspect of the Christian Renaissance, that were the concomitant of these intellectual considerations. The ways in which Manetti, and then, in turn, Ficino, and Pico "come to terms with the very Judaic religious tradition with which [their] humanistic study of Hebrew confronted [them]" (p. 734) are also dealt with at length in chap. 16. Though relying somewhat on previous work by scholars with a knowledge of Hebrew, e.g., U. Cassuto, the integrative way in which Trinkaus treats Hebraism as an intellectual enterprise and historical phenomenon and challenge makes his book especially worthy of note in the present context.

15. Geiger, *Studium,* is the best discussion of the various proponents and opponents of Hebrew studies in the period before 1550 and of the nature of their quarrel; his treatment of Reuchlin was to be expanded into the standard biography and even revised after that. See also, though, Maurer, "Reuchlin," for other views of the great humanist.

16. The standard survey of sixteenth–century Hebraism is Rosenthal's "Rise of Christian Hebraism." Its virtue consists not really in the listing of names and dates, but in the extensive passages from the leading Hebraists that Rosenthal has translated. These give the reader a sense of the Hebraists' purposes and motivations. See also, more recently, Jerome Friedman, "Sebastian Münster, the Jewish Mission, and Protestant Antisemitism," *Archiv für Reformationsgeschichte* 70 (1979): 238–59.

17. This is hardly the place to enter into a disquisition on the Spanish Inquisition; that would be beyond the scope of this work. But the currents in northern Europe did have their mirror in Spain, since crypto–Judaism among *conversos*

had become a major issue in the fifteenth century. Some inquisitors had recourse to the *Mishneh Torah* on questions of practice. See Baer, "Christian Spain," 2:390–93.

18. For a discussion of instances of such teaching in sixteenth–century Germany, see E. Zimmer, "Jewish and Christian collaboration in Sixteenth Century Germany," *JQR* 71 (1980): 69–88.

19. "Nostrates Judaei vel invidia, vel imperitia ducti Christianum neminem in eorum lingua erudire velint idque recusant cuiusdam Rabi Ami auctoritate, qui in Thalmud ita dixit: Non explanantur verba legis cuiquam gentili eo quod scriptum est: qui adnuntiat verba sua Jacob, praecepta sua et iudicia sua Israel, non fecit similiter omni genti." Quoted by Geiger, *Studium,* p. 16, n. 2. R. Ammi's statement is found at TB *Ḥagigah* 13a; the scriptural reference is to Ps. 147:19-20a. (In the Munich and Vatican codices, this statement is assigned to R. Assi, but the biblical proof-text parallels the Latin version more closely; the printed editions, e.g., Pesaro 1513, Bomberg 1548, and Vilna, attribute the dictum to R. Ammi, but cite only verse 20 (in its entirety). Incidentally, the Tosafot ad loc. base their ruling on verse 19.) Maimonides' own view differs somewhat. In a responsum to the students of R. Ephraim of Tyre that forms the basis for *Hilkhot Melakhim* 10:9-10, he affirms categorically the halakhic status of the dictum by R. Yoḥanan (*Sanh.* 59a) that an idolator who engages in the study of Torah incurs the penalty of death. Yet, vis-à-vis Christians, he adopts a more lenient pose. By contrast to Muslims, he notes, they believe that the authority of the Hebrew Scriptures is intact and enduring. As such, they are less likely to lead the unwary astray with their confutations and to bring the Jewish population into danger. Consequently, they are not to be subsumed under those idolators who are to be prevented from studying Torah. In fact, Maimonides looks forward to their being moved to convert, having received instruction in the correct understanding of the Torah: "ve-im ya'amidum 'al hap-perush han-nakhon, efshar she-yaḥzeru le-mutav." *Teshuvot ha-Rambam,* ed. Jehoshua Blau, (Jerusalem, 1957), no. 149, pp. 284-85. On this passage, see also Twersky, *Introduction,* pp. 452-53 and n. 234.

20. On Christian humanism, see Kristeller, *Renaissance Thought,* p. 86ff. and passim, as well as Spitz, "Humanism in the Reformation." On Calvin as a humanist, Harbison makes the following observation: "Calvin made a sound classical education the foundation of the curriculum in his Genevan Academy," despite the loss of interest in studying the secular classics that he experienced after his conversion. Erasmus and Luther were each "more generally revolutionary in his own way," but Calvin maintained a continuity with the past, "because he was more objective in his approach to scholastic, juristic, and humanistic learning . . . and because he was more catholic in his intellectual tastes." *The Christian Scholar,* pp. 145–46.

Hanna Gray's "Renaissance Humanism" has application far beyond its immediate confines; the pattern it describes was followed even in the seventeenth–century Netherlands. In her subsequent "Valla's *Encomium,*" Gray defines the term 'Christian humanism' as follows: "[It] directs secular studies and methods toward religious ends." For such figures as Valla, "to prove the compatibility of secular learning and Christianity, to show that the methods of rhetoric were needed for theology was enough; it was not required that the one be pursued for the sake of the other." (P. 51.) That, we know, would come later.

21. For this and some of the foregoing, see: Moore, "Christian Writers," p. 215; and Momigliano, "Ancient History and the Antiquarian," p. 76f.

22. Manuel, "Israel and the Enlightenment," *Daedalus* 111 (1982):33–52, esp. pp. 35ff.

23. Manuel, *The Religion of Isaac Newton,* pp. 49, 86.

NOTES TO PART I

1. J. J. Woltjer, "Introduction," in *Leiden University,* p. 1.

2. G. J. Hoenderdaal, "The Debate about Arminius outside the Netherlands," ibid., p. 156.

3. J. Van Den Berg's brief study in Dutch of Jewish–Christian relations, "Joden en christenen," (partially translated in Toon, pp. 137–53) does not approach the issue quite in this way, but it is clear from his description of anti–Jewish efforts that internal Christian struggles had an effect on the Jews. I have not seen the chapters by Nijenhuis in the new *AGN* (vol. 6 [1979]) [mentioned by Emery and Swart in *AHN* 12 (1980), p. 142, in their annual "Survey of Recent Historical Works on Belgium and the Netherlands Published in Dutch"], where he most probably addresses this question. Incidentally, these surveys are to be recommended as extremely useful.

4. S. J. Fockema–Andreae, "De Nederlandse Staat," pp. 146, 187; Foster, "Liberal Calvinism," p. 2; J. Van Den Berg, "Church and State Relations," pp. 35ff. On the Regents (and on almost any other aspect of the Dutch seventeenth century), see C. R. Boxer, *The Dutch Seaborne Empire: 1600–1800.* See also, most recently, H. A. Enno van Gelder, *Getemperde Vrijheid,* passim, showing how decentralization promoted toleration. The "General Crisis of the Seventeenth Century" question, which has indeed engaged the attention of so many, is not of particular applicability to our discussion.

5. Geyl, *The Netherlands,* 1:78f.

6. Foster, "Liberal Calvinism," p. 14.

7. Fockema–Andreae, "De Nederlandse Staat," p. 14.

8. The extent of Calvinist influence on Dutch culture has been variously interpreted. See: Huizinga, *Dutch Civilization,* pp. 47–61, who leans toward the idea of cultural freedom from Calvinist influence; Geyl, *The Netherlands,* 1:63–83, a more balanced perspective, perhaps, if not even leaning to the other side; K. H. D. Haley, *The Dutch in the Seventeenth Century,* pp. 109ff. On the other hand, see the comment by K. A. Swart in Krantz and Hohenberg, eds., *Failed Transitions,* p. 47: "Initially, bourgeois secularism, with its appreciation of comfort and confidence in man's ability to improve his mundane condition, was strongly opposed by Calvinist preachers dwelling upon original sin. But in the course of the seventeenth century Calvinism accommodated itself to the age's secularism. The extraordinary popularity of the poet Jacob Cats, who held that pursuit of gain did not necessarily impede the pursuit of godliness, reflects this accommodation, and testifies to the deep inroads made by bourgeois secularism into Dutch Cal-

vinism." The most far–reaching discussion of this question may be found in R. B. Evenhuis, *Ook dat was Amsterdam,* 2:257–310. While it is not our purpose to enter into a discussion of this topic here, it is clear that the Church's interpretation did not dictate such artistic and intellectual tastes completely. It did, however, because of its stridency, make its presence felt in almost every aspect of culture. Note also Johan Goudsblom, *Dutch Society,* pp. 15–18.

9. Fontaine Verwey, "The Netherlands Book," p. 32.

10. See I. Schöffer's essay in *Algemene Geschiedenis der Nederlanden* (henceforth *AGN*), 6:4ff. for one of the best and most succinct discussions of the issues.

11. Foster, "Liberal Calvinism," p. 18; and Frederic Platt, "Arminianism," in *Encyclopedia of Religion and Ethics,* 1:808 (and 809ff.) for the articles and their meaning.

12. On the issue of the relationship between Church and state, see Schöffer, 6:11ff., and Douglas Nobbs, *Theocracy and Toleration,* passim. It is not possible here to detail the complexity of Nobbs's presentation.

13. Jan & Annie Romein, *De Lage Landen bij de zee,* p. 364. Nobbs is generally cautious on the use of the word "theocracy."

14. This is one of many opinions, obviously. It was not necessarily a term used by contemporaries. Frederick Henry's moderation with respect to the Remonstrants was shown early and consistently: local prerogatives made it possible for Amsterdam, in 1631, to readmit the Remonstrants; for the Vroedschap to have Barlaeus and Vossius installed as the first two professors in the Athenaeum Illustre in 1632; to permit the opening of the Remonstrant Seminary in 1634, despite protests from the Calvinists; and for Vondel, on his way to becoming a Catholic, to celebrate the city of Amsterdam in *Gijsbrecht van Amstel,* a play which was to become an institution, in 1637.

15. See Geyl, *The Netherlands,* 1:65 and 222.

16. Huizinga, *Dutch Civilization,* p. 74.

17. H. Brugmans, *Opkomst en Bloei van Amsterdam,* p. 137f. Also, Evenhuis, 2:181, n. 230. We are not referring here to the kind of Arminianism shown in the ceremonial conformity imposed by Archbishop Laud on the Anglican church, but rather to what would later be characteristic of the approach of the Cambridge Platonists, and to what Laud himself advocated: freedom with respect to doctrine. Laud and G. J. Vossius were, after all, great friends.

18. Friedrich, *The Age of the Baroque,* p. 104.

19. Romein, p. 371.

20. Emile G. Léonard, *A History of Protestantism,* 2:249.

21. See, generally, Peter Burke, *Venice and Amsterdam;* and Paul Zumthor, *Daily Life in Rembrandt's Holland,* pp. 229ff.

22. The largely middle class origins of the *predikanten* themselves must be noted, however, as well as the fact that most remained middle class. Many were the sons of ministers and most generally contented themselves with the attractiveness and the good living that the ministry provided for those qualified. As such, one cannot view the *predikanten* as either upwardly mobile or concerned with falling from their secure position.

23. Romein, p. 371.

24. Geyl, 1:209. Other uses of this idea in England and America are suggested by the studies of B. S. Capp and J. F. Maclear. The framework and characteristics of this mode of thought will be further discussed in II, but it is beyond the scope of the present work to go into the non–Dutch manifestations in any detail.

25. Gomarus, quoted in Nobbs, p. 18.

26. Geyl, 1:213.

27. Similar usage can be seen elsewhere in Europe at this time, particularly in Britain. See further below, passim.

28. Harrison, *Arminianism,* p. 23.

29. Joost van den Vondel, *Pascha* (1612); cited in Meijer's intro. to Grotius's *Remonstrantie,* p. 31, n. 59.

30. Grotius, *Briefwisseling,* 5:55 (#1715 [August 17, 1632]).

31. On Huygens, see Conrad Busken Huet, *Het Land van Rembrand,* II, 1, 141ff.; on Cats, see n. 32. Meijer, in his intro. to the *Remonstrantie,* p. 31, has said that the theme "Israel" deserves a detailed study. On these writers and Dutch culture generally, see J. L. Price, *Culture and Society* or J. Presser's chapter in *AGN,* 6:360–83.

32. Geyl, 2:22 and 24. *AGN,* 7:2.

33. On the idea of myth, see C. A. Tamse, "The Political Myth," in *Britain and the Netherlands,* 5:1–18. Busken Huet, II, 2, p. 24, n. 47. See also Gans, *Memorbook,* pp. 77–83, for an extensive and intelligent discussion of this whole theme.

34. *Concordantie,* offte Verghelijckinghe/ Der ghesegende en affvallige staet deser Vereenighde Nederlanden/ beyde in Politie ende kercke/ Met den staet der Israeliten/ wanneer hen Godt het beloofde Canaan ingegeven hadde/ ende zy 'tzelve door ongehoorsaemheyt hadden vorlooren, n.p., 1631. (Knuttel, #4159; also mentioned in G. J. Renier, *The Dutch Nation,* p. 143.)

35. *Concordantie,* pp. 16, 17, 12, 16, and 17ff., combined from a rambling polemic. Is. 30:1 is cited on the title page.

36. Ibid., p. 6.

37. Joseph Lecler, *Toleration and the Reformation,* 2:241f.; see also Gebhardt's note in Uriel Acosta, *Die Schriften,* p. 242, n. ad XIX. 28: "*Idolatria* ist bei den

Marranen das terminus technicus für die katholische Religion." Schoeps, however, in *The Jewish–Christian Argument,* p. 190, n. 73, mistakes the source of Limborch's indignation: Limborch reacts as an *Arminian* to the charge of idolatry by Orobio.

38. See further below, in III and in the Appendix.

39. Geyl is very careful on this point, 1:215: "Philology was an indispensable auxiliary to theology . . . Vossius' international reputation as an authority on antiquity, and as an exponent of its literary laws, was unconnected with his ideas on predestination." At the height of Remonstrant controversy in 1618, Vossius's work on Pelagianism had the propagandistic goal that I assume for his later work on idolatry. With regard to the earlier work, see C. S. M. Rademaker, "Gerardus Joannes Vossius (1577–1649)," in *Acta Historiae Neerlandica* 4:230f.

40. Clemens M. Bruehl, "Scaliger," 12 (1960):206.

41. Romein, p. 371.

42. *ERE,* 1:814, s.v. "Arminianism."

43. Schöffer, "The Batavian Myth," *Britain and the Netherlands,* 5:78–101; Rembrandt has often been mentioned, incidentally, as a forerunner of the reconciliation between Christian and Jew. See, esp., Landsberger, *Rembrandt, the Jews and the Bible,* chapter 3.

44. For the idea of "entrepôt," de la Fontaine Verwey, *Netherlands Book,* p. 37: "storehouse"; Huizinga's idea of the mediator in his famous essay, "The Netherlands as Mediator Between Western and Central Europe," in *Dutch Civilization,* pp. 138–57; and, more recently, C. G. Gibbs, "The rôle of the Dutch Republic as the intellectual entrepôt of Europe in the 17th and 18th Centuries," *BMGN* 86 (1971), pp. 323ff.; Jan De Vries, *The Economy of Europe in an Age of Crisis, 1600–1750,* pp. 120–22, uses this idea in speaking about commercial exchanges.

45. S.v. "Arminianism," in *ERE,* 1:810.

46. Charles Wilson, *The Dutch Republic,* p. 154. Also, s.v. "Arminianism" in *ERE,* 1:814. For a solid traditional view of "observation" as the method of many Dutchmen of the Golden Age, see C. V. Wedgwood, "The Golden Age of the Dutch Republic," 1:280ff.

47. Cf. Bruehl, "Scaliger," 13 (1961):54ff., and Bangs, *CH* 42:16.

48. H. R. Trevor–Roper, "The Religious Origins of the Enlightenment," *The European Witch Craze,* p. 207. One might oppose the Aristotelianism of the Calvinists to the method of the Stagirite himself. Aristotelianism may have been breathing its last in the 1630s in Holland, but Aristotle was, in some respects, reborn there, at this period, in Descartes and his method—which became a subject of major disputes in the Netherlands and elsewhere after mid–century, yet "was preserved and continued by Arminian patronage." Ibid.

49. See Fisch, p. 187. Cf. Jacques Basnage, *Histoire des Juifs* (1716), 9:999. Grotius is reported there to have pointed out Menasseh's works to his learned

friends as very useful for understanding Scripture. In his *De jure belli ac pacis,* Grotius wrote: "In order to see what is the knowledge which the books of the Old Testament contain, the Hebrew writers may help us no little; and especially those who were best acquainted with the discourses and manners of their countrymen."; quoted in Isaac Husik, "The Law of Nature, Hugo Grotius, and the Bible," *HUCA* 2 (1925):398. Vossius once characterized the Talmud as "a work containing many things not unworthy of being known, but so covered with lies and falsehoods, that surely here, if anywhere, that saying of Epicharmus has a place: remember to be skeptical [*memneso apistein*]." *Theses theologicae,* ed. 3, p. 253f. Vossius never really abandoned his general policy of caution and incredulity, nor was he unusual in that respect.

50. H. R. Trevor–Roper discusses the concept "Republic of Letters" in his essay "The Religious Origins of the Enlightenment," repr. in his *European Witch Craze,* pp. 202–3.

51. Sir George Clark's *The Seventeenth Century* discusses this, pp. 288–305, as does Huizinga, *Dutch Civilization,* pp. 33–46.

52. On developments in the Netherlands, see: Huizinga; and Geyl, *The Netherlands* 1 :76–77 & 215–16, and, more generally, 1:63–70. Of particular worth is Geyl's distinction in chapter 4 between "native traditions" and "Baroque" as the two great poles in this conflict. On the continuing influence of the Greco–Roman classics. see: Highet, *The Classical Tradition,* esp. pp. 291–92; and Clark, p. 299: "The classics were still the mainstay of serious study"; also, ibid., pp. 270–73.

53. See Gray, "Renaissance Humanism," esp. p. 506.

54. Leon Roth, "Hebraists and non–Hebraists of the Seventeenth Century," *Journal of Semitic Studies* 6 (1961): 220. The biblicism of the century is not, of course, our general concern here; that a distinction must be drawn between general biblicism and Hebraist scholarship was recognized by Harold Fisch in his book on English Biblicism, *Jerusalem and Albion,* p. 14, n. 2. Baroway, "Tudor–Jacobean Hebrew Studies," is also suggestive.

55. On the derivative nature of much of the study of rabbinic literature and on the inherent possibility of confusion, see: Jaap Meijer, "Hugo Grotius' Knowledge of Hebrew." For the background and dynamics of this process with regard to the Greco–Roman classics, see R. R. Bolgar's masterful *The Classical Heritage and its Beneficiaries,* pp. 329–79.

56. Foster, "Liberal Calvinism," p. 11, attributing the phrase to Kuyper. Cf. Moore, p. 251.

57. Cf. Meijer's intro. to Grotius's *Remonstrantie,* p. 23. See also S. W. Baron, "Calvin and the Jews."

58. Grotius's *De Veritate,* which appeared in a Latin translation in 1627, made frequent and explicit reference to it. Vossius, in his *Theses Theologicae,* also indicated that the conversion of the Jews was a sign of the imminent coming of

Christ. See pp. 221–23, quoting Rom. 11:25. These orations dated from the years 1615–19.

59. See further below in part III.

60. Eekhof, *Theologische Faculteit,* p. 44*f.

61. Meijer's intro. to the *Remonstrantie,* p. 30. See also, s.v. "Arminianism" in *ERE,* 1:814. *De Statenvertaling: 1637–1937,* pp. 84–85, indicates how the Remonstrant point of view was systematically excluded from the translation.

62. Grotius, *Briefwisseling,* 9:20f. (#3414 [Jan. 6, 1638]).

63. Meijer's intro. to Grotius's *Remonstrantie,* p. 64 (trans. Jacob Meijer, "Hugo Grotius' *Remonstrantie,*" *JSS* 17: (1953):141. See, e.g., *Briefwisseling,* 9:506 (#3708 [Aug. 7, 1638]).

64. De Vries, p. 119; also now, especially, Jonathan I. Israel, *The Dutch Republic and the Hispanic World, 1606–1661,* pp. 77, 134–43 and passim. Israel calls attention to the role of the Amsterdam Sephardim, in circumventing the restrictions, as "a group particularly involved in the Iberian trade" (p. 135). On this latter question, see, particularly, Israel, "Spain and the Dutch Sephardim, 1609–60," *SR* 12 (1978):1–61.

65. J. C. H. Lebram, "Hebräische Studien," pp. 350–51, 356 and passim.

66. On Drusius, Lebram, "Hebräische Studien," pp. 332–36 and Diestel, pp. 422–25.

67. See Fuks, "Brievenboek."

68. Lebram, "Hebräische Studien." pp. 332–33.

69. On Amama and his humanism, see Lebram, "Ein Streit um die Hebräische Bibel und die Septuaginta," *Leiden University,* p. 47, and Fuks, "Franeker," pp. 59–62.

70. On Polonus, see S. Stein, and H. F. Wijnman.

71. Bernays, *Scaliger,* pp. 122–24.

72. Bruehl, "Scaliger." esp. 13 (1961):55–65. But excellent balance is found in J. H. Waszink, "Classical Philology," *Leiden University,* pp. 160–75, passim, and H. J. de Jonge, "The Study of the New Testament." ibid., 65–110, and the lit. cited there.

73. "Debet esse valde peritus Iudaismi, qui Iudaeo volet reprehendere & refutare. . . . docti sunt & subtiles Iudaei, sunt convincendi ex Thalmud, non ex Novo Testamento, ridebunt; mirum est neminem rei illi studere, miserum quid nos Christiani contra alios scribamus & nemo contra Iudaeos; ils exposent bien subtilement l'Escriture, il fait beau lire leurs livres, il y a beaucoup d'esprit . . ." *Scaligerana,* p. 130.

74. "Lisez les bons auteurs, la Métamorphose d'Ovide, le Thalmud, Illa sunt necessaria ad Biblia." Jonge, p. 84, and Bruehl, 12:212f.

75. Guttmann, "Einfluss." pp. 223–24, n. 4, has the quotation: "[Moreh han–nevukhim] non potest satis laudari. Ego non tantum illum librum, sed etiam omnia illius Magistri opera tanti facio, ut solum illum inter Judaeos desiisse nugari dicam."

76. From the preface, as are all the quotations that follow. See Meyer, "Bradford," as well.

77. See further in I, n. 130, on typologies.

78. Ziskind's interesting article, "Petrus Cunaeus on Theocracy, Jubilee and the Latifundia," *JQR* 68 (1978): 235–54, approaches the author from a different vantage point.

79. "Fuit tamen ex hac scriptione nobis perquam suavis voluptas. Recolebamus enim ea studia, quibus in adolescentia quondam mire dediti fuimus. Juvabat identidem cogitare, quantopere animum nostrum delectavisset Hebraismus, cum Biblica volumina, Rabbinorum commentarios, atque alia multa, quae erudite a Judaeis scripta sunt, evolveremus. Cujus sane operae nunquam nos poenituit."

80. See 1:18, which appears to have found echoes in Spinoza's *Tractatus,* chapter 5.

81. See: *Jugurtha* 10. 6.

82. On this point, see Ziskind, p. 237, 239 and passim.

83. Ziskind, pp. 252–53, on the basis of Cunaeus's letters.

84. ". . .agnovisse Deum conditorem suum . . . atque . . . coelestem doctrinam tam feliciter ad suos propagavit, ut jure eum Maimonides *'ammudo shel 'olam* (Hebrew letters are used here) *columen atque stabilimentum seculi* appellet." It may be pointed out that Cunaeus generally seems to aim at clarity in his translations, and that the translation here expands on the original words.

85. The lexicon *Arukh* is the work of Nathan ben Yeḥiel of Rome (1035–1106). It was made use of by virtually every one of the scholars under discussion.

86. Exceptions are his remarks about Kara (2:2) "that most accurate author Rabbi Joseph, whose commentaries . . . are of inestimable value"; on Rabad, however, he thinks that "though he was a diligent critic (*animadversor*) of the failings of sagacious Maimonides, he was wont to substitute the kind of things that have more the semblance of solid reasoning than the force of it, [so that] the investigations lose their effect" (1:17).

87. RSV translates here: "Behold, the days are coming, says the Lord, when I will punish all those who are circumcised but yet uncircumcised—Egypt, Judah, Edom, the sons of Ammon, Moab, and all who dwell in the desert that cut the

corners of their hair; for all these nations are uncircumcised, and all the house of Israel is uncircumcised in heart."

88. See Scholem, *On the Kabbalah and its Symbolism,* pp. 94–98 and 123–129.

89. This issue was not new with Cunaeus, of course. Bellarminus, the Catholic polemicist, had raised it in his *magnum opus, De Controversiis Christianae fidei adversus hujus temporis haereticos* (1586); he had been answered by Junius in the 1601 *Animadversiones.* Cunaeus's treatment of the issue is really rather superficial, though his conclusions are of interest to us.

90. Meijer, ed., *Remonstrantie,* p. 55.

91. Though there is a reference to "Abodazara," ed. Meijer, p. 108.

92. Baron, *History,* 15:391–92, n. 34, and text, pp. 27–28.

93. Meijer (in *JSS* 17), p. 94.

94. "Iudaei ex quo Patria exsules infestis dominis serviunt, haud dubie ad calumnias patent." Grotius, *Briefwisseling,* 7:577 (#2884 [Dec. 12, 1636]).

95. W. J. M. van Eysinga, *Hugo Grotius,* p. 126.

96. Grotius, *Remonstrantie,* p. 112.

97. Ibid., p. 108.

98. "Neque omnibus neque nulli credendum est." Grotius, *Briefwisseling,* 7:579 (#2884).

99. Meijer, *JSS* 17:96. The phrase is from Jer. 31:28 (AV).

100. Grotius, *Remonstrantie,* p. 113. For another perspective on the *Remonstrantie,* see Swetschinski's unpubl. Brandeis Univ. dissertation, *The Portuguese Jewish Merchants of Seventeenth–Century Amsterdam: A Social Profile,* (1980), pp. 43–58. His major emphasis is on the discrepancy between Grotius's proposals and "the Amsterdam reality," arguing that Grotius "exhibits far more blatant Christian sensitivities than ever appeared in the lawbooks of Amsterdam," and trying to show, in sum, "how out of touch with reality" Grotius was (p. 47).

101. Meijer apparently relied on Roth's imprecise translation rather than on the Latin text, which, curiously enough, he manages to print in a footnote, p. 62f., n. 27. See Roth, *Menasseh ben Israel,* p. 60, and his general discussion of the Grotius–Menasseh relationship, pp. 146ff. See, also, Menasseh's letter to Grotius, in the *Briefwisseling,* 9:774–76 (#3900 [Dec. 25, 1638]).

102. See pp. 106-7.

103. Löwenstamm, "Grotius' Stellung," pp. 298ff.; and Knight, *Grotius,* pp. 167–82, esp. 179ff.

104. "Deum . . . & precibus, & jejuniis, certant placare: nec exaudiuntur."

105. "Peccatum illud contempti Messiae."

106. Meijer, "Grotius' Knowledge of Hebrew," p. 140, remarks that the annotations of 1640 are sometimes "completely at variance with the original argument," but he does not account for this.

107. Meijer, (in *Historia Judaica* 14):144, but see Baron, *History* 15:390, n. 31, and Knight, *Grotius*, p. 254f. Also see, e.g., Grotius, *Briefwisseling*, 9:247f. (#3554 [Apr. 30, 1638]), with some remarks that can only be based on an original inspection of the *Mishneh Torah*.

108. "Apud Maimonidem libro de Idololatria."

109. The studies by Lachs and Rosenberg need correction in a number of places. The implication by Rosenberg, p. 84, about the sequence of events between the appearance of Grotius's work and Vossius's fails to take account of the intimate contacts between Vossius the Elder and Grotius and of the likelihood that Grotius was alerted to the importance of *'Avodah Zarah* by Vossius even before Dionysius's treatment appeared. Moreover, there is insufficient attention to the differences among the several editions. Our discussion may be found on p. 61.

110. A detailed conspectus of editions is Jacob ter Meulen's standard *Liste Bibliographique* (1950). Prior to 1646, there had already been at least four editions, some in several printings, and with variations. The Harvard Law Library has a complete collection. The annotations of the later editions were, for all practical purposes, additions that could not be inserted into the body of the text without further altering the typeset, in the way that the revisions had been integrated into the expanded editions of 1631. A fuller treatment follows.

111. Trans. Kelsey.

112. On Selden, see, for now, Herzog; a new study is a desideratum.

113. Grotius, *Epistolae* (1687), #1520, 14 September 1641.

114. "Collatis Christianis constitutionibus nostris Iudaica dogmata confutabo." One wonders exactly what he proposed to do; it is difficult to know.

115. Grotius, *Briefwisseling*, 7:1 (#2495, 1 Mar. 1635); 7:223 (#2644, 25 June 1635); 7:92 (#2554, 14 April 1636); 7:581 (#2885, 12 Dec. 1636). One would do well to examine Grotius's letters more carefully than Meijer has. Roth seems to conceal more than he reveals when he uses them in his study of Menasseh, but Meijer obviously did little independent work. To be sure, very little of the critical edition of the letters had appeared when Meijer was doing his work. Yet, as Baron has reminded us, 15:392, n. 34, (and his remark predates the appearance of the most recent volumes), the letters are a valuable source. The references to rabbinic literature in the letters became more frequent and polished as time progressed, even to the extent of a mention of some sources for which no translation yet existed, as far as I can tell.

116. Diestel, *Geschichte*, p. 431; and see also Haentjens, pp. 31–32.

117. "Baptizet eam in nomen proselytarum, id est, in eam religionem, quam profitentur proselytae."

118. Moore, p. 222.

119.

> . . . COCCEJUS, ut alter Jason,
> Sopito serpente, in dias luminis oras
> Effert hoc vellus. . . .

120. " . . . si ex ipso Talmude ejus autoritas convellatur: veraeque & solidae testamentis veteris explicationes adhibeantur, & ex antiquis magistris roborentur." See also Rengstorf, 1:476–77 and Meijer, ed., *Remonstrantie*, pp. 25–26.

121. " . . . novem est quod molior: ostendere nempe cognitionem Talmudis, Thalmudicorumque scriptorum, ad Novi Testamenti illustrationem insignem lucem afferre."

122. Reuchlin, of course, had had the same complaint a century and a quarter earlier: the Jews begrudge Christians any information on rabbinics.

123. See *Makk.* 10b.

124. Lebram, "Hebräische Studien," p. 341.

125. It will be remembered that Erpenius had acquired some of that Oriental treasure trove from Borelius. See above, p. 38.

126. Juynboll, chapter 1, pp. 1–10 passim. Yet compare J. Brugman, "Arabic Scholarship," *Leiden University*, p. 209.

127. Jonge, in *Leiden University*, p. 87.

128. The quotations and outline are from l'Empereur's *Oratio inauguralis*, pp. 20, 23, 25–26, 43, 40.

129. Reference in Fuks, "Franeker," p. 64, n. 30. On the leanings toward scholarship rather than theology even among academic controversialists, Fuks remarks justly that "many orientalists drew themselves up on the side of philology." (p. 55).

130. On the general history of typology, in its patristic, medieval, and Reformation background, see: Thomas M. Davis, "The Traditions of Puritan Typology," pp. 11–45; and the superlative annotated bibliography by Bercovitch, pp. 249–337. See also: Mason I. Lowance, Jr., *The Language of Canaan: Metaphor and Symbol in New England from the Puritans to the Transcendentalists*, pp. 1–40.

131. Article 36 of the *Confessio Belgica* reads as follows: "We believe that our God, because of the depravity of the human race, has appointed kings, princes, and magistrates, willing that the world be governed by laws and policies, so that the dissoluteness of men might be restrained, and all things carried on among them with good order and decency . . . And their office is, not only to have regard to and watch for the welfare of the civil state, but also that they protect the sacred ministry, and thus may remove and prevent all idolatry and false worship." Quoted

by Hoenderdaal, "Debate," *Leiden University,* p. 156–57, n. 22. L'Empereur's was a thoroughly Calvinist position.

132. Jonge, in *Leiden University,* p. 94.

133. *Scaligerana,* p. 128.

134. We have not examined l'Empereur's 1641 edition and commentary on Bertram's *De Republica Ebraeorum* (a later title for the *De Politia*).

135.

O videant caeci veram sine tegmine lucem!
Horreat ô tenebris obruta corda videns!
Magna, in laude Dei, tua laus erit, INDUPERATOR:
Quando tuo dium semine germen erit.

136. The Hebrew text may be found in Baneth's edition of Maimonides' letters, *Iggerot ha–Rambam,* 1:79. Buxtorf makes its thrust appear harsher that does the original, and, in the second sentence, makes the remark appear biographical. The original reads as follows: "If you waste your time on the interpretations and inner connections [i.e., *pilpul*] of the Gemara, and on those things that we freed people from [studying], time will be lost and little benefit will accrue." Kapaḥ's tr., p. 134, varies slightly.

137. Peter Toon, *Puritan Eschatology,* p. 23.

138. B. S. Capp, *Fifth Monarchy Men,* p. 190.

139. Ibid., p. 166.

140. B. S. Capp, "Godly Rule," *Past and Present* 52 (1971):114.

141. Capp, *Fifth Monarchy Men,* pp. 232ff.

142. Van Den Berg, in Toon, *Puritan Eschatology,* p. 153.

143. Brian G. Cooper, "Academic Re–Discovery of Apocalyptic Ideas," *Baptist Quarterly* 18 (1959–60):359.

144. J. F. Maclear, "New England and the Fifth Monarchy," *William and Mary Quarterly,* 3rd ser., 32 (1975):228, n. 6. I am grateful to Prof. Stephen J. Stein for this reference.

145. Toon, pp. 141, 128, cites Nuttall, dating the letter to 1649. It is from 8 April 1640 and is not really assessed at its full value by either Toon or Nuttall.

146. Van Den Berg, in Toon, p. 140.

147. Ibid.

148. Ibid. See the reference to Vossius, supra, n. 58. It is a more traditional view that Vossius holds; among other citations, he makes reference there to Augustine's letter to Hesychius (#197). On Episcopius, also see Rengstorf,

1:474–75, who quotes him to the effect that it is because of a misconception on the part of the Jews about the nature of Christianity that they refuse to be converted—they get their impressions from Roman Catholicism. In other words, a new impetus from Calvinism, which sees itself as truth, and, therefore, as capable of new initiatives and new accomplishments, will succeed in bringing about the Jews' conversion.

149. Baron, *History,* 15:27.

NOTES TO PART II

1. Recent surveys of Sephardic Jewish life in Amsterdam include: G. Nahon, "Amsterdam, métropole occidentale des *Sefarades* au XVIIe siècle," *Cahiers spinoza* 3 (1980): 15–50; Henri Méchoulan, "Un regard sur la pensée juive à Amsterdam au temps de Spinoza," ibid., 51–66, (the remainder of the volume also being of interest); the introduction by these two authors to their translation of Menasseh ben Israel, *Espérance d'Israel* (Paris, 1979), pp. 15–34; J. Kaplan, "The Portuguese Jews in Amsterdam: From Forced Conversion to a Return to Judaism," *SR* 14 (1981):37–51; and Daniel M. Swetschinski, "Kinship and Commerce: The Foundations of Portuguese Jewish Life in Seventeenth Century Holland," ibid., pp. 52–74. Ralph Melnick's short *From Polemics to Apologetics: Jewish–Christian Rapprochement in 17th Century Amsterdam* (Assen, 1981), which contains some useful observations, is based on extracts from the relevant sources, a few of them translated for the first time.

2. Meijer, ed., *Remonstrantie,* p. 26.

3. "Non sunt expellendi, lucrum afferunt, deinde ab illis discimus." *Scaligerana,* p. 129.

4. Kayserling, *Menasseh,* p. 11, is suggestive.

5. *Vikkuaḥ Shiv'ah Harim,* p. 24. Vossius, *Epistolae,* no. 193, p. 213 (9 February 1633). The addressee is mistakenly identified by the editor as Conrad Vorstius, who was neither a physician nor still alive at this point in time.

6. Nat, *Studie,* p. 9.

7. Bloom, *Economic Activities,* p. 22, n. 101. See also Swetschinski, pp. 8–38, esp. p. 35, as well as chapter III in general, on this and the following.

8. Meijer, ed., *Remonstrantie,* pp. 21–22. On Coster in general, see G. J. Jaspers, "Schets van Abraham Costerus' leven en werken," *NAK* 57 (1976):31–61.

9. Hirschel, "Cultuur en Volksleven," in Brugmans and Frank, p. 497.

10. Verborgene eygenschappen inde Heylighe Schriftuer / als in een verseghelt Boeck / in beyde Testamenten / soo wel int Nieuwe als Oude verseghelt / nootwendich om weten / tot opbouwinghe van den Tempel des vreden / voor Heydenen / Joden / Christenen / ende Mahumedisten. Geschreven aen de Eerwaerdighe Rabbinen van de Synagoge des Stede Amsterdam. Door J. H. J. van der Ley. (Amsterdam: the Widow of Ioris Veselaer, 1626), pp. 10, 6–7.

11. In a statement quoted by Meijer, ed., *Remonstrantie,* p. 23.

12. Van Den Berg, "Eschatological Expectations," in Toon, p. 142, summarizing.

13. "Homonymously" [Gk. is used] must express Voetius's opinion, articulated elsewhere as well, that, while Menasseh did not engage per se in debating Christians, his writings certainly went against Christian teachings.

14. Voetius, *Exercitationes & Bibliotheca Studiosi Theologiae* (Utrecht, 1644), pp. 545–46.

15. See Prins, "Freedom of the Press," pp. 158–165, and, again, for the 1660s, pp. 166–71. For anti–Christian disputations and polemic on the part of Jews, a preliminary list is Judah Rosenthal, "Anti–Christian Polemic," esp. 2:169–172 and, in a supplementary list, 3:433–39, no. 253, the 1650 disputation of Menasseh ben Israel with a Calvinist dominee. Further reference to Voetius, incidentally, can be found in F. Secret, "Notes" (1965), pp. 157–59.

16. Ancona, "Komst der Marranen," Brugmans & Frank, p. 212. See also Rivkin, "the Da Costa Circle," pp. 10–18 and John Lightfoot's preface to Broughton's *Works* (1662).

17. Zilverberg, "Beelthouwer," p. 158, n. 6.

18. Quoted by Hillesum, "Porta Veritatis," p. 339.

19. Grotius, *Remonstrantie,* article 25 (Meijer, pp. 118–19 and 126).

20. Mendes dos Remedios, *Os Judeus Portugueses em Amsterdam,* Appendix IV, p. 195. There is also a paraphrase by Wiznitzer, "Merger Regulations," p. 124. On the rabbis and the *Mahamad,* the comment by Ancona, "Komst der Marranen," in Brugmans and Frank, p. 269, is suggestive: "Dat de maämad zich boven de rabbijnen stelde . . . was niets niews." The tenor of the *Mahamad*'s authority is captured best by this article:

"12. A mamad tera auturidade e supiridade sobre todo e nenhuma pesoa nem pesoas poderaõ yr contra as resulucoens que dito mamad tomar nem firmaraõ papel nem papeis pera encontralos. E os que o fizerem emcoreraõ em pena de herem por que finalmente se ordena e entende que ho mamad a de ser supremo no governo da nacaõ de Kaal . . ." [Pieterse, *de Barrios als Geschiedschrijver,* p. 158].

21. Ancona, "Komst der Marranen," p. 262, and, more extensively, in his "Delmedigo, Menasseh ben Israel, en Spinoza," pp. 131–32. On censorship by the *Mahamad,* see further Swetschinski, pp. 412–36, for selected cases, including Delmedigo.

22. "Plane . . . alia quam studia animo agitat [Manasses], Lusitanis nihil, ob paupertatem synagogae, Doctori suo persolventibus. Nempe si Judaeis fides, (ut videntur mihi verum dicere) sese in urbem receptis, nostri illis esse familiares, negotiatio etiam saepe communis, ut facile fuerit nostris, omnes eorum artes bonas, malas, cognoscere. Sed nostri vel ad clavum sedent, vel eos habent favitores & amicos. Quare non operosum fuit siquid periculi, vel apud nos, vel in Hispaniis etiam oboriretur, illis in luto relictis, vel profunda potius palude, emergere opera eorum, qui & his, & terris aliis plus possent."

23. Discussed also above in part I, p. 57 and n. 101.

24. Vossius, *Epistolae,* no. 372 (1 Jan. 1640 [old style]), p. 345. (Unmentioned here, incidentally, is the laxity in missionizing that Vossius decries often enough elsewhere.)

25. Inter alia, see Morteira's students' introduction to *Giv'at Shaul,* p. 2b, speaking of his many "responsa" to gentiles on various questions. Jacob Sasportas, who came to Amsterdam from North Africa in 1651, while he seems to have approved of this kind of apologetics, criticized one of Morteira's responsa of this type, arguing that Morteira was too willing to bend the halakhah to make it more palatable for Christian ears. Other rabbis too, possibly members of the Ashkenazic community, took in hand the instruction of Johannes Leusden, a Hebraist of great renown and the author of the *Philologus Hebraeo–Mixtus* and other learned works; the evidence here is not concrete, however. See Zwarts, *Hoofdstukken,* pp. 142–43 and criticism of his view by Hirschel, "Leusden," p. 25, nn. 5, 7.

26. See above on Sforno, I, p. 78. For Maimonides' view, see above, Intro., n. 19, and below, p. 111.

27. Levita, *Massoret ham–Massoret,* ed. Ginsberg, trans., p. 100.

28. On this episode, see Swetschinski, pp. 412–20.

29. Luzzatto, approbation to Delmedigo, *Sefer Elim,* p. [2b]. See also Ancona, "Delmedigo," pp. 130–33. The view of Delmedigo on secular culture is summarized by Barzilay, *Between Reason and Faith,* p. 209. See also Barzilay, *Delmedigo,* pp. 92ff., 307ff., and 315–22.

30. Gray, "Renaissance Humanism," p. 503.

31. Ben–Sasson, "Reformation in Jewish Eyes," [Heb.], p. 78 [17]. The English version reads differently and does not convey the flavor accurately, p. 264.

32. Jacob le–Vet hal–Levi, responsum no. 49, text in Gebhardt, *Uriel da Costa,* p. 185.

33. Barzilay, *Between Reason and Faith,* p. 215.

34. Quoted in Ben–Sasson, "Reformation," p. 63 [2]; see also p. 78 [17].

35. Vossius and his family did not arrive in Amsterdam until the fall of 1631; there is no record of any earlier contact between them and the rabbis of that city. However, a 1626 letter from Vossius to Buxtorf, Sr., included a translation of several passages from the *Mishneh Torah.* Whose translations these were is unclear from the reference in the Amsterdam University Library *Catalogus der Handschriften,* 7:107, no. 716b. Dionysius, of course, was to tutor his family in Hebrew after having been trained by Menasseh ben Israel.

36. On the study of Maimonides in the Jewish school curriculum, the basic sources were collected by Simḥah Assaf in his *Mekorot le–Toledot ha–Ḥinnukh*

be–Yisrael, 4 vols.; see 4:251, where Assaf notes that even children plowed directly into the *Mishneh Torah* for their study of Jewish law. 2:144–45 shows "Rambam, Ḥelek Alef" as a regular part of the daily schedule. 1:155 has Shabbetai Bass's famous 1680 description of the Amsterdam Talmud Torah; Bass mentions "Maimoni" as being studied in the upper grades. In general, Amsterdam educational practice was (along with so much else) modelled on that of Italy [A. Shochat in *Entsiklopedyah Ḥinnukhit,* 4:409] and, in Italy, *Madda', Ahavah,* and *Zemanim* formed the halakhic portion of the curriculum. Yehudah Avida', "Maimonides' Code as a school–book" (Hebrew), *Areshet* 3 (1961):31 notes that even when the contents of the [school] editions containing these first three books were modified, no part of *Madda'* was ever omitted. This is demonstrated proof of its currency.

37. Baron, *History,* 13:405, n. 22. On the presence of Hebraists' works in Jewish libraries, see below, p. 140. Lara's Maimonidean translations were two: *Da lei divina* (Amsterdam, 1652) [*Yesode hat–Torah*] and *Moralidad y Regimento de la vida* (Hamburg, 1662) [*De'ot*]. M. B. Amzalak's introduction to his reprint of the former (Lisbon, 1925) lists these and Lara's other works, as well as Samuel da Silva's trans. of *Hilkhot Teshuvah* (Amsterdam, 1613); see pp. ix–x.

38. On the date of Aboab's departure, see Pieterse, *de Barrios,* pp. 71–72. On Aboab's relation to Herrera and thus to Sarug, see his preface to the translation *Sha'ar hash–Shamayim,* and Altmann, *Eternality,* p. 17 and refs., n. 54. Scholem mentions the translation of this work into Latin; see, *Sabbatai Ṣevi,* p. 68, n. 95; see also p. 522 and n. 126 there. The Lurianic eschatological "Vision of redemption from the gentiles" propagated by Sarug is reviewed by Scholem, pp. 25–27. Yet Aboab's own pronouncement at the time of the Sabbatian movement about the compatibility of the "popular devotional revival" with "the Law and our Tradition" (Scholem, quoting Sasportas, *SṢ,* p. 522) is but a reflection of the general balance, in Aboab's own sympathies and interests, and even in the interests of Aboab's colleagues Menasseh and Aguilar, between halakhah and aggadah, despite Aboab's and Aguilar's support for Shabbetai Tsevi.

39. On Herrera, see, most recently: A. Altmann, "Lurianic Kabbala in a Platonic Key: Abraham Cohen Herrera's *Puerta del Cielo,*" in the forthcoming proceedings of the conference on Jewish Thought in the Seventeenth Century, held at Harvard University in March 1982.

40. See Ancona, "Komst," p. 255 and Pieterse, *de Barrios,* p. 62, and 159 (#18), and 160 (#22).

41. Pieterse, *de Barrios,* p. 110.

42. Text in Kayserling, *Aboab,* Heb., p. 10: "tarti aḥare sherirut ve–ra'ayonim zarim . . . baḥanti mishpatekha u–maasti 'osehem; ha–ḥonef ve–ha–rasha' ahavti ve–hishtaḥaveti le–'ovedehem . . ." Now, "ha–ḥonef ve–ha–rasha'" could be a derogatory usage for Jesus, but the plural object of "le–'ovedehem" makes this problematic.

43. *Catalogus . . . Librorum . . . Abuab* (1693) (copy in the library of the Jewish Theological Seminary in New York). Some discussion, with errors, in Marx, *Studies*, pp. 210–11. A *conspectus raisonné* of this catalogue is clearly a desideratum and will provide a more informed look at Aboab's intellectual prosopography.

44. On polemical literature, and Isaac Troki, see Kaplan, "Morteira," p. 22. Again, on Jewish reluctance to publish polemics, Yerushalmi, *Spanish Court,* pp. 354–55.

45. Franco Mendes, *Memorias,* p. 25, l. 27.

46. Aboab, *Parafrasis,* pp. [i–iv], 6, 7.

47. Coch, it will be remembered, had written that the Jews have a purgatory, but Menasseh, for one, would disagree [*De Creatione,* problem 21]. This does not mean that Aboab supported the idea of a purgatory in the same way as Coch understood it.

48. Altmann, "Eternality," pp. 12 & 20–23.

49. Altmann has inferred from the initials *shin, lamed, mem* written by the copyist that the other disputant was Morteira; on the other hand, Teicher had suggested previously that Menasseh was more likely the other central figure, while Morteira had issued the *pesak* in favor of the eternalist side. Altmann, "Eternality," p. 5; Teicher, "Why was Spinoza Banned," p. 43–44. Altmann's distinction, as to general character and views, between Aboab and Morteira becomes harder to maintain now that it appears more likely that Morteira himself was of Portuguese New Christian background, if not birth. (See Kaplan, "Morteira," p. 10, and Salomon, "Morteira," pp. 139–41, summary).

50. Altmann, "Eternality," p. 22.

51. Ibid., p. 22 and text A, 11. 210–12, p. 15.

52. Roth, *Menasseh,* pp. 50, 56, 223, 287, etc. ("rival"). I have not seen Aboab's poem to the *De la Resurrección,* as no photocopy could be made from the fragile Klau Library copy.

53. Altmann, "Eternality," Text C, #8, 11. 20–31, pp. 87–88.

54. On Morteira's position, see Salomon, "Morteira," pp. 138–39.

55. Altmann, "Eternality," Text A, l. 204, p. 50.

56. Cited in Kaplan, *Orobio* (diss.), p. 277 and p. 619, n. 12.

57. Zunz, *Zur Geschichte und Literatur,* p. 234.

58. Silva Rosa, *Geschiedenis,* p. 66.

59. See Wiznitzer, *Colonial Brazil,* p. 171, I. S. Emmanuel, "Brazilian Jewry," pp. 60–61, and Zwarts, s.v., *NNBW,* 7:14.

60. Meijer, *Enc. Sef. Neer.*, 1:22–23, Mendes dos Remedios, pp. 60–67 and Fuks, *Manuscripts*, 2:84–86 and 2:229–30 (nos. 176 and 422) are discrepant lists of his manuscripts.

61. On Orobio, see J. Kaplan's 1978 Hebrew University dissertation *Isaac Orobio de Castro and His Circle* (offset); and Gans, *Memorbook*, p. 85. On Aguilar, see also J. Kaplan, "The Role of Rabbi Moshe d'Aguilar in his Contacts with the Refugees from Spain and Portugal in the XVIIth Century," in the *Proceedings of the Sixth World Congress of Jewish Studies*, Heb. sec., 2:95–106, which discusses these letters to Orobio and is essentially reproduced in the diss., albeit with more extensive notes, pp. 212–19 and nn., pp. 558–67.

62. Quoted by Kaplan, with comment on Aguilar's harsh stance and his possible awareness of its harshness, and with the observation that, though Aguilar cites Maimonides in support, his view is contravened by the more accurate text of Maimonides that was unknown to the Amsterdam reading public and, indeed, by the very thrust of the Maimonides' statement. See Kaplan, pp. 216–17 and p. 565f. nn. 30–32.

63. The list in Mendes dos Remedios, pp. 60–67, still provides useful information. Kaplan's article does not entirely supplant it. The letter to Antwerp is cited by Kaplan in his diss., p. 620f., n. 19.

64. Partial text in Gebhardt, *da Costa*, pp. 195–97.

65. The remarks from the "Advertencia ao Lector" of the *Dinim de Sehitá e Bedicá* are quoted by Mendes dos Remedios, p. 61.

66. The two views are represented by Silva Rosa, *Geschiedenis*, p. 50, and Ancona, "Komst," pp. 270 and 255–56, and, in greater detail, in Ancona's "Delmedigo, Menasseh," pp. 130–33.

67. Saraiva, "Vieira, etc.," p. 44.

68. Roth, p. 106.

69. Ibid.

70. Later he was reinterred at Ouderkerk, in the communal cemetery. See Kaplan in *KS* 54 (1979):611–13 on the date of his death. It will be evident that the foregoing account is, inevitably, indebted to Roth, whose biography, though in need of revision, is still quite sound. The biographical notice of Menasseh in the Méchoulan & Nahon tr., *Espérance d'Israel*, pp. 35–69 is a well–taken recent treatment.

71. Ancona, "Delmedigo, Menasseh," p. 124; Hebrew text, n. 1.

72. See above, I, p. 91.

73. Roth, p. 44, without advancing a source, makes this five years.

74. Unless otherwise specified, the quotations that follow are taken from either the prefaces or the dedication, to either the Spanish or the Latin edition, as will

be clear from the context; there is no pagination in the volumes for this preliminary material. The added reason here suggested is Maarsen's, "Wetenschap en Letterkunde," Brugmans and Frank, p. 527. I have generally followed Lindo's translation of the Spanish text, though, often, for clarity or precision, I have made my own version.

75. Roth, p. 88, summarizes and surveys these.

76. Ancona, "Delmedigo, Menasseh," pp. 123–30 and appendices; also Ancona, "Komst," pp. 259–60 and 262. Ancona discusses the earlier Delmedigo case as the first such instance in Amsterdam and draws the connection. See also Swetschinski, diss., pp. 412ff.

77. Roth, p. 123, says about Caceres that he had been awarded a licentiate in law at some Spanish university before coming to Amsterdam.

78. Benayahu, *Haskamah,* p. 121, considers the approbation for Delmedigo to have been "reshut," voluntary, and that the "ḥovah," the "obligatory" one, was instituted in 1639 by the *Mahamad.* The approbations for the Spanish *Conciliator* are clearly "ḥovah," however.

79. Roth, p. 320, n. 2, writes that because the support of the Frankfurt rabbinate was considered necessary, it is improbable that the imprint is false. See n. 3 there, for a summation of Hillesum's position in *Het Boek,* 1928, which is clearly in error.

80. Hahn, *Yosef Omets,* pp. 261–84, esp. p. 271.

81. See Gans, *Tsemaḥ David hash–Shalem* (1691 ed.), pt. 1, under the year 5393.

82. The extract may be reviewed above, p. 111.

83. Hahn, *Yosef Omets,* p. 271, mentions one Jacob Schweinfurt as the person who persuaded him to take up its study.

84. Hillesum, "Bijdrage," pp. 353–55 and 352–63, discusses Menasseh's printer's marks, but makes no reference to Günzburg. He does not stop to analyze their significance at all, in fact. Menasseh's title page to the *Pene Rabbah* is also omitted from Hillesum's discussion, incidentally. The significance of its border with the four verses on which it draws, Cant. 5:5; Is. 22:22; Cant. 7:14; and Jer. 40:4, should not escape us. Menasseh was already engaged in messianic speculation at that point and was obviously a receptive audience for Günzburg's preaching.

85. Menasseh's use of the verse was noted even by Isaac Troki, the Karaite leader, in Lithuania. Maarsen, "Wetenschap en Letterkunde," Brugmans and Frank, p. 526.

86. See A. Altmann's forthcoming essay on Herrera for a discussion of contemporary usage of "true kabbalah." I thank Prof. Altmann for pointing this out to me.

87. See Baron, 15:60–61 and nn.

88. "Tu enim . . . linguae sanctae Professor meritissimus, e nobili progenie oriendus, in Cabalistica speculatione doctissimus, a multis annis Hebraeorum concionator egregius."

89. ". . . Per universum orbem habitantibus, ubi divina Scriptura summe veneratur."

90. "Dum enim jampridem majorum nostrorum ditione ob peccata extorres agitamus, quid majus optare possumus, quam ut munere eorum, sub quibus vivimus, facultas nobis sit tranquille & innocenter vitam transigendi?"

91. "Quippe non ignoro, arduam esse rem occultos Sacrae Scripturae sensus scrutari & dijudicare; eoque majoribus ingeniis argumentum hoc fuisse relinquendum. Sed rursum occurrebat, ubi pietas adsit, & bene de publico merendi voluntas, qualemcumque laborem a bonis hominibus probari. Id ego dicere possim, me hic nec laedere quenquam, nec Religioni a nobis dissentientium obloqui studuisse."

92. "Et quia familiare huic saeculo est, etiam illis obtrectari, qui in neminis offensam, & consilio omnes juvandi scribunt, consultum putavi, postquam publice hoc opus consecrassem Potentissimis Hollandicae Westfrisiaeque Ordinibus, & Amplissimis hujus Vrbis Consulibus, privatim quoque aliquem deligere, cujus sub nomine scripta mea tutius in lucem prodirent."

93. "Neque ideo velim adeo me quis omnium rerum ignarum credat, quasi dedicando te adstringi putem ad assentiendum in omnibus quae hic scripsi. Scio vix inter ejusdem religionis homines convenire. Quanto minus inter eos, quibus haud levis est dissensio."

94. Blok, "Humanistes," pp. 56–57.

95. "Quomodo potuit homo Judaeus melius de Christianis mereri, quam colligendo et unum in opus transferendo, quidquid olim omnes Hebraeorum doctores scripsere?"

96. ". . .et ipse vitae integrae vir est et procul a malignitate aliorum suae religionis, quippe qui nusquam Christianis in suo opere insultet."

97. The Vossius–Barlaeus letter is quoted but not analyzed in Hillesum, "Porta Veritatis," p. 342. Blok, "Barlaeus I," pp. 194–95, discusses an additional letter by Barlaeus to the curator van der Myle.

98. It is Copy 3 in the Klau Library collection.

99. The preface will be discussed in the part III, under a consideration of the overall character and career of the translator.

100. Maarsen, "Wetenschap en Letterkunde," p. 527, and Prins, "Drukpersvrijheid," p. 156, whom he is obviously following, make the mistaken assumption that Vossius had actually used the expression and condemned the work.

101. Compare Jacob Sasportas's remarks in his proofreader's postscript to Menasseh's 1651 *Nishmat Ḥayyim;* he views much of Menasseh's prior activity as having been anti–Christian: "He raced forth in rage to counter [the statements] of the nobles of Bashan [i.e., Christian scholars] and to purge [such views] from their midst. . . . and he showed courage in appropriating what is useful and [thus] placing harm at a remove. With his logical presentation [of the Jewish view] against our enemies who rise against us, he shattered the jaws of injustice, severing and snapping their arguments as a thread of tow is snapped at the whiff of flame . . ." ("yaruts yitmarmer le–'umat abire bashan le–shaleaḥ otam la–'azazel . . . ve–higbir ḥayalim be–hakravat ham–mo'il u–ve–harḥakat han–nezek. be–hitpalsefuto shibber metale'ot 'avel neged oyevenu hak–kamim 'alenu u–vittek nittek sevaratam ke–hinnatek . . . petil hanne'oret be–hariḥo esh . . .")

102. Prins, "Drukpersvrijheid," pp. 156ff.

103. Hahn himself says in his approbation that he had known for a long time that Menasseh was a righteous man, a saintly one, a man beyond suspicion of putting out anything improper: "ish kadosh hu she–ḥezkato she–eno motsi davar she–eno metukkan mit–taḥat yado." Zacuto's letter is dated "the last day of August 1632."

104. For Counter–Remonstrant readers, see Hillesum, "Menasseh," p. 152.

105. See Sorbière's *Sorberiana,* p. 148, for the clue to the younger Vorstius's having been the translator. (Menasseh, by the way, knew Latin well enough to have made the translation himself. Franco Mendes, *Memorias,* p. 22, says he knew Greek and Latin "perfectly." Sorbière suggests that he did not and Blok assumes from this that some of Menasseh's friendships were due to his need to have his works translated. There is only a grain of truth in this, for Menasseh's need was a far larger one, to disseminate knowledge as broadly as possible, especially through personal contact.) Méchoulan, "Le problème du Latin chez Menasseh," *SR* 14 (1980):1–6, which examines the question of Menasseh's Latin with respect to *De termino vitae* and its publication, does not pretend to show the extent of Menasseh's fluency.

106. *De creatione,* p. [62].

107. "Sed dicere non possim, quam multi quoque e contrario invidiae succo turgidi, calumnijs suis ac quantum in se erat evertere prorsus sint conati."

108. " . . . ut multum commodare Christianis potest, sic etiam cupit: itaque hoc nomine nonnulla etiam invidia laborat apud suos." Vossius, *Epistolae,* #185, p. 208, 14 Nov. 1632. This is possibly one source for Silva Rosa's view that "men kon het niet goed verdragen, dat deze Rabbijn, ofschoon op streng orthodox standpunkt staande, zich op het gebied der profane wetenschappen bewoog en zich van de Christelijke theologie op de hoogte stelde." But this would apply to all the Amsterdam rabbis, not Menasseh alone. Menasseh gave the appearance more than the rest did, however, of pursuing Christians. Teicher, "Spinoza Banned," p. 44, argued that Menasseh's "enforced leisure" gave him time to work

on the *De creatione* and implies that Menasseh's opinions on the eternality of punishment controversy brought this about. The statement by Menasseh does not substantiate this in quite the way Teicher would like, for "succisivis & subsecundariis horis" need not mean those of an "enforced retirement"; they can be understood simply as "in my spare time," in other words, apart from the routine course of events, including work on *De resurrectione*.

109. Menasseh's prospective patron was David Wilhelm, whom he addresses as a counselor of the Prince of Orange. Wilhelm was also Constantijn Huygens's brother–in–law. On Wilhelm, see further, Méchoulan, "À propos de la visite."

110. Blok is certainly correct in pointing out, "Humanistes," p. 20, and "Barlaeus II," p. 106f., that the last line has frequently been mistranslated, as if it had read "ut . . . sic." [His discussion of "pietas universalis" is on p. 29, n. 44. Blok draws no significant connections between Barlaeus's remarks and Menasseh's own.] Mistranslations include M. H. Gans's (*Memorbook* (Engl.), p. 41). My translation: "True things [the lines before speak of Menasseh's ancestors and the "verba . . . sensaque Talmudicae relligiosa Scholae"] are pleasing; the author is pleasing for his excellent efforts; and that piety of a dissimilar faith [the piety of which Menasseh had spoken (cf. Blok, "Humanistes," p. 29, n. 44)] is pleasing. It is for everyone to worship God. It is not for one age or one people to be pious, we believe. If we have different understandings of things, let us, for [the sake of] God live as friends (there is an ambiguity, recognized by Barlaeus's critics, in the form "Deo," which might be taken, with "amici," as "friends to God"; see Blok, "Barlaeus II," pp. 88ff.), and let erudition [lit., a learned mind] be valued everywhere at its own worth. This is the sum total of my faith. Believe this [yourself], Menasseh! Thus I am a [believer] in Christ, thus will you be a son of Abraham." (Cf. Blok, "Humanistes," p. 21 and n. 56 and "Barlaeus II," p. 91f. and n. 171 on "Christiades," etc. Cf. also, on the subsequent Barlaeus–Vedelius exchanges about "pietas," "Barlaeus II," esp. pp. 86–87.)

111. See additional proof of this intolerance in his statement in the *Vindiciae* quoted by Blok, "Barlaeus II," pp. 88, 90 [error in pagination]. See also "Barlaeus I," p. 195 and "II," p. 107f.

112. " . . . hoc propositum mihi fuit, sedulo omnia tractare ex sententia veterum sapientum: quippe qui cum a prophetarum temporibus propius abfuerint, vel hoc nomine in pretio esse mereantur."

113. Hillesum, "Bijdrage," p. 360, mention's Barlaeus's informant by name, but does not draw these connections. The younger Vorstius would also be the translator of *Hilkhot Yesode hat–Torah*.

114. Prins, "Drukpersvrijheid," pp. 159–62. Censorship never became imposed from the outside.

115. ". . .quod Manassis Judaei opusculo de creatione carmen praeponuit, quo pietatem etiam agnosceret in homine Judaeo, Deoque etiam servire fateretur." Vossius, *Epistolae,* #308, p. 301, 12 July 1637.

116. Prins, "Drukpersvrijheid," p. 173, n. 20. The refusal to hire Menasseh came on 10 Jan. 1636, more than six months after the publication of *De creatione.*

117. Jacob le–Vet hal–Levi, Responsum no. 49, in Gebhardt, *Uriel da Costa,* p. 185.

118. Ibid.

119. *De Resurrectione,* pp. 241, 311, and 313.

120. Zilius was a Remonstrant who studied at Amsterdam until 1630 and in 1632 defended his thesis in Amsterdam under *Barlaeus!*

121. *De Resurrectione,* p. [8, a & b].

122. "Unum Deum colimus, ejus praeceptis nos subjicimus, & post hujus vitae difficultates meliorem vitam exspectamus." Quoted also by Blok, "Barlaeus I," p. 200.

123. "Certe scopus, quem mihi propositum habui, bonus fuit, minimeque vituperari meretur: nam semper studui ad verum collimare, & celebriorem reddere nominis divini gloriam, ac proinde etiam spero opus hoc meum aequioribus rerum aestimatoribus gratum, acceptumque fore." Ibid., p. 346.

124. Roth, *Menasseh,* p. 167.

125. "Si non idem in omnibus sentimus, quid vetat singulos suo abundare sensu, & Deo probare conscientiam, nec minus iis omnibus bene velle, qui nullis volunt male?"

126. "[Patres], . . . quibus si in omnibus assentiri non potes, talia tamen sunt, ut majore scientia perficere intellectum & veritatis priscae studiosum recreare queant."

127. *Humanists & Humanism,* p. 59, #29.

128. Menasseh would use this poem again, Anslo having died and Menasseh omitting his name, for the *Nishmat Ḥayyim* of 1651, the expanded Hebrew version of *De Resurrectione.* Anslo would appear only as an "ahuv asher le–'anvetanuto histir panav mimmenu," 'a beloved friend who out of modesty hid his name from us', the word "ahuv" denoting a great deal, especially in its parallel to "Amicus" here.

129. Hillesum, "Bijdrage," pp. 358–61. Indicative, though, of the kind of reception such works met with are Grotius's remarks on his reading of the *De Resurrectione,* "magno meo cum fructu, tum ob vera bene defensa, tum ob Iudaeorum opiniones satis fatuas magni magistri confessione melius quam antehac detectas." Menasseh was considered "the great teacher," but the clarity of his "statements about doctrine" ("confessio" is probably to be understood in this sense rather than as an "acknowledgment" that "certain" Jewish opinions are foolish) left open the possibility of condemnation by Christians. Grotius, *Briefwisseling* 8:682, #3321 31 Oct. 1637].

130. Maarsen, "Wetenschap en Letterkunde," p. 528.

131. Fuks, "Wat Heeft Menasseh . . . Geschreven en Gedrukt," p. 331; Hillesum, "Bijdrage," p. 363; and Roth, *Menasseh,* p. 79, all contribute to the picture. For a summary view of the work, see Baer, *Galut,* pp. 77–82.

132. "Hunc populum, hanc urbem quis neget esse Dei?" Quoted by Blok and identified as Barlaeus's, "Humanists," p. 31, n. 59.

133. Grotius, *Briefwisseling,* 9:801, Appendix no. 7 [4 June 1638].

134. Preface to *Conciliator,* Pt. II.

135. Beverovicius's letter was printed by Menasseh in the volume itself. On the dating, see also Méchoulan, "Le problème du latin."

136. "Nihil hic dicere decrevi, quo Christiana religio impugnetur: eo minus quia ex ejus Doctoribus plurimi, non aliam in hac controversia quam Rabbinorum plerique, amplexi fuere opinionem."

137. "Doctissimum te a me nominari, nullus mirabitur; amicissimum multi, tam hujus, quam illius Religionis, in unum tamen Israelis Deum credentis, homines; postquam invaluit apud nonnullos, nullam posse amicitiam consistere, nisi inter juratas circa Divina mentes."

138. "Quaeso, [Pharisee], dic mihi, si ego Christianus essem, quid fuisses dicturus? Planum est, dicturum te, foedissimum me esse idololatram, & cum Jesu Nazareno Christianorum doctore poenas vero Deo soluturum, a quo defeceram." Limborch, *De veritate,* p. 351; Gebhardt, *Uriel da Costa,* p. 117, ll. 14–16.

139. "Domum & visitas meam, tuamque me adeuntem honorificè habes."

140. " . . . de se ipse testatur, Hebraeo & origine, & religione, usus magistro."

141. "Voluntatem honesta cupientium, oportet animos in societatem trahere."

142. "Debemusque aliquid discere, ut doceamus; quod sublato generis humani consortio fieri nequit. Viva vox amplius, quam oratio, potest: quando oculis plus, quam auribus, dare solemus: &, ut porro menti Senecae insistam, Longum iter est per praecepta; breve, & efficax, per exempla."

143. "Nos, Doctissime Ansloti, bonae tantum conscientiae pretio ducti, virtutis porro calcemus, ipsis vel invitis, semitam, suoque vivere genio permittamus; persuadentes nobis, non è maligno talia effutire animo, verum è fragilitate quadam humana; . . ."

144. At the end of the actual treatise, Menasseh deals more fully with virtue and its origin and with why most men fall more easily into vice. The origin of virtue, he says (p. 136), lies in "bona educatio & doctrina"; it continues with having appropriate companions. Menasseh offers an elaborate discussion of Mishnah *Avot* 1:6–7: " 'aseh lekha rav u–kene lekha ḥaver ve–al titḥaber la–rasha'," and finally falls back on a "lectio bonorum librorum." He provides a list of Jewish authors from whom the reader may choose, and it is broadly

inclusive. Of particular interest to us are the mention of Joseph Delmedigo among kabbalists, the *Mishneh Torah* at the head of works on "jure civili & criminali, ritibus, & caeremoniis," and, among others far more famous at present to us, Jacob le–Vet hal–Levi. All the standard chronicles are there as well, including Ibn Verga's *Shevet Yehudah* and David Gans's *Tsemaḥ David.*

145. "Tuum erit, quia meritis debetur tuis. Tuum erit, quia affectus erga me tuus postulat; jam ab eo tempore, quo in Hebraeis ac Chaldaeis literis, cognoscendisque Rabbinorum monumentis me potissimum duce uti voluisti: in quibus eo ingenio, illaque industria, tantus evasisti, ut Doctor ipse de te non gaudeat modo, sed etiam glorietur: doctissimi verò homines, cum aliis nominibus, tum isto etiam, Te ament, mirentur, atque etiam colant."

146. "Faxit Deus Omnipotens, ut amor feliciter duret, & inconcussus maneat adversum omnes minantes scopulos, quamvis ringente invidorum caterva. Boni non secundum multitudinem faventium aestimantur, aut judicantur, cum sibi ipsis pretium constituant."

147. Roth, *Menasseh,* p. 66 (pun intended?). On this event, see Méchoulan, "À propos de la visite."

148. Roth, *Menasseh,* pp. 53–57 and Gebhardt, *Uriel da Costa,* pp. 212–22.

149. See Silva Rosa's comment, "Geschiedenis," p. 49, on the language issue with regard to polemics.

150. "Id est poenitentia; quia si ceciderimus, poenitudine ductis porrigit manum, eos sublevat, iterumque pro misericordia sua in gratiam recipit, sicuti parentes solent liberos, ubi seriò emendationem pollicentur." *De Fragilitate,* "Preface to the Reader," p. 10.

151. The few known details of Anslo's life (1612–1643) are given by Wijnman, *NNBW* 9:26–27. He was a cloth merchant of Norwegian ancestry, the son of the famous Mennonite preacher Cornelis Anslo (1592–1646), whose portrait was sketched by Rembrandt about 1640. His marriage was celebrated in verse by Vondel, his wife's great-uncle, who wrote that Anslo brought into the match "wat hy in de boecken las / Wat hy leerde van de stommen / Wat hy uyt de heyligdommen / Van de ware wijsheyt brocht / En met lust en arbeydt socht." (Vondel, *Werken,* 3:485). The range of his rabbinic interests included the *Levush* of Mordecai Jaffe; the Prague edition of this from his estate is now in the Rosenthal Library in Amsterdam. Anslo was also one of a number of people—G. J. Vossius was another—who received Arabic manuscripts from Christian Ravius, also noted as a Hebraist, after the latter's Constantinople trip in 1639. But Anslo's library was full of books and manuscripts in Orientalia and other areas too; as for the Hebrew materials, Gentius called it the envy even of the Jews.

152. See Roth, *Menasseh,* p. 64, for a description of Menasseh's daily activities during this period.

153. This translation comes, again, from Bloom, *Economic Activities,* p. 22, n. 102. See Méchoulan, "À propos," for a French translation of the complete oration. See II, n. 7 above.

NOTES TO PART III

1. Grotius, *Briefwisseling,* no. 3781 (Sept. 30, 1638) and no. 3823 (Oct. 30, 1638).

2. See, first of all, Vossius the Elder's lament in a letter to Grotius shortly after Dionysius's death [Grotius, *Briefwisseling,* 5:201 (no. 1890 [Nov. 12, 1633])] and Grotius's incredibly moving letter of consolation [ibid., 5:206ff. (no. 1895 [Nov. 20, 1633])]; Isaac Vossius's remarks and references in his preface are more than mere brotherly affection. In general, see Rademaker, *Gerardus Joannes Vossius,* p. 218f.

Grotius's earlier estimation that Dionysius was destined for fame is but one indication of such a likelihood [*Briefwisseling,* 5:74 (no. 1794 [Oct. 22, 1632]).] See also, though, Bang, Salmasius, and others in Chauffepié, s.v. "Vossius," nn. [C] and [F], and Vondel's threnody and his consolation, *Werken,* 3:398–401.

3. Ibid., 5:198 (no. 1886 [Oct. 19, 1633]), remarking to G. J. Vossius on the potential value of Dionysius's translation of Reyd's history (see below), "multa talia e domo tua in utilitates publicas veniant, ut bonas artes amantibus incipias *etiam per liberos* prodesse. . . ." (Italics mine.)

4. Gerardus Joannes Vossius, *De Historicis Latinis,* pp. [xxv, xxvii]. Vossius also expressed (p. [xxx]) the hope that his children would follow the method and example of their maternal grandfather, Junius, who had been G. J. Vossius's teacher at Leiden. On Junius, see Meijer, "Grotius' Knowledge of Hebrew," p. 134f.

5. See the Appendix below.

6. Vossius, *De Hist. Lat.,* p. [xvi], and *De Theol. Gent.,* p. [vi]. Also, Arnaldo Momigliano, "Creuzer and Greek Historiography," *Contributo Alla Storia Degli Studi Classici* (Rome: Edizioni di Storia e Letteratura, 1955), p. 236, and his quotation from Vossius's *Ars Historica* of 1623; and Paul Dibon, *La philosophie néerlandaise au siècle d'or* (Amsterdam: Elsevier, 1954), p. 226f. And see below, p. 176 and n. 61.

7. Rademaker, *Vossius,* p. 193ff.; Dibon, p. 239; Momigliano, "Creuzer," p. 235; and, in general, P. Grootens, "De Betekenis van Vossius' *Ars Historica,*" *Historisch Tijdschrift* 20 (1941):237–74, esp. 248ff. and 260ff. Wilamowitz, p. 31, extends the influence of the *De Hist. Gr.* and *De Hist. Lat.* to the nineteenth century. An excellent summary of Vossius's life and work is Rademaker's lecture, "The Correspondence of Gerardus Joannes Vossius (1577–1649)," in *Humanists and Humanism in Amsterdam,* pp. 33–39.

8. Busken Huet, II, 2:156.

9. Edith G. Kern, *The Influence of Heinsius and Vossius,* pp. 100–138.

10. Joost van den Vondel, *Cinq Tragedies,* p. 29.

11. Busken Huet, II, 2:156. In his correspondence and in the prefaces to his works, Vossius never failed to call attention to and bemoan his many responsibilities and distractions. (The reader is reminded of Maimonides' account of his working day in the oft-quoted letter to Ibn Tibbon.) Vossius had only the night hours left to him for study and scholarship, and even thought at one point of using the title *Noctes Amstelodamenses* for his work; he discarded it as insufficiently specific. *De Theol. Gent.,* p. [xi]f.

12. Vossius, *De Hist. Lat.,* p. [xxvii]. See also the entries under G. J. Vossius in the manuscript catalogue of the Amsterdam University Library, nos. 82–101, including compositions on such subjects as predestination, grace, original sin, and free will. Vossius wrote in the *Ars Historica* about the applicability of history to the study of religion: "ex [historia] disci, quid de Christo, quid de christianae religionis controversiis, olim ecclesia Dei senserit: denique innumeris ejusdem exemplis ad virtutes ad pietatem in Deum, exstimulari animos nostros." quoted in Dibon, p. 227.

13. See above, I, n. 39, and the citation there; and Nobbs, p. 59.

14. Vossius, *De Hist. Lat.,* p. [xi]: "Historia omnis, & otiosos oblectat, & negotiosos instruit, tum ad vitam privatam bene beateque degendam: tum ad eandem in imperio domi bellique prudenter componendam." Furthermore, the very title of his inaugural lecture at the Athenaeum in 1632 is indicative: *De Historiae Utilitate* (*Opera,* 4:92–99, esp. pp. 97–98, on the usefulness of history for theology).

15. Vossius, *De Theol. Gent.,* p. [xii]: "impensius publicis semper studuerim commodis." Also, Dibon, p. 248, who summarizes: "A la suite de Lipse, un Grotius, un Vossius et un Barlaeus ne cesseront de rappeler la prééminence, au sein de la *sapientia,* de la philosophie pratique sur la philosophie speculative."

16. Vossius, *De Theol. Gent.,* pp. [vi–vii] and Rademaker, *Vossius,* p. 250. It may be remarked in passing that indispensable for any demonstration of truth, be it religious or secular, at this period was a dazzling display of virtuosity and erudition, and these qualities Vossius possessed in abundance. Yet he himself was dissatisfied with this method alone, as he indicated to Grotius in explaining why it was taking so long to complete the work: "Miraberis, scio, non posse me manum tollere de tabula. Sed primo satis visum ex prisca historia adducerem, quae ad religionis gentilis primordia et progressum pertinerent. Postea non sum visus mihi sat utilem operam publico navaturus, nisi mentem humanam adducerem quoque ad veri numinis cultum. Itaque juvit per omnia me naturae opera diffundere inque iis considerare Dei bonitatem, potentiam ac sapientiam. Valde enim ab iis dissentio, qui inanem naturae speculationem arbitrantur." Grotius,

Briefwisseling, 9:256 (no. 3558 [May 2, 1638]) Vossius tried never to lose sight of the essence of the argument, even if there was a mass of detail.

17. Rademaker, "Vossius," in *AHN,* 4:225.

18. Cf. Isaac Vossius's cantankerous comments on the Jews and their knowledge of Hebrew—or the lack thereof—in his *Variarum Observationum Liber,* p. 270ff.

19. G. J. Vossius had already acquired at least a rudimentary knowledge of Hebrew at Leiden, where it was part of the course of study. He knew enough to use Hebrew words and phrases in his works. In the preface to the *De Idololatria,* p. [i], it is said that Dionysius had, in general, tutored Isaac and his brother Gerardus. We can assume that this tutelage included their Hebrew studies.

20. The citation is given more fully in I, n. 49.

21. H. J. Koenen, *Geschiedenis der Joden in Nederland,* p. 473; Rademaker, *Vossius,* p. 213, n. 490; and, esp., Blok, "Humanistes," p. 17f.

22. Vossius, *Epistolae,* 1:293 (no. 295, Dec. 20, 1636). Some of the sentiments here resemble Grotius's; worth noting also are Vossius's comments on the history of Jewish calamities and his bemoaning "quam levi amictu Judaei exeant tela nostra; atque id hac in urbe Amstelodamensi magis etiam cognovi quam ante." His move to Amsterdam heightened his former zeal. In this same letter, in the portion omitted after "convertendis," is his rationale for Dionysius's activity. On this see further below, n. 49.

23. Salo W. Baron, "The Historical Outlook of Maimonides," *History and Jewish Historians,* p. 111f. On other aspects of Maimonides' historiosophical position, see the essays by Y. Y. Ross and Y. Ben–Sasson in *Ḥevrah ve–Historyah,* pp. 529–542 and 543–630.

24. Maimonides' account in *'Avodah Zarah,* chapter 1, of the founders' articulation of the fundamental principles of Judaism is more than a historiographic complement or rounding out of his essentially theological treatment of them in *Hilkhot Yesode hat–Torah.* It is pivotal to his explanation of them and to his overall design, and he uses a somewhat daring approach. He does not just contrast two sets of principles, those of idolatry and those of Judaism, i.e., religion. It is in the primary context of a discussion of idolatry that he gives his summary historical exposition of the fundamental principles of Judaism, illuminating their meaning, even more clearly than before, precisely through that which is their negation. In this way, he can argue that Judaism rests not only on positive affirmations but also and more fundamentally perhaps, on the rejection of idolatry, properly understood for what it is. Additionally, it may be remarked that Maimonides considered himself exceedingly well versed in idolatry; see his "Letter on Astrology" and, esp., his *Guide,* 3:29: "The meaning of many of the laws became clear to me and their causes became known to me through my study of the doctrines, opinions, practices, and cult of the Sabians [i.e., pagans]."

25. Vossius, *De Theol. Gent.*, p. [ix]; Maimonides' definitions of the *ḥasid* and of the prophet include both facets.

26. Vossius, *De Theol. Gent.*, p. [ix]f. Compare Dionysius's trans. of Maimonides' "ve–nateshu kol darkhe ha–emet" (*'Avodah Zarah* 11:18, p. 160f.): "relicta, quae ad veritatem ducit, via."

27. Ibid., p. [vi]. The differences between the two men and their ideological and religious viewpoints should not be underestimated, however. Maimonides was a twelfth–century spokesman for revealed religion, understood and elaborated philosophically; Vossius, a seventeenth–century expositor of "natural religions," not yet the Deist version, but one with God and His revelation through nature still at its core. See Rademaker, *Vossius,* p. 250, on G. J. Vossius's correspondence with and influence upon Herbert of Cherbury, a forerunner of Deism. See also, again, Blok, p. 20f., on "natural religion" and Barlaeus, and our comments in II, above, passim.

28. Vossius, *De Theol. Gent.*, p. [x].

29. Vossius had early defended himself against the then rampant charge of Pelagianism, one that was often directed against the Remonstrants. Menasseh, as we have established, also was anxious to clear the Jews of these charges.

30. Vossius, *De Theol. Gen.*, p. vii. In general, he had seen another purpose of his work as the illustration of Scripture: "eo multa etiam complectar, quae scripturis faciant illustrandis" (*Epistolae,* 1:299, no. 304, Apr. 18, 1637).

31. Ibid., p. [xii].

32. See the Appendix.

33. Some of this can be gleaned from Isaac Vossius's preface to the printed edition (Dionysius himself apparently did not write any preface or introduction). But see also a letter from l'Empereur to Dionysius included in the corpus of the elder Vossius's *Epistolae* (2:109, no. 169, May 1, 1633), asking him to look over some of his work (his Benjamin of Tudela, inter alia) because of Dionysius's skills in languages and theology. Barlaeus pronounced an ode at Dionysius's funeral that was reproduced at the front of the printed edition of *De Idololatria.* In it, Barlaeus speaks of all those who stood in awe of the young man's achievements, "Et proprium Maimon mox stupuisset opus." On Dionysius's work with Golius, see the Vossius *Epistolae,* 1:162 (#124, Aug. 18, 1630); in sending a copy of the *De Idololatria* to Golius, 1:393 (no. 442, Mar. 14, 1642), Vossius *père* writes of the work: "Gratum fore spero, imo scio, pro amore, quo vivum, non modo ut Praeceptor discipulum, sed pene, ut Parens filium complecti solebas." And Cunaeus, too, was a great family friend, to whom Dionysius sent his works (1:213, #192, Jan. 24, 1633). His father wrote of the gift: "Scio non ingratum tibi munusculum fore, quia sic familiam nostram amas."

34. Vossius, *Epistolae,* 1:159 (#122, June 8, 1630, to Pococke); 1:383 (#425, Nov. 23, 1641, to Pococke); 1:386 (#430, Nov. 26, 1641, to Casaubon).

35. Surely at the elder Vossius's bidding. See Blok, "Barlaeus I," pp. 192–93, n. 58, for the composition of the preface; we may assume, however, that Isaac Vossius, in signing his name, indicates his own reworking.

36. *De Idololatria,* pp. 73, 165.

37. For the exchange, see Vossius, *Epistolae,* 1:209 (#186, Nov. 26, 1632) and 2:92 (#140, Feb. 15, [1632] 1633).

38. Ibid., 1:382 (#423, Nov. 22, 1641) and 1:383 (#424, Nov. 23, 1641).

39. See, for example, the letter of Jacobus Skytte to Dionysius in the *Epistolae* 2:88 (#135, Nov. 14, 1631) and his father's remarks 1:[191], no. 159 (Feb. 1, 1633).

40. Though he had proposed translating Reyd as early as 1629, he did not complete the project until late August 1633; the *Conciliator,* which was clearly begun by August 1632, was not ready for the press until mid–August 1633, though, in the *De Idololatria,* Vossius refers to that work as having been translated "ante menses paucos"; the notes on Caesar, which were also begun by 1629 and may have been substantially complete by August 1632, awaited further manuscripts from Puteanus and some help from Meursius.

See Grotius, *Briefwisseling* 5:156 (#1862, July 28, 1633), Vossius *père* to Grotius, on the Reyd translation: "the work is just being finished up; another week or two and it will be done," and Grotius's response (5:175, #1872, Aug. 19, 1633): "There will be no handier (*promtius*) source for a knowledge of *respublica nostra et ejus actus.*" A year earlier, Grotius had already written of the project: "et nostratibus et externis utilissime et probavi et probo." (Ibid. 5:74, #1794, Oct. 22, 1632). Cf. Ibid. 5:182, #1877, Sept. 22, 1633. See also Vossius, *Epistolae* 1:139 (#104, June 30, 1629) on both Reyd and Caesar (the latter called "deliciis suis, cujus dictionem ut assequi possit, impense elaborat." On Caesar, see further ibid., 1:182 (#149, Sept. 4, no year given, but virtually identical with #181, p. 206, dated only to the year 1632, both to Puteanus). The request for additional manuscripts reads in part: "Dionysio . . . decretum, Caesarem, scriptorem sibi perfamiliarem, plurimis locis à se castigatum, ac notis illustratum, edere in lucem. Eam ad rem usus est uno alteroque Manuscripto, & editionibus vetustis, . . ." The elder Vossius's letter to Meursius (at Dionysius's request) is #238 (1:248), Sept. 25, 1632.

41. Vossius, *Epistolae* 1:208 (#185, Nov. 14, 1632), to Simon Bellimontius, about Menasseh and Dionysius: "At tanto mihi gratior [Menasseh], qui eo utor pène familiariter; magis etiam filius Dionysius, non sine emolumento literarum Hebraearum, quamvis jam ab sexennio (i.e., since 1626), ut nostis, studiosus fuit."

42. The opening "ut magis Ecclesiae studia iuvaret" can hardly be applied to the Calvinist establishment; it must include the Remonstrant branch, equally legitimate spokesmen in G. J. Vossius's mind for the larger truth of Calvinism. See also below, n. 48.

43. Blok, "Barlaeus I," pp. 192–93, n. 58, on the basis of an unpublished letter of G. J. Vossius to his son Isaac (Amsterdam Univ. Library MS. J 88c, Oct. 28, 1641), writes that "the preface . . . was actually written by [Isaac's] father Gerard."

44. This is different from the term "uytvluchten," and even sounds different from the comments by Grotius quoted at the opening of this chapter.

45. This parallels Menasseh's own statement, of course.

46. Thirty "questions" are lacking in the Latin, as well as numerous lines, such as we have seen above. (The list of Menasseh's works that is prefaced to the Latin *De Resurrectione* mentions the number thirty.) As for those great men who served him as "examples," we can assume that he has in mind l'Empereur and Coccejus, and many of those mentioned above.

47. Vossius, *Epistolae,* 1:225 (no. 210).

48. Ibid., 1:223 (no. 207); this parallels, but does not necessarily echo, Menasseh's use of "doctissimi" in his dedication. Also see *Epistolae,* 1:224 (no. 209, Oct. 6, 1633), to Meursius, to whom he adds, "Si minus ex hoc opere quicquam haurire sit, quod studia tua juvare possit, poteris donare Academiae nostrae Theologo, (the theological faculty (!), after they had counseled rejection), vel alii amicorum, omnino invenient theologi quod discant. Pauci enim Rabbinos legunt, vel intelligunt; At noster ille Manasses Ben–Israel (id enim Conciliatori nomen est) omnem prope aetatem in hujusmodi scriptoribus trivit." Note the use of "studia tua juvare," similar as it is to Isaac Vossius's claim about Dionysius's hope "ut Ecclesiae studia iuvaret," and also G. J. Vossius's expectation that everyone can learn something from this work. Most interesting of all is Vossius's sense that very few theologians either read or understand the rabbis. Roth's identification of the work as the earliest such version is on p. 144.

49. Ibid., 1:293 (no. 295, Dec. 20. 1636): "Hoc fine jam Thalmudicis & Rabbinicis totum se dare coeperat *ho makarites* Dionysius meus." Cf. above, n. 22.

50. Ibid., 1:231 (no. 215, Jan. 3, 1634).

51. Ibid., 1:393 (no. 441, Mar. 15, 1642).

52. Ibid., 1:209 (no. 186, Nov. 26, 1632), to Laud (Cf. above, n. 37): "Argumentum foecundum, & in quo Notas plusculas addendo, varia ostendi eruditio possit." The "rich subject–matter" was an important consideration.

53. Ibid., 1:231 (no. 215, Jan. 3, 1634). "Jam Maimonidem de Idololatria ex Hebraeo fonte in Latinam linguam a se derivatum Commentario redditum illustriorem, communicare Reipubl. literariae gestiebat." Note the similarity of the use of "illustrior" to several instances cited earlier.

54. Here, of course, are the views of Heinsius and Coccejus, not those of l'Empereur.

55. See, for example, the citations in Blok, "Barlaeus I," pp. 186–87 and nn.

56. G. J. Vossius saw the following linkage between classical studies and others: "Nec enim extra res Hebraeas ulla est Historiarum, quae meliora vel uberiora prudentiae, justitiae, fortitudinis, aliarumque virtutum exempla praebeat, quam Graeca & Romana." *Epistolae,* 1:202, no. 174, n.d., no addressee (Grotius?).

57. For the background and method of Lipsius and Scaliger, see the articles in *Leiden University* by Oestreich and Jonge and, especially, J. H. Waszink's "Classical Philology," ibid., pp. 165–67.

58. G. J. Vossius, *De Historicis Latinis*, p. 2: "What is more perfect than Tacitus's *Annales?*"

59. Vossius, *Epistolae*, 1:228 (no. 213, Dec. 10, 1633).

60. Vossius tends to prefer the "veteri codices" to the vulgate manuscripts, but nowhere does he arrive at any classification scheme or stemmatic guideline. That would be reserved for the eighteenth century. In short, Vossius has no theory of textual criticism that can be articulated; he produces no real *recensio*. He relies on probability, parallel and style, not to mention the authority of his predecessors. He also relies on his own lights: I think, I believe, I approve, I reject, I praise, I condemn, I wish, and so on.

61. The Delphin Classics edition of Caesar gives a good conspectus of how Vossius was treated by the eighteenth and nineteenth centuries. This quotation is in Vossius's note on *BGall* 6:10.

62. Preface to *De Idololatria*, p. [iii].

63. On the "necessary subordination of substance to form and ornament," and on the concern with speaking "appropriately, of suiting style and manner to subject, aim, and audience": "The imitation of stylistic and of ethical models is spoken of in identical terms." Gray, "Humanism," pp. 498–500 and 506. The whole idea of "argument from example and from authority," such emphases as that on variety, and the humanists' "insistence on representing general types or conveying universal lessons through the concrete" and through particulars (and the relationship, both substantive and formal, of these to rhetoric) go back into the earliest Renaissance (p. 506). What is new here is that it was the rabbis who now became the examples and the authorities, their diction having been replaced with a classical "purity and grandeur." Under the influence of l'Empereur, who, as noted earlier, stressed the unity between his translation and his commentary, Vossius too attempts to persuade his audience through both his translation and what Gray called "the philological and documentary evidence [that] may appear conclusive" (p. 511).

64. Vossius, *Epistolae*, 2:234 (no. 346, April 18, 1642).

65. Ibid., 1:209 (no. 186, Nov. 26, 1632), to Laud; 1:164 (no. 128, Sept. 30, 1637); and 1:382 (no. 423, Nov. 22, 1641).

66. *De Theologia Gentili*, p.[7a], and Isaac Vossius's preface to the 1700 edition of the work.

67. *De Idololatria*, p. 21, on *'Ikkarim* 2:28 and 3:18 (there is a cross–reference in Albo himself from the former locus to the latter). Compare *Conciliador*, Question 103 (on Exodus 20:5). (See Albo *'Ikkarim* [Husik, ed.] 3:158–59, with a reference to Maimonides, *Hilkhot 'Avodah Zarah*, chapter 1.

68. The reference to Baḥya ben Asher on p. 16 (ad 1:8) is not to be found in the printed editions of that commentator.

69. Vossius also knew the various scholiasts, and the Byzantines, such as Tzetzes and Eustathius.

70. Vossius, *Epistolae,* 1:150 (no. 113, Mar. 16, 1630); and 1:291 (no. 291, Sept. 21, 1636 to Crocius, about Coch): "virum amo et eadem mens erat filii, quod Maimonides ejus luculentis indiciis ostendent." Also 1:376 (no. 412, June 29, 1641, to Coch himself): "Amavi te & aestimavi jam ab eo tempore, quo Brema ad me misisti primum, ut arbitror, ingenii tui foetum" (i.e., the *Sanhedrin* commentary). "Quem quanti fecerit *ho makarites* Dionysius meus . . . saepius ex ipso lectis tuis audivi, & non sivit posteritatem plane ignaram esse judicii sui in notis ad Maimonidem de Idololatria."

71. He also connects the Arabic: "*syr* [in Arabic characters] est *ivit, profectus est.* unde *sira* [Arabic characters] iter, profectio."

72. See above, III, n. 4.

73. P. 182.

74. There was also, incidentally, a copy of Ḥayyun in Aboab's library.

75. Johann Benedict Carpzov, *Disputationes Academicae* (Leipzig, 1699), Disputation IV, p. 133.

76. Vossius, *De Idololatria,* p. 12.

77. Carmilly, "External and Internal Censorship," p. 11.

78. G. J. Vossius, *Epistolae,* 2:110 (no. 169, May 1, 1633), to Dionysius ("Mi Dionysi").

79. In one instance, Vossius does react rather sharply, we must point out. Maimonides had mentioned a particularly repulsive practice associated with Peor–worship. Vossius cites Rashi's exegesis of Num. 25:33 and identifies this as the "common view (*opinio*)" of all the rabbis. "No way can I accept this," he says: "Quam probare neutiquam possum." Repulsive practices were avoided by pagans too, he says, giving a few examples. And yet, even here, his goal was to find support for Maimonides' assertion, and his long, involved annotation attempts to do so (3:2, pp. 37–38).

80. See p. 201.

81. Vossius, *Epistolae,* 2:80 (no. 121, Sept. 25, 1630). This referred to the history of Tamerlane that an inquirer had written him about; Vossius's teacher Golius would edit the work by the Arabic historian 'Arabshah in 1636 (Leiden: Elsevier).

82. "Crudele multis videtur sacrificare liberos. Et sane est. Nihil tamen certius, quam gentiles immolasse suos liberos. Id Ægyptios fecisse, testis Athenaeus. . . . Carthaginenses quoque, Phoenicum colonos, hunc morem recepisse, docent Dio-

dorus . . . & Trogus. Etiam Ennius de iis: *Ille suos Divis mos sacrificare puellos.* Quid gentium alias persequar? . . ." (p. 79).

83. The reference Vossius gives to II.9.4 is obviously a misprint.

84. Compare Vossius's note on *lo titgodedu* (12:13, p. 172).

85. "*Quia solent eae ad cultum fieri. she–ḥezkatan shel 'avodat kum hen 'asuyin.* De voce *ḥazakah* consule Davidem de Pomis. Iurisdictionem & possessionem denotat. Item consuetudinem & receptum morem. unde *ma'amidin et ha–adam 'al ḥezkato* statuunt hominem super consuetudinem suam, i.e., judicant eum *'al ma'asav hat–tovim o ha–ra'im she–heḥezik bam yamim rabbim, secundum opera bona aut mala, quibus assuevit, multo tempore.*" (7:8, pp. 91–92).

86. See pp. 182-83.

87. See the partial citation above, p. 199.

88. These annotations are on 2:6–7, pp. 27–29.

89. Compare Coccejus's reference to Sixtus Amama in his preface to *Sanhedrin* as "rei literariae columini egregio," 'the most distinguished pillar of the Republic of Letters'.

90. We have quoted this passage above, p. 209.

91. See the partial treatment above, pp. 216.

92. See above, p. 190. Yet see ad 1:9, p. 17, on the interpretation of *anshe veto* as 'converts'. Vossius rejects this on the basis of grammar, despite support for it in Epiphanius.

93. We may point out again that the citation does not correspond to the text of Baḥya ben Asher ad loc. in the printed editions.

94. Compare the translation of the other instance of "harḥakah" and the annotation there (6:13, pp. 84–85), discussed above. See p. 202.

95. See above, pp. 199-200.

96. Albo, as it happens, quotes this halakhah from Maimonides.

97. The passage that Vossius is referring to must be the one in 18:25, however: "Shall not the judge of all the earth do justly?"

98. As an indication of the milieu in which this was read, it is of interest that one correspondent of G. J. Vossius's focused on this single remark. It was de Dieu, who expressed his own particular delight at Dionysius's defense of Jesus' divine nature. *Epistolae* 2:228, no. 338, Mar. 25, 1642.

99. Cf. the earlier note on "adoratio," pp. 6–7 (see above, p. 199), though Vossius makes no cross–reference.

100. See Twersky, *Introduction,* p. 519.

101. S. Ettinger, "Jews and Judaism in the Eyes of the English Deists of the Eighteenth Century (Hebrew)," *Tsiyyon* 29 (1963):185. Spencer himself was probably without Hebrew.

102. Roth, *Menasseh,* p. 144.

103. P. 147.

104. Menasseh, *Vindiciae Judaeorum,* p. 136; "Dorstius" is an obvious misprint; and see below, pp. 246-47.

105. See, for example, his comment (n. 30, pp. 73–74) on Maimonides' characterization of the wise man (5:15) as one of modest bearing attired in *tallit* and *tefillin.* Vorstius quotes passages from TB *Shabbat,* chap. 2, Maimonides' *Hilkhot Tefillin* 4:24, TB *Yoma,* and TB *Ḥullin* 91, and makes additional references to TB *Berakhot* 7 and 14, and *Menaḥot* 39, 43 "& c," all of which tend to support the view that the *tefillin* help promote modesty and wisdom. The *Yoma* passage is the only one referred to by the Hebrew commentators here. One of those in *Berakhot* is cited by the *Kesef Mishneh* on the *Hilkhot Tefillin* passage. Vorstius was obviously able to operate independently.

106. Other remarks disparaging of the rabbis are those speaking of their "dictatorship" (p. 78, n. 4), of their twisting everything to their point of view ("ad placita sua") (p. 76, n. 2). On Moses, see pp. 103–4, n. 20, and passim, chapters 7 and 8. On the law, see pp. 121–23, nn. 2 and 3, the latter trying to disprove the rabbinic interpretation of the verse "Non est in coelis" (Deut. 30:12).

107. ". . .ut contra pertinacem horum mortalium incredulitatem asseramus miraculosam Iesu nostri doctrinam: nam omnia in hoc capite allata eò fere collimant, ut enervent divinissima nostri Messiae opera, . . ."

108. "Ridiculè etiam fides ejusmodi legato, qui ipse nesciat à quo missus sit, olim habita fuisset & etiamnum haberetur à Judaeis: aequiores hîc Christianos habebunt Mosaicae prophetiae aestimatores." Vorstius subsequently heaps further scorn upon the view of "the author of the *Tipheret Israel*" [R. Judah Löw ben Bezalel (c. 1525–1609), whose work dates from 1599], "among others," that Moses' lack of knowledge of whom he had spoken with proved the excellence and perspicuity of his prophecy.

109. "Rapsodiis aut scribarum statutis," Vorstius's phrase, is probably to be taken to refer to aggadah and halakhah respectively, that is, not merely to the different kinds of Jewish literature in which investigations of the elements of religion are contained, but also to the totality of their methods (10:1, pp. 139–41, n. 2).

110. "Sed malunt hi mortales odio & praejudicio excaecati inani spe se suosque pascere, quam veri Messiae imperio colla subdere."

111. "Non ut inde aliquid oblectamenti capiat Christianus lector, sed potius discat Iudaica abominari deliria, & religionis suae firmamenta ex iis petere."

112. It is of interest that this translation, which had a popularity—even Menasseh used it, as we have indicated above—was roundly criticized by the Hebraist audience for its inaccuracies.

113. "...habet quandoque speciosa interpretamenta, quae vel illustrandae historiae sacrae, vel Hebraeorum ritibus ac traditionibus explanandis facere possunt."

114. Vorstius uses this term several times; see above, pp. 240 and 243. For Vossius on "aestimatio," see above, p. 174. Menasseh, especially, entreats his audience as learned individuals to be fair and impartial in judging his arguments. See above, pp. 130, 139, 150, 157, and below, p. 280.

115. Beyer, *Gentius,* p. 12.

116. "Inter [Hebraeos] vir omni doctrina incomparabilis Rabbi *Moseh Meimonides* viguit & ipsis vigentibus vigebit: vivus enim claruit eximiè & plurimorum animos fabularum tenebris obrutos illuminavit; mortuus vero ea, quae omni aevo permagno usui esse possint, reliquit."

117. "Sic & homines in hoc officiorum genere Deum imitari oportet, quod maxime est necessarium, uti & in antecedentibus reliquis pietatis officiis supra generatim enumeratis."

118. Ibid., pp. 83–84.

119. We may compare the treatment of the proselyte by each of the three. See Vossius, pp. 138–39 (our discussion, above, pp. 218-19); Vorstius, pp. 54, 55; Gentius, pp. 91–92. In this instance, Vorstius is quite straightforward, merely making passing reference to the subject and sending the reader to Maimonides' discussions in *Melakhim* 10, *Issure Biah* 14 and *Yevamot* 11:2, before going on himself to discuss the actual matter at hand, the question of martyrdom to which the *ger* who observes the Noachide commandments is not obligated. Vossius had sent the reader to Grotius's *de Jure* 1:16 for more light on the subject. Gentius refers to no other source, but gives an elaborate account of the different kinds of proselytes, including one category of his own, those who consider this life and the things of the world transitory.

120. Meir Benayahu, *Haskamah u–reshut,* p. 45.

121. H. G. Enelow, "Isaac Belinfante," p. 7f.

122. Yerushalmi, *Spanish Court,* p. 136.

123. Mention is made of these poems in: Brugmans and Frank, *Geschiedenis der Joden in Nederland,* p. 479; Jaap Meijer's edition of Hugo Grotius's *Remonstrantie,* p. 61; and M. H. Gans, *Memorbook,* p. 79. The pointing and translation here are mine.

124. Their poems appear together in, for example, Ya'akov Yehudah Leon, *Alabanças de Santitad* (Amsterdam, 5431 [1671] and Joseph Penso de la Vega, *Asire hat–Tikvah* (Amsterdam, 1673); their formal approbations were prefixed together

(among those of others) to two works of Abraham Israel Pereyra, *Certesa do Caminho* (Amsterdam, 1666) and *Espejo de la Vanidad del Mundo* (Amsterdam, 5431 [1671]).

125. *Meme Yisrael* was found in Aboab's library. Aboab was accepting the specific and open invitation to make use of its contents that Najara had extended in the subtitle to the work. The subtitle reads: "a collection of poems, satires, lyric epistles, and forceful speeches that I had written in my youth ['yeme ḥorpi' may also suggest 'the days when I was ostracized'] [offering] opinion and counsels [or, perhaps, 'on account of my views' or, generally, 'when I was reviled by public opinion'], sending waters all over the land [var. on Job 5:10] to beloved friends . . . [so that] whoever wishes to slake his thirst may lap up the water with his tongue, [var. on Judg. 7:5] drinking it like water from a brook by the wayside [Ps. 110:7], and may forget his poverty and misery [Prov. 31:7], and also that the young man may draw upon it—any youth who wishes may fill the office [sc. 'of poet', var. on 1 Kings 13:33] and wield the writer's pen [var. on Judg. 5:14] to [produce] elegant phrases [Gen. 49:21] and to send choice presents and gifts to others [Esth. 9:19, 22] in beautiful language." Poem *ḥet,* p. 142a, is the one plagiarized. With respect to the subtitle, though the sending of "manot", 'gifts' (in other instances called "teshurot") was a feature of the literary enterprise in which Aboab was engaged, surely there were other considerations on his mind besides style and sociability.

126. On the relations between Najara and Onkeneira, see: A. M. Habermann, *A History of Hebrew Liturgical and Secular Poetry* (Hebrew), 1:234f.; also, 1:278. Najara's poem, in my translation, is as follows:

The day a bow appeared in the thickness of your palm, 1
  And strength upheld the purity of your palm,
Your splendrous presence rested over my tent,
  Which was filled with light by your singing.
My heart was moved [to speak] of the wisdom of your song
  And the power of your great achievement.
Yet my thoughts were unable to give a song in response,
  Because the sweep of your anger was too high and mighty.
I did not believe the rumor while I might yet 5
  Eat honey from the honeycomb of your [hive].
Behold! I, the humble one, as long as I live, I shall hold onto
  The palm branch of your friendship and not forsake you.
Take, will you, a gift from one who greatly longs for you;
  Is his heart not, indeed, scorched by your fiery sparks?
I would better fill up a day in the courtyards of your song
  Than behold the glory of your form or face.
My dark night you turned into day, dear friend,
  The day a bow appeared in the thickness of your palm. 9

The phraseology in line 3 is based on Ps. 45:2 and Esth. 10:2. The phrase "tuv . . . sikhlekha" is an obvious play on "sekhel–tov," meaning "wisdom."

127. In his commendatory poem to Menasseh ben Israel's *De la Resurrección de los Muertos,* Aboab calls Menasseh "dodi." There is an obvious link between "nigletah" in line one and "yegaleh" in line four. In the opening line, "nigletah" ("was revealed") should be taken to mean appeared; in the fourth, "yegaleh" ("will or would reveal") is to be rendered idiomatically as 'revealing', 'uncovering', or 'bringing out into the open [something previously hidden]', that is to say, 'interpreting'. Aboab would again use the verb 'galah' with the sense of 'bringing out the hidden' in another commendatory poem written some thirty years later. For Ya'akov Yehudah Leon, the translator of the Psalms into Spanish, Aboab would write: "To a people speaking the vernacular you have indeed revealed [that which was] concealed in your hidden store of glorious splendor (*hod!*)." Leon, *Alabanças,* p. [14]. Also in *Migdol David* (see list), Davidson, *Thesaurus,* 486 [letter] *heh.*

128. A collateral example to Aguilar's distinction making is found in the commendatory poem of Samuel de Casseres for Saul Levi Morteira's *Giv'at Shaul* (Amsterdam, 1645 [Warsaw, 1901]), p. 35. Casseres called his poem "korban bikkurim," "an offering of first fruits." (Casseres was, incidentally, one of Morteira's star pupils and later delivered the eulogy at his funeral.) He wrote as follows:

אם כל גדולי לב הלא יובאו
תוך מאסר דומה בחבלי עוני,
על כי פאר הרב לספר לאו,
מה יעשה יתוש אשר כמוני?!
אך מחשבות לבי בעוז יקראו:
עורי לשוני נא וקומי רני'!,
כי מעשי הרב אשר גברו
הן הם כבוד שמו יאמרו....

An even more striking parallel to Aguilar's poem is found in a roughly contemporaneous Italian collection recently uncovered by Dan Pagis and discussed in his "Liturgical Poetry in Seventeenth–Century Italy: A Hebrew Manuscript" [Hebrew], *Kiryat Sefer* 50 (1975):306. The reader can easily appreciate the stylistic affinities.

יש לומדי ספר רבים יחכמו,
אך לא כמשפט דרכיהם יכונו.
הלב והלשון יחדו נלחמו,
כי תוך לבבם רעתם יצפנו.
. . .
אתה בדת אל חי, השר, חכמת,
משפט דבריה פעל פעלת,
. . .

129. Cf. Aguilar's "Approvaçaõ" to Pereyra's *Espejo de la Vanidad,* p. 2b.

130. "Sefarim barim," "pure books," is an interesting parallel to Aboab's usage "bor kappekha," 'the purity of your palm'.

131. Grotius, *Briefwisseling,* 9:775, no. 3900 [Dec. 25, 1638]; Vossius, *Epistolae* 2:270, no. 406.

NOTES TO PART IV

1. G. J. Vossius, *Epistolae* 2:270–71 (no. 406, 7 May 1645). Gentius had also corresponded at an earlier period with Isaac Vossius. (Amsterdam University Library Manuscript Catalogues, vol. 4, s.v. 'Gentius'. 12 June 1640, from London [RK M87]).

2. The existence of the position in Oriental languages is mentioned by Beyer, *Gentius,* p. 97, n. 'q'. On the situation of Hamburg Jewry, see: Kellenbenz, *Sephardim,* pp. 45–51, 99–103; and Graetz, *Geschichte* (3rd Ed.) 10:15–24, esp. 10:19–23.

3. De le Roi, *Evangelische Christenheit,* 1:113. Hensen, *Die hamburgische Kirche,* p. 48, contains a brief biography, showing that, having been pastor of St. Peter's from 1626, Müller was appointed "Senior," that is to say the chairman of the Ministerium, the Lutheran hierarchical council, in 1648 and held this position till his death. Elsewhere, he is reported to have held "friendly discussions" with Abraham Farrar (d. 1663), a friend of Menasseh [Roth, *Menasseh,* p. 118].

4. A complete quotation of his remarks is to be found in Reils, "Beiträge," pp. 398–400 and an abridged one in Kayserling, *Sephardim,* pp. 311–12.

5. Reils, "Beiträge," pp. 395–406.

6. There is no evidence indicating why Blaeu did not publish both volumes.

7. He does not cite the lines or give a source reference, so it was impossible to verify this.

8. "Vos quoque, Proceres nobilissimi, cum pari studio Judaeorum gentem habeatis, laudatissimo more atque exemplo, pietate potius servare, quam severa disciplina excludere, eos tanquam perditas Christi oviculas colligere, quam dissipare mavultis."

9. "Nec tamen diffitemur esse in hoc ipso autore nonnulla, in quibus Iudaeum fuisse agnoscas, nos iis omnibus in notis aliquando abunde, Deo juvante, occurremus."

10. Beyer, *Gentius,* pp. 100–1.

11. Ibid., pp. 98–102, n.

12. "Passim extollit Judaeorum innocentiam, virtutes, rectitudinem, felicitatem, contrario autem scelera Christianorum, quod in innocentes Judaeos machinati sunt, plenis buccis decantat."

13. The incident with the *Conciliator* is an interesting parallel.

14. Beyer, *Gentius,* pp. 103–4. Selden's reply is on pp. 105–6.

15. On these see: Roth, *Menasseh,* pp. 158–64; Saraiva, "Vieira"; and Popkin, "Menasseh and la Peyrère."

16. Sorbière, *Sorberiana,* pp. 147–78.

17. Schorsch, "From Messianism," pp. 195–200.

18. On the sequence, Wolf, *Menasseh's Mission,* p. 151.

19. Trans. Schorsch, "From Messianism," p. 191.

20. *Pace* Schorsch, p. 199. Incidentally, the translator's preface by Moses Wall should not be overlooked. There is another important comparison between the *Conciliator* and the *Hope of Israel:* in Gen. Quest. 45 (Lat.) [68 (Span.)] the interpretation of "yikkehat" at Gen. 49:10 (the 'Shiloh' passage) corresponds to chapter 34 of *Hope.*

21. Franco Mendes, *Memorias,* p. 24, 11. 3–5 & 18–22, and n. 61, p. 155–56, which fails to give a complete analysis of what happened. Also, see Roth, *Menasseh,* pp. 223 and 330, n. 45, for all that was known before this edition appeared.

22. *De Fidelitate et Utilitate Judaicae Gentis,* mentioned in a letter of February 1655, is almost certainly identical with the body of the *Humble Addresses.* Though the title was Latin, the work itself was said to be in English. See: Roth, *Menasseh,* p. 336, n. 33; pp. 34–42, n. 7; and the additional note on this, p. 354; also, Wolf, *Menasseh's Mission,* p. xxxviii.

23. See Menasseh's *Vindiciae Judaeorum,* pp. 143-44.

24. Roth, *Menasseh,* p. 226 and p. 340, n. 2.

25. Roth, *Menasseh,* pp. 340–41, n. 3.

26. "Nostram gentem Iudaicam vestro patrocinio defenditis atque protegitis, imo nos vestro libertatis Asylo, Imperatorie plane propugnatis." On Ferdinand, see Graetz, *Geschichte,* 3rd ed., 10:47.

27. Cf. above in II, n. 21. Sasportas's criticism was not directed at Menasseh, but at Morteira, in 1652–53. See his *Ohel Ya'akov,* no. 17 and the inadequate summary by Maarsen, "De Responsa," pp. 128–29. Sasportas views the purposes of the Christians as destructive and says that, if Jews with inadequate preparation should be cautioned away from the *Mishneh Torah,* as Karo recommended, all the more so should Christians. Sasportas also distinguishes between what rational argument, such as the Hebraists use, achieves and what the tradition propounds; he defends the Maimonidean text against what he believes is too lenient an interpretation by Morteira.

28. The bibliography by Dienstag is to be used with caution.

29. See Schoeps, *Philosemitismus,* for his characterizations of different types of such individuals. The dating of the classification is far too rigid. See pp. 1, 137–41.

30. Steinschneider, "Christliche Hebraisten," 1:50.

31. De le Roi, *Evangelische Christenheit,* 1:155.

32. See *Shevet Yehudah,* (Shoḥat, ed.), pp. 78ff.; (Gentius, tr.), pp. 173ff. As for Mendelssohn himself, he would translate Menasseh's *Vindiciae Judaeorum* and prefix to it a noteworthy apologia of his own. Alexander Altmann's commentary on this work in the Jubilee Edition of Mendelssohn has just appeared, but was unavailable for discussion here. The same applies to two other significant works that have appeared recently, David Katz's *Philo-Semitism and the Readmission of the Jews to England* and Yosef Kaplan's monograph on Isaac Orobio de Castro.

BIBLIOGRAPHY

MAJOR PRIMARY SOURCES

Aboab da Fonseca, Isaac. *Catalogus librorum.* Amsterdam, 1693.

———. *Parafrasis.* Amsterdam, 1681.

Aguilar, Moses Rephael d'. *Tratado da immortalidade da alma* [1639]. (Coimbra, 1934). [= *Biblos* 10 (1934):488–99.]

Buxtorf, Johannes, Jr., tr. *Doctor Perplexorum* Mosis Maimonidis. Basel, 1629.

Coccejus, Johannes. *Duo Tituli Thalmudici Sanhedrin et Maccoth.* Amsterdam, 1629.

Cunaeus, Petrus. *De Republica Hebraeorum.* Leiden, 1617.

"G. N.," tr. *Canones Poenitentiae.* Cambridge, 1631.

Gentius, Georgius. Meimonidis [*sic*] *Canones ethici.* Amsterdam, 1640.

———. *Historia Judaica.* Amsterdam, 1651.

Grotius, Hugo. *De Veritate Religionis Christianae.* Leiden, 1627; 1640.

———. *De Jure Belli ac Pacis.* Amsterdam, 1625, etc.

L'Empereur, Constantinus. *Talmudis Babylonici Codex Middoth.* Leiden, 1630.

———. *Clavis Talmudica.* Leiden, 1634.

———. *De legibus Ebraeorum forensibus* [*De Damnis,* i.e. TB *Bava Kama*]. Leiden, 1637.

———. *Oratio inauguralis de linguae Hebraeae dignitate ac utilitate.* Leiden, 1627.

Menasseh ben Israel. *Pene Rabbah.* Amsterdam, 1628.

———. *Conciliador.* Frankfurt and Amsterdam, 1632.

———. *Conciliator.* Translated by Dionysius Vossius. Amsterdam, 1633.

———. *De creatione problemata xxx.* Amsterdam, 1635.

———. *De resurrectione mortuorum.* Amsterdam, 1636.

———. *De termino vitae.* Amsterdam, 1639.

———. *De fragilitate humana.* Amsterdam, 1642.

———. *The Hope of Israel.* London, 1650.

———. *Nishmat Ḥayyim.* Amsterdam, 1651.

———. *Humble Addresses.* London, 1655.

———. *Vindiciae Judaeorum.* London, 1656.

Vorstius, Guglielmus. Maimonidis *Constitutiones de fundamentis Legis.* Amsterdam, 1638.

———. Abravanelis *De Capite Fidei.* Amsterdam, 1638.

———. *Chronologia Sacra–Profana.* Leiden, 1644.

———. *Capita de R. Elieser.* Leiden, 1644.

Vossius, Dionysius. Reidani *Belgarum . . . annales.* Leiden, 1633.

———. Caesaris *Commentarii* [1632–33]. Amsterdam, 1697.

———. Maimonidis *De Idololatria* [1632–33]. Amsterdam, 1641.

Vossius, Gerardus Johannes. *Epistolae.* London, 1690.

———. *De Theologia Gentili.* Amsterdam, 1641.

BIBLIOGRAPHIC AND REFERENCE AIDS

Aa, A. J. van der. *Biographisch Woordenboek der Nederlanden.* 12 vols. [N.p.,] 1852–78.

Amsterdam—Nationale tentoonstelling van het boek. *Catalogus van boeken in Noord–Nederland verschenen van de vroegsten tijd tot op heden.* The Hague, 1911.

Amsterdam—Universiteit—Bibliotheek. *Catalogus der Handschriften.* Vols. 4 & 7. Amsterdam, 1916 & 1923.

Amsterdam—Universiteit—Bibliotheek. *Catalogus van de tentoonstelling der Universiteitsbibliotheek.* Amsterdam, 1932.

Bercovitch, Sacvan. "Annotated Bibliography." In *Typology and Early American Literature,* edited by S. Bercovitch, pp. 249–337. N.p., 1972.

Bie, J. P. de and Loosjes, J., eds. *Biografische Woordenboek van Protestantische Godgeleerden in Nederland.* 6 vols. The Hague, 1919–49.

Buck, H. de. *Bibliografie der Geschiedenis van Nederland.* Leiden, 1968.

Chauffepié, Jacques Georges de. *Nouveau dictionnaire historique et critique.* 4 vols. Amsterdam, 1750–56.

Davidson, Israel. *Thesaurus of Mediaeval Hebrew Poetry.* 4 vols. [1928–33.] Repr. ed. with an introduction by J. H. Schirmann. New York, 1970.

Dienstag, Jacob I. "Christian Translators of Maimonides' *Mishneh Torah* into Latin." In *Salo Wittmayer Baron Jubilee Volume,* pp. 287–310. Jerusalem, 1975.

Encyclopaedia Judaica (1931). S.v. "Christliche Hebräisten," by A. Spanier.

Encyclopaedia Judaica (1971). S.v. "Hebraists, Christian," by Raphael Loewe.

Fabricius, Johann. *Historia bibliothecae Fabricianae.* 6 vols. Wolffenbuttel and Helmstadt, 1717–24.

Fuks, L. and Fuks–Mansfeld, R. G. *Hebrew and Judaic Manuscripts in Amsterdam Public Collections.* 2 vols. Leiden, 1973.

Jerusalem—Jewish National and University Library—Institute of Microfilmed Hebrew Manuscripts. *Reshimat tatslume kitve hay–yad ha–'ivriyyim bam–makhon* (List of Photocopies in the Institute). Vol. 2. Jerusalem, 1964.

Jöcher, Christian Gottlieb. *Allgemeines Gelehrten–Lexicon.* 4 vols. [Leipzig, 1750–51.] Repr. ed. Hildesheim, 1960–61.

Kayserling, M. *Biblioteca Española–Portugueza–Judaica.* Repr. Edited by Yosef H. Yerushalmi. New York, 1971.

Knuttel, W. P. C. *Catalogus van de pamflettenverzameling berustende in de Koninklijke Bibliotheek.* 9 vols. in 11. The Hague, 1889–1920.

Me–otsrot sifriyyat Ets Ḥayyim/Montezinos le–yad bet ham–midrash hay–yehudi hap–portugali "Ets–Ḥayyim", Amshterdam [Treasures from the Library Ets Haim/Livraria Montezinos of the Portuguees Israëlietisch Seminarium Ets Haim, Amsterdam]. Catalogue of an Exhibition in the Jewish National and University Library, Jerusalem. Edited by Raphael Weiser and Joseph Kaplan. Jerusalem, 1980.

Mencke, Johann Burchard. *Compendiöses Gelehrten–Lexicon.* Leipzig, 1715.

Molhuysen, Philip C., ed. *Nieuw Nederlandsch Biografisch Woordenboek.* 10 vols. Leiden, 1911–37.

Muller, Frederick. *Bibliotheek van Nederlandsche Pamfletten.* 3 vols. Amsterdam, 1858–61.

Nahon, Gérard. "Les Marranes espagnols et portugais et les communautés juives issues du marranisme dans l'historiographie récente (1960–1975)." *REJ* 136 (1977):297–367.

Nicéron, Jean Pierre. *Mémoires pour servir à l'histoire des hommes illustres dans la république des lettres avec un catalogue raisonné de leurs ouvrages.* 4 vols. Parma, 1728–39.

Paquot, Jean Noël. *Mémoires pour servir à l'histoire littéraire des dix–sept provinces des Pays Bas.* 3 vols. Louvain, 1762–70.

The Portuguese Jews of Amsterdam in the Seventeenth Century. Catalogue of an Exhibition at the Jewish National and University Library. Jerusalem, 1975.

Rodriguez de Castro, José. *Biblioteca española.* Madrid, 1781.

Rosenthal, Judah. "Anti–Christian Polemic from its Beginnings to the End of the 18th Century" [Hebrew]. *Areshet* 2 (1960):130–79 and 3 (1961):433–39.

Steinschneider, Moritz. *Bibliographisches Handbuch über die theoretische und praktische Literatur für Hebräische Sprachkunde.* 2nd ed. Jerusalem, 1973.

———. *Christliche Hebraïsten.* [1896–1901.] Repr. ed. Hildesheim, 1973.

———. *Die Hebraeischen Übersetzungen des Mittelalters und die Juden als Dolmetscher.* [Berlin, 1893.] Repr. ed. Graz, 1956.

Tijdeman, J. *Remonstrantsche Broederschap—Biographische Naamlist.* Haarlem, 1847.

Wolf, Johann Christoph. *Biblioteca hebraea.* 4 vols. Hamburg and Leipzig, 1715–33.

OTHER PRIMARY AND SECONDARY SOURCES

Acosta, Uriel. *An Example of a Human Life.* Translated from the German of Carl Gebhardt by Helen Lederer. Cincinnati, 1958.

———. *A Specimen of Human Life.* New York, 1967.

———. *Die Schriften des Uriel da Costa.* Translated and edited by Carl Gebhardt. Amsterdam, Heidelberg, and London, 1922.

Ainsworth, Henry. *Annotations Upon . . . Genesis.* [Amsterdam,] 1616.

Algemene Geschiedenis der Nederlanden. Vols. 6–7. Utrecht, 1953–54.

Altaner, Berthold. "Die fremdsprachliche Ausbildung der Dominikaner–missionare während des 13. und 14. Jahrhunderts." *Zeitschrift für Missionswissenschaft* 23 (1933):233–41.

———. "Zur Kenntnis des Hebräischen im Mittelalter." *Biblische Zeitschrift* 21 (1933):288–308.

Altmann, Alexander. "Eternality of Punishment: A Theological Controversy Within the Amsterdam Rabbinate in the Thirties of the Seventeenth Century." *Proceedings of the American Academy for Jewish Research* 40 (1972):1–88.

———. "William Wollaston: English Deist and Rabbinic Scholar." *Transactions of the Jewish Historical Society of England* 16 (1945–51 [1952]). Repr. in his *Studies in Religious Philosophy and Mysticism.* Ithaca and London, 1969.

Ancona, J. d'. "Delmedigo, Menasseh ben Israel en Spinoza." *BMGJWN* 6 (1940):105–42.

Anglo–Dutch Historical Conference. *Britain and the Netherlands.* Edited by J. S. Bromley and E. H. Kossmann. 5 vols. London, 1960–75.

Arkin, Marcus. *Aspects of Jewish Economic History.* Philadelphia, 1975.

Assaf, Simḥah. *Mekorot le–Toledot ha–Ḥinnukh be–Yisrael.* 4 vols. Tel Aviv, 1925–42.

Aston, Trevor, ed. *Crisis in Europe: 1560–1660.* New York, 1965.

Avida, J. "Maimonides' Code as a school–book" [Hebrew]. *Areshet* 3 (1961):31–47.

Azevedo, J. Lucio d'. "Judeus portuguêses na disperção." *Revista de História* 4 (1915):105–27.

Baer, Yitzhak. *A History of the Jews in Christian Spain.* 2 vols. Translated by Louis Schoffman et al. Philadelphia, 1961–66.

———. *Galut.* New York, 1947.

Balaban, Meir. "Hugo Grotius und die Ritualmord." *Festschrift zu Simon Dubnows 70–em Geburtstag,* pp. 87–112. Berlin, 1930.

Ball, Bryan W. *A Great Expectation: Eschatological Thought in English Protestantism to 1660.* Leiden, 1975.

Bangs, Carl. *Arminius: A Study in the Dutch Reformation.* Nashville and New York, 1971.

———. "'All the Best Bishoprics and Deaneries'; The Enigma of Arminian Politics." *Church History* 42 (1973):5–16.

———. "Dutch Theology, Trade, and War: 1590–1610." *Church History* 39 (1970):470–82.

Barbour, Violet. *Capitalism in Amsterdam in the Seventeenth Century.* The Johns Hopkins University Studies in Historical and Political Science, vol. 67. Baltimore, 1949.

Barnet, L. D. *El Libro de los Acuerdos.* Oxford, 1931.

Barnouw, A. J. and Landheer, B., eds. *The Contribution of Holland to the Sciences.* New York, 1943.

Baron, Salo W. "The Historical Outlook of Maimonides." *Proceedings of the American Academy for Jewish Research* 6 (1935):5–113. Repr. in his *History and Jewish Historians,* pp. 109–63. Philadelphia, 1964.

———. "John Calvin and the Jews." *Harry Austryn Wolfson Jubilee Volume,* pp. 141-63. Jerusalem, 1965.

———. "Medieval Heritage and Modern Realities in Protestant–Jewish Relations." *Diogenes* 61 (1968):32–51.

———. *A Social and Religious History of the Jews,* 2nd ed. 17 vols. to date. New York, 1952–.

Baroway, Israel. "Toward Understanding Tudor–Jacobean Hebrew Studies." *JSS* 18 (1956):3–24.

Barzilay, Isaac. *Between Reason and Faith: Anti–Rationalism in Italian Jewish Thought, 1250–1650.* The Hague, 1967.

———. *Yoseph Shlomo Delmedigo* (*Yashar of Candia*). Leiden, 1974.

Basnage, Jacques. *Histoire des Juifs.* New, enl. ed. 9 vols. The Hague, 1716.

Ben–Sasson, H. H. "The Reformation in Contemporary Jewish Eyes." In *Proceedings of the Israel Academy of Sciences and Humanities* 4 (1969–70):239–326. Jerusalem, 1971.

Ben–Sasson, Yonah. "Mishnato ha–Historit shel ha–Rambam." In *Ḥevrah ve–Historyah,* ed. Yeḥezkel Cohen, pp. 529–42. Jerusalem, 5740 [1979–80].

Benayahu, Meir. *Haskamah u–reshut bi–defuse Venetsyah* [Copyright, Authorization and Imprimatur for Hebrew Books Printed in Venice]. Jerusalem, 1971.

Bernays, Jacob. *Joseph Justus Scaliger.* [1855]. Osnabrück, 1965.

Bertram, Bonaventure Corneille. *De Politia Judaica.* Geneva, 1574.

Besso, Henry V. *Dramatic Literature of the Sephardic Jews of Amsterdam in the Seventeenth and Eighteenth Centuries.* New York, 1947.

Bible. O. T. Psalms. Hebrew and Spanish. 1671. . . . Alabanças de santitad, tradución . . . Por el haham Yahacob Yehuda, Leon . . . Amsterdam, 5431 [1671].

Blau, Joseph Leon. *The Christian Interpretation of the Cabala in the Renaissance.* Port Washington, New York, 1965.

Blok, F. F. "Caspar Barlaeus en de Joden: De Geschiedenis van een Epigram." *NAK* 57 (1977):179–209 and 58 (1978):85–108.

———. "Quelques Humanistes de la Jerusalem de l'Occident." In *Humanists and Humanism in Amsterdam,* pp. 9–32. Amsterdam, 1973.

Bloom, Herbert. *The Economic Activities of the Jews of Amsterdam in the Seventeenth and Eighteenth Centuries.* Williamsport, Pa., 1937.

Bolgar, R. R. *The Classical Heritage and its Beneficiaries.* Cambridge, 1958.

Bonfil, R. "The Nature of Judaism in Raymundus Martini's *Pugio Fidei*" [Hebrew]. *Tarbiz* 40 (1971): 360–75.

Bots, Hans, ed. *Constantijn Huygens: zijn plaats in geleerd Europa.* Amsterdam, 1973.

Box, G. H. "Hebrew Studies in the Reformation Period and after: their place and influence." In *The Legacy of Israel,* edited by Edwyn R. Bevan and Charles Singer, pp. 315–76. Oxford, [1927]. Corrected repr., 1965.

Boxer, C. R. *The Dutch in Brazil, 1624–1654.* Oxford, 1957. Repr. ed. Hamden, Conn, 1973.

———. *The Dutch Seaborne Empire: 1600–1800.* New York, 1965.

Brown, Virginia. *The Textual Transmission of Caesar's Civil War.* Leiden, 1972.

Bruehl, Clemens M. "Josef Justus Scaliger: Ein Beitrag zur geistesgeschichtliches Bedeutung der Altertumswissenschaft." *Zeitschrift für Religions– und Geistesgeschichte,* 12 (1960):201–18. and 13 (1961):45–65.

Brugmans, Hendrik, and Frank, A., eds. *Geschiedenis der Joden in Nederland.* Vol. 1. Amsterdam, 1940.

Brugmans, H. *Geschiedenis van Amsterdam.* Utrecht and Antwerp, 1973.

———. *Opkomst en Bloei van Amsterdam.* Amsterdam, 1944.

Burke, Peter. *Venice and Amsterdam.* London, 1974.

Busken Huet, Conrad. *Het Land van Rembrand.* 2nd ed., rev. Haarlem, 1886.

Cahiers spinoza 3 (1980):9–170. [A collection of articles under the title "Spinoza et les juifs d'Amsterdam, Marranes et Post–Marranes."]

Capp, B. S. "Godly Rule and English Millenarism." *Past and Present* 52 (1971):106–17.

———. *The Fifth Monarchy Men.* Totowa, New Jersey, 1972.

Cardozo, de Bethencourt. "Lettres de Menasseh ben Israel à Is. Vossius, 1651–1655." *REJ* 49 (1904):98–109.

Carmilly–Weinberger, Moshe. "External and Internal Censorship of Hebrew Books." *Jewish Book Annual* 28 (1970–71):9–16.

Carter, Alice Clare. *The English Reformed Church in Amsterdam in the Seventeenth Century.* Amsterdam, 1964.

Clark, G. N. *The Seventeenth Century.* 2nd ed. Oxford, 1949; 1960.

Clarke, M. L. *Classical Education in Britain, 1500–1900.* Cambridge, 1959.

Classical Influences on European Culture A.D. 1500–1700. Proceedings of an International Conference held at King's College, Cambridge, April 1974. Edited by R. R. Bolgar. Cambridge, 1976.

Coccejus, Johannes. "Oratio de causis incredulitatis Judaeorum." In his *Opera omnia theologica* 8:12–21. Amsterdam, 1675.

Colie, Rosalie L. *Light and Enlightenment: A Study of the Cambridge Platonists and the Dutch Arminians.* Cambridge, 1957.

Concordantie, offte Verghelijckinghe/ Der ghesegende en affvallige staet deser Vereenighde Nederlanden/ beyde in Politie ende kercke/ Met den staet der Israeliten/ wanneer hen Godt het beloofde Canaan ingegeven hadde/ ende zy 'tzelve door ongehoorsaemheyt hadden vorlooren. N.p., 1631.

Cooper, Brian G. "The Academic Re–Discovery of Apocalyptic Ideas in the 17th Century." *Baptist Quarterly* (London) 18 (1959–60):351–52. and 19 (1961–62):29–34.

Cotterell, Geoffrey. *Amsterdam: The Life of a City.* Boston, 1972.

Court, Pieter de la. *The True Interest and Political Maxims of the Republic of Holland.* London, 1746. Rep. ed. New York, 1972.

Cragg, Gerald R. *The Cambridge Platonists.* New York, 1968.

Crane, Iohann Guilielmus de. "Oratio de vossiorum Iuniorumque familia." In *Annales Academiae Groninganae,* 1819–20 [1821].

Creveld, M. van, ed. *The Rise of the Dutch State, 1559–1648.* Jerusalem, 1972.

Davis, Thomas M. "The Traditions of Puritan Typology." In *Typology and Early American Literature,* edited by S. Bercovitch, pp. 11–45. N.p., 1972.

Delmedigo, Yosef Shlomo. *Sefer Elim.* Amsterdam, 1628–29.

De Vries, Jan. *The Economy of Europe in an Age of Crisis, 1600–1750.* Cambridge, 1976.

———. "On the Modernity of the Dutch Republic." *Journal of Economic History* 33 (1973):191–202.

Dibon, Paul. "La philosophie néerlandaise au siècle d'or." Vol. 1. Amsterdam, 1954.

———. "L'Université de Leyde et la République des Lettres au 17e siècle." *Quaerendo* 5 (1975):5–38.

Diestel, Ludwig. *Geschichte des Alten Testaments in der christliche Kirche.* Jena, 1869.

Dillen, J. G. van. "Amsterdam's Rôle in Seventeenth–Century Dutch Politics and its Economic Background." In *Britain and the Netherlands,* edited by J. S. Bromley and E. H. Kossmann, 2:133–47. Groningen, 1964.

———. *Van Rijkdom en Regenten.* The Hague, 1970.

———. "Vreemdelingen te Amsterdam in de Eerste Helft der Zeventiende Eeuw." *Tijdschrift voor Geschiedenis* 50 (1935):4–35.

Dort, The Articles of the Synod of. Translated by Thomas Scott. Philadelphia, 1856.

Dumbauld, Edward. *The Life and Legal Writings of Hugo Grotius*. Norman. Okla., 1969.

Eeghen, I. H. van. "De gereformeerde kerkeraad en de joden te Amsterdam." *Amstelodamum,* maandblaad 47 (1960):169–74.

Eekhof, Albert. *De Theologische Faculteit te Leiden in de 17de Eeuw.* Utrecht, 1921.

Emmanuel, I. S. "New Light on Early American Jewry." *American Jewish Archives* 7 (1955):3–64.

———. "Seventeenth–Century Brazilian Jewry: A Critical Review." *American Jewish Archives* 14 (1962):32–69.

———. "Yedi'ot ḥadashot 'al hak–kehillah hap–portugezit me–Amsterdam." *Otsar Yehude Sefarad* 6 (1963):160–82.

Encyclopedia of Religion and Ethics. Edited by James Hastings. S.v. "Arminianism," by Frederic Platt.

Enelow, H. G. "Isaac Belinfante: An Eighteenth Century Bibliophile." In *Studies in Jewish Bibliography and Related Subjects in Memory of Abraham Solomon Freidus (1867–1923),* pp. 5–30. New York, 1929.

Ettinger, S. "The Beginnings of the Change in the Attitude of European Society Towards the Jews." *Scripta Hierosolymitana* 7 (1964):193–219.

———. "The Jews and Judaism as seen by the English Deists of the 18th century" [Hebrew]. *Tsiyyon* 29 (1964): 182–219.

Evenhuis, R. B. *Ook dat was Amsterdam.* 4 vols. to date. Baarn, 1965–.

Eysinga, W. J. M. van. *Hugo Grotius.* Basel, 1952.

Fisch, Harold. *Jerusalem and Albion.* London, 1964.

Fockema–Andreae, S. J. "De Nederlandse Staat onder de Republiek." *Verhand. Kon. Ned. Akad. afd. Letterk.*, n.s. 68, no. 3 (1961, Amsterdam).

Fontaine Verwey, Herman de la. "Willem Jansz. Blaeu as a publisher of books." *Quaerendo* 3 (1973):141–46.

———. "Humanism in Holland: The Heirs of Erasmus." *Quaerendo* 4 (1974):261–64.

———. "The Netherlands Book." In Wytze Gs. Hellinga, *Copy and Print in the Netherlands.* Amsterdam, 1962.

———. "Rembrandt as a book–illustrator." *Quaerendo* 3 (1973):3–19.

Foster, Herbert Darling. "Liberal Calvinism; The Remonstrants at the Synod of Dort in 1618." *Harvard Theological Review* 16 (1923):1–37.

Franco Mendes, David. *Memorias.* Edited and with an introduction by L. Fuks and R. G. Fuks–Mansfeld. Assen, 1975. [= *SR* 9, no. 2 (July 1975)].

Fremantle, Katherine. *The Baroque Town Hall of Amsterdam.* Utrecht, 1959.

Freudenthal, J. *Spinoza: Leben Und Lehre.* 2nd edition. Edited by Carl Gebhardt. Heidelberg, 1927.

Friedman, Jerome. "Sebastian Münster, the Jewish Mission, and Protestant Antisemitism." *Archiv für Reformationsgeschichte* 70 (1979):238–59.

Friedrich, Carl J. *The Age of the Baroque: 1610–1660.* Vol. 5 of *The Rise of Modern Europe.* Edited by William L. Langer. New York, 1952.

———. *The Baroque Age.* In *Perspectives in Western Civilization: Essays from Horizon,* edited by William L. Langer, 1:238–55. New York, 1972.

Fuks, L. "Het Hebreeuwse brievenboek van Johannes Drusius jr.: Hebreeuws en Hebräisten in Nederland rondom 1600." *SR* 3 (1969):1–52.

———. "Hebreeuws en Hebräisten in Franeker in de 17e en 18e eeuw." In *Travels in the World of the Old Testament.* Studies presented to . . . M. A. Beek, pp. 50–70. Assen, 1974.

Fuks, Leo and Fuks, Rena. "Jewish Historiography in the Netherlands in the 17th and 18th centuries." In *Salo Wittmayer Baron Jubilee Volume,* pp. 433–66. Jerusalem, 1975.

Fuks, L. "Wat Heeft Menasseh ben Israel Geschreven en wat is Ervan Gedrukt." *Het Boek* 46 (1957):330–35.

Funkenstein, Amos. "Hemshekhiyyut ve–ḥiddush be–maḥshevet ham–meah hash–sheva' 'esreh u–ve–madda'eha." *Proceedings of the Israel Academy of Sciences and Humanities,* vol. 6, no. 6. Jerusalem, 5781 [1980–81].

Geiger, Ludwig. *Das Studium der Hebräischen Sprache in Deutschland von Ende des XV. bis zur Mitte des XVI. Jahrhunderts.* Breslau, 1870.

Gans, Mozes Heiman. *Memorboek.* Baarn, 1971. [Eng. trans. *Memorbook,* 1977].

Gelder, H. A. Enno van. *Getemperde Vrijheid.* Groningen, 1972.

———. "Nederland geprotestantiseerd?" *Tijdschrift voor Geschiedenis* 81 (1968):445–64.

Gesellschaft zur Förderung der Wissenschaft des Judentums. *Moses ben Maimon, Sein Leben, Seine Werke und Sein Einfluss.* 2 vols. Leipzig, 1908–14.

Geyl, Pieter. *The Netherlands in the Seventeenth Century.* 2 vols. London and New York, 1961–64.

Gibbs, C. G. "The role of the Dutch Republic as the intellectual entrepôt of Europe in the seventeenth and eighteenth centuries." *BMGN* 86 (1971):323–55.

Goudsblom, Johan. *Dutch Society.* New York, 1967.

Grabois, Aryeh. "The *Hebraica veritas* and Jewish–Christian Intellectual Relations in the Twelfth Century." *Speculum* 50 (1975):614–34.

Graetz, Heinrich. *Geschichte der Juden.* 3rd ed. by Marcus Brann. Leipzig, [1897–1911].

Graupe, Heinz Moshe. *Die Statuten der drei Gemeinden Altona, Hamburg und Wandsbek.* 2 vols. Hamburg, 1973.

Gray, Hanna H. "Renaissance Humanism: The Pursuit of Eloquence." *Journal of the History of Ideas* 24 (1963):497–514.

———. "Valla's Encomium of St. Thomas Aquinas and the Humanist Conception of Christian Antiquity." *Essays in History and Literature* Presented . . . to Stanley Pargellis. Chicago, 1965.

Grootens, P. "De Betekenis van Vossius' *Ars Historica.*" *Historisch Tijdschrift* 20 (1941):237–74.

Grotius, Hugo. *Briefwisseling.* 10 vols. to date. Edited by P. C. Molhuysen and B. L. Meulenbroek. The Hague, 1929–.

———. *De Veritate Religionis Christianae.* New edition. The Hague, 1734.

———. *Remonstrantie nopende de ordre dije in de landen van Hollandt ende Westvrieslandt dijent gestelt op de Joden.* Edited and with an introduction by Jaap Meijer. Amsterdam, 1949.

Gui, Bernard. *Manuel de l'inquisateur.* Edited and translated by G. Mollat. Vol. 2. Paris, 1964 [1927].

Guttmann, Jacob. "Der Einfluss der Maimonidischen Philosophie auf das christliche Abendland." In: Gesellschaft zur Förderung der Wissenschaft des Judentums. *Moses ben Maimon.* Edited by J. Guttmann. Vol. 1. Leipzig, 1908.

Habermann, A. M. *A History of Hebrew Liturgical and Secular Poetry* [Hebrew]. 2 vols. Ramat Gan, 1970.

Haentjens, A. J. *Hugo de Groot als Godsdienstig Denker.* Amsterdam, 1946.

Haley, K. H. D. *The Dutch in the Seventeenth Century.* London, 1972.

Harbison, E. Harris. *The Christian Scholar in the Age of the Reformation.* New York, 1956.

Harrison, A. W. *Arminianism.* London, 1937.

Henriques de Castro Mz., D. *Keur van grafsteenen op de Nederl.–Portug.–Israel. Begraafplaats te Ouderkerk aan den Amstel.* Leiden, 1883.

Herrera, Abraham Cohen. *Bet Elohim.* Translated by Isaac Aboab. Amsterdam, 1655.

Herzog, Isaac. "John Selden and Jewish Law." [1930]. In his *Judaism: Law & Ethics,* pp. 67–79. London, Jerusalem, and New York, 1974.

Highet, Gilbert. *The Classical Tradition.* London and New York, [1949] corr. repr., 1967.

Hillesum, J. M. "Bijdrage tot de biliographie van Menasseh ben Israel's geschriften." *Het Boek* 16 (1927):353–63.

———. "Menasseh ben Israel." *Het Boek* 5 (1916): 145–52.

———. "De 'Porta Veritatis' van Jacob ben Amram." *Het Boek* 17 (1928):335–46.

Hirschel, L. "Jan Pietersz. Beeldthouwer en de rabbijnen." *Vrijdagavond* 6 (1930):210–11 and 227–28.

———. "Jodocus Hondius en Hugh Broughton: Bijdrage tot de kennis der eerste hebreeuwsche uitgaven in Amsterdam." *Het Boek* 17 (1928):199–208.

———. "Johannes Leusden Als Hebraist." *SR* 1 (1967): 23–50.

———. "Uit de Voorgeschiedenis der Hebreeuwsche Typographie te Amsterdam." *Jaarboek Amstelodam* 31 (1934):66–79.

Holt, P. M. *A Seventeenth Century Defender of Islam: Henry Stubb (1632–76) and his Book.* London, 1972.

———. "The Study of Arabic Historians in Seventeenth Century England: The Background and the work of Edward Pococke." *Bulletin of the School of Oriental and African Studies, University of London* 19 (1957):444–55.

———. "The Treatment of Arab History by Prideaux, Ockley and Sale." In *Historians of the Middle East,* edited by Bernard Lewis and P. M. Holt, pp. 290–302. *Historical Writing on the Peoples of Asia.* Vol. 4. London, 1962.

Hoornbeek, Johannes. [*Teshuvat Yehudah.*] *sive, Pro convincendis, et convertendenis Judaeis.* Leiden, 1655.

Horst, D. J. H. Ter. *Isaac Vossius en Salmasius.* The Hague, 1938.

Houtte, J. A. Van. *Economische en Sociale Geschiedenis Van de Lage Landen.* Zeist and Antwerp, 1964.

Huizinga, J. H. *Dutch civilisation in the seventeenth century and other essays.* Selected by Pieter Geyl and F. W. N. Hugenholtz. Translated by Arnold J. Pomerans. New York and Evanston, 1969.

Humanists and Humanism in Amsterdam. [Catalogue of an Exhibition in the Trippenhuis, Amsterdam, 20–25 August 1973.] Amsterdam, 1973.

Husik, Isaac. "The Law of Nature, Hugo Grotius, and the Bible." *HUCA* 2 (1925):381–419.

Hyamson, Albert. *The Sephardim of England.* London, 1951.

Ibn Verga, Solomon ben Judah. *Schevet Jehudah.* 2 vols. Heb. and Ger. Edited and translated by M. Wiener. Hannover, 1855–56.

Israel, Jonathan I. *The Dutch Republic and the Hispanic World, 1606–1661.* Oxford, 1982.

Jeannin, Pierre. *L'Europe du Nord–Ouest et du Nord: Aux XVIIe et XVIIIe siècles.* Paris, 1969.

Jensen, Wilhelm. *Die hamburgische Kirche und ihre Geistlichen seit der Reformation.* Hamburg, 1958.

Jong, M. de. "O 'Tratado da Immortalidade da Alma' de Moses Rephael de Aguilar." *Biblos* 10 (1934):488–99.

Jong, O. J. de. *Nederlandse Kerkgeschiedenis.* Nijkerk, 1972.

Jonge, H. J. de. *Daniel Heinsius and the Textus Receptus of the New Testament.* Leiden, 1971.

Juynboll, Wilhelmina M. C. *Zeventiende–eeuwsche beoefenaars van het arabisch in Nederland* . . . . Utrecht, 1931.

Kamen, Henry. *The Rise of Toleration.* New York and Toronto, 1967.

Kaplan, Joseph. *Isaac Orobio de Castro and His Circle.* Ph.D. dissertation, Hebrew University, 1978.

———. "On the Death Dates of Members of the Nunes Henriques Family, and of Three Important Rabbis of Amsterdam." *KS* 54 (1979):611–13.

———. "The Portuguese Jews in Amsterdam: From Forced Conversion to a Return to Judaism." *SR* 14 (1981):37–51.

———. "Rabbi Saul Levi Morteira's Treatise 'Arguments Against the Christian Religion'" [Hebrew]. In *Studies on the History of Dutch Jewry,* edited by Jozeph Michman, 1:9–32. Jerusalem, 1975.

———. "The Role of Rabbi Moshe d'Aguilar in his Contacts with the Refugees from Spain and Portugal in the XVIIth Century." In *Proceedings of the Sixth World Congress of Jewish Studies,* Heb. sec., 2:95–106.

Karpeles, Gustav. *Geschichte der Jüdischen Literatur.* 2 vols. 3rd ed. Berlin, 1921. Repr. ["4th"] ed. Graz, Austria, 1963.

Katz, David S. *Philo–Semitism and the Readmission of the Jews to England 1603–1655.* Oxford, 1982. [Not consulted]

Kaufmann, David. "Elia Menachem Chalfan on Jews Teaching Hebrew to Non–Jews." *JQR,* o.s. 9 (1897):500–508.

———. "Der 'Führer' Maimûni's in der Weltliteratur." *Archiv für Geschichte der Philosophie* 11 (1898):335–74. Repr. in his *Gesammelte Schriften,* edited by M. Brann, 2:152–89. Frankfurt am Main, 1910. Heb. tr. in his *Meḥkarim bas–sifrut ha–'ivrit,* pp. 214–38. Jerusalem, 1965.

Kayserling, M. "Un conflit de la communauté hispano–portugaise d'Amsterdam: ses conséquences." *REJ* 53 (1901): 275–76.

———. "Les correspondants juifs de Jean Buxtorf." *REJ* 13 (1886):260–76.

———. "Les Hébraisants Chrétiens du XVIIe siècle." *REJ* 20 (1890): 261–68.

———. "Une histoire de la littérature juive de Daniel Levi de Barrios." *REJ* 32 (1896):88–101.

———. *História dos Judeus em Portugal.* Translated by G. B. Corrêa da Silva and Anita W. Novinsky. With an introduction and notes by Anita Novinsky. São Paulo, 1971.

———. "Isaac Aboab, The First Jewish Author in America." *Proceedings of the American Jewish Historical Society* 5 (1897):125–36.

———. "The Life and Labours of Menasseh ben Israel." Translated by F. de Sola Mendes. In *Miscellany of Hebrew Literature,* edited by A. Löwy, pp. 1–96. London, 1877. Rep. Ed. Westport, Conn., 1972.

———. *Rabbi Yitzhak Aboab hash–Shelishi.* [*Hag–Goren* 3 (1902):155–74].

———. *Sephardim: Romanische Poesien der Juden in Spanien.* [Leipzig, 1859]. Repr. ed. Hildesheim and New York, 1972.

Kellenbenz, Hermann. *Sephardim an den Unteren Elbe.* Wiesbaden, 1958.

Kern, Edith G. *The Influence of Heinsius and Vossius upon French Dramatic Theory.* Baltimore, 1949.

Kleerkooper, M. M. and van Stockum, Jr., W. P. *De Boekhandel te Amsterdam voornamelijk in de 17e eeuw.* 2 vols. The Hague, 1914–16.

Kluxen, Wolfgang. "Die Geschichte des Maimonides im Lateinischen Abendland als Beispiel Einer Christlich–Jüdisch Bewegung." *Judentum im Mittelalter.* Edited by Paul Wilpert. [Miscellanea Mediaevalia, vol. 4]. Berlin, 1966.

———. "Literargeschichtliches zum lateinischen Moses Maimonides." *Revue de Theologie Ancienne et Mediévale* 21 (1954): 23–50.

Knight, William Stanley MacBean. *The Life and Works of Hugo Grotius.* London, 1925.

Kobler, Franz. *A Treasury of Jewish Letters.* 2 vols. London, 1952.

Koenen, H. J. *Geschiedenis der Joden in Nederland.* Utrecht, 1843.

Kossmann, E. J. "The Development of Dutch Political Theory in the Seventeenth Century." In *Britain and the Netherlands,* edited by J. S. Bromley and E. H. Kossmann, 1:91–110. London, 1960.

Krantz, Frederick, and Hohenberg, Paul M., eds. *Failed Transitions to Modern Industrial Society: Renaissance Italy and Seventeenth Century Holland.* Proceedings of the First International Colloquium of the Interuniversity Centre for European Studies, April 18–20, 1974. Montreal, 1975.

Kristeller, Paul Oskar. *Renaissance Thought.* A revised and enlarged edition of "The Classics and Renaissance Thought." New York, 1961.

Lachs, Phyllis S. "Hugo Grotius' use of Jewish Sources in 'On the Law of War and Peace'." *Renaissance Quarterly* 30 (1977): 181–200.

Lamont, William M. *Godly Rule: Politics and Religion, 1603–60.* London, 1969.

Landsberger, Franz. *Rembrandt, the Jews and the Bible.* 2nd ed. Philadelphia, 1961.

Lebram, J. C. H. "Hebräische Studien Zwischen Ideal und Wirklichkeit an der Universität Leiden in den Jahren 1575–1619." *NAK*, n.s. 56 (1975–76):317–57.

Lecky, W. E. H. *History of the Rise and Influence of the Spirit of Rationalism in Europe.* 2 vols. [London, 1865;] Rev. ed. New York, 1890.

Lecler, Joseph. *Toleration and the Reformation.* 2 vols. Translated by T. L. Westow. New York, 1960 and London, 1960.

Leiden University in the Seventeenth Century: An Exchange of Learning. Edited by Th. H. Lunsingh Scheurleer and G. M. H. Posthumus Meyjes. Leiden, 1975.

Léonard, Emile G. *A History of Protestantism.* Vol. 2: *The Establishment.* London, 1967.

Levy, Hartwig. *Die Entwicklung der Rechtsstellung der Hamburger Juden.* Hamburg, 1933.

Levy, S. "English Students of Maimonides." *Miscellanies of the Jewish Historical Society of England* 4 (1942):61–84.

Ley, Jan Hendrik van der. *Verborgene Eijgenschappen inde Heylighe Schriftuer.* Amsterdam, 1626.

Lieberman, Saul. *Shkiin.* 2nd ed. Jerusalem, 1970.

Lowance, Mason I., Jr. *The Language of Canaan: Metaphor and Symbol in New England from the Puritans to the Transcendentalists.* Cambridge, Mass. and London, England, 1980.

Löwenstamm, Arthur. "Hugo Grotius' Stellung zum Judentum." *Festschrift zum 75–jahrigen Bestehen des Jüdisch–Theologischen Seminars* [Breslau]. (Breslau, 1929), 2:295–302.

Löwenstein, Leopold. "Die Familie Aboab." *MGWJ* 48 (1904):661–701.

Maarsen, I. "De Responsa Als Bron Voor de Geschiedenis der Joden in Nederland." *BMGJWN* 5 (1933):118–46.

Maccoby, Hyam. *Judaism on Trial.* London and Toronto, 1981.

Maclear, J. F. "New England and the Fifth Monarchy." *William and Mary Quarterly*, 3rd ser. 32 (1975):223–60.

Manuel, Frank. "Israel and the Enlightenment." *Daedalus* 111 (1982):33–52.

———. *The Religion of Isaac Newton.* Oxford, 1974.

Martin, Raymond. *Pugio Fidei adversus Mauros et Judaeos.* Edited by Joseph de Voisin. [Leipzig, 1687.] Repr. ed. Farnborough, England, 1967.

Marx, Alexander. *Studies in Jewish History and Booklore.* [New York, 1944.] Repr. ed. Westmead, England, 1969.

Maurer, Wilhelm. "Reuchlin und das Judentum." *Th. Lit. Z.* 77 (1952):533–44.

McGee, J. Sears. *The Godly Man in Stuart England: Anglicans, Puritans and the Two Tables, 1620–1670.* New Haven and London, 1976.

McNeill, John T. *The History and Character of Calvinism.* New York, 1954.

Méchoulan, Henri. "À propos de la visite de Frédéric–Henri, prince d'Orange, à la synagogue d'Amsterdam." *LIAS* 5 (1978):81–86.

———. "Lorsque Saumaise consultait Menasseh Ben Israël: Deux lettres inédites du rabbin d'Amsterdam à l'humaniste de Leyde." *SR* 13 (1979):1–17.

———. "Menasseh Ben Israël au centre des rapports judéo–chrétiens en Hollande au XVII° siècle dans une lettre inédite d'Isaac Coymans à André Colvius." *SR* 16 (1982):21–24.

———. "Le problème du Latin chez Menasseh Ben Israël et quelques implications religieuses et politiques à propos d'une lettre inédite à Beverovicius." *SR* 14 (1980):1–6.

———. "Quelques remarques sur le Marranisme et la rupture Spinoziste." *SR* 11 (1977):113–25.

Meijer, J. *Encyclopaedia Sefardica Neerlandica.* Amsterdam, 1949.

———. "Hugo Grotius' Knowledge of Hebrew." *Historia Judaica* 14 (1952):133–44.

———. "Hugo Grotius' *Remonstrantie.*" *JSS* 17 (1955):91–104.

Meijer, Reinder P. *Literature of the Low Countries.* Assen, 1971.

Melkman, Jozeph. *David Franco Mendes, a Hebrew Poet.* Jerusalem, 1952 and Amsterdam, 1952.

Melnick, Ralph. *From Polemics to Apologetics: Jewish–Christian Rapprochement in 17th Century Amsterdam.* Assen, 1981.

Menasseh ben Israel. *Conciliador.* Part II. Amsterdam, 1641.

———. *The Conciliator.* Translated by E. H. Lindo. [1842.] Repr. ed. New York, 1972.

———. *Esperança de Israel.* Amsterdam, 1650.

———. *Espérance d'Israel.* Translated with an introduction and notes by Henri Méchoulan and Gérard Nahon. Paris, 1979.

———. *Of the term of life.* Translated by Thomas Pocock. London, 1709.

———. *Thesouro dos Dinim.* Amsterdam, 1710.

Mendes dos Remedios, J. *Os Judeus Portugueses em Amsterdam.* Coimbra, 1911.

Merḥavyah, Ḥen–melekh. *Hat–talmud bi–rei han–natsrut.* Jerusalem, 5731 [1970].

Meursius, Johannes. *Athenae Batavae.* [Leiden, 1625.] Repr. ed. Westmead, England, 1970.

Meyer, Isidore S. *The Hebrew Exercises of Governor William Bradford.* Plymouth, Mass., 1973.

Michman, Dan. "Tenufah Ḥadashah be–Ḥeker Yahadut Holand." *Bi–Tefutsot hag–Golah* 15 (1973):100–104.

Michman, Jozeph, ed. *Studies On the History of Dutch Jewry.* Vols. 1—. Jerusalem, 1975—.

Molhuysen, P. C. *De Bibliothek van Hugo de Groot in 1618.* [Nederlandsche Akademie van Wetenschappen, Afd. Letterkunde (Mededeelingen), n.s., vol. 6, no. 3.] Amsterdam, 1943.

Molko, Yitshak Raphael. "Sephardic Communities in the Diaspora: Amsterdam" [Hebrew]. *Otsar Yehude Sefarad* 4 (1961): 59–77.

Momigliano, Arnaldo. "Ancient History and the Antiquarian." In his *Contributo Alla Storia Degli Studi Classici,* pp. 67–106. Rome, 1955.

Moore, George Foot. "Christian Writers on Judaism." *Harvard Theological Review* 14 (1921):197–254.

Morteira, Saul Levi. *Giv'at Shaul.* Edited by Joseph Schein and Eliezer Platt. Warsaw, 1901.

———. *Vikkuaḥ Shiv'ah Harim.* Amsterdam, 1767.

Moses ben Maimon. *Da lei divina.* Translated by David Cohen de Lara. Second printing with an introduction by Moses Bensabat Amzalak. [Amsterdam, 5412 (1652).] Lisbon, 1925.

———. *Le Livre de la Connaissance.* Translated by Valentin Nikiprowetzky and André Zaoui. Paris, 1961.

———. *Mishneh Torah.* Vol. 1. Translated by Simon Glazer. New York, 1927.

———. *Mishneh Torah.* Vol. 1. Translated by Moses Hyamson. Jerusalem, 1965.

———. *Mishneh Torah.* Vol. 1. Saul Lieberman, general editor. Jerusalem, 1964.

Müller, Johann. *Judenthumb.* Hamburg, 1644.

Müller, Lucian. *Geschichte der Klassischen Philologie in den Niederlanden.* Leipzig, 1869.

Murray, John J. *Amsterdam in the Age of Rembrandt.* Norman, Okla., 1967.

Najara, Israel. *Meme Yisrael.* Venice, 1599.

Nat, Jan. *De studie van de Oostersche talen in Nederland.* Purmerend, 1929.

New Cambridge Modern History. Vol. 4. The Decline of Spain and the Thirty Years War, 1609–1648/59. Cambridge, 1970.

Newman, Louis I. *Jewish Influence on Christian Reform Movements.* New York, 1925.

Nobbs, Douglas. *Theocracy and Toleration.* Cambridge, 1938.

Ogilvie, R. M. *Latin and Greek; a History of the Influence of the Classics on English Life from 1600–1918.* London, 1964.

Pagis, Dan. "Liturgical Poetry in Seventeenth Century Italy; A Hebrew Manuscript" [Hebrew]. *KS* 50 (1975):228–312.

Parkes, James. "Early Christian Hebraists." *Studies in Bibliography and Booklore* 4 (1959):51–58 and 6 (1962):11–28.

Pennington, D. H. *Seventeenth Century Europe.* London, 1970.

Pereyra, Abraham. *Espejo de la Vanidad del Mundo.* Amsterdam, 5431 [1671].

Pieterse, Wilhelmina C. *Daniel Levi de Barrios als Geschiedschrijver van de Portuguees–Israelietische Gemeente te Amsterdam in Zijn 'Triumpho del Govierno Popular'.* Amsterdam, 1968.

———. *Livro de Bet Haim do Kahal Kados de Bet Yahacob.* Assen, 1970.

Pimientel, Abraham hak–Kohen. *Sefer Minḥat Kohen.* Amsterdam, 1668.

Popkin, Richard H. "The Historical Significance of Sephardic Judaism in 17th Century Amsterdam." *American Sephardi* 5 (1971): 18–27.

———. "Jewish Messianism and Christian Millenarianism." In *Culture and Politics From Puritanism to the Enlightenment,* edited by Perez Zagorin. Berkeley, 1980.

———. "Menasseh ben Israel and Isaac La Peyrère." *SR* 7 (1972):59–63.

———. "Philosophy and Polemics in the Manuscripts of Ets Haim" [Hebrew]. *Studies on the History of Dutch Jewry* 3 (1981):55–63.

———. "Spinoza and La Peyrère." In *Spinoza: New Perspectives.* Edited by Robert W. Shahan and J. I. Biro. Norman, Okla., 1978.

Popper, William. *The Censorship of Hebrew Books.* 1899. Repr. edited with an introduction by Moshe Carmilly–Weinberger. New York, 1969.

Price, J. L. *Culture and Society in the Dutch Republic During the 17th Century.* London, 1974.

Prins, Izak. "De Oud–Hollandsche Drukpersvrijheid ten Opzichte van het Joodsche Boek." *BMGJWN* 5 (1933):147–76.

———. *De Vestiging der Marranen in Noord–Nederland in de zestiende eeuw.* Amsterdam, 1927.

Rabinowitz, R. N. *Maamar 'al hadpasat hat–Talmud.* Jerusalem, 1952.

Rademaker, C. S. M. "The Correspondence of Gerardus Joannes Vossius (1577–1649)." In *Humanists and Humanism in Amsterdam,* pp. 33–39. Amsterdam, 1973.

———. *Gerardus Joannes Vossius (1577–1649).* In *Acta Historiae Neerlandica* (Historical Studies in the Netherlands) 4:217–23. Leiden, 1970.

———. *Gerardus Joannes Vossius (1577–1649).* Zwolle, 1967.

Rankin, Otto Shaw. *Jewish Religious Polemic.* Repr. Ed. New York, 1970.

Recife, Brazil—Kahal Kadosh sur Israel. *Livro de Atas das Congregações Judaicas Zur Israel em Recife e Magen Abraham em Mauricia, Brasil, 1648–1653.* Rio de Janeiro, 1955.

Reijnders, Carolus. *Van "Joodsche Natiën" Tot Joodse Nederlanders.* Amsterdam, 1970.

Reils, H. "Beiträge zur Ältesten Geschichte der Juden in Hamburg." *Zeitschrift des Vereins für Hamburgische Geschichte* 2 (1842):357–424.

Rengstorf, Karl Heinrich and Kortzfleisch, Siegfried von. *Kirche und Synagoge: Handbuch zur Geschichte von Christen und Juden.* 2 vols. Stuttgart, 1968–70.

Renier, G. J. *The Dutch Nation.* London, 1944.

Reusch, Franz Heinrich. *Der Index der verbotenen Bücher.* 3 vols. [1883–85.] Repr. ed. Aalen, 1967.

Révah, I. S. "Les Écrivains Manuel de Pina et Miguel de Barrios et la censure de la communauté Judéo–Portugaise d'Amsterdam." *Otsar Yehude Sefarad* 8 (1965): LXXIV–XCI.

———. "Aux Origines de la rupture spinozienne: nouveaux documents sur l'incroyance dans la communauté judéo–portugaise d'Amsterdam a l'époque de l'excommuncation de Spinoza." *REJ* 123 (1964):358–431.

———. *Spinoza et le Dr. Juan de Prado.* Paris and the Hague, 1959.

———. "Spinoza et les hérétiques de la communauté judéo–portugaise d'Amsterdam." *Revue de l'histoire des religions* 154 (1958): 173–218.

Riemersma, Jelle C. *Religious Factors in Early Dutch Capitalism, 1550–1650.* The Hague and Paris, 1967.

Rivkin, Ellis. *Leon da Modena and the "Kol Sakhal".* Cincinnati, 1952.

Rogier, L.–J., and Brachin, P. *Histoire du catholicisme hollandais depuis le XVIe siècle.* Paris, 1974.

Roi, J. F. A. de le. *Die evangelische Christenheit und die Juden.* Vol. 1. Karlsruhe and Leipzig, 1884.

Roldanus, Cornelia Wilhelmine. *Coenraad van Beuningen: Staatsman en Libertijn.* The Hague, 1931.

Romein, Jan and Annie. *De Lage Landen bij de zee.* Utrecht, 1949.

Roorda, D. J. "The Ruling Classes in Holland in the Seventeenth Century." In *Britain and the Netherlands,* edited by J. S. Bromley and E. H. Kossmann, 2:104–32. Groningen, 1964.

Rosenthal, Frank. "The Rise of Christian Hebraism in the Sixteenth Century." *Historia Judaica* 7 (1945):167–91.

Rosenberg, A. W. "Hugo Grotius as Hebraist." *SR* 12 (1978):62–90.

Ross, Ya'akov Yehoshu'a. "Ha–Rambam ve–hak–kedmah—hat–tefisah ha–historit shel ha–Rambam." In *Ḥevrah ve–Historyah,* edited by Yeḥezkel Cohen, pp. 529–42. Jerusalem, 5740 [1979–80].

Rossi, J. B. de. *Bibliotheca Judaica Antichristiana.* [Parma, 1800.] Repr. ed. Amsterdam, 1964.

———. *Historisches Wörterbuch der Jüdischen Schriftsteller und Ihrer Werke.* Translated from the Italian by C. H. Hamberger. Amsterdam, 1967.

Roth, Cecil. *A History of the Jews in England.* Third ed. Oxford, 1964.

———. *A History of the Marranos.* Philadelphia, 1932. Repr. ed. New York, 1966.

———. "Immanuel Aboab's Proselytization of the Marranos." *JQR* 23 (1932–33):121–62.

———. *The Jewish Contribution to Civilization.* New York, 1940.

———. *The Jews in the Renaissance.* Philadelphia, 1959. Repr. ed. New York, 1965.

———. *A Life of Menasseh Ben Israel: Rabbi, Printer, and Diplomat.* Philadelphia, 1934.

———. "A List of Books from Menasseh Ben Israel's Stock" [Hebrew]. *Areshet* 2 (1960):413–14.

———. *Studies in Books and Booklore.* Westmead, Farnborough, England, 1972.

Roth, Leon. "Hebraists and Non–Hebraists of the Seventeenth Century." *Journal of Semitic Studies* 6 (1961):204–21.

———. *Spinoza, Descartes, and Maimonides.* New York, 1963.

Rowen, Herbert H., ed. *The Low Countries in Early Modern Times.* New York, 1972.

Rubio y Lluch, Antonio. *Documents per l'historia de la cultura catalana mig–eval.* 2 vols. Barcelona, 1914–21.

Sa'di. *Rosarium politicum.* Translated and annotated by Georgius Gentius. Amsterdam, 1651.

Salomon, H. P. "Haham Saul Levi Morteira en de Portugese Nieuw–Christen." *SR* 10 (1976):127–41.

———. "The 'De Pinto' Manuscript: A Seventeenth–century Marrano family history." *SR* 9 (1975):1–62.

Santa Companhia de Dotar Orphas e Donzelas. *Reglement.* Amsterdam, 1862.

Saraiva, A. J. "Antonio Vieira, Menasseh ben Israel, et le cinquième empire." *SR* 6 (1972):25–56.

———. *Inquisição e Cristãos–Novos.* Porto, Portugal, 1969.

Sasportas, Jacob. *Ohel Ya'akov.* Amsterdam, 1737.

———. *Tsitsat Novel Tsevi.* Edited by I. Tishby. Jerusalem, 1954.

Scaligerana. Editio Altera . . . Edited by Johannes Dalläus. Coloniae Agrippinae [Rouen], 1667.

Schneppen, Heinz. *Niederlandische Universitäten und Deutsches Geistesleben.* Münster, 1960.

Schoeps, Hans–Joachim. *Barocke Juden–Christen–Judenchristen.* Munich and Bern, 1965.

———. *The Jewish–Christian Argument.* Translated by David E. Green. New York, 1963.

———. *Jüdische Geisteswelt.* Cologne, 1960.

———. *Philosemitismus im Barock.* Tübingen, 1952.

Schöffer, I. "The Batavian Myth during the Sixteenth and Seventeenth Centuries." In *Britain and the Netherlands,* edited by J. S. Bromley and E. H. Kossmann, 5:78–101. The Hague, 1975.

———. "Did Holland's Golden Age Co–incide With a Period of Crisis?" In *Acta Historiae Neerlandica* (Historical Studies in the Netherlands) 1:82–107. Leiden, 1966.

———. *A short history of the Netherlands.* Amsterdam, 1973.

Scholberg, Kenneth R. "Miguel de Barrios and the Amsterdam Sephardic Community." *JQR* 53 (1962):120–59.

Scholem, Gershom. *Sabbatai Ṣevi, The Mystical Messiah: 1626–1676.* Princeton, 1973.

Schorsch, Ismar. "From Messianism to *Realpolitik:* Menasseh ben Israel and the Readmission of the Jews to England." *Proceedings of the American Academy for Jewish Research* 45 (1978):187–208.

Secret, F. *Les Kabbalistes Chrétiens de la Renaissance.* Paris, 1964.

———. "Notes sur les Hébraïsants Chrétiens, I: Léon de Modène et Gisbert Voetius." *REJ* 124 (1965):157–59.

Seeligmann, Sigmund. *Bibliographie en Historie.* Amsterdam, 1927.

———. "Die Juden in Holland." *Festkrift i Anlednung af Professor David Simonsens 70–aarige Fødselsdag.* Copenhagen, 1923.

Septimus, Bernard. "'Better under Edom than under Ishmael': The History of a Saying" [Hebrew] *Tsiyyon* 47 (1982):103–11.

Seven Sages. Hebrew. Mishle Erasto. Translated by Isaac Uzziel. Edited by Avraham Almaliḥ. [Sifriyyat Mekorot 7.] Jerusalem, 1975.

Shetter, William Z. *The Pillars of Society: Six Centuries of Civilization in the Netherlands.* The Hague, 1971.

Shulvass, Moses A. *The Jews in the World of the Renaissance.* Translated by Elvin I. Kose. Leiden and Chicago, 1973.

Sigonio, Carlo. *De Republica Ebraeorum.* 1574. [in Ugolino. *Thesaurus.*]

Silva Rosa, J. S. da. *Alfe Menasheh;* Catalogus der Tentoonstelling in het Portugeesch Israëlitisch Seminarium "Ets Haïm" te Amsterdam . . . Amsterdam, 1927.

———. *Geschiedenis der Portugueesche Joden te Amsterdam, 1593–1925.* Amsterdam, 1925.

———. *Iets over den Amsterdamschen Opperrabbijn Isaac Aboab.* Amsterdam, 1913.

———. "Over de Verhouding Tusschen Joden en Niet–Joden in de Republiek der Vereenigde Nederlanden Gedurende de 17e en 18e eeuw." *Nieuw Israëlietische Weekblad* 58, nos. 5–9 (1922).

Simonsohn, Shelomo. "Books and Libraries of Mantuan Jews, 1595" [Hebrew]. *KS* 37 (1961–62):103–22.

———. *Toledot hay–Yehudim be–Dukasut Mantovah* [History of the Jews in the Duchy of Mantua.] 2 vols. Jerusalem, 1962.

Smit, J. W. "The Netherlands and Europe in the Seventeenth and Eighteenth Centuries." In *Britain and the Netherlands,* edited by J. S. Bromley and E. H. Kossmann, 3:13–36. London and New York, 1968.

Sokolow, Nahum. *Barukh Shpinozah u–Zemano* [Baruch Spinoza and his Time; a study in philosophy and history]. Paris, 1928/29.

———. *History of Zionism, 1600–1918.* 2 vols. in 1. 1919. Repr. ed. New York, 1969.

Sonne, Isaiah. "Leon Modena and the Da Costa Circle in Amsterdam." *HUCA* 21 (1948):1–28.

Spinoza, Benedict de. *Opera.* Edited by Carl Gebhardt. Heidelberg, n.d.

———. *Theological–Political Treatise.* Translated and with an introduction by R. H. M. Elwes. London, 1883. Repr. ed. New York, 1955.

Spitz, Lewis W. "Humanism in the Reformation." In *Renaissance Studies in Honor of Hans Baron.* Edited by Anthony Molho and John A. Tedeschi. De Kalb, Ill., 1971.

De Statenvertaling: 1637–1937. Haarlem, 1937.

Stein, Siegfried. "Phillipus Ferdinandus Polonus, A Sixteenth–Century Hebraist in England." *Essays Presented to J. H. Hertz,* pp. 397–412. London, 1943.

Stevenson, Edward Luther. *Willem Janszoon Blaeu, 1571–1638.* New York, 1914.

Strauss, Leo. *Spinoza's Critique of Religion.* Translated by E. M. Sinclair. New York, 1965.

Swart, K. W. *The Miracle of the Dutch Republic as Seen in the Seventeenth Century.* Inaugural Lecture, University College, London, 6 Nov. 1967. London, 1969.

Swetschinski, Daniel M. *The Portuguese Jewish Merchants of Seventeenth–Century Amsterdam: A Social Profile.* Ph.D. dissertation, Brandeis University, 1980.

———. "Kinship and Commerce: The Foundations of Portuguese Jewish Life in Seventeenth Century Holland." *SR* 14 (1981):52–74.

Tchernowitz, Gershon. *The Jewish–Gentile Relationship According to Maimonides* [Hebrew]. New York, 1950.

Teicher, J. L. "Maimonides and England." *Transactions of the Jewish Historical Society of England* 16 (1952):97–100.

———. "Why Was Spinoza Banned?" *Menorah Journal* 45 (1957):41–61.

Tels–Elias, L. J. "De Resolutie van de staten van Holland van 12 Juli 1657 en de civiele status van de Nederlandse Joden." *BMGJWN* 8 (1960):56–57.

Temple, William. *Observations Upon the United Provinces of the Netherlands.* Edited by George Clark. Oxford, 1972.

Tex, Jan den. *Oldenbarnevelt.* 5 vols. to date. Haarlem, 1962–.

———. *Oldenbarnevelt.* 2 vols. Translated from the Dutch by R. B. Powell. Cambridge, 1973.

Thijssen–Schoute, Caroline Louise. *Uit de Republiek der Letteren.* Gravenhage, 1967.

Tideman, J. *De Remonstrantie en het Remonstrantisme.* Amsterdam, 1851.

Toon, Peter. *Puritans, the Millennium and the Future of Israel: Puritan Eschatology 1600 to 1660.* Cambridge and London, 1970.

Trevor–Roper, H. R. *The European Witch Craze of the Sixteenth and Seventeenth Century and Other Essays.* New York and Evanston, 1969.

"Trevor–Roper's General Crisis of the Seventeenth Century: A Discussion." *Past and Present* 18 (1960):8–42.

Trinkaus, Charles. *In Our Image and Likeness: Humanity and Divinity in Italian Humanist Thought.* 2 vols. Chicago, 1970.

Twersky, Isadore. *Introduction to the Code of Maimonides ("Mishneh Torah").* [Yale Judaica Series, vol. 22]. New Haven and London, 1980.

———. "Rabbi Joseph Ashkenazi and the *Mishneh Torah* by Maimonides." In *Salo Wittmayer Baron Jubilee Volume,* Hebrew Section, pp. 183–94. Jerusalem, 1975.

Ugolino, Blaesio. *Thesaurus antiquitatum sacrarum* . . . 34 vols. Venice, 1744–69.

Uit den Bogaard, M. Th. *De Gereformeerden en Oranje Tijdens Het Eerste Stadhouderloze Tijdperk.* Groningen and Jakarta, 1955.

Ullmann, Salomon. "Geschichte der Spanisch–portugiesischen Juden in Amsterdam im XVII. Jahrhundert." *Jahrbuch der Jüdisch–Literarischen Gesellschaft* 5 (1907):1–74.

Van Den, Berg, J. "Church and State Relations in the Netherlands." In *Lowland Highlights: Church and Oecumene in the Netherlands,* pp. 32–39. Kampen, 1972.

———. "Joden en Christenen in Nederland gedurende de zeventiende eeuw." *Verkenning en bezinning,* vol. 3, no. 2. (September 1969). Kampen, 1969.

La Vie et l'Oeuvre de Grotius (1583–1645). Catalogue of an Exposition. Paris, 1965.

Vlekke, Bernard H. M. *Evolution of the Dutch Nation.* New York, 1945.

Voetius, Gisbertus. *Exercitationes et Bibliotheca Studiosi Theologiae.* Utrecht, 1644.

Vondel, Joost van den. *Cing Tragédies.* Edited by Jean Stals. Paris, 1969.

———. *Werken.* 4 vols. Amsterdam, 1929.

Vossius, Gerhard Johann. *De Historicis Latinis.* Leiden, 1627.

Vossius, Gerhard Johann. *Theses Theologicae et Historicae.* 3rd ed. (1st ed., 1628). The Hague, 1658.

Vossius, Isaac. *Variarum Observationum Liber.* London, 1685.

Wagenaar, Jan. *Amsterdam, in zyne opkomst, aanwas, geschiedenissen, voorregten, koophandel, gebouwen, kerkenstaat, schoolen, schutterye, gilden en regeeringe.* 4 Vols. Amsterdam, 1760–1802. Repr. ed. Alpen aan den Rijn, 1971–72.

Walde, Bernhard. *Christliche Hebräisten Deutschlands am Ausgang des Mittelalters.* Münster, 1916.

Wansink, H. "Holland and Six Allies: The Republic of the Seven United Provinces." In *Britain and the Netherlands,* edited by J. S. Bromley and E. H. Kossmann, 4:133–55. The Hague, 1971.

Waxman, Meyer. *A History of Jewish Literature.* 5 vols. New York, 1933, reprinted 1960.

Wedgwood, C. V. "The Golden Age of the Dutch Republic." In *Perspectives in Western Civilization: Essays from Horizon,* edited by William L. Langer, 1:270–87. New York, 1972.

Weil, Gérard E. *Élie Lévita.* Leiden, 1963.

Wijnman, H. F. "Philippus Ferdinandus, Professor in het Arabisch aan de Leidse Universiteit, de eerste Oost–Europese Jood in Nederland (1599)." *Jaarbericht ex Oriente Lux* 19 (1965–66): 558–80.

Wilamowitz–Moellendorff, Ulrich von. *Geschichte der Philologie.* [1921.] Repr. ed. Leipzig, 1959.

Wilensky, Mordecai. *Shivat hay–Yehudim le–Angliyyah.* Jerusalem, 1943.

Wilson, Charles. *The Dutch Republic and the Civilization of the Seventeenth Century.* New York, 1968.

———. "Rebellion, liberty and nationhood." *The Age of Expansion: Europe and the World 1559–1660,* edited by Hugh Trevor–Roper, pp. 95–108. New York and London, 1968.

Winkelman, Petrus H. *Remonstranten en Katholieken in de eeuw van Hugo de Groot.* Nijmegen, 1945.

Wiznitzer, Arnold. *Jews in Colonial Brazil.* New York, 1960.

———. "The Merger Agreement and Regulations of Congregation Talmud Torah of Amsterdam (1638–39)." *Historia Judaica* 20 (1958):109–32.

———. *The Records of the Earliest Jewish Community in the New World.* New York, 1954.

Wolf, Lucien. *Menasseh Ben Israel's Mission to Oliver Cromwell.* London, 1901.

Yardeni, Miriam. "The Jews in French Historiography of the Sixteenth–Seventeenth Centuries" [Hebrew]. *Tsiyyon* 34 (1969):145–88.

———. "Judaism and Jews as seen by the French Protestant Exiles in Holland (1685–1715)" [Hebrew]. In *Studies in the History of the Jewish People and the Land of Israel* 1:163–85. Haifa, 1970.

———. "The Solution of the Jewish Problem in European Utopianism of the 16th–18th centuries" [Hebrew]. In *Studies in the History of the Jewish People and the Land of Israel* 2:133–48. Haifa, 1972.

———. "La Religion de la Peyrère et 'Le rappel des Juifs'." *Revue d'histoire et de philosophie religieuses* 51 (1971): 245–59.

Yates, Frances A. *Giordano Bruno and the Hermetic Tradition.* New York, 1969.

Yerushalmi, Yosef Hayim. "Conversos Returning to Judaism in the 17th Century, Their Jewish Knowledge and Psychological Readiness" [Hebrew]. *Fifth World Congress of Jewish Studies, Divre hak–Kongres.* 2:201–9.

———. *From Spanish Court to Italian Ghetto: Isaac Cardoso: A Study in Seventeenth–Century Marranism and Jewish Apologetics.* New York and London, 1971.

———. "Professing Jews in Post–Expulsion Spain and Portugal." In *Salo Wittmayer Baron Jubilee Volume,* pp. 1023–58. Jerusalem, 1975.

Zilverberg, S. B. J. *Geloof en geweten in de zeventiende eeuw.* Bussum, 1971.

———. "Jan Pieterszoon Beelthouwer (± 1603 – ± 1669) en de Joden." *SR* 3 (1969):156–67.

Zimmels, H. J. *Die Marranen in der Rabbinischen Literatur.* Berlin, 1932.

Zimmer, Eric. "Jewish and Christian Hebraist Collaboration in Sixteenth Century Germany." *JQR* 71 (1980):69–88.

Zinberg, Israel. *A History of Jewish Literature.* Vols. 1–6. Translated and edited by Bernard Martin. New York, 1972.

Ziskind, Jonathan R. "Petrus Cunaeus on Theocracy, Jubilee and the Latifundia." *JQR* 68 (1978):235–54.

Zumthor, Paul. *Daily Life in Rembrandt's Holland.* Translated by Simon Watson Taylor. New York, 1963.

Zunz, Leopold. *Die Gottesdienstliche Vorträge der Juden, historisch entwickelt.* 2nd ed. revised by N. Brüll. Forward by M. Steinschneider. Frankfort am Main, 1892.

———. *Zur Geschichte und Literatur.* Vol. 1. Berlin, 1845.

Zwarts, Jacob. "Die Eerste Rabbijner en Synagogen van Amsterdam naar Archivalische Bronnen." *BMGJWN* 4 (1928):147–271.

———. *Hoofdstukken uit der Geschiedenis der Joden in Nederland.* Zutphen, 1929.

Indices

INDEX OF BIBLICAL PASSAGES

New Testament Passages

INDEX OF PASSAGES from *De Idololatria* and *Hilkhot 'Avodah Zarah*

INDEX OF TITLES

Mishnaic Tractates:

Babylonian Talmud:

Midrashic and Other Tannaitic Literature:

Other Rabbinic and General Titles:

GENERAL INDEX

CENTER FOR JEWISH STUDIES

HARVARD JUDAIC MONOGRAPHS

1. *David Kimhis: The Man and the Commentaries*, by Frank Talmage

2. *Studies in Medieval Jewish History and Literature*, edited by Isadore Twersky

3. *Decoding the Rabbis: A Thirteenth-Century Commentary on the Aggadah*, by Marc Saperstein

4. *Hispano-Jewish Culture in Transition: The Career and Controversies of Ramah*, by Bernard Septimus

HARVARD JUDAIC TEXTS AND STUDIES

1. *Rabbi Moses Naḥmanides (Ramban): Explorations in His Religious and Literary Virtuosity*, edited by Isadore Twersky

2. *Jewish Thought in the Sixteen Century*, edited by Bernard Dov Cooperman

3. *Christian Hebraists and Dutch Rabbis: Seventeenth Century Apologetics and the Study of Maimonides' "Mishneh Torah,"* Aaron L. Katchen